Rebirth

Reconstruction Reconsidered

Series Editors

J. Brent Morris and Hilary N. Green

REBIRTH

Creating the Museum of the Reconstruction Era and the Future of the House Museum

JENNIFER WHITMER TAYLOR

THE UNIVERSITY OF
SOUTH CAROLINA PRESS

Published by the University of South Carolina Press
Columbia, South Carolina 29208

uscpress.com

Printed in the United States of America

Library of Congress Cataloging-in-Publication Data can be found at http://catalog.loc.gov/.

ISBN: 978-1-64336-558-9 (hardcover)
ISBN: 978-1-64336-583-1 (paperback)
ISBN: 978-1-64336-581-7 (ebook)
DOI: https://doi.org/10.61162/DUHG4620

open carolina

The inclusion of this book in the Open Carolina collection is made possible by the generous funding of the University of South Carolina Libraries.

To the past, present, and future docents of the Woodrow Wilson Family Home and the Museum of the Reconstruction Era

Contents

List of Illustrations

Acknowledgments

This book required infinite support from numerous institutions, public history practitioners, historians, family, and friends. The journey began with my parents in the 1980s. My late father, Gary, loved history and film and instilled in me a passion for both. He knew nothing of public history's definitions or theories yet was and will always be the first public historian in my life. If my father was a muse, my mother Linda provided the foundation, work ethic, and confidence required to complete a manuscript ten years in the making. She also took me to all the free museums she could find in our community and when we traveled. When I felt overwhelmed or mentally blocked, I found shelter in the support of my husband, Robert; the smiles of our son, Jenson; and cuddles with our dogs, Lennon (bless his perfect soul) and Biscuit. To my husband, thank you for being my ride or die, twenty years legally. It's hard to believe this book consumed half of our marriage. My brother pledged boldly and truthfully that he would never read my book. I appreciate our candid relationship, shared experience, and mostly healthy sibling rivalry, and his letting me work in his shop on extended stays in Kentucky. So many family members encouraged me along the way, including the Watkins, Robert's family and the Kohls clan, and I am grateful for their support. My lifelong friends outside of academia—Felicia, Libby, Margaret, Julie, and Jessica—never wavered in their belief that I would complete this book. This is also true of my neighbors Mike and Mindy, who championed me over the last six years.

Strong institutions and peers along my scholarly voyage made a tremendous impact on me as both a person and a historian. I would like to thank my comrades in the history department at the University of South Carolina, many of whom were in my cohort and/or endured unfounded imposter syndrome and a volatile market alongside me: Rochelle Outlaw, Candace Cunningham, Robert Greene, Caitlin Mans Sharpe, Kate McFadden, Megan Bennett, and Brian Robinson. They provided friendship and intellectual support when I was at my most vulnerable and inspired me often. I am thankful to have met Erin Holmes and my southern feminist historian soulmate Jennifer "Bingo" Gunter, both of whom are my biggest cheerleaders and help me make sense of academic life, womanhood, and southernness. I am especially grateful to my dissertation committee, Wanda Henricks, Robert Weyeneth, and Susan Courtney, all of whom gave me tremendous guidance when I first began this project. Wanda was an invaluable resource on Black women's history and critical to the evaluation of Historic Columbia's content and tour as a predominantly white institution. Susan's South on Film course gave me unique training and prepared me to look at the visual text *The Birth of a Nation* in new ways. Bob brought his sharp preservationist eye as a committee member and continues to be a wonderful mentor in his retirement through the National Council on Public History. I am indebted to Allison Marsh for her guidance and friendship as committee chair and my longtime adviser. She taught me the kind of academic public historian I want to be—an active practitioner and a caring mentor who guides students toward being the best public historians they can be. I would like to thank the University of South Carolina Press and acquisitions editor Ehren Foley, who spent years supporting me in completing the project and expediting publication as tenure and promotion loomed. Anonymous peer reviewers from the fields of public history and Reconstruction dramatically improved this manuscript as well. Bruce Baker, in particular, offered thoughtful and detailed feedback that infinitely strengthened the book.

In the midst of assaults on history education and an ever-shrinking market, I managed to land in Duquesne University's history department in 2017, which provided me overwhelming support for the book and a public history program with institutional partnerships that make it a joy to be a practitioner. Most vital has been my departmental mentor, Jay Dwyer, who read the manuscript draft cover to cover. His keen editorial skills brought a complicated intersectional conversation far outside of his field of Latin American history to publication quality. My chair, John Mitcham, not only reviewed my book proposal but also solicited course releases and released funds to help me bring the final project to fruition. A fellow southerner (though it took me about six months to convince the Georgian that my upper South origins were legit), John made his devotion to this project clear when he started bringing me Duke's mayonnaise, not well-stocked in Pittsburgh, from his trips home. My public historian colleague Stephanie Gray cheered me on at every phase of the publishing process, asked smart questions, and helped me think out ideas, organize, and stick to writing schedules. She is a delightful partner in building a nationally recognized public history program. The book also would not be possible without the generous support of my dean, Kris Blair in the McAnulty College and Graduate School of Liberal Arts, and the Wimmer Family Foundation, which funds pre-tenure research. Four graduate assistants from Duquesne provided excellent aid in manuscript tasks that emerged. Amanda Seim, Sydney Yates, and Deanna Berryman worked diligently to find Reconstruction museums in the past and present. Amanda also edited and finalized the transcriptions of docent oral histories that I had only partially transcribed for the dissertation. In addition Deanna tracked down permissions for images used in the book and provided historiographical research and analysis for post-reviewer revisions. Glenna Van Dyke assisted in contacting docent narrators and transferring ownership of their oral histories to the Department of Oral History at the University of South Carolina Libraries. I would also like to thank our department administrative assistants, Kelly Kovalsky and Sam Hicks-Gandy, who handled payments for research trips, student workers, and images for the book and in general make my job easier every day. Special thanks to Sam, who gifted me a tiara when I completed peer-review revisions. I happily wore it to announce publication and my teaching award and have tucked it away to honor Stephanie's future book milestones.

Of course, no historian succeeds without the aid provided by archivists. The staff of the South Caroliniana Library, including Graham Duncan and Nathan Saunders, director of the Department of Oral History Andrea L'Hommedieu, and Libby Shortt, formerly of the Woodrow Wilson Presidential Library and Museum, proved no exception. I would like to thank the public historians and docents who shared their time and skills with me at Wilson homes across the South: the Presidential Library and Museum, the boyhood home in Augusta, and S Street. Research at these sites would not have been possible without funding from the Institute for Southern Studies and Institute for African American Research at the University of South Carolina.

Most important, I am filled with gratitude that docents of the Museum of the Reconstruction Era (MoRE) at the Woodrow Wilson Family Home, who turned an exhibit into an experience, disclosed their stories to me. I especially would like to acknowledge Heather Bacon-Rogers for her continued friendship and updates about the MoRE and Historic Columbia. Any criticism docents may perceive in this work reflects on my shortcomings as their trainer. I must recognize the MoRE interpretive and exhibit teams circa 2014 as well: Ann Posner, James Quint, Fielding Freed, Sarah Blackwell, John Sherrer, and Robin Waites. They taught me a great deal about working with volunteers, how to use the MoRE in education and programming, and the preservation history of Wilson's childhood home. Similar to the visitors and docents of the MoRE, I, too, was taught a Dunning School interpretation in AP US history by my favorite high school teacher, who also happened to worship Woodrow Wilson. As such I am incredibly thankful that Robin, Historic Columbia's visionary leader, gave me the opportunity to work on this revolutionary historic house museum, took my expertise seriously, and paid me appropriately. Greater still, she offered the docents and me the chance to correct our miseducation and complicate the history of "great men." She will be sorely missed after her retirement in June 2024.

Introduction

On the crisp Saturday morning of February 15, 2014, dozens of people gathered between a magnolia tree and the front steps of a blue, Italianate Victorian era house in Columbia, South Carolina. The crowd awaited entry into the childhood home of Woodrow Wilson. The historic house museum (HHM) shuttered its doors to the public nine years prior. A ribbon strung across the home's porch signaled the last formal barrier in presenting the reinterpretation and rehabilitation of the eighty-year-old HHM. From its inception as a presidential home in the 1920s, the Woodrow Wilson Family Home (WWFH) allowed visitors via tours to explore the teenage years of the twenty-eighth president of the United States. Yet with one slice of a yellow ribbon that President's Day, the WWFH severed it ties to the shrine approach common in HHMs. Armed with a revolutionary reinterpretation, the WWFH officially opened as the first museum of Reconstruction in the nation. The new interpretation overthrew the traditional HHM narrative of elite white men in an attempt to fill the enormous gap between academic and public knowledge of Reconstruction. Historic Columbia, the organization that administers the home, reimagined the outdated HHM model of docent-guided tours heavily dependent on period rooms. The preservationist group installed a twenty-first-century exhibit reliant on panels and a minimalist approach to displaying artifacts. The organization launched an innovative semiguided tour led by vetted docents trained to interpret the biracial space that the Wilsons and their employees occupied, with the goal of exploring the biracial democracy created by Reconstruction. In the process of blending two seemingly unconnected subjects, the post–Civil War world and a teenager named Tommy who would become president, the museum created complex and at times contested conversations about freedom, citizenship, white domestic terror, systemic racism, hero worship, and memory in South Carolina, the South, and the nation.

Rebirth is the first comprehensive study of the MoRE at the WWFH, believed to be the first Reconstruction museum in the country. Reconstruction as a field is rich in historical assessment and revisionism but not in areas of public interpretation until the last decade. That the MoRE is the first museum of Reconstruction is an institutional claim by Historic Columbia that I have been unable to refute through internet research, examination of National Park Service (NPS) sites, and familiarity with the literature on museums.[1] Both the NPS and the American Association for State and Local History recognize the museum as such on their websites.[2] Although museums partially focus on Reconstruction as part of their timeframe or housed temporary exhibits on the era, no museum prior to the MoRE focused on the history of Reconstruction. I cannot rule out that there may have been a Reconstruction museum that has disappeared from the record, most likely during the prolific, community-centered Black museum movement of the 1960s and 1970s. As Andrea Burns argues, tracing and analyzing the movement has proven difficult because it was so vast geographically, economically, culturally, and politically. In addition scholarship on Black public history can be challenging to find, since, as Pero Gaglo Dagbovie notes, the term is rarely used, and though African American public history first appeared in 1980s, it was often synonymous with Black history. Furthermore, the specialization of Black public history, with its own methodology and objectives, has not followed the same trajectory as general public history.[3]

An early form of Black public history began in the late 1820s and lasted into the early twentieth century, when Black urban elites on the East Coast included exhibits as part of their work with churches, literary societies, and benevolent groups.[4] Two generations of founders followed, heavily influenced by the "Negro canon," a literary term describing the Black history, culture, and art produced between 1915 and 1960 and often taught at historically Black colleges and universities.[5] Critical to this first wave countering white supremacist narratives was Carter G. Woodson, the "father of Black history" and arguably the first Black public historian who provided academic scholarship to a mass Black audience through the Association for the Study of Negro Life and History, Negro History Week, and Negro History clubs, kits, books, and extension courses. At the same time the American Legion Auxiliary saved Woodrow Wilson's home in Columbia, Black churches, club women, and professionals such as teachers, librarians, and social workers relied on the association's programming, as well as field trips to Frederick Douglass's DC home and Harpers Ferry. After World War II, Black neighborhood museums, or what Burns describes as alternative "free spaces," frequently operated between the private and public sphere of storefronts or apartments.[6] Amid the mid-century civil rights movement, the first public museums that were both established and maintained by the Black community and dedicated to long-term exhibition and research in Black history, culture, and pride appeared. This movement, inspired by 1940s radicalism and 1960s Black nationalism, expanded the Negro canon and Black pride. Greater interest in African history and Pan-Africanism fueled the "aesthetic" of the Black museum movement.[7] In the late 1970s, these museums expanded, and a second generation of new public museums materialized, as did the Association of African American Museums. Forced to be resourceful and flexible and lacking professional staff, these independent, grassroots Black museums and their collections successfully countered mainstream museum and educational institutions by controlling and presenting complex, radical narratives that reimagined power, memory, and identity. In the 1980s and 1990s, Black museums faced financial strains that forced some museums to close their doors.[8] It is this period in which, I suspect, a Reconstruction museum could have emerged and disappeared.

Those Black museums that remained changed dramatically, more closely resembling traditional and professionalized institutions that rely on elite fundraising, expansion, and new buildings that removed them from communities they initially served. Though they still pushed back against the Eurocentric model of the museum, Black museums forged new relationships with academia, on the precipice of institutionalizing public history and Black history as a field of study. Those museums that survived operated amid urban problems of renewal and gentrification, housing shortages, and unemployment and epidemics of crack, violence, over-policing, and mass incarceration.[9] In the last three decades, a third generation of commemorative museums and a revived national museum movement appeared, culminating in the Museum of African American History and Culture on the National Mall. In the South, cultural tourism helped inspire a surge of "safe icon" museums devoted to important figures like Harriet Tubman and Martin Luther King Jr.; however, Black women, such as educator Nannie Burroughs, who were vital to the intersection of women's and civil rights activism remain largely overlooked. Less well-known and more "revolutionary" subjects like Marcus and Amy Jacques Garvey and Nat Turner remain nearly untouchable.[10] Opposition from the Black museum movement, the Smithsonian, and white conservatives to a federal museum on the National Mall delayed its opening by decades.[11] Since 1988 experts estimate that there are over two hundred Black museums ranging from those devoted to significant individuals to aspects of culture, slavery, baseball, civil rights, and military service.[12]

Since the MoRE's opening and during Reconstruction's sesquicentennial, other sites are interpreting Reconstruction, especially in South Carolina but across the nation as well. In 2015 the state-run North Carolina History Center on the Civil War, Emancipation, and Reconstruction received its first $500,000 grant, but it will not open until 2027. Five years after the MoRE reopened, the National Constitution Center, which possesses original copies of the Thirteenth, Fourteenth, and Fifteenth Amendments, claimed that its new permanent exhibit, "Civil War and Reconstruction: The Battle for

Freedom and Equality," was the "first exhibit devoted to exploring the constitutional debates from the Civil War and Reconstruction."[13]

The MoRE is also part of a growing movement to commemorate Reconstruction in South Carolina, making the state a leader in Reconstruction public history. Not until 2016 did the NPS finally expand from a partial Reconstruction narrative at two sites: the Nicodemus, Kansas, National Historical Site, a freedmen's town established as Reconstruction eroded, and the Andrew Johnson National Historical Site in Greeneville, Tennessee.[14] The NPS, formed in 1916 during the Progressive Era and Wilson's administration, in general was slow to preserve sites of Black history, especially those related to more radical Black thinkers and activists.[15] In the late twentieth century, the NPS sought more inclusive narratives, particularly around the Underground Railroad and civil rights movements, culminating in the Beaufort Reconstruction Monument.[16] In October 2016 Reconstruction historians Kate Masur and Gregory Downs completed a Reconstruction-era theme study for the NPS, a prerequisite for adding a new site. Based on this research, the scholars asked President Barack Obama in a *Washington Post* opinion piece to designate a Reconstruction monument in Beaufort County, South Carolina. In his final days in office, Obama used the Antiquities Act to fulfill their request, naming four properties to the Reconstruction Monument. The NPS's first Reconstruction site in Beaufort was a victory fifteen years in the making. The South Carolina Sons of Confederate Veterans campaign derailed the first attempt to designate a site there in 2002.[17] Since 2010 the Historic Mitchelville Freedom Park, a nonprofit on nearby Hilton Head Island, works to preserve and commemorate the first self-governed freedmen's community, which was destroyed in a 1893 hurricane.[18] The South Carolina Department of Archives and History launched a permanent digital exhibit on Reconstruction.[19] Reconstruction 360, a web and mobile application designed by South Carolina Educational Television, expands digital interpretation to increase understanding of the Reconstruction era for the public, students, and educators. A concise and interactive, place-based case study model, the first module dissects the widely misunderstood history of "40 Acres and a Mule." It brings to digital life the early battle over land and labor waged in Beaufort county, now home to the NPS Reconstruction park, that Willie Lee Rose described in *Rehearsal for Reconstruction: The Port Royal Experiment*. Reconstruction 360 continues to grow its primary-source-driven documentaries and lesson plans via new modules.[20] The South Carolina State Museum updated its permanent exhibit to include a modern interpretation of Reconstruction and its impact in the twenty-first century. In 2018 the museum hosted a Reconstruction exhibit with elements reminiscent of the MoRE, which borrows its legislative desk and chair and red shirt from

State Museum. Both sites display a Democratic straight ticket from the 1876 election and a wooden ballot box. The State Museum also hosts an online Reconstruction exhibit.[21] For over a decade the MoRE, as well as other local, state, and federal projects operating in South Carolina, led the initiative to interpret Reconstruction for the public. Together they show the South and the nation the value of commemorating Reconstruction, the nation's first Black civil rights movement, in a time of increased Black disenfranchisement and social justice activism.

The MoRE docents became the first tour guides in the country to interpret a museum devoted to Reconstruction and were critical to the success of the semiguided tour of the permanent house exhibit. Eleven docent oral histories anchor the manuscript, amplifying the voices of vital frontline labor that are too often erased in public history literature driven by studies of audience and their identity. As cultural institutions increasingly compete with the leisure and tourism industry, museums have embraced interactive and multimedia exhibits as well as explored more diverse, inclusive narratives and social advocacy. In *The Participatory Museum*, Nina Simon postulates that the audience-centered institution should be as relevant, useful and accessible as a shopping mall or train station.[22] Now museums apply atmospherics, manipulating the environment to affect people's behavior in their architectural, interior, and exhibition design as well as in commercial or leisure spaces.[23] Attending a museum, like other leisure activities, also affirms identity. John Falk argues a person's "self-aspects" (or "i"dentities), such as being a family member, impact leisure choices more than race, religion, or gender ("I"dentities), especially when matched with convenience and affordability. His theory marked a contextual turn in visitor studies away from a focus on the length of visits to identify and define five types of visitor identity: explorer; experience seeker; professional/hobbyist; recharger, who looks for a therapeutic or rejuvenating experience; and facilitator, who encourages learning. Emily Dawson and Eric Jensen criticized Falk's "short-term" identities as reductionist and shaped by a "behaviorist market research framework." Though he rightly argued "long-term" identities did not fully explain visitors' leisure choices, he neglected them all together.[24] The importance of Falk's identities lies in their contribution to understanding how visitor motivations complement demographic factors such as gender, sexuality, age, race and ethnicity, education level, ability/disability, and the complexity of socioeconomic status that also shape attendance and experience. A new contextual turn is needed to research nonvisitors and aid museums in attracting this previously ignored group. Scholarship shows, and public historians know, that adult museum visitors are younger, white professionals, often wealthier and more educated than the general population. Families are numerous, but minorities, those with disabilities, and non-English speakers are rare.[25] In the case of Black museums, at least 20 percent of their visitors are non-Black, while Black visitors rarely make up more than 10 percent of primarily white-centered museums' guests. Art museums receive the harshest criticism with respect to accessibility. Nonvisitors view galleries and the ability to interpret their collections as for elites only.[26] Although they lack a grounding in museum theory, absent audiences likely understand that museums solicit diverse audiences not as an attempt to promote inclusiveness but as a form of hegemonic messaging intended to shape societal norms based on white middle- and upper-class ideals.[27]

In the late 1970s and early 1980s, public history and museum practitioners began asking important questions about the limited training docents received and their motivations in volunteering at museums.[28] Volunteer docents who worked with the public on the front lines of an institution were not considered a professional force. Consequently, interpreters struggle to professionalize their field within public history. As such the mediated learning and experiences of paid and volunteer staff remain understudied in the museum field.[29] Scholarship that incorporates docents often centers the visitor experience during a tour or the perspective of the trainers or full-time staff rather than giving these interpreters their own voice and agency. For example, *The Museum Educator's Manual* appeared in 2009 as a step-by-step handbook for a "team approach" to volunteer management and the three Rs: recruitment, recognition, and retention of docents. A solid training manual, it offers no docent perspectives.[30] A notable exception most relevant to the MoRE training is Shawn Halifax's reflective essay on the training at McLeod Plantation Historic Site, a former Sea Island cotton planation once occupied by Confederate artillery officers and the 54th Massachusetts United States Colored Troops. As a trainer Halifax found a gap in interpretive scholarship for practitioners that was accessible yet methodological and offered solutions on the psychological and pedagogical hurdles docents faced when interpreting the legacy of slavery. The site, which opened a year after MoRE and also depicts Reconstruction, required new training protocols and professionalization, supported by Charleston County Parks.[31] McLeod trained four paid interpreters in methods based on the National Association for Interpretation's interpretive philosophy, which stresses research skills, knowledge of audience/behavior, and a foundational theme across interpretation. Docents received a contextual narrative connecting primary and secondary sources and attended multiday workshops on themes and visitor resistance and response. They spent the last two months creating a tour lasting forty-five to sixty minutes.[32]

Case studies demonstrate patterns of docent resistance that emerged with the interpretive training at MoRE and are elucidated in several chapters of this book. Docents at San Francisco's Haas-Lillienthal House rejected a 1993 "counter-tour" that followed the "invisible life" of a fictional, 120-year-old man. The docents felt undermined by the museum's effort to create a fictional life with artifacts and docent-told stories that created a false "historical presence." Similar to the volunteer docents at Historic Columbia who contested the reinterpretation of Wilson's early life, some docents participated, while others refused.[33] Akin also to the Wilson house, the 2001 reopening of the Campbell House tour in Spokane, Washington, moved away from a tour based on décor and objects to one with larger themes of class, gender, and labor. At both sites docents struggled with the complicated script and its difficult interpretive material. At Campbell House docents broke character during vignettes placed within the tour and gave visitors the wrong information.[34] When the Fernbank Museum of Natural History in Atlanta hosted the American Museum of Natural History's traveling exhibit the Genomic Revolution from June 2004 through January of 2005, the museum adopted a peer training model for undergraduate students, who possessed an existing framework of knowledge and were on payroll. The success of the MoRE at the WWFH depended on the paid weekend staff, who were often graduate public history students, and well-educated volunteers.[35] These studies offer glimpses at the docent experience, foreshadowing docent resistance to HHM counter-tours that move away from elite, white narratives and deemphasize static objects and decorative arts.[36] This book illuminates the voices of ten volunteers and six paid weekend staff who completed short written surveys and ten oral histories at a "reinterpret or perish" turning point in HHM history.

As the title *Rebirth* seeks to convey, the book expands our understanding of a key debate emerging within the last decade in the museum studies field. Put simply, there are too many HHMs, many of which are outdated and some of which cannot be saved.[37] The MoRE reinterpretation grew out of an attempt to make a former HHM that was a decorative art shrine to Woodrow Wilson relevant as well as distinctive from the three other HHMs devoted to the former president. My research into Wilson's childhood living in three southern states helped to answer docent questions about how the regional experience shaped him, his family, and his leadership. It also led to new interpretations of Wilson's Reconstruction experiences with a biracial government and community that will add to the robust literature on his life.[38]

The MoRE joins other HHMs revolutionizing interpretation with counternarratives and unorthodox approaches as called for in a 2015 issue of *Public Historian* that looked to reimagine the HHMs inundating the landscape. The Weeksville Heritage Center in Brooklyn and the home of

Matilda Joslyn Gage, a more progressive and lesser-known contemporary of Susan B. Anthony, exemplify sites choosing inclusion and eschewing white men and elites to contest "biased systems of power and narrow histories."[39] The MoRE, the Weeksville Center, and the Gage home are not "object-rich" or vignette focused. They abandoned decorative arts to address "the trauma inflicted by social and political invisibility."[40] Like the MoRE, the Weeksville Center tells "a needed counterculture narrative" about a free Black community first founded in 1838 a decade after New York eradicated slavery. Both sites commemorate the creation of schools, churches, and other institutions by their respective Black communities through "creativity, entrepreneurship, and self-sufficiency" in the post-emancipation era. The MoRE and the center tackle continued oppression after liberation rather than focus on one of these "two extremes" that dominate the historic representation of Black communities. They both juxtapose questions about freedom with "unfreedom."[41] MoRE weekend docent Jennifer Gunter was "fascinated with the idea of freedom." In thinking about the concept of emancipation, she asked, "Some men in Washington D.C. say you're free. What do you do? What's next? . . . How do you be free? What does that entail?"[42] Both sites share slavery as the visitors' "default reference point," which create patterns of assumption that free individuals were enslaved. But the center counters the HHM model of "elite architecture" and conveys the "normalcy" of freed peoples' daily lives better than a presidential home ever could. Yet, both stress that people built and maintained routines to their lives surrounded by "families, jobs, procuring food, leisure" that counter the traditional "aberrant" narrative of enslavement, poverty, and criminalization.[43] Where the MoRE only implies it, Gage informs its visitors of two rules: "Check your dogma at the door" and "Think for yourself." This is a wise warning for a site that comes out swinging with a "dialogical model" centered first on reproductive rights, which was part of a decision to use Gage's ideas and writings about social justice rather than a traditional lens of domesticity. With dialogue as the driver of the interpretation, the volunteer facilitators at Gage's home also resemble MoRE docents.[44]

This project's title also reflects a conversation with the theoretical literature on how museum visitors receive and contest power. *Rebirth* comes from its engagement with three texts on power, including a theoretical study of the modern museum, *Birth of the Museum*. The MoRE exhibited the other two visual works, the 1915 white supremacist epic *The Birth of a Nation* (dir. D. W. Griffith, 1915) and a modern-day response, *The Rebirth of a Nation* (2007), by the Black artist DJ Spooky. His film and the MoRE are both attempts to contest and invert unilateral dominant messages of power in traditional public spheres. For more than a century, museums and their ordered collection of objects, as well as theaters, parks, and libraries, managed the social behavior and conduct of their visitors with a surveilling white gaze. One of these unidirectional, dominant cultural messages disseminated both in museums and in *The Birth of a Nation* in response to a demographically changing United States was white supremacy. The MoRE's semiguided tour disrupts the one-way system of a docent talking at guests as they are guided in a linear fashion on a timed tour. Instead visitors are free to construct the meaning in their museum visit by exploring and discussing topics of interest to them.[45]

The reinterpretation of the MoRE revolutionizes the conventional models of the HHM and the presidential shrine, though it is only one approach to modernizing these traditional, ideological spaces. The MoRE also stands in stark contrast to the overproduced Old South plantation HHM and tells an interracial story of the past. For over a century, the nostalgia-driven heritage industry in the South and HHMs devoted to elites across the nation emphasized the beauty of the home and its objects, displacing a narrative about slavery and the social relations that existed between biracial communities. Fascination with the plantation as a site of leisure began in the late nineteenth century when elite northern men purchased plantation ruins to evoke, not replicate, antebellum experiences and construct what Daniel Vivian calls a "new plantation world." This "second Yankee invasion" of South Carolina's Lowcountry, which lasted through the New Deal era, transformed plantations into sites of recreation and leisure, first as hunting clubs and retreats and eventually as lavish rehabilitated and landscaped sports estates with modern amenities. There new owners enacted the fantasy consumed by the nation on film, in novels, and in print media. The local and national press embraced these restorations, cementing these plantation sites as significant and central to the region's history. Moonlight and magnolia plantation tourism, or "selling the South," arose during this period, emphasizing the big house and erasing slavery.[46] Though sites of extreme violence, tourism flourished and plantations became settings of lavish weddings, complete with docents in hoopskirts, furnished antebellum homes, and opulent landscaping that masked the labor of slavery and daily interracial interactions with what Tara McPherson describes as a "a southern mise-en-scène of imagined hospitality."[47] The twenty-first century, though, brought significant changes in interpretation to a limited number of plantations that finally welcomed Black visitors as an "imagined audience," such as McLeod Plantation Historic Site.[48] Just as films and novels contributed to the moonlight and magnolia tourism, modern films centered on slavery, such as *Lincoln* (dir. Steven Spielberg, 2012), *Django Unchained* (dir. Quentin Tarantino, 2012), and *12 Years a Slave* (dir. Steve McQueen, 2013), as well as social movements, including the removal of Confederate iconography from public spaces and Black Lives Matter and George Floyd protests, inspired a new "slave-centric" retelling that overturned the dominant narrative. Still, most of the nearly four hundred public plantations across the South host tourists that are white, affluent, and over fifty and at best market "roots" or genealogy tourism to Black communities. These sites often include slave cabins, which come off as nothing more than outbuildings and place markers, denied the status of homeplaces and absent of intimate family and community experiences that render their mostly anonymous occupants as objects within the plantation economy. The most dramatic transformation in what Melaine Harnay calls the "plantation turn" is that of Whitney Plantation on Louisiana's famed River Road. One time known as Millionaire Row for its long line of plantations, more than a dozen today make up a "neo-plantation economy." As with MoRE and Reconstruction, the Whitney claims to be the first museum of slavery. In contrast, the owner of a nearby plantation Houmas offered the site as a home for Confederate statues removed from New Orleans in 2018.[49]

The Whitney tour disrupts traditional white plantation narratives in its spatial organization and emphasis on memorial sculpture. Using a new materialist approach, the concept that "knowledge is generated in material-semiotic ways," Dorota Golanska contends the tour is an "aesthetic encounter" where visitors are immersed in learning via the landscape, the inhabitants, the violence, and the context of the transatlantic slave trade.[50] The tour begins at Anti-Yoke Baptist Church, founded by freed people, where visitors watch a film on Whitney's renovation and archival research, heavily anchored in Work Projects Administration (WPA) slave narratives. Here visitors encounter Woodrow Nash's *Children of Whitney* installation of sixty clay sculptures of children. Other memorials with powerful but traumatic history abound throughout the tour, such as sixty ceramic skulls on steel rods representing those decapitated in an 1811 German Coast slave revolt. When possible the memorials name the members of the enslaved community, whether insurrectionists, two thousand children who died between 1823 and 1863, or people trafficked.[51] One of the most potent artifacts is a rusted jail that leaves visitors feeling trapped, baking in the sun, and reflecting on the myth of benevolent masters evoked at other plantation museums. Visitors first glimpse the big house, which they tour briefly at the end of the tour, from behind the jail's bars.[52]

The book explains how the MoRE centered a Black narrative of Reconstruction. There were "competing visions of Reconstruction" from the beginning, both as a plan for reunion and in the emerging historical narratives that shaped the memory of the sectional crisis and Civil War. These competing visions came from political autobiographies, textbooks, popular novels, local celebrations, reform movement gatherings, and even material culture. This process, W. Fitzhugh Brundage argues, was "one of the major American cultural projects of the late nineteenth and first half of the twentieth centuries." The space overturns what Bruce Baker, in his study of Reconstruction memory in South Carolina, called a "white supremacist narrative of Reconstruction." It overshadowed a Black created and centered counter narrative in the public sphere, helping to buttress Jim Crow and divide Black and white workers. This connectedness between the Lost Cause and the white supremacist narrative of Reconstruction is why docents often use the language of the Lost Cause to describe their own historical memory of Reconstruction or what Brundage defines as the "social construction of historical identity." For most white Americans, Reconstruction demonstrated freedmen were ill-prepared for the vote, citizenship and equality with whites. Furthermore, a crooked North and excessive federal intervention corrupted the South.[53] The MoRE disrupts the white supremacist narrative that the Red Shirts were heroes rather than a paramilitary force that violently ended Reconstruction.[54] Poised to come to terms with its long history of white supremacy and white domestic terror, the United States is learning, albeit slowly, its Reconstruction history. The museum provides a blueprint for making HHMs reparative sites that confront white supremacy and train their frontline staff in teaching contested history. These conversations remain vital to American democracy in the wake of the January 6, 2021, insurrection at the US Capitol and attacks on teaching Critical Race Theory and racism in classrooms.

In October 2020 Historic Columbia formally changed the name of the Wilson home to the Museum of the Reconstruction Era at the Woodrow Wilson Family Home. By originally capitalizing on the name of Woodrow Wilson rather than Reconstruction, the HHM escaped the backlash that befell the 2002 attempt to make Beaufort, South Carolina, the home of the NPS's first Reconstruction-focused site.[55] The nation had yet to confront systemic racism in its public spaces. The Confederate flag still waved boldly on the grounds of the South Carolina State House, five blocks from Wilson's childhood home. Statues to Robert E. Lee and other Confederate leaders were untouchable. The thought of renaming buildings at Princeton University, where Wilson served as president, and other commemorative efforts praising him had gained little traction. However, the public's mood regarding these issues of historical memory shifted dramatically in the summer of 2015 following the horrific massacre of nine Black parishioners at Mother Emanuel AME Church in Charleston, South Carolina.[56] On June 22, less than week after the shooting, Governor Nikki Haley called for the Confederate flag to be removed from the capitol grounds after decades of debate.[57] Living just outside of Columbia, shooter Dylann Roof saw the flag regularly. Pictures circulated of him with it. He visited McLeod Plantation two months before the massacre and took three pictures in front of a slave cabin and the big house and at the African and African American cemetery, "desecrating" the site and leading to new training on active shooters and white nationalist symbols. He flashed racist symbols during his trial and defended his actions after his death sentence.[58] Subsequently, "great men" in the American history pantheon, their flaws more visible, sustained scrutiny. Impromptu crowds toppled Confederate iconography in public spectacle. Vandalism continued as state legislatures blocked legal removal with heritage protection acts and President Donald Trump issued an executive order criminalizing monument defacement. These were symbolic acts in the war against systemic racism, levied against monuments long weaponized by white supremacy movements, but they contributed to an environment where Historic Columbia could finally rename the WWFH the Museum of the Reconstruction Era.[59]

This reckoning with the legacy of white supremacy and its commemoration on the public landscape intensified during the Trump administration. In August 2017 white supremacist, far right, and alt-right groups descended on Charlottesville, Virginia, for a Unite the Right Rally to protest the removal of a local Robert E. Lee statue. This resulted in the death of counter-protester Heather Heyer and accelerated monument removal.[60] The heated and violent clashes over the commemoration of white supremacy peaked alongside a mainstream Black Lives Matter movement in the summer of 2020. Protests erupted across the country and globe following the murder of George Floyd and death of Breonna Taylor at the hands (and knees) of police. These deadly encounters directly followed the lynching of Ahmaud Arbery.[61] Some mayors removed controversial statues while their residents slept to avoid threats and counterprotests. Others bypassed their state legislatures by finding loopholes such as transferring public land to private ownership. The culmination of the national debate and removal took place along Monument Avenue in Richmond, Virginia. Protesters toppled Jefferson Davis's statue, and the city eventually removed Stonewall Jackson. However, the most powerful moment in the sequence of events was when locals projected George Floyd's image, "BLM," and the protest slogan "No Justice, No Peace" on the Robert E. Lee statue's pedestal. The protest art evolved to include famous Black historical figures and other victims of police brutality. Witnessing this spectacle on Monument Avenue felt like the end of Confederate and white supremacist iconography in public spaces. More than 100 Confederate monuments, markers, and memorials disappeared from the landscape. Regrettably, more than 2,400 remain, a third of them statues.[62]

Historic Columbia renamed the MoRE in the wake of these protests, mere months before unmasked, white paramilitary forces attempted a coup d'état at the US Capitol. On January 6, 2021, these men and women sought to stop formal congressional approval of the Electoral College votes legally required to make Joe Biden the president a few weeks later. Outraged Trump supporters, in their red "Make America Great Again" apparel and furry horn hats, provided cover for more organized militia and helped lay siege to the Capitol.[63] One hundred forty-five years prior, white Democrats committed to ending Republican and Black Reconstruction in South Carolina gathered around the State House in Columbia prepared to assault Republicans who claimed they were the legitimate victors amid a disputed election plagued by white terror and fraud. Like Trump, Governor Wade Hampton spoke to the mob and convinced them to disband, demonstrating his control over the white populace. For months the federal military presence kept the Republican house in power in name only while Hampton's Democrats maintained their own government. On April 3, 1877, President Rutherford B. Hayes ordered those troops to depart.[64]

The process of creating and implementing the MoRE's reinterpretation, centered on a Reconstruction narrative, is more than a case study of one solution to public history's conundrum of HHM oversaturation. It helps us understand and connect to the country's larger, evolving dialogue on race and systemic white supremacy. The evolution of the MoRE's interpretation is also another example of a highly contested, nationwide historical reckoning that is revising history across our public landscapes and in our public institutions to teach a more accurate representation of a whitewashed past. *Rebirth* traces the transformation of the WWFH from an eighty-year-old presidential shrine celebrating Wilson's teenage years in Columbia to the nation's first museum of the Reconstruction era. The tour of the HHM uses the lens of Thomas Woodrow "Tommy" Wilson's childhood to reveal for its public audiences the joy and hope of Reconstruction and how the period, and the white memory of it as a failure, might have shaped President Wilson. The MoRE's reinterpretation upends the conventional model of the HHM as presidential shrine. Trained docents facilitate a semiguided tour that navigates visitors through a permanent panel exhibit with each room in the HHM devoted to a key theme. The tour and exhibit juxtapose a comprehensive history of Reconstruction with the Wilson family's timeline of moving to the first home that they ever owned and joining the Presbyterian community in postwar Columbia. At the tour's conclusion, docents help visitors unravel a fifty-year history of white supremacy and domestic terror that was both political and racialized. Together they dissect the complex intersection of Reconstruction memory and historiography with Wilson's presidency. White terror and election fraud dismantled the socioeconomic and political gains of Black Americans during Reconstruction and buttressed Jim Crow, a codified legal and cultural system of apartheid in the United States that Wilson defended, which endured until the mid-twentieth-century civil rights movement.

Rebirth shows managers and staff of historic sites at predominantly white institutions how to lead docents and visitors during controversial interpretive transitions, center Black narratives, and train frontline docent staff to interpret white supremacy. As such the book focuses on paid and volunteer docents ranging in age and education who gave tours for Historic Columbia, the parent preservationist organization that administers the MoRE and three other HHMs. My analysis of docent training demonstrates the importance of mandatory language and cultural sensitivity exercises for all docents as part of an inclusive practice. I conclude that trained public historians and volunteer docents with advanced degrees were most successful in delivering a counternarrative tour that challenged public perceptions of Reconstruction and what a presidential home should highlight. Until recently HHMs limited or excluded narratives that were not elite or white and had great difficulty discussing white supremacy.[65] Yet MoRE docents were successful in interpreting racialized and political terrorism. Some even questioned their own privilege as white docents discussing racialized violence against Black Americans. The examples I include of interpretive debates that took place between Historic Columbia's leadership and docents offer tools for dialogue and revision to improve exhibits and tours while respecting the expertise that docents provide.

The book also reveals how public history methodology can fill silences in the historical record about both the Black experience during Reconstruction as well as lives of so-called great men, who for centuries have driven the HHM movement. The chapter "Aren't I a Citizen? Interpreting the Lives of Black Women and Domestic Workers in Historic House Museums" demonstrates how incorporating historical literature, census records, and architectural and image analysis into the tour and exhibit as well as docent training can illuminate the lives of unknown domestic workers. Local Columbia history and my analysis of the interpretations at the three other HHMs devoted to Wilson answered new docent-inspired questions about President Wilson's childhood that are of value to Wilson scholars. Docent queries included how Wilson's parents felt about slavery and the Confederacy, which political party they supported, and how a southern upbringing during the Civil War and Reconstruction shaped the future president. For example a Black legislator, Beverly Nash, represented Tommy Wilson's district at a time the teenager developed a deep interest in government. Building on my research for the MoRE's primary exhibit film, *Rebirth* is also a revisionist history, reviving the question of how Wilson felt about his White House screening of the white supremacist film *The Birth of a Nation*. The film's Civil War and Reconstruction-era setting is South Carolina, which was the same state that Wilson experienced the first US civil rights movement.

Finally I illuminate the transformative power of MoRE's interpretation for docents and the majority of visitors. Some docents ultimately used their training and tours to combat their own biases and indoctrination regarding the Lost Cause and white supremacist narratives of Reconstruction, shaped from the inaccurate public history and education of their past. The majority of visitors often consumed this same false narrative that convinced generations of white Americans that Reconstruction was corrupt and needed to fail. Their tour evaluations reveal an eagerness to learn about Reconstruction at a Wilson HHM. Interpreting history with negative political or cultural implications for many white visitors risks backlash from that demographic. A national example and worst case scenario of audience "expectation distortion," when an exhibit contradicts visitor memory and knowledge, was the scrapping of the Smithsonian's original *Enola Gay* exhibition. It was interpretively sound but filled with historical complexity that posed difficult questions about the atomic bomb on the fiftieth university of its deployment. However, in the twenty-first century, a growing number of museums refuse to be held hostage by the public relations dangers that revisionist interpretations and updates previously posed among some white audiences and supporters. The MoRE joins a burgeoning movement to reframe museums not as sites of neutrality (as many white audiences view them) but as spaces that are inherently political and multivocal.[66] MoRE visitor evaluation data determined expectation distortion from the change in focus from Wilson to Reconstruction to be minimal. Often visitors failed to realize that myths of Reconstruction need correcting and did not know they wanted Reconstruction content until after they received it.[67]

The MoRE actualizes twenty-first-century theories of visitor identity and visitation patterns that reimagine how docents and visitors exchange information. Visitors negotiate and conflate the perspectives of both institution and self, in turn becoming a self-styled museum docent.[68] Although Historic Columbia selected a dominant scholarly message about Reconstruction for the MoRE, both docent and visitor communicate and receive messages, negotiate their identity, and create and modify memory. This process enables the MoRE tour to resolve some of the most common complaints about museums: they are static sites of institutional power that do not represent their visitors. By adopting an original theme and reinterpretation, the MoRE demonstrates that HHMs can present multiple views and encourage visitors to challenge authoritative voices, even those of the museum.[69] The visitors' choice to move between panels, artifacts, and interactives at their discretion democratizes the tour experience. These movements, made possible by the semiguided tour, the conversational nature of the tour's design, and open-ended questions, create original, individualized tours for every visitor. In this way the MoRE remains unfinished, as new meanings always are being constructed by visitors based on their individual life experiences and ideologies. The visitor transforms into a self-made docent.

An example of this interplay at work is how the MoRE corrects the interpretation of Reconstruction built on the false narrative that it was a disastrous punishment for white southerners and warranted a violent response. This reinterpretation is possible because many white visitors now abhor the political and domestic terrorism ending Reconstruction, once celebrated as part of a white supremacist narrative of the era. The first modern museums regulated and monitored visitors for middle-class decorum via the surveying eye of other guests and staff. Today this same style of surveillance by visitors and docents, who no longer accept white supremacist violence as a mainstream or respectable response to Reconstruction, silences or challenges the antiquated ideology of their peers. Visitors perform their identity and surveillance in response to the institutions' visual signs or messages. They may nod in approval at panel text highlighting Black political participation. Or they may ask a question about new information or previous incorrect information they learned, demonstrating that their identity and ideology are evolving. For example, white southern visitors and docents shared stories about being taught that Wade Hampton III and his Red Shirts were heroes by their schools or by their family who admired a Red Shirt among their clan. Some visitors may visually or physically reject the performance of a white supremacist narrative of Reconstruction with an eye roll, verbal response, or walking away. Guests, accordingly, curate a dynamic tour in real time based on what they learn and encounter as part of this institutional performance.[70]

Many of the sources for my book and the questions that I answer herein emerged from the year and a half that I served as lead facilitator for the MoRE's reinterpretation and reopening. In helping create the first museum of Reconstruction, I began to ask: What can future Reconstruction sites and outdated HHMs learn from the MoRE? What missteps should these institutions steer clear of, and what issues should they be prepared to address? What new scholarship can be produced at HHMs revising their interpretations? As I worked closely with Historic Columbia docents, I drew my own conclusions about a question that the museums studies field has largely ignored: What should the role and expectations of a docent be? To address these questions, I rely on a rich, diverse collection of primary sources mined from both manuscript and film archives and new sources created as part of the practice of public history, including oral histories, tour scripts, and tour experiences.

The primary method used to tell the MoRE's story and answer my questions is oral history with docents. Historic Columbia relies on paid and volunteer docents to conduct the tours of its four HHMs: the Robert Mills House, the Hampton-Preston Mansion, the Mann-Simons site, and the MoRE. At the time of the MoRE's reopening, paid docents, often from the public history program housed at the University of South Carolina, filled the busier weekend schedule. Volunteer docents, the weekend staff coordinator, and, as necessary, other staff guided tours Monday through Friday. For my research ten volunteers and six paid weekend docents completed a preliminary survey. Eleven of them went on to participate in oral interviews. One of those docents requested anonymity in their oral history, which I granted. While anonymity in oral history practice is frowned upon, the docent's voice and expertise were more important than their identity. To truly understand the power of Reconstruction memory and how issues of race influence white docents and public history, docents must feel comfortable having these contentious but necessary conversations. Renowned oral historian Donald Ritchie cites a case where Palestinian women were not identified because of political conditions. Had a large number of the docents chosen to give anonymous oral histories, the validity of the research perhaps could be questioned. Fortunately, that was not the case.[71]

I also analyze public history primary sources produced at Historic Columbia, including both records related to the WWFH before the reinterpretation and materials produced during its transformation into the MoRE. Historic Columbia's emails and administrative files proved vital in tracing tour development, training procedures, and docent assessment. In addition I examine my personal experiences serving as lead facilitator from November 2013 until May 2015. My responsibilities included crafting the semiguided tour, training volunteer and paid docents, and serving on the interpretive team as we finalized the exhibit. The interpretive team at the time of my hire comprised six of Historic Columbia's full-time staff: Ann Posner (volunteer manager), James Quint (education coordinator), Fielding Freed (director of historic house museums), Sarah Blackwell (director of programs), John Sherrer (director of cultural resources), and Robin Waites (executive director). As lead docent for fourteen months, I gave over half of the MoRE tours, processed visitor evaluation data, presented those results monthly, and offered strategies to docents for improvement. My hire was part of a larger collaboration between Historic Columbia's interpretive team and experts at the University of South Carolina: Drs. Daniella Cook (education), Allison Marsh (public history), Kendrick Clements (Wilson history), and Tom Brown (Reconstruction and public memory). My facilitator position evolved in the year after MoRE reopened. When combined with the number of paid weekend docents and scholarly consultants, it demonstrates the close working relationship between Historic Columbia and the University of South Carolina's history department and public history program, one of the first in the nation when it was formed in 1975.[72] As the lead facilitator position phased out, my research expanded to site visits of the three other Woodrow Wilson HHMs. Retracing Wilson's childhood, I traveled in Staunton, Virginia, and Augusta, Georgia, to evaluate their exhibits and tours. My last stop was in Washington, DC, to the Woodrow Wilson House, a National Trust for Historic Preservation HHM where the president died.

My experience in many ways mirrors that of Amy Tyson at Minnesota's premier living history attraction, Minnesota Historical Society's Historic Fort Snelling, which resulted in her book *The Wages of History: Emotional Labor on Public History's Front Line*. Similar to me, Tyson began her work as a living history interpreter and researcher at the same time she was a graduate student. She also conducted thirty-two interviews with frontline workers and managers, though mine were a blend of part-time paid docents and volunteers. While only one MoRE narrator chose anonymity, Burns assigned narrators a pseudonym. She also relied on unique archival materials, including institutional memos, work schedules, training notes, interpretive materials, and electronic files, with the support of fort staff.[73]

Rebirth also integrates a variety of archival primary source material. This includes collections at the Woodrow Wilson Presidential Library, located next door to his first childhood home in Virginia. Most relevant were documents related to Edith Galt Wilson's support for the establishment of the Staunton HHM. I consulted four manuscript collections at the South Caroliniana Library at the University of South Carolina, where records of the local American Legion Auxiliary and their efforts to save Wilson's Columbia home in the 1920s are held. The university's Moving Image Research Library also provided footage of a 1926 Red Shirt parade celebrating the end of Reconstruction in Columbia, which is used in a MoRE exhibit film. The last chapter on President Wilson's screening of *The Birth of a Nation* draws heavily on film analysis and the National Archives digitization of silent era films, including Griffith's and a response film by Black director Oscar Micheaux titled *Within Our Gates* (1920). This chapter, centering the MoRE's last exhibit film, *The Legacy of Woodrow Wilson and Reconstruction*, required working across the disciplines of history and media studies to contextualize a film central to the dual narrative of Reconstruction and Wilson.

This book is primarily a public and oral history monograph about historic house museums and Reconstruction. I wrote for public history practitioners, especially docents, oral historians, and those working with contested spaces. However, executive directors and museums studies specialists in education and interpretation will benefit immensely from this study in best practices. In addition the book traverses the terrain of southern history, historic preservation, women's history, presidential history, and film and media studies. Dismantling a shrine preserved by white clubwomen to President Wilson to interpret the gains and promise of Reconstruction for Black citizens in South Carolina as well as show how white supremacy and racialized violence brought the period to a tragic end required all of these instruments of knowledge.

I have divided *Rebirth* into two parts. Part I, "Bait and Switch?," traces the origin of the Woodrow Wilson Family Home as a presidential shrine in the 1920s, its redesign between 2005 and 2014, and the subsequent docent training process. Part II, "Interpreting Silences, Violence, and Memories," provides a deeper dive into four interpretive spaces and exhibits within the home. Each chapter serves as a concise case study of four themes either absent in most HHM interpretation or difficult to discuss because of the subject of white supremacy and violence against African American people. These examples center on the lives of Black people as they made their way through a new free labor system, the continuous white supremacy campaign that ultimately ended Reconstruction in South Carolina in 1876, and the memory of Wilson's Progressive Era presidency through 1920.

The first chapter traces the 1920s origins of the MoRE at the WWFH in Columbia as a presidential shrine. In the wake of World War I, the local unit of the American Legion Auxiliary saved the home from demolition as part of a larger campaign by white women's organizations to commemorate the Lost Cause, white supremacy, and segregationist leaders along the southern landscape. The chapter lays the foundation of the MoRE as a typical "great white man" HHM and shrine that defined the preservation movement since Ann Pamela Cunningham arranged purchase of Mount Vernon in the 1850s. The chapter also uncovers the fiscal challenges the Legion Auxiliary faced to preserve the home, made worse by their failure to secure public and financial support from Wilson's widow, Edith Galt. Instead she devoted most of her commemorative energies to her husband's birthplace in Staunton, Virginia, now the location of his private presidential library. In 1961 she donated his last residence with her in Washington, DC, the President Woodrow Wilson House, to the National Trust for Historic Preservation. The chapter situates the MoRE within all four of Wilson's HHMs, all located in the South. Three of them were where a young boy known by his family as Tommy lived long before he became president. In 2001 Historic Augusta, Inc., opened the last one, a decorative-arts-centered shrine. The Wilsons lived in a Presbyterian manse, now the Boyhood Home of President Woodrow Wilson, during the Civil War and early Reconstruction before moving to Columbia.

Chapter 2 details how redesigning the WWFH into the MoRE upended the outdated structure of HHMs. The WWFH overturned traditional assumptions about HHMs, namely the need for a fully guided tour, period room furniture vignettes, and original artifacts. The Wilson home itself became the primary artifact, allowing for an interpretation focused on a specific place and period: Reconstruction-era Columbia. Thematic panel exhibits line each room, most of which contain a small number of objects from Historic Columbia's collection owned by the Wilson family or material culture related to Reconstruction. The MoRE emphasizes a people-centered approach to interpreting objects rather than an object-centered approach dominant in HHMs.

The final chapter of part I, "Docent Training: Unlearning the Lost Cause and Reconstruction Memory," focuses on rarely studied docents, encouraging future examination of their experiences and training. The MoRE's unconventional redesign upended the traditional model of an HHM. The unexpected panel exhibit, the horrific nature of some of the subject matter, and visitor expectations of a guided tour resulted in the decision to maintain the use of docents to interpret a semiguided tour. Historic Columbia reinvented docent education and their training process for the MoRE. Not only did the organization offer a variety of required workshops covering history, public history best practices, and racial and cultural sensitivity training, but it also evaluated and thoroughly vetted each docent to conduct tours. The majority of Historic Columbia's volunteers did not complete the training process. Most docents rejected the new home and training because they disliked the Reconstruction-heavy script or the time-consuming and rigorous evaluation demands. The docents who excelled were those who worked in education or held advanced degrees and were primarily women. Over time some recalcitrant docents embraced the changes once they saw the museum's success or learned that the interpretation had evolved based on feedback from MoRE docents. Although numerous docents came into the process having learned the Lost Cause or elements of a white supremacist view of Reconstruction, many of them used the training and their tours to overturn these biased or inaccurate preconceived notions. Remarkably those docents "reconstructed" their memory of Reconstruction and taught visitors to do the same. However, docent resistance, which mostly came from volunteers, demonstrates the importance of professionalizing docent interpretation.

Part II showcases thematic case studies, beginning with "Aren't I a Citizen? Interpreting the Lives of Black Women and Domestic Workers in Historic House Museums." This chapter focuses on the MoRE within the context of HHMs, especially southern ones, and their tradition of limiting or excluding narratives of nonelite whites. Chapter 4 describes how the MoRE incorporated historiography, census records, architecture, image analysis, and docent training to give greater agency to unidentified domestic workers and Black women educators discussed throughout the home. But in the effort to illuminate the lives of working-class domestics, some docents and visitors succumbed to the *Downton Abbey* effect, which blinded them to the unique racial circumstances that affected workers' lives beyond their economic and social status. However, the MoRE's interpretation of Black experiences proved far more successful than other Wilson homes at that time, which employed either annihilation or relative incorporation. Those outdated interpretive modes, which remain common at plantation sites, either avoid Black narratives or include them intermittently; nonetheless, as a radical HHM, the MoRE fell short because the interpretation avoided the violence and sexual exploitation experienced by Black women during Reconstruction. Nor did the docent training adequately prepare MoRE docents to discuss this unsettling history with visitors when necessary.

Set in the context of the assault on the US Capitol on January 6, 2021, chapter 5 addresses best practices for interpreting white supremacy and domestic political terrorism. The chapter presents the MoRE's interpretation of the end of Reconstruction in South Carolina and the violence of Red Shirts—the statewide paramilitary force that used fraud and violence to return white Democrats to power in 1876. White supremacist artifacts and images from Reconstruction, combined with docent-guided open-ended questions, facilitate visitor dialogue about the Red Shirts and their predecessors, including the Ku Klux Klan. The room's exhibit introduced Reconstruction-era violence to some white visitors for the first time. Script revisions, docent evaluations, and docent oral histories show that docents were at their most comfortable and successful in this challenging space. For some, discussing white violence against Black citizens made them acutely aware of their own white privilege as well as their family and community ties to violence. The chapter is also a call to action to spark public dialogue and guide policymakers in addressing our nation's recent surge in paramilitary white nationalism and domestic terrorism. The exhibit demonstrates historical continuity by offering concrete examples from the distant past that are still recognizable today, including the inept federal and state responses that failed to stop contemporary white supremacist violence and political fraud.

Chapter 6, "Interpreting the Craft: Doing Reconstruction History," looks at the difficult transition that MoRE docents faced coming from the "Red Shirt room" to the final semi-guided space in the home. The bedroom that once belonged to Wilson's parents, signified by the couple's authentic bed, demanded a succinct but powerful denouement that tied the history and memory of Reconstruction to Wilson's presidency. The most successful docents focused on how history, specifically Reconstruction history, gets professionally made. Docents with advanced degrees, particularly in public history, crafted a narrative for visitors that explained and simultaneously revised the early twentieth-century Dunning School's academic defense of the Lost Cause and white supremacist narrative of Reconstruction, which was supported by Wilson as a historian. This choice to bring visitors up-to-date with current scholarship crafted by historians over the last fifty years serves as a modification of Hilary Iris Lowe's call for HHMs to adopt the interpretive techniques of literary house museums. These literary centered sites provide visitors with creative, interactive engagement experiences via books and their authors that continue to resonate long after the tour.[74]

The final chapter illuminates the challenges of interpreting memory, both of Reconstruction and Woodrow Wilson, as well as the white supremacy that is associated with both subjects. The chapter focuses on the exhibit film *The Legacy of Woodrow Wilson and Reconstruction*, its revision within the first year of opening, and its attempts to explain the importance of *The Birth of a Nation* to Wilson's presidency and Reconstruction memory. The debate that the exhibit film ignited made Historic Columbia acutely aware that most volunteer docents were reluctant to frame Wilson as a racist akin to fellow politicians from South Carolina, such as Benjamin Tillman or "Cotton Ed" Smith. However, in the wake of the 2015 Charleston massacre and nationwide student protests on college campuses addressing institutional racism, Wilson's memory and white supremacy came under attack. These events allowed Historic Columbia to address the issue of Wilson's relationship with white supremacy, which had been minimized by the original MoRE interpretation of the former president. Workshops with docents generated new conversations within the institution outside of public view, which often continued between docents and visitors in the public space of the MoRE.

The conclusion applies visitor evaluation data and reviews to assess the success of key arguments in each chapter. The chapter surveys the overwhelmingly positive responses from visitors to the Reconstruction narrative in the first year of opening. The conclusion also addressed the October 2020 name change from the WWFH to the MoRE, which resolved one of the chief criticisms raised by the tour review appearing in the professional journal *Public Historian* for its special issue on HHMs. The museum's name change met the energy of a nationwide effort to dismantle white supremacy commemorated in the public sphere that had flourished and faced fierce resistance since the MoRE reopened its doors in 2014. The conclusion closes with Historic Columbia's increased resolve to challenge white supremacist narratives and to teach Reconstruction history to the public.

The MoRE demanded relevancy as it shunned its presidential shrine origins and the partial political and social truths that style of interpretation sold. Rather than be trapped in a clichéd, dollhouse-style interpretation with voyeuristic vignettes that serve as a "repetitive time stamp" set to the average afternoon typically depicted in HHMs, the MoRE answered the call of Franklin Vagnone and Deborah Ryan, self-described historic house museum anarchists, to turn these sites "upside down and inside out" for the sake of survival.[75] When the deteriorating home closed in 2005, the WWFH was guilty of all these charges. But with the MoRE's reopening, Historic Columbia produced an exhibit and tour that when combined with the voices of public historians, docents, and visitors serve as a guide to revolutionize the obsolete house museum. The process of this transformation from presidential shrine to Reconstruction museum simultaneously demonstrates the unique challenges of correcting alternative memory and the boundaries of discussing violence and oppression perpetuated against Black citizens by white Americans. The difficulty lay not only in initiating conversations with the public but also in promoting honest dialogues and best practices within the institution itself.

In illuminating the voices of the docents in conversation with staff and visitors, this book provides valuable insight into how this revolutionary reinterpretation of Reconstruction at a presidential shrine succeeded and at times failed on the front lines. I recall that conflicted anonymous docent, who was excited to be a part of the MoRE "as it transformed into the nation's first museum of Reconstruction" but not in the historical record. Since college the docent felt both North and South knew almost nothing about this period of American history. The native South Carolinian knew personally that white southerners often espoused the Lost Cause and a negative interpretation of Reconstruction. The docent recognized they were a part of a Reconstruction reckoning and, I suspect, worried that their views, progressive by standards of the Jim Crow era, might one day be antiquated or used against them. Yet this docent boasted that "in Columbia, South Carolina and in the "state that was the first to secede from the Union" is the "first museum dedicated to Reconstruction, which I think is wonderful."[76] The MoRE is no longer the sole museum or site devoted to Reconstruction in the state, but the first of many in South Carolina attempting to atone for its Reconstruction sins.

PART I

Bait and Switch?

CHAPTER 1

Building Shrines

Women Gatekeepers and Making the President Southern

On February 11, 1929, Ruth Cappelmann, who was leading the campaign by the Columbia unit of American Legion Auxiliary to save Woodrow Wilson's childhood home from demolition, wrote to former First Lady Edith Galt Wilson asking her to attend the dedication of the Woodrow Wilson Boyhood Home in the summer of 1930. Cappelmann reached out to Edith Wilson on at least three occasions, only ever receiving responses from John Randolph Bolling, Wilson's secretary and brother. Bolling politely responded that the First Lady expected to be abroad but would "make every effort to attend" if those plans changed. Wilson, with only a few weeks' notice, declined an earlier luncheon invitation the previous month.[1] Cappelmann probably hoped Wilson would be an enthusiastic supporter of efforts to save the president's Columbia home. Little did she know that Wilson was about to donate her influence, time, and personal belongings to her husband's birthplace in Staunton, Virginia. Despite never meeting, both women continued their work within the historic house museum movement and reflected a broader pattern of commemorative labor by women and their various associations. Both Cappelmann and Edith Wilson established historic house museum shrines to the twenty-eighth president of the United States. However, the two museums sanctioned by Wilson's widow would become her husband's most prominent.

The 1920s origins of the Museum of the Reconstruction Era at the Woodrow Wilson Family Home in Columbia, South Carolina, occurred at the intersection of two commemorative movements, a larger campaign across the South by middle-class and elite white women's organizations that often advanced the Lost Cause narrative and celebrated segregationist leaders as well national trends within the historic house movement to preserve presidential shrines. The American Legion Auxiliary (ALA) formed in 1919 to support the American Legion via the women's sphere. Congress chartered the legion earlier that year as a patriotic veteran's organization. It aided World War I veterans socially and economically as well as promoted Americanism and the preservation of the memory and history of the war. By 1920 the ALA had spread to forty-five states with 1,342 units, and by 1923 the legion was the largest veterans' organization. The membership of the legion, which was segregated in the South, comprised primarily white, middle-class conservatives.[2] The ALA was a patriotic version of the many women's voluntary associations of the era, variously organized around literary, social reform, philanthropic, and/or hereditary interests. These associations were well-organized, with boards of directors and trustees, and achieved astounding feats of fundraising, making them incredibly successful at installing their narrative on the public landscape. Memberships often overlapped and grew rapidly as evidenced by the Daughters of the American Revolution (DAR). Formed in 1890 after the Sons of the American Revolution denied them entry, within five years, DAR grew from a few members to a membership higher than the Sons of the American Revolution or the Sons of the Revolution. These clubwomen were interested in local history, which patriotic and hereditary societies like the ALA and the DAR strengthened. These mostly elite, white women of the New South, without suffrage or federal support, built monuments and a foundation for what historian W. Fitzhugh Brundage calls "collective historical memory" that offered them the power to make historical narrative and levy cultural authority. While they celebrated a past distinct from the nation, these women and the HHM movement both promoted reunification.[3]

The Columbia unit of the ALA emerged in a post–World War I world when women's groups were gradually losing members and control of public history to the state. Patriotic and hereditary groups like the ALA willingly united with the state, however, to subsidize the cost of creating archives and museums, which held the documents and artifacts required to draft future historical narratives of the South.[4] In the 1920s and 1930s, the MoRE was a typical "great white man" house museum and presidential shrine that exemplified the HHM preservation movement from its inception when Ann Pamela Cunningham arranged purchase of George Washington's Mount Vernon in the 1850s. The Mount Vernon Ladies' Association saved George Washington's residence and created the model for the HHM movement. This effort and the Monticello campaign, fashioned as Mount Vernon 2.0, demonstrated the politics of preservation, which promoted unity as regional tensions threatened to bring the United States to war in the antebellum period and the North and South reconciled following Reconstruction.[5] The crusade for Monticello, surprisingly, had strong connections to Woodrow Wilson, whose election in 1912 marked the first of a southern Democrat to assume the presidency since the Civil War, as well as the return of a nationally reconciled Democratic Party. As governor of New Jersey, Wilson endorsed the 1912 testimony of Maud Littleton, wife of Rep. Martin Littleton (D-NY), before Congress to rescue Monticello from private ownership. Wilson's secretary of state, William Jennings Bryan, eventually convinced fellow Democrat Jefferson Levy, the owner of Monticello, that selling would commemorate and protect a fragile Democratic coalition built by Wilson. Key to this reunification process was eliminating "the last vestiges of white sympathy for Reconstruction" via the Dunning School and films such as *The Birth of a Nation*, which, combined with southern tourism and monument building, became what Karen L. Cox called a "culture of reconciliation." Thus Monticello was but "another dimension of the post-Reconstruction effort to recover the Old South."[6]

The effort to save two of Wilson's boyhood homes began in the middle of a surge in commemoration, including HHMs, that fostered a patriotic spirit and the greater mission of Americanization. By the 1890s preservation efforts rescued two historic homes vulnerable to ruin per year. The movement expanded with the rise of the automobile, until HHMs numbered more than four hundred by 1933, stretching from the East Coast to the first cabins of the West. In the decade after World War I, commemoration expressed loyalty to the nation-state, a process that accelerated during the 1930s and 1940s and brought the federal government into national memory making.[7] Amid this boom the American Legion, proponents of "100% Americanism" and those strongly committed to preventing subversion, joined the Americanization effort. The legion and its Committee on History Investigation campaigned to revise the national narrative and school curriculum to promote a triumphant historical account starring great white men descended from Western European stock. The legion viewed the budding US empire as a noble endeavor and World War I as necessary. Part of this crusade, a thousand-page, two-volume 1926 textbook, *The Story of Our American People*, failed to meet scholarly rigor established by professional historians, lacked readability, and could not reconcile the overall theme of Americanization with the nation's sectionalism, racial and immigration history, and penchant for empire. The book presented Wilson as an Anglo-Saxon president who desired peace but prepared for war to protect democracy and who unified his cabinet, leading southerners back onto the political stage. The legion abandoned the project, which George Lewis likened to the 1776 Commission, a response to Nikole Hannah-Jones's 1619 Project, that argued exceptionalism and heroism should be privileged in history. The legion also displayed a disrespect for its own auxiliary by relegating women to fashion or jokes about aging and ignoring auxiliary activities in publications. The Richland County ALA unit in Columbia was remarkable in its success at saving and administering the Wilson home, because few units participated in lobbying and, when they did, education and welfare were center. Where the textbook failed, the Richland ALA's effort to save and preserve Wilson's home was a perfect project to support the legion's Committee on History Investigation.[8]

The MoRE's foundation stemmed from the same shrine worship movement that inspired the preservation of the Wilson homes scattered across the South. As the Roaring Twenties neared its end, white women and their patriotic women's organizations saved Wilson's home in Columbia and the manse he was born in in Staunton, Virginia. The Richland ALA unit and Ruth Cappelmann faced fiscal challenges in preserving Wilson's home, made worse by their failure to secure a celebrity endorsement and financial support from Edith Wilson. Instead the First Lady assumed control of how and where Wilson's memory and legacy would be interpreted in HHMs. She devoted most of her commemorative energies to her husband's birthplace in Staunton, now the location of his private presidential library. Staunton's close proximity to Washington, DC, permitted Edith and birthplace secretary Emily Smith to cultivate relationships with political elites. Edith also supplied both original Wilson artifacts and connections to grow a $100,000 endowment. Then, in 1961, she donated her husband's residence with her in Washington, the President Woodrow Wilson House, and the majority of her belongings to the National Trust for Historic Preservation. Through the efforts of middle-class white clubwomen and Edith Wilson, three HHMs decorated with period furniture and Wilson material culture enshrined the twenty-eighth US president by the 1960s, demonstrating the popularity of HHMs.

Four decades later, the one HHM Edith Wilson did not actively support, the Woodrow Wilson Family Home in Columbia, closed its exhibit amid the home's disrepair. By that time a new Wilson HHM opened in Augusta, Georgia, hoping to fill a historiographical gap with Woodrow Wilson's southern upbringing during the Civil War and Reconstruction. In 2001, under the leadership of Erick Montgomery, Historic Augusta, Inc., opened the fourth and latest Wilson HHM as another decorative arts shrine located in the Augusta Presbyterian manse that Wilson occupied for a decade in Georgia. Montgomery's history of the Wilson family's time during the Civil War and early Reconstruction before the family moved to Columbia in 1870 supports and helped inspire parts of the reinterpretation at the MoRE—that the future President Woodrow Wilson was distinctly southern and unreconstructed. By the time Wilson arrived in Columbia, he was a typical southern teenager, with characteristics he developed while living in Augusta. Today the sites in Staunton, Augusta, and Columbia interpret Wilson's boyhood in the South as slavery was eroding and when his father Joseph Wilson's career was blossoming, rather than the president's. However, the Woodrow Wilson Boyhood Home (WWBH) tour in Augusta stopped short of its revisionist potential by not connecting Wilson's positive childhood experience to the era of Reconstruction and minimizing the significant professional gains his father made by supporting the Confederacy and slavery during the war.

The Woodrow Wilson Family Home's Origins as Presidential Shrine

In 1933 the leading museum expert Laurence Coleman acknowledged the shrine origins of the HHM movement. The homes "chosen to survive" were those "where celebrity is born, where fame makes its home, where art or science labors in erstwhile obscurity, where important incidents occur, where death visits the great."[9] In the twenty-first century, HHM staffs struggle to break the hold that fame and a whitewashed national unity have over their sites as well as to address modern institutional challenges. First, HHMs are too numerous. As birthplaces and properties of elites shrouded in outdated interpretations of the past, HHMs often lack diversity and relevancy.[10] The MoRE broke new ground by deconstructing the Wilson shrine and reinventing the ideal American image typically found there. Instead Wilson's home illuminates the patriotism of Black Americans working toward political, economic, and social equality when he was a teenager living in Reconstruction-era Columbia. This continues a process underway at the nation's most prestigious presidential homes and reputable southern institutions, such as Mount Vernon and Monticello. By adopting the interpretive style of social historians, these HHMs now present more inclusive narratives that also incorporate nonwhite and working-class people in an attempt to provide a more holistic encounter with the past and its people and expand the museum-going audience. New interpretations of slavery at Monticello's Mulberry Row and Whitney Plantation as well as a variety of tours available on the immigrant experience in New York's Lower East Side Tenement Museum reflect some of these more successful attempts.[11]

The MoRE could never entirely shed its presidential shrine origins. Historic Columbia chose instead to combine institutional history and neighborhood architecture at the beginning of the tour to tell this origin story. Docents and visitors depart the gift shop to start the tour and pass Township Auditorium, the structure that sparked the movement to save Wilson's home. The tour lacks enough time to tell the full account of how white women's organizations, namely the local unit of the ALA, saved the home despite fierce competition from Wilson's birthplace in Staunton for resources, funding, and status. The Woodrow Wilson Family Home first opened in 1933 to the public, and for the next eighty years it functioned as a presidential shrine. Although the 2014 reinterpretation at MoRE would shed this foundation, Historic Columbia believed it important to include the museum's origins and combine them with the Wilsons' local movements and the evolution of the neighborhood as a "teaching tool."[12]

The American Legion Richland Post No. 6 and its women's auxiliary led the campaign to stop the destruction of Wilson's home and replace it with Township Auditorium on the property. The state's ALA first celebrated

Wilson's teenage years by placing a memorial tablet outside the home in 1925.[13] However, women's organizations and club leaders turned out in droves to support the ALA in preserving the home three years later. The president of the auxiliary in Columbia, Ruth Cappelmann, along with clubwomen such as Ann Cathcart, led the effort to save the home by first stopping its demolition and then campaigning for legislation and fundraising to transform it into a memorial. Cappelmann circumvented competition from a Wilson film documentary fundraiser and then lobbied the American Legion to place the home under the direct care of the state ALA and open it as a museum. Several of the foremost women from the auxiliary administered care for the Wilson home for the next thirty-five years, while Cappelmann served as caretaker for three decades.

Ruth Cappelmann established an early role in saving Wilson's childhood home on its original property. As president of the local ALA, she signed the agreement in August 1928 that negotiated a deal to purchase the dwelling for a one-dollar down payment, halting its immediate demolition. The agreement required paying in cash the remaining balance of one thousand dollars to the Auditorium Committee, owners of the home and lot, within thirty days and moving the house off the property.[14] In September 1928 Columbia's American Legion and Legion Auxiliary appointed Cappelmann, Cathcart, Francis Lumpkin, and Agnes McMaster, four future chairwomen of the Wilson home, as auxiliary representatives to discuss the best way to remove the house.[15] But less than a week later, the women changed the legion's position, resolving to preserve the home where it stood on Hampton Avenue in a way favorable to the auditorium trustees.[16]

The campaign to save Wilson's home immediately generated statewide interest and demonstrated how critical women's organizations were.[17] At the time, there were only four HHMs in the state of South Carolina. Three of them were administered or owned by the United Daughters of the Confederacy (UDC), the DAR, and the Colonial Dames. Two owned by the Charleston Museum opened not long after the Wilson home in the 1930s.[18] Approximately 115 organizations across the state emerged by late 1928 as enthusiastic champions of enshrining the Wilson home. Ninety-five organizations passed formal resolutions in support of the preservation effort by the end of October. South Carolina's American Legion, including its state president, seven posts, and seven sister auxiliaries, joined Columbia's unit in solidarity.[19] Columbia-based organizations sent about 20 percent of the total resolutions. One of these, the Richland County Federation of Women's Clubs, was led by Marie Jones, a future chairwoman of the Wilson home and wife of one of the auditorium trustees. An impressive six resolutions came from local teacher improvement and parent-teacher organizations, signaling a small but well-connected network of white women actively involved and influential in public education. At least ten counties with women's club wrote resolutions, including four book clubs, two Jewish organizations, music clubs, and study clubs. Rural women, too, came out in support, in the form of the Council of Farm Women in two counties. The community of Rock Hill forwarded an astounding seven resolutions supporting the project. White women's organizations led the charge there too, drafting over 60 percent of the resolutions. War-inspired women's organizations in the memorialization business also joined the ranks of the legionnaires. Thirteen chapters of the DAR and eight from the UDC, including Columbia's Wade Hampton unit, submitted resolutions. One DAR chapter confidently claimed that women's organizations in the state would financially support the restoration and upkeep of the home. Other noteworthy women's groups enlisted in the campaign: the Daughters of 1812, the Women's Christian Temperance Union, and Columbia's Junior League, League of Women Voters, and a Colonial Dames branch.[20]

Resolutions varied in focus but addressed six themes. The most popular, and especially important to women's clubs, was preserving the home as a shrine. Eleven clubs, including the state American Legion, three chapters of the UDC, and two Federation of Women's Clubs representing nine counties, referred to the home as such. Also prevalent among eleven organizations, mostly the war-related ones, was honoring Wilson as a war president. The other themes, in order of popularity, were the necessity of moving the auditorium to save the home, the historical value of the home, Wilson's significance as a southerner and Democrat, and the importance of supporting Americanism.[21]

The ALA campaign forged ahead in January 1929 in its effort to get a bill passed through the state legislature to preserve the Wilson home on its original site. The bill appropriated $35,000, with $6,000 allotted for repairs and renovations and the remainder for purchase of the house and land. The bill empowered the Historical Commission of South Carolina to make the purchase and create a "Woodrow Wilson Memorial Museum." Assuming a curatorial role, the commission developed the rules and regulations to procure or accept any historic relic, memento, or article related to the wars in which South Carolina and the nation engaged. The bill also proposed a close relationship with the Confederate Relic Room, operated by the local Wade Hampton chapter of the UDC in the State House. The third oldest museum in South Carolina, the relic room began collecting and preserving Confederate artifacts in 1896.[22] The plan called for the relic room to move to the Wilson house and become custodian of the site. The Columbia legion and auxiliary posts hoped for but failed to secure permission to build additions onto the Wilson property and to move the artifacts from the relic room to the Wilson home to the satisfaction of the Wade Hampton chapter. The auxiliary's legislative committee asked each unit to contact its legislator, even if at home for the weekend adjournment, and urged them to remain in contact with senators until the bill's passage. Units could also collaborate with other community groups.[23]

The bill passed March 7, 1929, but the reveling did not last long. After the legion and auxiliary celebrated with a tea at the Wilson house and the national commander of the American Legion lavished praise on Cappelmann for her "splendid work" in saving the home, the auxiliary immediately shifted into fundraising mode.[24] The unit donated the first $500 of $17,500 required in the bill and launched a campaign to raise half of appropriated funds, which benefited from the network of clubs that wrote resolutions and propelled several women into leadership. For three months, the executive committee of the Woodrow Wilson Purchase Fund (WWPF) met at the Chamber of Commerce in Columbia.[25] Cappelmann held the only position of power as a woman, rising from temporary secretary to elected secretary.[26] The committee authorized a weeklong publicity campaign ahead of a statewide campaign. Cappelmann invited the presidents of various clubs such as the DAR to meet with the group. The heads of pro–Wilson Home organizations across the state, often powerful clubwomen, served on the state executive committee along with the local officers of the WWPF committee. The state presidents of the Colonial Dames, League of Women Voters, American Legion, and ALA, as well as representatives from the SC Federation of Women's Clubs, Sons of Confederate Veterans, and nearly a dozen others, made up the committee.[27]

Two other auxiliary women active in the initial movement, Ann Cathcart and Francis Lumpkin, emerged as leaders. Lumpkin eventually became chairwoman of the Wilson home in 1938–39, followed by Cathcart the next year. Lumpkin and her sister-in-law Katharine Du Pre Lumpkin exemplify how women worked to support and occasionally reject the Lost Cause and white supremacist memory of Reconstruction. Katharine Lumpkin and the women in her family maintained close ties with Confederate women's organizations at various points of their lives, and her sister was the maid of honor in an annual reunion parade of the Red Shirts. Yet she began to reject her father's Lost Cause indoctrination after reading Thomas Dixon's *The Clansman* (1905) and attending a screening of *The Birth of a Nation*, as she recounts in her 1946 book, *The Making of a Southerner*. Francis married Bryan Lumpkin, Katharine's youngest brother, a white conservative who opposed her liberal political views and resisted integration. In the same decade that Katharine worked for the YWCA and built an interracial coalition with Black student secretaries in her role as the organization's national student secretary for the southern region, Francis began her work to save and manage the Wilson home.[28] Prior to her tenure as chair, Cathcart, next to Cappelmann, became the most vocal and active woman in the WWPF.[29] Cappelmann mostly took notes and observed during WWPF meetings. Cathcart presented new ideas and was a leader in fundraising. As counties began requesting quotas, she successfully pushed the local committee to hire a professional organizer for the state campaign.[30] The committee selected Cathcart as captain of the women's team for the house-to-house canvas to raise funds.[31] She organized the 180 chaperones accompanying 150 college students for Wilson Tag Day on May 8. She and Cappelmann along with two other WWPF members met with the governor to seek state funds. Cathcart was also part of a small group that met with the auditorium committee and unofficially secured the purchase of the lot for its original $28,000 price tag.[32]

House canvasing and Tag Day proved most lucrative, bringing the campaign within $600 of its goal. The WWPF raised $14,000 in a month, often playing to people's patriotism and Wilson's historic relationship with the community. Fundraising letters requested that recipients solicit ten other citizens to "rescue" the home as their patriotic duty.[33] A joint DAR and ALA benefit near the end of the campaign had an extensive program, including Wilson's childhood history, a poem dedication to his patriotism and good deeds, and "A History with Every Plant," a plant sale "pregnant with associations of the immortal Wilson," featuring items plucked from places where Wilson spent time.[34]

On June 20, 1929, the state of South Carolina became owner of Wilson's home, but the state ALA wanted administrative control. Initially the SC Historical Commission oversaw the house and procured the most prized Wilson artifact, the bed the president was born in.[35] With $1,000 remaining in appropriated funds, the bed arrived in time for the home's dedication during the legion's state convention in 1930. Alice Wilson McElroy, the president's niece, included a bureau and table in the sale because she felt ashamed for taking the money. She needed tuition to educate her children after the family returned from a long missionary trip in Japan.[36] Despite this success, during preparation for the convention and dedication, the state auxiliary petitioned the American Legion to be named custodians, along with the local Richland County legion post. The ALA argued it had launched the movement to save the home and was a war-centered organization and thus a natural steward. Additionally World War I veterans and their widows, more so than other citizens, felt bound to Wilson.[37] The legion ignored the proposal for eight months, which prolonged passage at the state convention for two years. The 1932 act required public entry for no more than twenty-five cents. Funds for upkeep would come from a $500 general legion fund and ALA unit donations, ranging from $38 to $82 a year.[38]

With the home under ALA control, Cappelmann continued to develop the Wilson site through her leadership in the ALA and other organizations. A founding member and vice president of the Crape Myrtle Garden Club, she secured two crape myrtle trees for landscaping.[39] She held the chair of the memorial for six consecutive terms and eight years overall (1956–62, 1964–66), by far the longest tenure, consecutive or otherwise. In her first year, she presided over a large reception held at the Wilson Home for the president's one-hundredth birthday on December 28, 1956. She also served as chair the last two years the auxiliary ran the home. Claiming that it could no longer care for the memorial, the ALA relinquished control to the Richland County Historical Commission in 1966.[40]

Ruth Cappelmann guided Woodrow Wilson's childhood home into and out of the ALA's charge, although other auxiliary women and women's organizations helped her in the fight. At the end of her tenure, she reflected on the importance of Wilson and his childhood home. It was the only home his parents ever owned. His parents and sisters were buried at the local Presbyterian church. Cappelmann prized the family artifacts she had played a role in acquiring for the collection: Wilson's bed, bureau, and table, his mother's Bible and silk quilt, and the desk and chair that he used as New Jersey's governor. In the end the work of Cappelmann and the ALA attracted the interest of *National Geographic* and Wilson's most noted biographer Arthur S. Link, who began to ask new questions about Wilson's childhood history.[41]

The Virginians

Despite the best efforts of Cappelmann and her successor Ann Cathcart, their passion to preserve Wilson's childhood home in Columbia could not match the influence of Edith Galt Wilson and Emily Smith in saving the Wilson birthplace in Staunton, Virginia. It was not for a lack of trying. Cappelmann eagerly wanted the support of Wilson, who brushed off her several letters of inquiry during the ALA's fundraising campaign. Cappelmann first reached out to learn more about President Wilson's life in Columbia from those who knew him best. John Randolph Bolling, Edith Wilson's brother and secretary, suggested Cappelmann contact Ray Stannard Baker, who was working on the authorized biography of the president.[42] Baker made clear how much Columbia influenced Wilson, that the president's years there were the "richest" and happiest of his childhood. He loved the home since it was planned by his mother and located a few blocks from the church where his father preached and his parents were buried. Baker opined that it would be a "great loss" if the "home so intimately associated" with Wilson's childhood was razed.[43]

Cappelmann did not realize when she first began to write to Wilson that Staunton was the real threat to ALA fundraising in the competition to be Woodrow Wilson's premier southern childhood home. Cappelmann likely viewed the Woodrow Wilson Memorial Society as the fiscal menace. Four months following the president's death in 1924, the Memorial Society released a ninety-minute compilation documentary, *The Woodrow Wilson Film Memorial*. It positively eulogized him and featured him delivering speeches, signing documents, and interacting with world leaders.[44] The film circulated the country as part of a fundraising campaign that benefited the Memorial Society, which also split the admission proceeds with local sponsors; however, the society was guaranteed at least fifty cents a head. In early 1929, society representative H.F. Drugan wrote to Cappelmann offering the ALA a chance to sponsor the film in advance of its tour in South Carolina. Cappelmann, perhaps believing the film would oversaturate the community with requests for Woodrow Wilson related donations, did not want the film to be associated with the ALA's campaign or screened in the region. She wrote the First Lady twice more about the film. Wilson had not viewed it but was aware of it. In the end, by remaining friendly with Dugan and helping him network, Cappelmann masterfully dodged his efforts to meet, finally declining sponsorship during a phone conversation. She also convinced the Memorial Society to limit their viewings and fundraising to Charleston until the ALA's campaign ended. Likely in exchange, Cappelmann arranged a meeting between Drugan and former Governor Richard Manning.[45]

The last contact came from Governor John Richards and Cappelmann, who both invited Wilson to the house's dedication in the summer of 1930. Wilson promised to "make every effort to attend" if not abroad, but she did not show.[46] Any interest she had in South Carolina seemed relegated to the Lowcountry. She visited Bernard Baruch's plantation, Hobcaw Barony, in coastal Georgetown and attended a 1930 New York performance of the Society for the Preservation of Negro Spirituals, a group formed in 1922 by Charleston's elite slave owner descendants to perform Gullah spirituals.[47] Even though Wilson lived in Staunton the shortest period during his infancy, the birthplace had the attention of his widow's philanthropy and support.

The local community saved both the Columbia and Staunton, Virginia, homes at roughly the same time in the 1930s; yet the manse where Wilson was born and spent the least amount of time, now part of the Woodrow Wilson Presidential Library and Museum, possesses the strongest claim to him. Wilson and his second wife, Edith Galt, saw themselves as Virginians.

As such Edith actively supported the preservation of the Staunton manse through large financial and artifact donations and fundraising. Wilson was one of eight US presidents from Virginia, placing him in the same lineage as founders George Washington and Thomas Jefferson. He cemented this status as one of Virginia's sons by attending law school at the University of Virginia. Wilson returned to Staunton on numerous occasions to visit his sisters and cousins attending Augusta Female Seminary (Mary Baldwin College). He also called on his beloved Aunt Marion, who had lived in Augusta, Georgia, during the Civil War and Reconstruction as he did.[48] He felt confident he could discuss any issue with candor in Virginia with other men of his "own race and breeding." Edith, native of Wytheville, Virginia, 150 miles southwest of Staunton, claimed Pocahontas and the state's first families in her lineage. Her family were slaveholders on a plantation in the eastern part of the state, and her father was a circuit court judge. Early in their courtship, Wilson grew so comfortable with Edith during a fireside conversation following dinner that he told her about his childhood in the South and of his father. Edith, who was far too young to recall Reconstruction, nonetheless spoke of the "heartache" of the period.[49] The couple's legacy as Virginians and southerners combined with the diligent work of Emily Smith, Staunton's more successful equivalent of Ruth Cappelmann, and Edith Wilson ensured the home in which Wilson was born would be preserved as the premier shrine to the president, today comprising a one-block museum and research center.

Edith Wilson's letters and donations demonstrate that she actively supported the preservation of the Staunton manse far more than the Wilson parents' privately owned home in Columbia. The presidential library contains over one hundred letters written by Wilson regarding her husband's birthplace. From its inception she was the honorary president of the Woodrow Wilson Birthplace Foundation (WWBF), but her presence was far more than honorary.[50] She displayed a silent leadership via advice and instructions to Smith. Wilson hid this private influence, exercised primarily in letters, behind the celebrity presence that she brought to public fundraising and events.

Smith's leadership skills, honed in a variety of organizations, as well as her social standing with the community made her essential to the founding and success of the Woodrow Wilson Birthplace site.[51] She felt a connection to Wilson because she belonged to the same church his father once pastored for, First Presbyterian. Smith's command originated in her position as president of the Garden Club of Virginia in 1928. She persuaded the club to restore the gardens at the manse, purchased by Mary Baldwin College following Woodrow Wilson's death in 1924. One of six women on

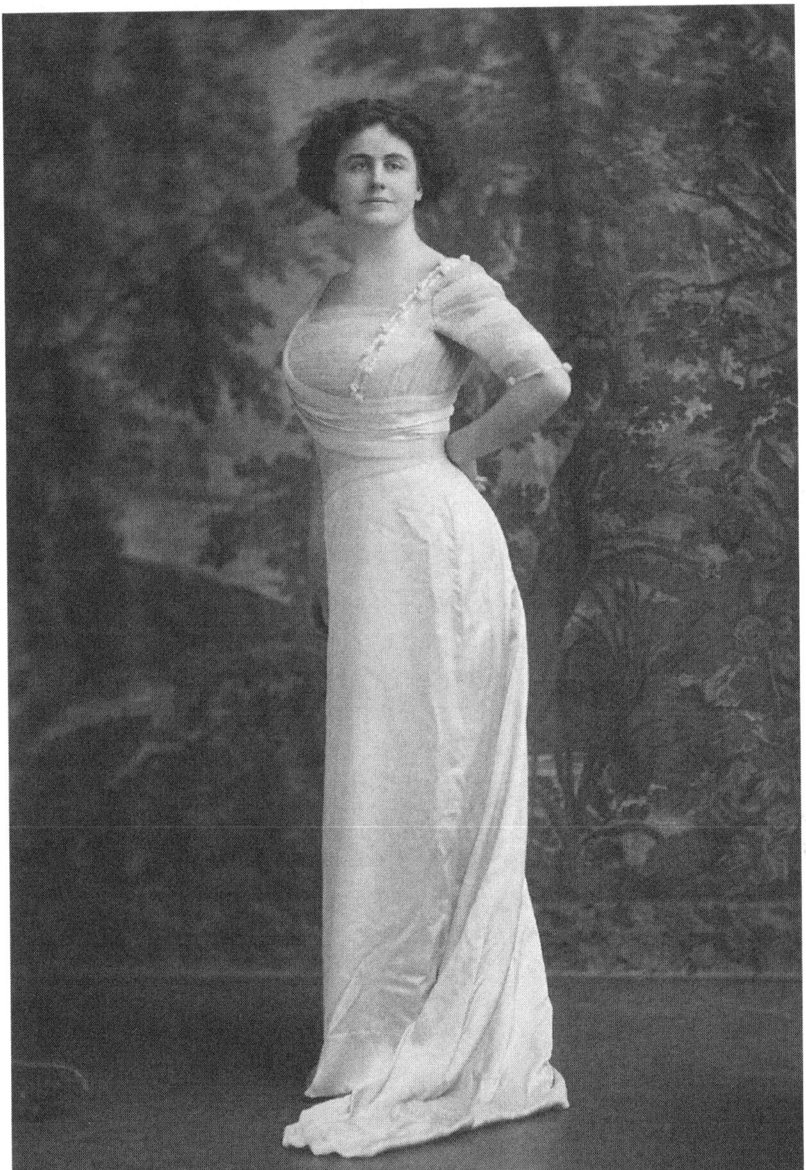

Figure 1. Edith Bolling Galt Wilson, full-length portrait, standing, facing front, hands behind waist, 1913. Courtesy of the Library of Congress. Edith Bolling Galt during Woodrow Wilson's presidency.

the restoration committee as well as the local chair, Smith led locals in the three-year restoration project, completed in 1934. Her club's Historic Garden Week, which she helped establish, raised more than $5,000.[52]

Preservation and commemoration moved slowly, despite the success of the gardens. However, Smith's collaboration with Edith Wilson began to blossom. Smith and Wilson probably met for the first time in the early 1930s and certainly by 1932, when Wilson attended a "dignified and impressive little ceremony" designating the manse a permanent memorial open to the public.[53] She carefully navigated her role, often working behind the scenes when she deemed it more appropriate.[54] She refused to affiliate her name to an early plan to request funds from the federal government for fear of "great embarrassment" should the petition be denied. She compromised, arranging a lunch for Smith and two fellow committee members, Virginia senator Harry Byrd and Adm. Cary T. Grayson, Woodrow Wilson's friend and doctor, to initiate discussion.[55] Always protective of the Wilson name, she avoided soliciting gifts in writing in case the WWBF board rejected the gift. As important as the president's widow was "to the success of the movement," Smith opined that she did not possess "the authority to form plans and appoint committees" on her own.[56] Not that it mattered much. Wilson continued to attend a variety of events to support the birthplace, but the Great Depression stifled momentum.[57]

A new energy surrounded the project after 1938 with the formation of the WWBF.[58] Nearly a decade after Columbia's campaign, a group of Stauntonians organized the foundation to purchase the property for conversion to a "national shrine." Mary Baldwin College could not afford the half-million-dollar memorial it envisioned.[59] The WWBF exploited its proximity to the nation's capital, meeting with and soliciting help from political elites. Staunton native Rose Hull, wife of Secretary of State Cordell Hull, became the foundation's president, while Judge Lawrence Groner, chief justice of Washington DC's Court of Appeals, served as chairman.[60] Smith simultaneously filled the assistant treasurer and secretary positions, and she continued to serve as the latter for sixteen years.[61] By July 1939 the WWBF owned the manse, secured through a $10,000 appropriation by the Virginia General Assembly and a $15,000 donation from the Woodrow Wilson Foundation of New York.[62] Wilson rejoiced, "It is good to know that at last the house is ours!! But that is only the first step. What we must now do is to gird our loins for the final one."[63]

By the busy tourist season of April 1939, the WWBF determined that it needed an endowment to maintain the home. Its dilapidated state meant cosmetic changes were no longer enough.[64] Despite abysmal funding, Smith, Wilson, and the local committee rejected the proposal to hire a campaign manager under the supervision of the ALA. Like in Columbia, the ALA could contact other state organizations and patriotic groups for support. Smith envisioned the WWBF committee controlling the endowment campaign as the UDC had done with Robert E. Lee's birthplace at Stratford Hall. With Chairman Groner's approval, Wilson offered Smith the chairmanship of Virginia's state endowment campaign and promised that the honorary power structure of officer positions would not interfere with Smith's work at the manse or ability to run the campaign. Smith reluctantly agreed.[65]

Wilson gave decorating, preservation, and administrative advice from the beginning and was actively involved in getting the home ready for a formal opening and dedication. She, Smith, and President Rose Hull all agreed to restore the house to its original condition before pursuing cosmetic updates like painting. With a low budget of $3,000 for furnishings, Wilson's focus turned to acquisitions.[66] Having made most of the monetary donations over the last decade, she halted all purchases to seek donations. To get the acquisitions rolling, she donated a bed, the lamp used by Wilson at the University of Virginia and in the White House, and twenty-seven pictures of his family and revered Virginians, including other presidents and Robert E. Lee. She also negotiated donations from her peers and family members, thus supplying the majority of the furniture and artifacts.[67] As the formal dedication, scheduled for May 4, 1941, approached, Wilson approved sinks and paint. She advised how to hang chandeliers, hide electrical connections on top of the mantels, and match materials effectively. She helped draft the invitation list, filled with Washington elites.[68] President Franklin Delano Roosevelt dedicated the "shrine to freedom" and brought national prestige to the day. Edith described as perfect the opening and the "lovely" furnishings she secured. The day's only flaw was the fringe on the big bed, which Wilson deemed too short.[69]

As Wilson feared would happen, World War II brought financial difficulties to the newly opened birthplace. This site held a large place in her "own small world" amid the uncertainty of war. Frugal spending and a new army hospital kept her and Smith optimistic. Fundraising for the home rather than the war proved difficult during rationing and seemed improper. She and a few supporters managed to raise fifty dollars to add to the foundation's measly thirty-three-dollar bank balance.[70] Wilson never promised specific donation amounts, but her financial contributions, along with Rose Hull securing a thousand-dollar donation from Nelson Rockefeller, kept the institution afloat.[71]

A generous gift of $25,000 from 20th Century-Fox Film Corporation in 1944 changed the WWBF's financial status by finally making a $100,000 endowment possible. Wilson's behind-the-scenes negotiations proved critical.

She likely offered extensive help with Fox's production of a Woodrow Wilson film, because the company wanted to give her $50,000 personally. She directed the money be given to the birthplace. Lest she give the appearance of commercializing her husband's memory, Wilson asked that press language originally referencing her donation as a gift be changed to place emphasis on Fox, Rose Hull, and building an endowment. Nonetheless, Wilson expected to attend any affiliated event. To her chagrin, she missed Fox's Woodrow Wilson film premiere on September 18, 1944, because she received only a few days' notice and had another engagement in South Carolina. She placed blame on the invitation committee, not Smith, but her irritation showed. She thanked Smith for sending the train schedule that "now I do not need."[72]

Despite Wilson's embarrassment at missing the Fox premiere, she remained heavily involved with the birthplace over the next decade. She influenced leadership and administration. She wrote Smith with advice, met with her and the board when possible, and aided in board member and officer selection. She facilitated the transition to a new cadre of leadership in 1949, including a new woman vice president of the WWBF, and proposed a change to the by-laws regarding trustees to make the organization run more smoothly. Wilson also raised funds and gave from her own pocketbook, wishing all the while she and Smith "had some of the Rockefeller millions."[73]

Edith's support waned, however, as the nation neared the centennial celebration of Woodrow Wilson's birth in 1856. She was overwhelmed with the number of centennial invitations flooding her mailbox. She missed more meetings but attended Staunton's major centennial celebrations.[74] On January 10, 1956, the birthplace converted the room that Wilson was born in (Columbia possessed the bed) into a temporary post office. It sold twenty-five thousand commemorative stamps on the first day. The day of the centennial, Wilson rode in the birthplace's most prized possession, the 1919 Pierce-Arrow limousine, her first artifact gift to the site in 1925. The president's "favorite car" broke down during the parade, forcing Wilson to transfer to another car.[75]

At the same time as Wilson's presence diminished, Smith grew even more prominent in the hierarchy of power. She became second vice president of the WWBF in 1954. Finally, in 1957, Smith accepted the presidency. She declined this position for two decades because she believed it was better for the site if nationally prominent figures held the top positions. Under Smith's tenure, President Dwight Eisenhower visited the home in 1960, prompting Wilson's most political and critical letter to Smith.[76] Edith was both "surprised" and "distressed" by Eisenhower's visit ten days before the presidential election, which she called "a political trick."[77] As a John F.

Kennedy supporter, she refused to be present on the grounds or be photographed with Eisenhower. She viewed it as disloyal to her husband. After the 1960 election, Wilson began plans to lure Kennedy to the site. She wrote to Jacqueline Kennedy, First Lady to First Lady. By late 1961 Kennedy verbally accepted Wilson's personal invitation to visit.[78] Both Wilson and Kennedy died before the visit could occur. Staunton held a memorial service for Edith Wilson on January 28, 1962. Wilson biographer Arthur S. Link spoke. Wilson, not surprisingly, gave $25,000 from her estate to the birthplace's endowment fund. Her enduring goal was to see the endowment reach $100,000. Before her death, Wilson secured a final critical donation of $17,000 from an unknown acquaintance, which pushed the fund over $100,000.[79]

Smith proved an excellent steward of Wilson's birthplace and legacy. She expanded the network of women's groups critical to Staunton's early success to keep the birthplace relevant after the old guard retired or passed away, and she secured a garage for the restored Pierce-Arrow.[80] She also drew Arthur Link further into the organization. Link served on the memorial commission and later the board of trustees.[81] He supported Smith's proposed education center, pushing for a corresponding exhibit with a room devoted to "photographic reproductions" of important Wilson letters and state papers and offered to select documents. Wilson artifacts were difficult to obtain, and Edith willed most of her items to S Street and the National Trust. Link donated a set of *The Papers of Woodrow Wilson* and recommended Wilson books, usually ones he authored, for sale at the birthplace. Link's son and namesake acted as chairman of the library's board of directors after the WWBF transitioned to a presidential library.[82]

Smith transformed Wilson's birthplace into a respected institution, although her vision surpassed her tenure. After thirty-five years of Wilson shrine-making, she was celebrated by the city of Staunton and the state of Virginia with a 1968 testimonial dinner.[83] The director of the American Association for State and Local History congratulated her for being that "one single individual" on a preservation and commemoration project who brought in and nurtured its many supporters. Even President Richard Nixon thanked her for her service to one of his favorite presidents.[84] However, Smith's dream of a Wilson education center, auditorium, museum, and library remained unrealized when she retired in 1973 as president emeritus. She died two years later.[85] In 2002 the WWBF changed its name to the Woodrow Wilson Presidential Library, an autonomous, independent presidential library free of the national library system's oversight. In the early aughts, the site began working on a new interpretation that incorporated Wilson's legacy and flaws, hoping to shed some of the birthplace's shrine orientation.[86]

The Mausoleum and President Woodrow Wilson House

Edith Wilson bequeathed her Washington, DC, home to the National Trust for Historic Preservation, but not until her death in 1961, giving her plenty of time to devote to Staunton. While bolstering Staunton, Wilson prepared the legacy for S Street, an extension of her presidential memory making begun with Staunton.[87] While Staunton celebrated her husband's birth and roots, S Street commemorated Wilson's presidency and the couple's final years in DC. The Wilson homes in Staunton, Augusta, and Columbia address Wilson's youth, but the President Woodrow Wilson House (PWWH) was Edith's vision of Woodrow's swan song. The home, purchased with Wilson's Nobel Peace Prize money, was six years old when the couple arrived in 1921. It supposedly changed little after 1924, when Wilson died, and included artifacts from his time as president. What Edith Wilson did not donate to Staunton fills this final home. The museum opened in 1963 and focuses on Wilson's Washington years and foreign policy from 1912 until 1924, a fitting choice since he was the only president to live exclusively in the nation's capital after departing the White House until Barack Obama. Recently the PWWH expanded its mission to include "regressive policies that institutionalized racism, segregation and the loss and obstruction of civil liberties."[88]

Edith Wilson's memory looms large in the home she occupied for forty years, though only thirty-five months were with Woodrow. She envisioned the home as a memorial to her late husband.[89] The sheer number of artifacts, many gifts and mementos from the White House, and Wilson's interment at the National Cathedral two miles away gives PWWH the interpretive feel of a mausoleum. Edith wanted a burial location befitting a global dignitary but ruled out Arlington at Wilson's request and Princeton since he left amid controversy. She dismissed the southern cities of his past, reasoning that he had rarely visited his former homes. In addition only Columbia's First Presbyterian Church held a Wilson family plot, which was full. Edith never considered burial alongside Wilson's first wife, Ellen.[90]

The mausoleum effect reflects Edith Wilson's narrative of memorialization, both celebratory and full of struggle. Lisa Lopez argues that "domestic spaces tend to become mausoleums—meaningful in their permanence, but petrified and lifeless in their presentations."[91] In the case of the PWWH, this petrified interpretation is intentional and authentic to Wilson's experience. PWWH docent Betty van Iersel noted that Wilson only had three good years with her husband before she became a caregiver. She felt compelled to fulfill this role out of a sense of duty not unlike her unique commitment to preserving her husband's memory in the HHM movement.[92] Though disability history is not a focus of the tour, the mausoleum effect is most prominent in the nurse's room, which separated Wilson's and Edith's bedrooms. One of the most peculiar items in the PWWH collection, an electroshock therapy machine used on Wilson, shocks visitors into imagining a time this was an accepted medical treatment for stroke-related ailments.[93]

A New Shrine for the Twenty-First Century

By the 1960s those closest to Woodrow Wilson, volunteers, organizations, and museum professionals had enshrined him in three historic house museums across the South. Edith Wilson proved vital in ensuring that his birthplace in Staunton possessed the strongest claim to his legacy and his Virginian roots. She curated his presidency and death by donating her Washington, DC, home to the National Trust, which gave the site instant legitimacy. At the turn of the twenty-first century, the least funded and celebrated of the HHMs, the Woodrow Wilson Family Home in Columbia, shuttered its doors for nearly a decade, renovating the home and preparing a radical new interpretation. In that vacuum a new HHM emerged in Augusta, Georgia, staking claim to Woodrow Wilson's southern upbringing during the Civil War and Reconstruction.

Southerners displayed an eagerness to save Wilson's homes, even if his northern residences, such as Prospect House at Princeton, failed to generate interest among preservationists. Presidential narrative drove the Wilson HHMs that originally opened as shrines. Today the sites in Staunton, Augusta, and Columbia not only anchor his identity in the South but also serve as a map tracing Joseph Wilson's career in the Presbyterian Church after he left Ohio for Virginia.[94] That career traversed the South. Thinking deeply about the elder Wilson's career, the impact of the Woodrow family, and Tommy Wilson's childhood in these communities illuminates a much clearer image of what it means to define President Wilson as a southerner. These homes as artifacts, and the rich material culture, exhibits, and interpretation within them, provide windows into Wilson's youth as well as how public historians have interpreted his southernness and the region's effect on his policies and racial views.

Wilson biographer Arthur Link and Ray Stannard Baker, who corresponded with Cappelmann and is frequently cited by Link, both identified the twenty-eighth president as a southerner.[95] His family and the first decades of his life in the South contributed to his distinctly southern characteristics. Writing Wilson's biography in the post–World War II Jim Crow era, Link labeled Wilson, like his fellow upper-class white southerners, as paternalistic in his attitude toward Black Americans. The only ideology that defined him more than his southernness was his Presbyterianism.[96] In 1909, before offering remarks on his interpretation of Gen. Robert E. Lee, Wilson wrote about his own regional identity:

> It is all very well to talk of detachment of view, and of the effort to be national in spirit and in purpose, but a boy never gets over his boyhood, and never can change those subtle influences which have become part of him, that were bred in him when he was a child. So I am obliged to say again and again that the only place in the country, the only place in the world, where nothing has to be explained to me, is the South. Sometimes, after long periods of absence, I forget how natural it is to be in the South, and then the moment I come, and see old friends again, and discover a country full of reminiscences which connect me with my parents, and with all the old memories, I know again the region to which I naturally belong.[97]

Wilson's election elated white southerners and represented national reunification among white people a half century after the Civil War. Wilson was the first southerner elected to the presidency since Zachary Taylor in 1848 and, other than Grover Cleveland's two nonconsecutive terms, the first from the Democratic Party since James Buchanan's disastrous tenure on the eve of the Civil War. Wilson's election signaled the resurgence of the South and the Democratic Party to national leadership and national reunion. A Presidential Library museum exhibit in 2015 reinforced the reunification narrative, though the panel "Washington Welcomes a Democrat to the White House" did not invite readers to consider how white Democrats resumed their powerful position in national politics by overturning Reconstruction and implementing Jim Crow terror and disenfranchisement.[98] President Wilson's South was constructed and controlled by white people, and thus white southerners loved him. The imagined community of white southerners, despite their support for slavery and racial apartheid, believed they were exceptional but also descended from enlightened Europeans, particularly the English. Their loyalty lay with two nations, for they were fiercely nationalistic but also proud of the Confederacy. Wilson represented this ideal well. His mother was born in Carlisle, England, and his father supported the Confederacy.[99]

The tension of reunion manifested itself when Wilson almost declined to speak at the fiftieth anniversary of Gettysburg on July 4, 1913. The absence of Black veterans or press affiliated with an event reuniting more than fifty-three thousand US and Confederate troops visually marked the end of the sectional conflict for white Americans. Wilson mentioned race only once in his speech and alluded to slavery only obliquely.[100] He made no mention of the four million Americans freed by the Thirteenth Amendment at the end of the war, which he likely remembered as an eight-year-old child living in Augusta, Georgia. Nor did he note the Jim Crow disfranchisement of Black southerners and a dormant Fifteenth Amendment that promised universal male suffrage back when he was just a teenager living in Columbia during Reconstruction.

The executive branch of the federal government forged a relationship with the UDC to facilitate national reunification via memorialization at Arlington National Cemetery. Both presidents William Taft and Theodore Roosevelt opened the White House to UDC presidents to discuss federal assistance in burying Confederate soldiers at Arlington and constructing a Confederate monument. Wilson completed the reconciliation process by attending the Arlington monument unveiling and accepting it as a gift from the UDC as a celebration of national unity. However, reunification between Wilson and the UDC predated his presidency. While Princeton's president, he judged the inaugural UDC essay contest on southern history, with a pro-southern slant, hosted by Columbia University in 1906.[101] Given Wilson's relationship with the organization, it is little wonder that South Carolina branches of the UDC worked to save the Columbia home.

The Woodrow Wilson Boyhood Home in Augusta was the last Wilson HHM created, opening on September 29, 2001. A Creel Foundation study focusing on the site's architecture, archeology, history, and landscape determined that interpreting Wilson's life as a southerner during the Civil War and Reconstruction would fill a noticeable gap in the Wilson historiography. Executive director Erick Montgomery's well-researched book illuminating Wilson's time in Augusta and the South, published by Historic Augusta, provided a source and opportunity to fill this gap as well as rich context for Wilson's southern ideology.[102] Montgomery relied heavily on a 1994 report by Historic Augusta and research focused on Wilson's parents and childhood communities. He retraced Wilson's time in Atlanta with a failed law firm, his relationship with future wife Ellen in Georgia, and Wilson's return to Augusta in 1911. Despite this invaluable resource, Augusta's tour and interpretation, developed by Montgomery, Dr. Lee Ann Caldwell of Augusta State University, and historic preservation planner Anne S. Floyd, falls short. Its interpretation of Wilson's southern influences omits several insightful observations made by Montgomery himself.[103]

The Augusta manse in which Wilson grew up transferred hands and changed functions for over a century. No longer able to afford the maintenance, Augusta's First Presbyterian Church sold the home in 1930.[104] Suggesting that the Wilson family liked the design of the manse, the Columbia home replicates several of its features: the gasolier, original slate mantels with faux marble, two closets, a storage space beneath the stairs, a back porch bathroom on each floor, and a two-story kitchen.[105] Subsequent owners modified the former manse into rental spaces, a florist shop, and the aptly named Woodrow Wilson Beauty Salon. In 1980, a year after being placed on the National Register, the site briefly opened as a private house museum displaying Victorian antiques. The city purchased Georgia's oldest presidential home on May 25, 1991, for $200,000 at auction at the request of the executive committee of Historic Augusta, Inc., which counted Mayor Charles A. DeVaney among its membership. Historic Augusta took ownership and responsibility for restoring and managing the public site.[106]

It took less than a decade to restore and interpret the last Wilson HHM. Arthur Link, a long supporter of the Staunton home, visited Augusta in May 1992 as the keynote speaker for the first Woodrow Wilson Symposium, held at the manse, the First Presbyterian Church, and Augusta State University. Historic Augusta hired professionals and formed committees to undertake the extensive and varied research and work required to restore the home to its beautiful 1860s form with remarkable attention to detail. This included analyzing paint, regraining, restoring faux marbling, hunting for appropriate period furnishings, and garden planning. The church loaned thirteen original pieces used by the Wilsons. Historic Augusta launched a three-million-dollar fundraising campaign for private and municipal funds. In 1995 the organization purchased the Supreme Court justice Joseph R. Lamar's boyhood home next door as a space for visitors and staff for the future museum. On the eve of the public opening, September 28, 2001, Historic Augusta hosted an inaugural gala attended by hundreds of supporters and nineteen descendants of Wilson's parents, Joseph and Janet.[107]

The manse tour omits insights about Wilson's Reconstruction experience in favor of immersing guests in Civil War–era Georgia.[108] The Civil War dominates the tour narrative more than any revision or addition to the historiographical gap of Wilson's childhood. The war constantly looms over the lives of the family. Four-year-old Wilson's first memory was of Abraham Lincoln's election. The tour narrative describes the "conversational setting" of the parlor as a public space likely made the war a hot topic among the family and their guests. Although no battles were waged in Augusta, injured soldiers received treatment a block away from the home. First Presbyterian transformed into a hospital in 1863, perhaps providing Wilson's two sisters with volunteer opportunities to nurse Union soldiers on the lawn or Confederate soldiers inside. Joseph even traveled with the Confederacy as a missionary for a summer. Tommy Wilson did not suffer much personally during the war. Montgomery believes that Joseph and Jessie sheltered him due to his age, and he came to see the daily life of the home front as normative.[109]

If Wilson's formative years took place in Augusta and his exposure to the Civil War was limited, then Reconstruction was the most influential period of his young life. Yet Reconstruction was not named nor connected to Wilson's childhood on the WWBH tour. In fact, the end of the war brought excitement to his routine. Wilson remembered the anxiety generated by rumors circulating that Gen. William T. Sherman would possibly target Augusta. Sherman never came. In the summer of 1865, Wilson rushed to see the defeated Confederate president Jefferson Davis, under arrest, when he rode by with his guards en route to Fortress Monroe. An unusually large crowd of Black residents also followed Davis's procession, perhaps to see with their own eyes the downfall of the Confederacy and the end of slavery in the South.[110] Incorporating how the Black community and Wilson's family viewed Davis's arrival, as both a sign of defeat and celebrity, would diversify the tour narrative with multiple perspectives of freedom and loss.

Montgomery's book and the tour say little about Reconstruction as a force shaping Wilson's youth even though his daily life as a child is illuminated. Wilson experienced a charmed postwar childhood. A series of four laminated pictures he drew, several of which are replicated in Columbia's exhibit, depict a happy kid. Wilson sketched wartime and postwar Augusta and its trains as they brought Federal troops and moved goods. He took field trips to manufacturing plants with his father just as they had done during the war and played on the tracks built for the first horse-drawn streetcars. His drawing of the Light Foot Base Ball Club lineup included two hot air balloons, his way of remembering a traveling balloon that came to town offering rides for twenty-two cents. He got his first taste of baseball and leadership with the Light Foot Club.[111] As president he convened meetings using parliamentary procedure in his stable's hayloft and created a constitution and bylaws for the team. He played with his next-door neighbors Joseph and Phillip Lamar, whose father was also a minister. In 1910 President Taft named Joseph Lamar to the Supreme Court. Before his inauguration Wilson wrote Lamar with fond, vivid recollections of playing with the brothers. When Wilson arrived in Washington, he visited with "Joe" for the first time since moving from Augusta.[112] Sharing the rich Reconstruction-era experiences of Tommy Wilson's life in the WWBH tour would refute the argument that Reconstruction was a disaster for white southerners. Furthermore, revising the tour's Civil War narrative into a discussion of how the Confederacy influenced Wilson's father and his career would illuminate what southernness meant to the Wilson family and how it was crafted by them.

Joseph Wilson's Career and Making a Southern Family

The most influential force in Wilson's young life was his family; however, the extent to which his mother's side of the family, the Woodrows, developed Wilson's southernness and bolstered his parents' prestige is more profound than the WWBH tour acknowledges. The tour introduces two Woodrow family members who helped the Wilsons plant deeper southern roots. Joseph presided over Dr. James Woodrow's wedding to Felixina Shepherd Baker in Georgia. Afterward First Presbyterian, which had been without a pastor for half a decade, offered to triple Wilson's salary in Staunton. James, the first Woodrow to head south, possessed the greatest intellectual prowess in the family. His work with the Confederacy and move to Columbia placed him and Joseph in similar ideological, intellectual, and social circles. After the Wilsons moved to Augusta, James's sister Marion Woodrow came for an extended stay, married James Bones in the manse, and moved to a home near the Augusta arsenal. The Boneses expanded and reinforced the Wilsons social connections and "position among the Southern aristocracy."[113] Their "tomboy" daughter, Jessie, played with Wilson and later introduced him to Ellen. During Reconstruction the pair attempted to convert the "wicked" Yankees they encountered into good Presbyterian people. Aunt Marion devastated the children with news that the troops next door at the arsenal fought against the South.[114] One early Wilson biographer claimed that the cousins also played "Cowboys and Indians" and "attacked" Black children. Painted up in pokeberry juice, wearing feathered headdresses, and armed with bows and arrows, the children waited near a Black settlement in the woods for "little darkies" headed to town packing wood on their heads. With cries of war, the pair launched their surprise attack, capturing no one and "consol[ing] themselves by remembering that kinky wool would not make attractive scalps to hang at their belts."[115] Whether true or not, that this anecdote appears in a biography published before Wilson's presidency demonstrates how accepted white supremacy was among white Americans, especially those from the South.

Wilson created other fond memories during Reconstruction as well. In 1866 he attended a new school run by Joseph Tyrone Derry, who served four years in the Confederate army. Although Derry thought Wilson an apathetic, below-average student, Wilson admired Derry enough to host him at the White House. Wilson remembered warmly the economic rebuilding of Reconstruction and arrival of the first horse-drawn streetcars. He and his friends made scissors out of crossed pens on the track.[116] In a 1909 speech celebrating Robert E. Lee's hundredth birthday, Wilson recalled seeing the defeated general during his three-day visit to Augusta in spring of 1870. He recalled the "delightful memory of standing, when a lad, for a moment by General Lee's side and looking up into his face."[117]

Despite the lessons learned in Augusta during the Civil War and Reconstruction, Wilson himself understood that the foundation of one's beliefs came from family and community. In a 1904 speech, he said home and family were "the first and most intimate and most important organization for the indoctrinating of the next generation." His father cautioned him that the mind was "not a prolix gut to be stuffed" but rather a "vessel made to transmute something."[118] Thus two Confederates, a soldier turned teacher and the other a sympathetic supporter from the home front, laid the cornerstone of Wilson's education and belief system. Joseph cultivated his son's intellect in the offices and parlors of these HHMs, imprinting the pastor's adopted southern, pro-Confederate ideology on young Tommy.

WWBH executive director Erick Montgomery declared that Augusta was where the "first Southern president following Reconstruction learned to be Southern" before "his destiny" took him north.[119] Yet the tour shares only a sliver of the wealth of knowledge about Joseph Wilson's transformation into southerner and Confederate sympathizer, which illuminates how deeply white supremacy penetrated Wilson's domestic sphere. The interpretation of his study directly confronts Joseph's Confederate and proslavery ideology. In an 1861 meeting, the Presbyterian Church split after the southern members of the church sided with the Confederacy. Joseph continued to work for the wealthy Augusta congregation within the newly formed southern branch. He left his fashionable neighborhood to travel with the Confederate army.[120]

Wilson's Confederate sympathies extended much further than the WWBH depicts. The war not only split the Presbyterian Church, but it also fueled Joseph's burgeoning career. He began to excel professionally in Virginia despite his northern roots. He developed his administrative skills as principal of Augusta Female Seminary (Mary Baldwin College) in Staunton in 1855–56 and as elected moderator of the Presbytery of Lexington, Virginia. In addition he pastored Black congregants. Joseph drew scores of new members into his Augusta congregation, including at least thirteen Black members his first year. For a brief period, he conducted segregated Sunday schools for Black members from First Presbyterian Church before they were absorbed back into the main church.[121] The Presbyterian Church's schism provided Wilson an opportunity to climb quickly into leadership positions and new levels of professional prestige he had been missing. The southern church withdrew after the General Assembly forbade assistance to rebellious states, which would be interpreted as treason in the South. The southern churches already believed the war to be an unjust attack on the right to maintain slavery. Wilson was not upset at the division. He watched the thrilling spectacle of the Southern Presbyterian Church electing new General Assembly representatives, including his position of permanent clerk in December 1861. The assembly elected him stated clerk a few years later, a position he held until 1898. In 1863 the Bible Society of the Confederate States hosted its first annual meeting with Wilson, and the First Presbyterian Church named him head of the Committee of Publication. At the next annual meeting, the society elected him to the board of managers. The year continued to be busy for the pastor. At the request of Columbia's Executive Committee of Domestic Mission of the Southern Presbyterian Church and with permission of his church, Wilson spent the summer as a missionary for the army. To support the war proved professionally lucrative, but as the WWBH tour noted, it put Joseph at odds with his northern family, especially his three brothers serving in military or government positions for the Union. However, his view aligned more with the Woodrow side of the family. James Woodrow, living in Columbia since 1861, was chief of the Confederate army's medical laboratory from 1863 until 1865. James Bones, his brother-in-law, ranked as a second lieutenant in the 19th Battalion Georgia Infantry.[122]

Joseph endorsed slavery and supported the Confederacy through all means available to him as a pastor except combat service. In a sermon in early January 1861 titled "Mutual Relation of Masters and Slaves as Taught in the Bible," which was circulated in the press, he addressed his "slaveholding brethren" and the "institution we are resolved to cherish." Wilson cut one sermon short, using his pulpit for a patriotic call to his congregation, specifically the women. He asked them to wrap paper cartridges in the munitions factory to meet an important deadline for an impending battle in Virginia under General Lee, whose troops did not have enough ammunition. Wilson's fascination with homefront production led to field trips with his son to see operations, an informal education in total war. Wartime Augusta produced gunpowder, pistols, textiles, army boots, and shoes. The canal and railroads stretching to Savannah, Atlanta, Columbia, and Charleston transformed the city into one the Confederacy's few manufacturing and distribution centers. Wilson was also a member of the Silver Greys, a group formed to defend and help the home front made up of approximately 117 men over the age of forty-five. He worked on behalf of soldiers, delivering letters to local infantrymen who were nearby on his trip to Staunton. He placed "tens of thousands" of copies of the New Testament and the Psalms in troops' hands, a performance of Confederate religion that women carried out as well as southern ministers. According to historian W. Scott Poole delivering the Bibles was an aesthetic ritual but also part of larger "ritual of devotion to the Confederacy" that conferred chivalry upon the troops and deemed them protectors of all things feminine, including a version of the South constructed as such. In addition Wilson served as a "special agent" with the Georgia Relief and Hospital Association before joining the board of superintendents and eventually becoming its chair. The relief organization established hospitals to treat soldiers, raised funds, and sent packages from loved ones to soldiers.[123] Wilson actively supported the Confederate cause and traveled frequently for war-related issues, topics that would have dominated conversation and household activity in the manse. The Wilsons did not simply watch helplessly as the war unfolded. Joseph Wilson enthusiastically embraced the changes in the church that came with secession and worked diligently to improve his professional and social standing through his contributions to the South's war effort and wartime opportunities that came his way.

When Reconstruction arrived, Wilson struggled to navigate its political waters. Other than serving on the education committee for the Augusta Orphan Asylum, his activism waned significantly following the war. When his father-in-law, Thomas Woodrow, planned a visit in late 1866, Wilson told him to be "prepared to preach a good deal." He joked that "my people will be greatly pleased to have you occupy my pulpit, even if you have voted the radical ticket!" Wilson quickly grew weary of the politics of Reconstruction. He cared "but little about the politics of the country" and had "lost all confidence" in both parties, which were "contending for the mastery of the North" in the name of party "not country." He turned his attentions instead to the "fate" of the church "amidst this strife of human passions." Foreshadowing the political and racial violence that would accompany the election of 1876, Wilson said, "I fear that much evil, possibly much blood shed, will come from their angry contentions for power. Meanwhile, we are here left in a state of most painful uncertainty and alarm." Even though they disagreed at times, Wilson looked forward to hearing his father-in-law's "honest" and "candid" political opinions.[124]

Wilson once more returned to his southern household when he moved the family from Augusta to Columbia, South Carolina, in 1870. After becoming a school board member for the Columbia Theological Seminary in February 1866 and its chairman in 1868, he attended the May 1870 meeting of the Southern Presbyterian General Assembly and learned the seminary, the primary institution of higher learning for the church, wanted him to fill a position as professor of pastoral and evangelistic theology and sacred rhetoric. He won the election, reaching the pinnacle of his career, during Reconstruction, no less. The prestigious position came with less income and no housing, but the church had spoken. The First Presbyterian Church released Joseph for the fall semester. In the move, his wife, Jessie, lost one sibling but gained another, trading Marion in Augusta for James, who also worked at the seminary and taught at South Carolina College in Columbia.[125]

Locals in Staunton and Augusta welcomed their native son's return near the time of his election and continue to commemorate Woodrow Wilson's visits in their contemporary interpretation. Scouting his appeal as a presidential candidate, the New Jersey governor arrived in Augusta for a two-day trip on November 18, 1911. Wilson explored the city with excited locals and on his own by foot. He attended receptions and dinners. He sat once again in the congregation of First Presbyterian Church and met with his old Sunday school teacher. He took an afternoon drive to his Aunt Marion's suburban neighborhood. He reminisced about the baseball team he helped found. The WWBH tour proudly recounts Wilson's lunch visit to the manse to corroborate that the president scuffed up the dining room table, the most prized artifact. He supposedly crawled underneath the table to search for decades-old scuff marks he left as a boy. Wilson received a brief reprieve from gladhanding while watching baseball star Ty Cobb lead a production at Augusta's Grand Theater. While talking with the local press afterward, Wilson, overwhelmed with childhood memories, said, "I am not thinking of myself as a man, but as a boy, I walked about this city this afternoon and visited many of the old familiar places, which brought back memories of the past. And, tonight, I don't wish to be disturbed from my thoughts of my boyhood. I still want to think of myself as a boy and not a grown-up." Wilson left on the night train to Savannah, thrust back into adulthood, a southerner posed to become the Democrat's candidate for president in 1912.[126]

One month after his election, Wilson celebrated his fifty-sixth birthday in his birthplace of Staunton. The interpretive materials at the Woodrow Wilson Presidential Library and Museum (WWPLM) boasts of the return of "the hometown boy who made good." Images depict downtown Staunton decorated in red, white, and blue bunting and Wilson on the porch of the manse, waving his hat to admirers. One picture of the crowd gathered to hear Wilson speak on the steps of Mary Baldwin College shows no Black southerners supporting the president-elect. Like his Gettysburg speech in 1913, the celebration of Wilson's election and the reintegration of the South did not include the Black community of Staunton. The WWPLM re-created the dinner for Wilson's fifty-sixth birthday at a reception dinner celebrating his sesquicentennial.[127]

Erick Montgomery called the relocation of the Wilsons to Georgia the "initial step in the making of the first Southern President following Reconstruction." The Presidential Library concurs that Wilson was "above all a

Southerner," because, as he said, he was "born Virginian. A man's lineage is more important than this linkage."[128] The comprehensive nature of the WWPLM leaves little time to question how Wilson's southern upbringing shaped him. Because Edith Wilson resided at the S Street home in DC for nearly four decades after her husband's death, her life and the nine years she devoted to Wilson define the mood of the Woodrow Wilson Home. Little of the material culture or docent interpretation addresses Wilson's life before becoming president much less his southern upbringing. The MoRE at the Woodrow Wilson Family Home in Columbia rectifies this omission in the first three Wilson shrines saved by Ruth Cappelmann, Emily Smith, and Edith Wilson. Although not saved by women or their organizations in the 1930s, the WWBH in Augusta, Georgia, and the research it yielded at the turn of the twenty-first century has provided much-needed insight into Wilson's southern rearing. Montgomery's scholarship presents a more complete picture of a southern boy named Tommy who became president. When properly applied, his evidence and research revises Wilson historiography, filling an important gap in questions of how race, the Confederacy, and Reconstruction shaped the president. Had Augusta employed this interpretation, its site, like the MoRE, would have made a radical transformation in an era of abundant HHMs.

CHAPTER 2

The Rebirth

Making the Museum of the Reconstruction Era

Smiling, I welcomed the dozen or so visitors standing outside of the flanker building on a sunny Saturday afternoon. The starting point of the tour for the Museum of the Reconstruction Era at the Woodrow Wilson Family Home, the flanker, now Historic Columbia's gift shop, sits adjacent to a home designed by Washington Monument architect Robert Mills. I shared that Woodrow Wilson's father, Dr. Joseph Ruggles Wilson, accepted a teaching position at the Columbia Theological Seminary, which operated in what is now known as the Robert Mills House and Grounds. We left the parking lot and crossed onto Taylor Street, where I took the opportunity to share, "We are taking a path similar to the one Dr. Wilson, and sometimes his son, Tommy, the future twenty-eighth president of the United States, would have taken nearly every day. You are walking in the footsteps of a president." This effort to immerse the audience in Tommy's world is the first step in introducing the dual narrative of the tour and a warning that this will not be a shrine tour. By the time guests reach the front porch, they understand the Wilson family as the lens through which we see this place and time, Reconstruction-era Columbia.[1]

Historic Columbia toppled traditional assumptions about historic house museums when it established the MoRE and shed its shrine origins. The new interpretation contested the need for a fully guided tour, period room furniture vignettes, and a large number of original artifacts. It also risked inciting visitor complaints about the tour being a bait and switch, exchanging Wilson presidential history for a Reconstruction lesson. Historic Columbia reimagined the way in which the docent and objects could be used to interpret the home, emphasizing the importance of time, space, and place. The MoRE experience transports visitors to Wilson's neighborhood in the 1870s. Wilson was only a teenager, witnessing the first experiment in a biracial democracy with Black leadership. MoRE docents entered the conversation during what Steven Conn calls a "second golden age" of museums that are more inclusive, less neutral on moral or social issues, and less wedded to objects. The first golden age ordered objects. The second uses them to educate and interpret social history.[2] MoRE docents agreed that object-filled rooms with imagined moments frozen in time did not produce a good tour. They embraced the home as the primary artifact, helping build a narrative around it, five Wilson objects, and a handful of material culture from the Reconstruction era. They incorporated interactive digital displays, most notably a digitized version of the 1872 bird's-eye map of Columbia drawn by Camille Drie. Not only did docents embrace an interpretation with fewer objects, but also the majority of visitors in the first year of reopening welcomed a new HHM experience. But the question remained whether an experimental semiguided tour, as opposed to a fully guided or self-guided one, was the most effective way to bring visitors into Tommy Woodrow Wilson's Reconstruction era world, crafted through his childhood home and the panels and objects displayed there. The semiguided tour, when combined with a pull-back method encouraging visitor exploration, was successful; however, the style of tour endured challenges with large groups, especially those consisting of visitors with different learning styles, and when docent fatigue and scheduling complicated logistics.

A Brief Synopsis of the Tour

The docent-led movement through the MoRE, room by room of the first and then second floor, appears traditional. However, the panel format and ability to explore without restriction creates an original HHM experience. The tour begins with a block-long walk from the Robert Mills Museum Shop to the Wilsons' front porch, where the docent provides an introduction. There docents disclose upfront the tour's unconventional design and the interpretation's focus on Reconstruction, the period following the Civil War and ending in South Carolina in 1876, through the eyes of Tommy Wilson. The dual narratives of Reconstruction and the Wilson family thematically link the room exhibits, and each room has its own topic relative to Reconstruction or the Wilsons and usually both. Transition and introductory room statements establish these subthemes and direct visitors to additional information available on panels and through artifacts. Visitor engagement points with the docent, generally built around an open-ended, thematic question, continue conversations surrounding these topics.

The tour script required that docents cover three critical components for each space: transition, room, and engagement statements. Inclusion of these statements illuminated an issue with personal ownership over one's tour and the divide between volunteer and weekend staff in control over the tour narrative. Brazier embraced the "stricter" script that limited the "freedom" to personalize her tour beyond fine-tuning based on visitor interest. She "didn't necessarily want to put too much of me into it." Morgan disagreed. In making the script hers, she brought in seminary history she used on her Robert Mills mansion tour and explored the themes of America's "rapid expansion" West and across the globe and the loss of interest in Reconstruction. "We just didn't give as a nation Reconstruction long enough to actually make change," Morgan argued. The America of the Civil War era took "generations to build," and the nation could not "change all of that, roll it back in twelve years." Though an institutionally trusted and popular guide, Morgan waited six months to be evaluated after completing the first training in January. She spent this time producing her own interpretive methodology and presentation.[3]

The first half of the tour takes place on the first floor, launching from the entrance hall (room 1) where visitors become acquainted with Woodrow Wilson's family. Panel images introduce Tommy, who sat for a portrait when he lived in Columbia, and his parents, Joseph and Janet Wilson; however, docents verbally present Tommy's older sisters, Annie and Marion; his younger brother Josie; and the presence of domestic workers.[4] The southeast formal parlor (room 2) orients the visitor to Reconstruction on the local, state, and, to a lesser degree, national levels. The study's (room 3) main theme is religion.

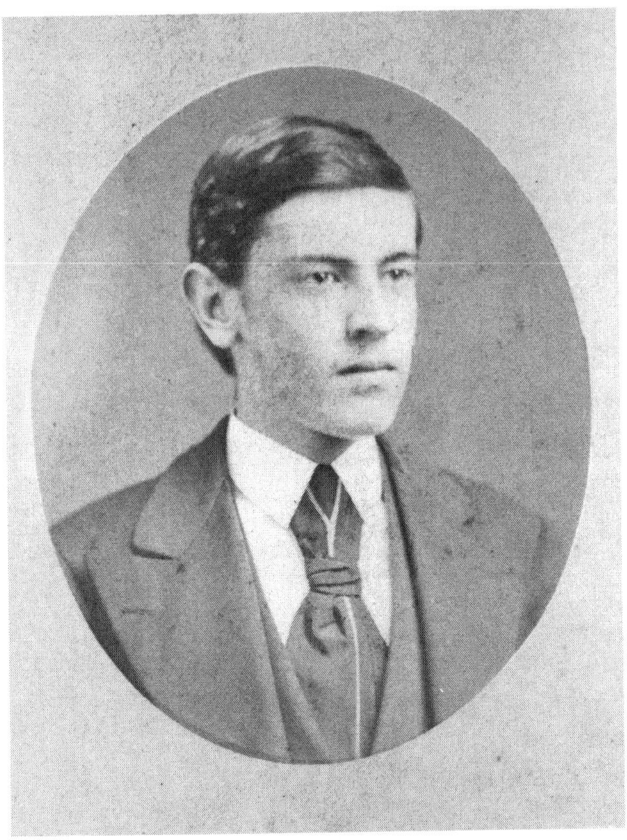

Figure 2. In 1873 Wilson sat for a portrait with the studio of Wearn & Hix. "Woodrow Wilson, head-and-shoulders portrait, facing right," courtesy of the Library of Congress.

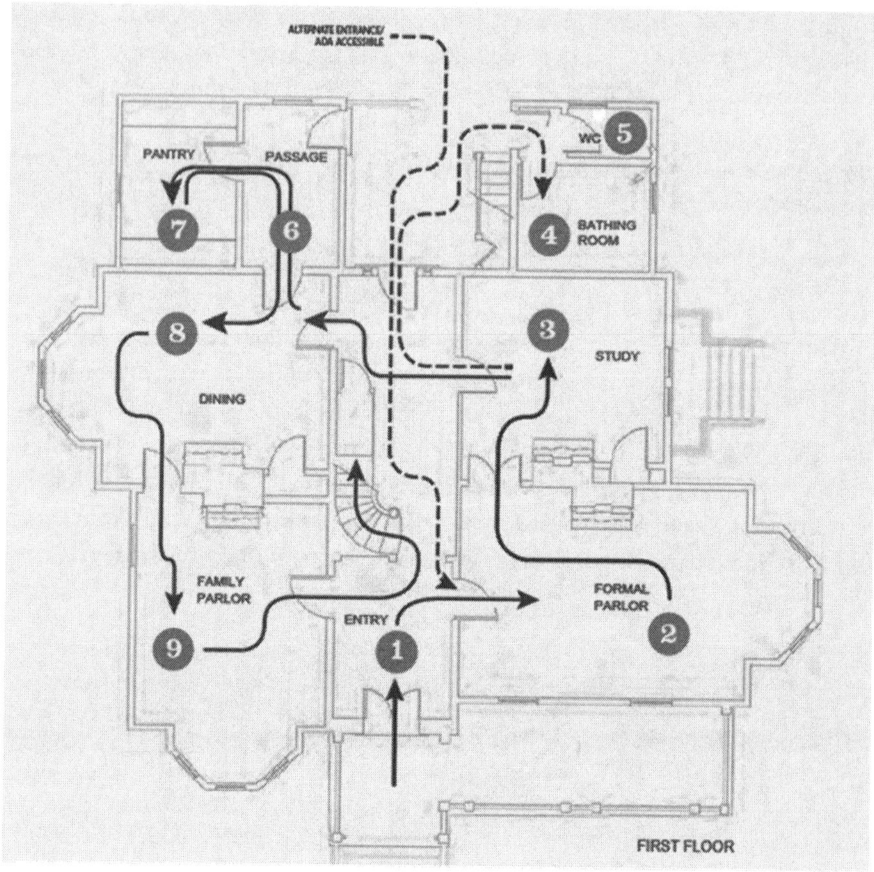

Figure 3. MoRE at the Woodrow Wilson Family Home Adult Tour Script First Floor Plan.

The Wilson family and their maternal in-laws, the Woodrows, were key figures in the southern Presbyterian Church. Reconstruction, however, also witnessed the proliferation of free Black churches. The pantry and passage (rooms 6 and 7), or butler's pantry, open conversations between docent and visitor about domestic labor and local merchants. Dialogue often trickles into the adjoining dining room (room 8), a space that considers family life, both the Wilsons' and that of Columbians at large. The final space, the southwest family parlor (room 9), explores the Reconstruction Amendments to the US Constitution ending slavery, providing citizenship, and granting suffrage to Black men. Citizenship takes center stage for five minutes via a short exhibit film and discussion about the Fourteenth Amendment, segregation, and contemporary issues of citizenship.[5]

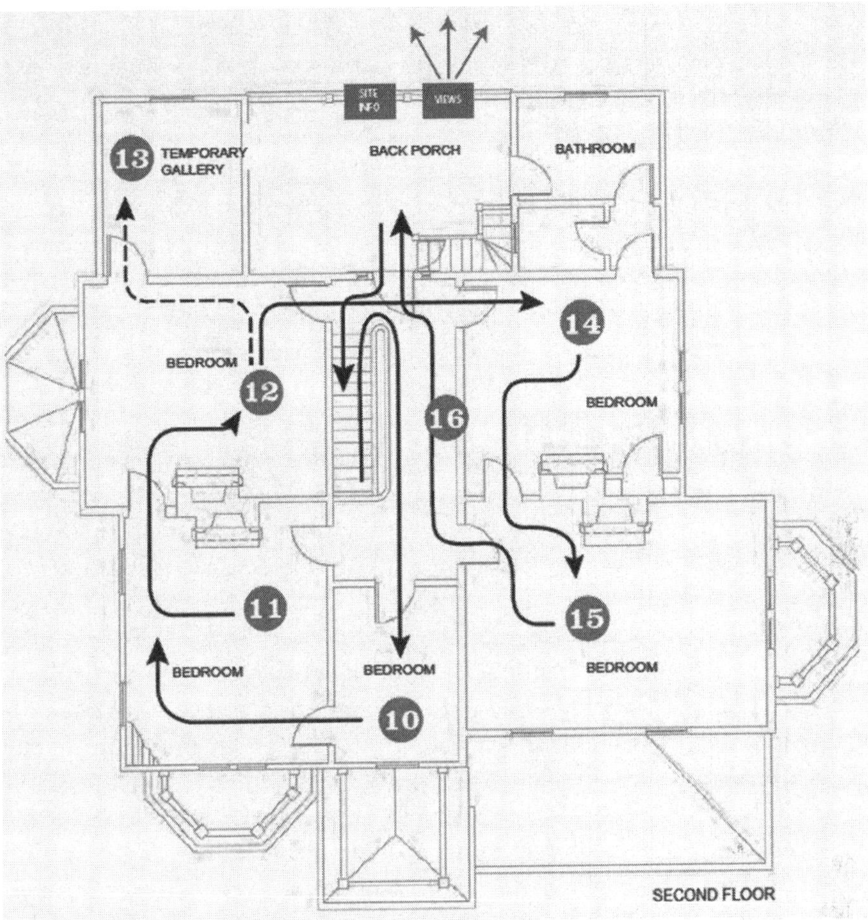

Figure 4. MoRE at the Woodrow Wilson Family Home Adult Tour Script Second Floor Plan.

The second half of the tour moves into the private spaces of the home in the bedrooms located on the second floor. Visitors stop first in Tommy's bedroom (room 10), which highlights young Wilson's passion for baseball and British politics as well as his education, a topic expanded in the northwest bedroom (room 12).[6] Its theme, "The Promise of Reconstruction," unveils the origins of an integrated public education system in South Carolina in 1868. The southwest bedroom (room 11) sandwiched between rooms 10 and 12, presents two aspects of the politics of Reconstruction: municipal services and the introduction of a temporary two-party system in the South. Republicans and Democrats of the era look vastly different to visitors than the parties they recognize today. The final two bedrooms (rooms 14 and 15) on the east side navigate the traumatic resolution to Reconstruction in South Carolina. These spaces address political terrorism at the hands of the Ku Klux Klan and Red Shirts as well as the complex and often incorrect ways Woodrow Wilson and Reconstruction have been remembered. If time permits, visitors explore the back porch before returning to the first floor for self-guided touring of the bathing room and water closet (rooms 4 and 5). Although fixtureless, these rooms include house rehabilitation videos as well as descriptive panels about each room's use. By opening access to these last two rooms that were private, additional spaces to the original home, the MoRE made spaces usually closed off from tours publicly available to visitors.[7]

Walking in the Footsteps of the President

Time and place were critical components of the new tour. Visitors purchased their tour ticket in the Robert Mills Museum Shop, Historic Columbia's gift shop located in a reconstructed flanker of the Mills home. Shop and house both bear the name of the famous architect who designed the residence, but during Reconstruction the Presbyterian Church's Columbia Theological Seminary occupied these buildings. The one-block journey to the MoRE commenced from this sacred space.[8] Both the preservation and rehabilitation of the premier artifact—the Wilson home—and patriarch Joseph Wilson's appointment to the seminary allowed the visitor to think immediately about the importance of time and place. This was a middle-class home constructed at the height of Reconstruction in Columbia and centered in a Presbyterian world.[9] Although the South was upended through Civil War and Reconstruction, Tommy's world retained some sense of normalcy through the ever-present Presbyterianism that rooted his childhood and bound his community together.[10] From the onset of the tour, docents immersed visitors in Tommy's Presbyterian environment. His father spent a decade at First Presbyterian Church in Augusta, Georgia, before moving the family to Columbia. Once in the capital, the Wilson family built their first home, just a block from the seminary. Visitors walked in Tommy's shoes by taking a path similar to the future president and his father.[11]

The tour invites guests to "imagine for a moment" Columbia during Reconstruction rather than docents telling guests about the Wilsons and Reconstruction in an abstract space. Docents illuminated what HHM anarchists Franklin Vagnone and Deborah Ryan call the "social and cultural construct" of Tommy's neighborhood during Reconstruction. This enables visitors to conjure this world and negotiate what their place within it, as well as the Wilsons', might have been.[12] Docents pushed both visitors and the interpretive team to consider the importance of the space within this world. Weekend staff docent Jennifer Gunter asked visitors to imagine the dirt roads, construction, and horses and buggies as they retraced Tommy's path in the 1870s. This was not a stretch for "realistic" people like volunteer docent Jean Morgan, who preferred immersion in the "real environment."[13] Pam Redfield, another volunteer docent, discovered a neighborhood anecdote and emphasized it to introduce Annie, Tommy's sister. Annie was neighbor to her future husband, Dr. George Howe Jr., for a few months while the Wilson home was being constructed. The Wilsons rented a house (today the Campbell-Bryce House) near the seminary and across the street from the Howes. Redfield's experience as a guide taught her that "visitors love these fun facts." Because of her approach, the tour clarified the spatial relationships of the neighborhood and Tommy's world, linking the seminary, the rental of the Campbell-Bryce House, and the Wilson's new home together.[14]

Docents and staff wanted the tour to be forthcoming about the focus on Reconstruction through Tommy Wilson's eyes and the tour's unconventional design. Visitors had likely heard that the MoRE was a departure from the traditional HHM from media coverage or the synopsis they heard in the gift shop.[15] When Historic Columbia revised the script in the summer of 2014, using Tommy as a lens to a time and place became the centerpiece of the MoRE's introduction. Months of tour experience by docents solidified the precise script language needed to convey this theme: "Today we will explore the teenage years of Woodrow Wilson and his family's experience in this city during Reconstruction. Thus, the Wilson family becomes the lens through which we see this place and time. By the end of the tour, you should have a greater understanding of the complexities of both Reconstruction and Woodrow Wilson."[16]

Consultant Annie Wright argued that the introduction gave visitors "a schema that new info can fit into."[17] This dual narrative grounded the tour and offered visitors the opportunity to consider how Reconstruction shaped the future president and how Wilson shaped the memory of the period. The layering of Reconstruction over Wilson moved beyond the traditional narrative of one or two people at the height of their prestige, which often silences marginalized groups occupying the home or local community. By using Tommy the teenager, not the president, as the main character, the experiences of his youth allowed visitor/docent inquiry into the Reconstruction era with its diverse cast of religious leaders, educators, politicians, and citizens.[18]

Most docents took great care to craft and present their explanation of the dual narrative and tour format upfront. Gunter emphasized that the MoRE is "a museum inside of a house and not a house museum." She used that as a stepping stone to then address the construction and rehabilitation of the primary artifact, the Wilson home.[19] Vagnone and Ryan, who lead an HHM anarchist movement, argue that these sites are having an "identity crisis" as to whether they are houses or museums.[20] The MoRE shows that some HHMs are both. Docent Doe wanted visitors to understand the tour's purpose at the beginning. She told them, "We are here to talk about and interpret this time in American history, this time in Southern history, particularly this time in Columbia, seeing it through the eyes of a family who lived here in the middle of this time period, a family who happened to have a son who became a president of the United States."[21] These efforts by docents minimized the bait-and-switch effect on visitors, who otherwise may have felt deceived, alienated, or suspicious of the museum.[22] Weekend staffer Halie Brazier stressed the focus on the president's teenage years, the world around him, and minimal material culture within the house. She "wanted to be frank and upfront" for the majority of guests who came for Woodrow Wilson and received a lesson on Reconstruction. She informed visitors, "There are plenty of other historic houses that do that" [solely focus on Wilson].[23] As chapter 1 explains, there are in fact three HHMs enshrined to Wilson, one a little over an hour away in Augusta, Georgia.

Wilson HHMs in Augusta, Columbia, and Staunton, Virginia, speak to a specific time and place in Tommy Wilson's development and through a southern and Presbyterian lens. However, the 2014 exhibit and tour installed in the MoRE employs these themes in order to uncover the misunderstood period of Reconstruction. In addition to the MoRE docent script narrative, an introductory panel in the entry hallway buttressed the importance of the time and place of Wilson's move during the period of Reconstruction, when "the entire community was working out the meanings of freedom in a post-slavery society." Completed in fall of 1871, the home was built "at the height of post–Civil War Reconstruction." But what did this mean for Tommy? The panel encouraged visitors to walk through the house and "think about how Tommy Wilson's experiences in Columbia may have shaped his ideas as the future 28th president of the United States."[24] Some docents used the dual narrative to ignite a conversation about the rhetorical question. Volunteer Kathy Hogan, seeking conversation over assumption, asked her tour in the entry hall: "If you were fourteen years old and living in this house and in this time and place how might it have impacted you?"[25] For her the home was "unique in that it tells the story of a time and place," specifically Reconstruction, a subject no other museum had been solely devoted to and that many people "want to sweep . . . right under the rug." Everyone should know about the time period, because "you cannot understand civil rights, you cannot understand current African American relations with Black Lives Matter, you cannot understand any of that . . . if you don't understand what preceded it."[26] Docents asked visitors to think critically about how living in

Reconstruction-era Columbia shaped Wilson, even if they struggled to answer those questions definitively for themselves.

The debate and ambiguity surrounding Reconstruction's influence on Wilson, particularly his racial and political views, trickled into other spaces as well. This manifested itself most prominently in the final space of the tour (room 15), which is discussed in the last chapter on the difficulties that the interpretive team and docents had in addressing white supremacy during Wilson's administration. However, a panel in the formal parlor, immediately following the entry hall, devoted to the politics of Reconstruction in Columbia and South Carolina offered an opportunity to think critically about how Wilson understood Black political power on a national and international level. Black Americans, including Republicans, voted for Wilson, a Democrat, because they believed his 1912 campaign message to support Black constituents. Wilson, however, believed segregation to be a moderate position in the South that eased racial tension. The president understood the segregationist policies of his southern cabinet members Albert Burleson, the postmaster-general, Josephus Daniels, secretary of the navy, and William McAdoo, secretary of the treasury and Wilson's son-in-law, all of whom segregated their offices and workspaces. Segregating federal offices in Washington, DC, sent a powerful message about federal support for Jim Crow and sparked protest.[27] Wilson's biographers have noted that he was no champion of ethnic nation-states or self-determination outside of Europe. However, colonized people in Africa and Asia shrewdly adopted Wilson's Fourteen Points and League of Nations rhetoric to legitimize their claims for independence and political freedom, ushering in an international "Wilsonian moment." These nationalists sent hundreds of documents to Wilson in Paris, petitioning him and other leaders for a hearing at treaty negotiations at Versailles and for statehood in the League of Nations. Wilson sided with the imperial allied powers of Japan, Great Britain, and France, ending the Wilsonian moment and prompting nationalists and elites to launch popular anticolonial, and often communist, campaigns across the Middle East and Asia in 1919. Asian imperialism endured, but this shift planted the seeds of its destruction. At home Black activists W. E. B. Du Bois and William Monroe Trotter, who campaigned against federal segregation and the racist film *The Birth of the Nation*, adopted this same language of self-determination.[28]

However, the MoRE, by exploring Wilson's childhood under a biracial democracy, adds a new layer of complexity to historians' assessments of his racial policies and philosophy of self-determination. Wilson was not naive or ignorant when it came to Black political power. As a teenager he witnessed a successful biracial state legislature and was represented by a middle-class

Black man. The story of William Beverly Nash is featured on a panel in the first large exhibit that the guests experience (formal parlor, room 2) on early rebuilding efforts of Reconstruction and Black representation. W. B. Nash was the senator for Richland County throughout Reconstruction, helping draft the 1868 state constitution and serving until domestic terror during the election of 1876 ended his tenure. Reconstruction's Thirteenth Amendment freed Nash, who went from enslaved to business entrepreneur during the period. Active in real estate, he owned a large farm and part of a brickyard.[29] Nash was a successful businessman when Wilson lived in Columbia and, more important, was his representative at a time when the future president developed a deep interest in government. Wilson knew well that Black political leadership came from economically successful representatives and produced legislative results.

Objecting to Objects

When Historic Columbia centered the Wilson home as the museum's primary artifact, it permitted an interpretation focused on a specific place and time period. Historic Columbia chose to leave the house exposed, displaying its rehabilitation rather than an overwhelming number of objects that distract from the restored faux graining, the reproduction gas-lighting system, and exposed paint layers and wallpaper. This corresponds to a twenty-first-century museum philosophy that treats the museum building as an object (and one that can be more significant than the objects housed inside). Louisiana's Old State Capitol Museum was a precursor to the MoRE's interpretation in that the structure became the key artifact and the exhibition included multimedia and flexible guided approaches. Both attacked their subjects first and foremost through the building. The Capitol Museum was the only museum in the world devoted exclusively to Louisiana politics, just as the MoRE was the first museum devoted to Reconstruction.[30]

By creating a panel-driven exhibit on Reconstruction in the capital city, Historic Columbia resolved issues related to its Wilson collection. The organization possessed the home and only five original Wilson family artifacts, a fraction of the material culture needed to complete traditional HHM period-room vignettes. This strategy enabled the MoRE to weave the history of Black Americans during Reconstruction into a minor story about the teenage years of Wilson. The MoRE's minimalist collection stands in stark contrast to the eight thousand artifacts maintained by the PWWH in Washington, DC. This includes much of his presidential collection of gifts from dignitaries and state officials as well as memorabilia. For example, Wilson and his second wife, Edith, brought with them from the White House the dip pen he used to declare war and a gold timepiece from the first president of Czechoslovakia. The couple also packed Pope Benedict XV's mosaic and, from Hollywood couple and Liberty Bond promoters Mary Pickford and Douglas Fairbanks, a graphoscope that magnified small works of art, photographs, postcards, and text. Today the National Archives houses most presidential gifts, but at that time there was no policy regarding their preservation.[31] With much of the Wilson estate donated to PWWH and his birthplace in Virginia, there was a lack of material culture available for the Columbia home. Historic Columbia's choice to minimize material culture in the MoRE was a product of the collection, but this move away from an object-centered approach also placed the museum within a larger trend of favoring a people-centered approach to interpreting objects.[32]

Museums possess a long history as repositories for objects and object-based epistemology where object meaning is generated through their systematic collection, classification, and arrangement. While giving the appearance of order, the grouping is unnatural in that it sterilizes any quirkiness about the objects and the world in which they operated. Spaces that were once intimate become staged and limit interaction. This "cult of the object" privileges comprehension of the artifact over how people lived in these environments. To reverse this and delve more deeply into the complexity of domestic spaces, sites must transcend the objects. In addition this ordering makes less sense as education replaces collecting as the primary function of museums overall.[33]

Museums, especially those with large or well-known collections, will continue to center objects, but others that may be smaller or newer are reducing or eliminating objects, often in favor of interactive audio and visual components. The drawbacks are that the remaining objects have to work harder to tell the story and provide less opportunities for alternative narratives.[34] However, in the case of the MoRE, decluttering and choosing objects that only had a connection to the Wilson family and Reconstruction emptied the space to make room for alternative narratives. The removal of objects produced a similar effect as that of the Mikhail Bulgakov House in Kyiv, Ukraine, when it painted its nonoriginal artifacts white to make the original artifacts stand out.[35] Volunteer Jean Morgan found herself pleased with historic preservation's evolution over the decades to highlight the authenticity of the space and material culture. The MoRE's objects are "authentic to that house, to that space, to that family," a point she emphasized on her tours. Tour and program coordinator Heather Bacon-Rogers concurred that reproductions and objects with no relationship to the house were "meaningless" in advancing the story.[36] The number of Wilson homes within a saturated HHM industry helped two docents explain why Historic Columbia chose a minimalist approach to objects to advance a Reconstruction narrative. Morgan blamed the limited objects on the competition between four

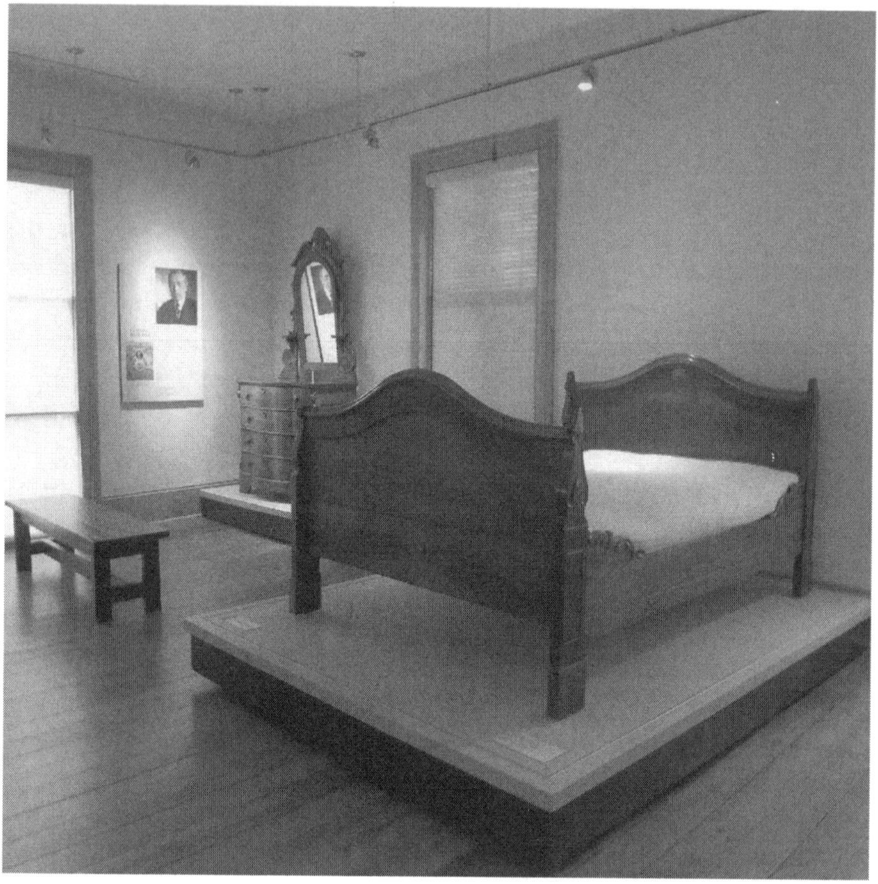

Figure 5. The bed Woodrow Wilson was born in and a family bureau. Wilson's niece, Alice Wilson McElroy, sold the items to the American Legion Auxiliary for the Columbia home in 1930. Courtesy Historic Columbia.

Wilson HHMs. She believed the Columbia house was "late to the game" of acquisitions rather than restricted from items Edith Galt Wilson intended to donate to the birthplace in Staunton or National Trust for Historic Preservation with her home in Washington, DC.[37] However, the local American Legion Auxiliary procured four of the five objects currently on display during the museum's early years.

To compensate for the reduction in objects and complement the panels, Historic Columbia incorporated digital interactives in the home. The organization digitized the bird's-eye map of Columbia drawn by Camille Drie in 1872 and placed the station in the formal parlor. It is the home's most successful interactive, allowing visitors to navigate and explore sites and structures significant to Reconstruction, the Wilsons' world, and Columbia. The script included specific instructions, demonstrations, and engagement questions because the interpretive team expected high levels of interaction. Guests continued to explore temporally and spatially Columbia and Wilson's community by zooming in and out on locations or searching by building name or subject.[38]

Docent oral histories clearly established that visitors were drawn to the map, physically engaging with the theme of space and time, but the level of popularity varied. Docents frequently expressed that visitors liked the map and used it to learn more about Columbia landmarks.[39] For Morgan the map was "a very physical representation" of Tommy's world, the spaces he occupied and walked to at a specific moment in time before the conveniences of modern transportation.[40] Bacon-Rogers agreed that guests could "triangulate" where Tommy lived and might have gone. The twenty-first-century connection to the past allowed visitors to "pretend" they were using their "iPad at home" and exploring "something old with something new." She speculated that all visitors, "every last one of them," engage with the map because "everybody has come from somewhere in the city," their hotel, their house, the zoo. They "are able to map how they got there and how different things looked."[41] Three other docents confirmed this observation, noting that guests wanted to position popular sites and places they had visited such as the State House, the University of South Carolina, or Elmwood Cemetery in relationship to the home and see the differences over time.[42] For other docents the map became a learning tool to direct visitors to other "great places," especially First Presbyterian Church, where Wilson's parents are buried. Then the visitors took it upon themselves to place their modern experiences in Columbia digitally in the 1872 version or to find other interests.[43] Bacon-Rogers described the map as a "special" interactive tool, "one of the best" in Historic Columbia's arsenal to bring Reconstruction into the twenty-first century.[44]

Several volunteer docents, however, argued that the map was hit or miss. They questioned how much learning or engagement was taking place as visitors pressed buttons, especially children.[45] While volunteer Doe witnessed more interest in the panels than the map, Bacon-Rogers thought the panel-heavy exhibit benefited from technological breaks. The weekend manager speculated, and volunteer docent interviews confirmed, that map ambivalence was an anomaly. It stemmed from docents not demonstrating the map properly, if at all, and moving to another room, which discouraged play. Docents needed to be at ease using the tablet-like tool to help visitors feel comfortable. Bacon-Rogers adamantly declared of her tours, "When I say 100 percent of people look at that map, I mean 100 percent."[46] Hogan agreed that demonstrating the tool to visitors was critical. Even one of the two volunteer docents who claimed that only locals showed interest in the map admitted to

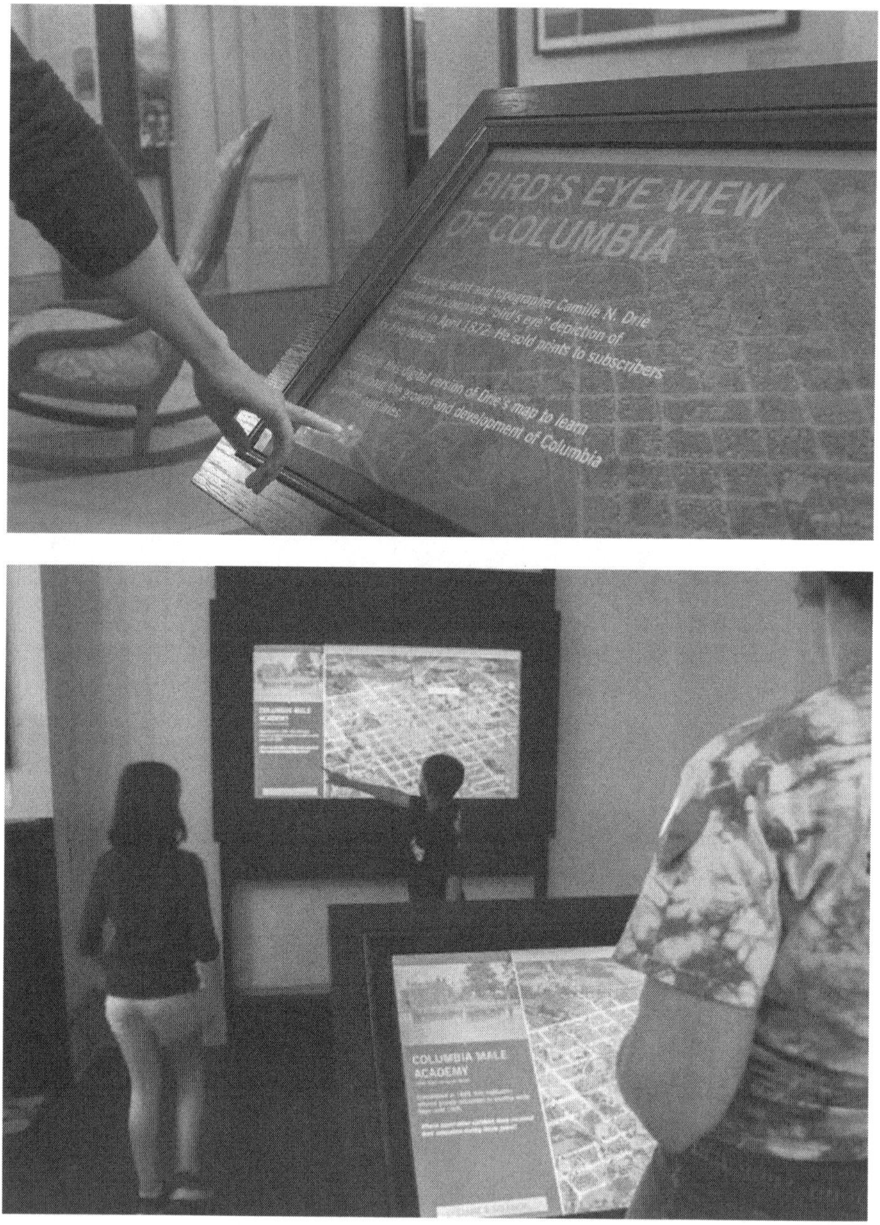

Figure 6. Digitized interactive of bird's-eye map of Columbia drawn by Camille Drie in 1872.

not spending much time with visitors and the tool. Another docent attributed lukewarm interaction to a lack of children, who are more likely to play with interactives than adults, and smaller groups, who were more attached to the docent.[47]

The lack of objects posed few problems for docents on MoRE tours, although it was a concern before opening. Two docents on weekend staff worried about a lack of material culture in the home. Bacon-Rogers thought visitors might complain, and some did. She led tours on the weekend at the busiest time. Laughing, she disclosed that "the no furniture, we hear a lot about." But like volunteer Kathy Hogan, Bacon-Rogers found people appreciated that the objects the MoRE did display were "genuine articles" and family pieces chosen in a "more deliberate way." Weekend staff docent Erin Holmes primarily feared that the absence of objects would affect her interpretation style of blending architecture and material culture, her areas of expertise as a PhD student. However, she discovered "a much stronger framework and more touchstones for the visitors to connect to when they didn't have an object in front of them." By blending architecture "extensively" throughout her tour with the required transition, room, and engagement statements, she easily illuminated the primary artifact.[48] Two docents never had any concerns about the scarcity of objects. One had no previous exhibit to compare the new interpretation to, unlike senior docents, who gave old material-culture-heavy tours before the 2005 closure of the home. Brazier saw a "museum not a period house" and a nontraditional tour that added to Historic Columbia's museum repertoire. The organization's Hampton-Preston mansion "was chock full of objects," she argued, but people "couldn't even get close to a vast majority of things so those aren't necessarily effective." She found the images and the information on the text panels "more akin to her style of learning."[49]

No longer bound by the weight of rooms inundated with material culture, docents chose to ignore some material culture and privilege other objects to strengthen and advance their narrative. If an object seemed out of place or forced on the MoRE tour, docents bypassed it. For one docent it was the birth bed where Tommy was born in Staunton, located in the bedroom devoted to the memory of both Reconstruction and Wilson. Another docent detoured exhibit items in the formal parlor, such as the rocking chair, which seemed to be a contrived effort to fit a Wilson family object in the space.[50] While some objects could be easily skipped, two areas, the study and the bedroom detailing the end of Reconstruction, possessed social objects capable of initiating conversation or connecting strangers. The study, filled with the majority of family objects, is the most popular object-based engagement point because the personal objects are items familiar to most museumgoers:

a family pew from the Wilson's church and matriarch Jessie's Bible set and quilt. The first edition copy of Charles Darwin's *On the Origin of Species*, not a Wilson artifact, is also popular.[51] Weekend staff docent Casey Lee said visitors were drawn to room 14's red shirt, worn by a member of the paramilitary forces committed to returning power to the Democratic Party in 1876, because of its connection to the larger narrative in the house. Some visitors may have more interest in the family pieces replicated in traditional HHMs, like the bed, and ask more questions about Wilson; however, other visitors are drawn to Reconstruction and objects not normally seen in HHMs, such as an 1876 fraudulent tissue ballot or the red shirt. As explained in chapter 5, the red shirt and tissue ballot are examples of provocative social objects because of their connection to political and racial violence and election fraud.[52]

Historic Columbia compensated for the absence of Reconstruction-era or Wilson-related material culture with a few well-selected reproductions. Docent responses were mixed. Bacon-Rogers thought the reproduction clothing in Tommy's room was "fantastic" and afforded a "direct connection" because people could "hold them and handle them and understand the type of clothing he was wearing."[53] Gunter disagreed, noting that, while cute and hands-on, the clothing distracted from bigger concepts that children are fully capable of grasping if not overshadowed by dress-up and picture taking. This philosophy extended to the reproduction stereoscopes in the education bedroom. The question for Gunter was "Why are we having fun?" The lasting legacy of public education created during Reconstruction and the brief integration of the University of South Carolina were far more important themes set up to be discussed in this space. Thus she waited for guests to finish looking at images before she spoke about these critical topics.[54]

Several docents expressed that the MoRE changed the way they thought about HHMs needing objects and period rooms. Four guides favored interpretations that deemphasized objects to advance a narrative of historical importance rather than one of a particular family or a period furniture lesson. Three docents specifically named the MoRE as their favorite of the four houses administered by Historic Columbia because of its Reconstruction theme and move away from furniture. Volunteer Cyndy Storm chose to specialize in the MoRE because she preferred talking about the home within the context of Reconstruction in Columbia over "telling a family story" and pointing out "old furniture." What volunteer John Clark liked most about the house was its lack of objects, not "the same old same old . . . house with all this stuff." For Gunter, Reconstruction was far more interesting than looking at the possessions of the middle class or wealthy. The reinvention of the Wilson HHM changed expectations too. Bacon-Rogers summarized

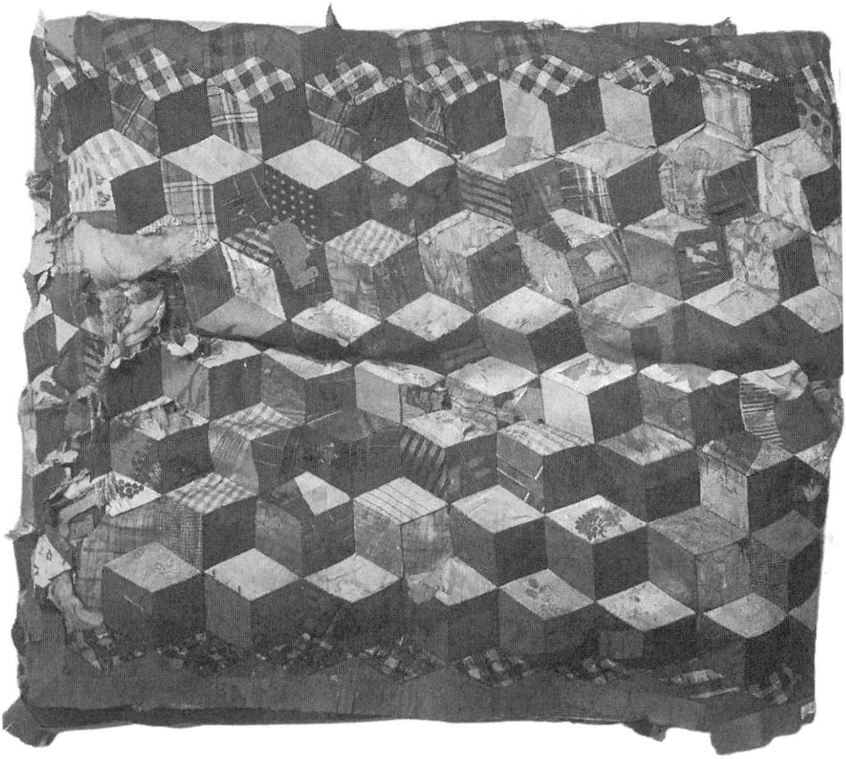

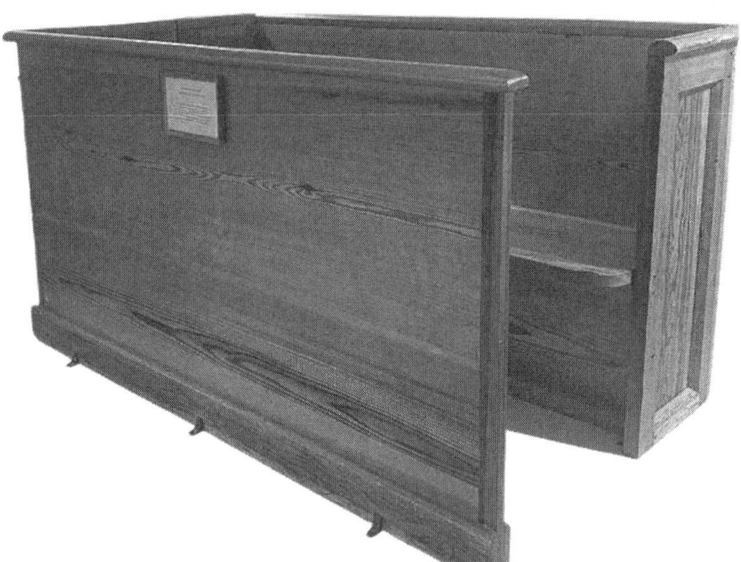

Figure 7. The quilt and pew are original items belonging to the Wilson family and displayed in the study. Courtesy of Historic Columbia.

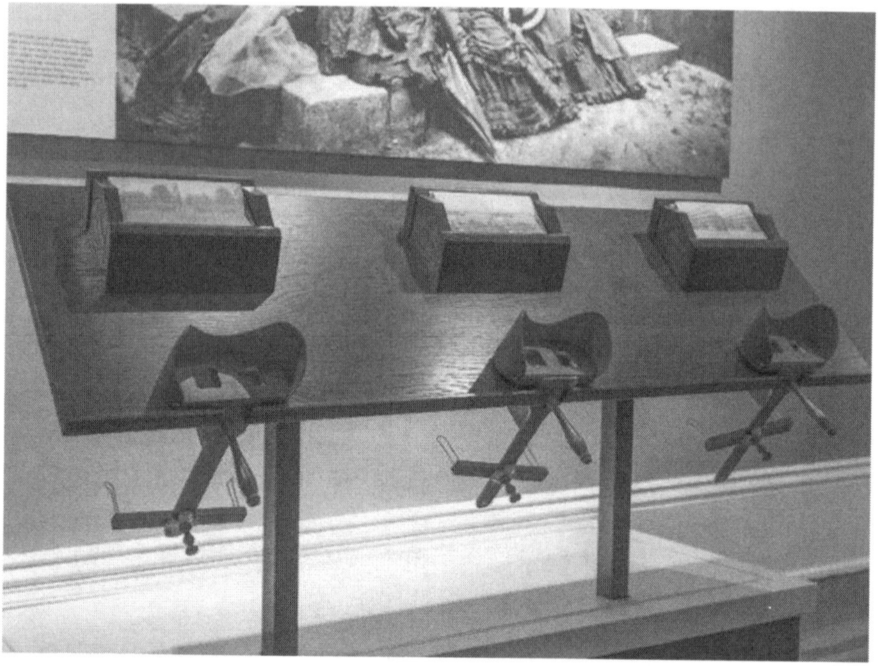

Figure 8. Reproduction stereoscopes. Courtesy of Historic Columbia.

her changed philosophy: "Just a pretty house museum doesn't do it for me anymore."[55]

MoRE visitors arrived expecting an abundance of material culture based on their understanding of traditional HHMs and museums. However, guests are not disappointed by fewer objects. In her everyday conversations outside of volunteering, Storm warned prospective guests interested in period furniture about what they will find inside the MoRE.[56] But the majority of docents, particularly volunteers who work during the week, received no complaints from guests about the lack of objects.[57] One factor was that docents and gift shop staff told visitors upfront about the limited number of objects. When docents explained on the front porch that guests would not see rooms "crammed full of furniture that you look at from a distance," visitors nodded in agreement or out of politeness, because they had generally been informed by the gift shop manager before purchasing tickets.[58] Weekend staff protocol required telling visitors a blanket statement that the MoRE was not a furnished, traditional house museum. Rather it was a "museum in a house, not a house museum."[59] Visitors were thus prepared to show interest in the artifacts to which they were exposed. Of 556 respondents on the visitor survey, when asked what information they found most interesting, nearly half selected what the tour guide told them (45.5 percent). But only 3 percent of visitor interest separated the panels (23.38 percent) and artifacts (20.68 percent) in second and third place.[60]

No amount of preparation nor well-conducted tour can persuade some visitors to abandon their preconceived notions about object-filled HHMs. Clark heard a few comments but, as a docent tapped for interpretive team meetings, knew that objections manifested themselves more often in the visitor evaluations solicited by docents at the end of the tour. Despite the positive response to artifacts on the survey, disappointment at a lack of objects was the number one criticism of the home written in the comments section. From opening through January 2015, eighteen comments, or just over 5 percent of the 337 total comments, referenced objects, furniture, or artifacts. However, 6 of those, or one third, were positive statements. Artifacts were "loved," "captivating," or "interesting and helpful." One evaluator "appreciated how the home was not over crowded with ramdom [*sic*] artifacts." Although 14 comments called for more objects, their absence did not distract visitors from enjoying the tour. They appreciated that original artifacts were hard to come by as well as the focus on Reconstruction. For two respondents the exhibit films played in the home helped compensate, as did the "great" guide for one visitor. Although it was "a bit spartan" or "bare" in some visitors' eyes, four visitors wanting more material culture still called the museum "wonderfully done," "well worth the visit," "so fantastic," and "overall a very enjoyable experience."[61]

Docent experiences reinforced the affirmative visitor comments. A visitor might enter a museum not wanting a nontraditional HHM experience, but they often left satisfied. When visitors expressed displeasure or made comments, docents often converted them into fans of a new kind of HHM experience, or they otherwise went on to enjoy the tour.[62] One weekend Bacon-Rogers led a group that had not been told the blanket statement. "They came to see a pretty house. Plain and simple," she recalled. The first thing they asked was "Where is the furniture?" But by the time she entered the pantry and dining room, they began "to finally forget about the furniture, completely," and "were fully engaged in the material."[63] They ultimately "enjoyed the unconventional house tour" once they explored and understood that "the pieces that were chosen were meaningful and directly related to the family." The experience inspired them "to want to find other such houses and museums."[64] What Bacon-Roger's story indicated, and another volunteer confirmed, is that visitors forget about the furniture once immersed in the tour.[65]

Whether giving tours during the week to smaller audiences or to larger groups on the weekend, docents found the objects mattered less when visitors received an unexpected experience. Clark's "general perception" was that visitors left the MoRE "very happy with what they've seen there, as enthusiastically happy" as with other tours of HHMs he gave, if not more so. Visitors got "something they did not expect," new information. That was "what we do here . . . a high proportion of it is new to almost everybody who goes here." Bacon-Rogers acknowledged that the tour would not please everyone, but "nine times out of ten we've given them such a different experience that they are thrilled with what we've done."[66] They are transported to a different type of museum where uncomfortable topics can be teased out. She saw visitors purchase tickets for the tour expecting another furnished home. She continued: "They realize we are special. We're covering a topic that a lot of people don't want to talk about. That they never thought that they would come to a museum just to talk about something that was going to make them uncomfortable. But I think we're making people uncomfortable in a way that's making an impact."[67]

The curatorial choices made for the MoRE situated it within recent institutional shifts where collections became secondary to sites and missions that sought greater political relevancy. Like other historical museums courting diverse audiences or presenting one historical event, the MoRE's design carved a space for the Black experience of Reconstruction. It also turned the HHM origins of preserving the lives of great men on its head by using Wilson to show the white supremacist response to freedom rather than enshrining him.[68] The MoRE's Reconstruction narrative thrust the HHM into membership in what Steven Conn calls a "second golden age" for museums, where moral compasses, inclusive narratives, and ideas have rendered objects secondary. With a less structured tour providing physical access, particularly to objects previously forbidden, visitors felt less forced to focus on objects and were more inclined to use them to support questions and analyze the narrative.[69]

Death of the Docent?

The difficulty of Reconstruction as subject matter, the exhibit's text-heavy panels, and traditional expectations of a guided tour for house museums resulted in the decision to maintain the use of docents to interpret the twenty-first-century museum with a semiguided tour. The script temporarily toyed with three scenarios, one for a single-docent tour, another where docents offered transitions between spaces only, and a final option for unaccompanied visitors. However, the interpretive team privileged a single-docent tour for consistency, and so that tours could be constructed based on visitor interest ascertained in the walk from the gift shop.[70] For the semiguided tour, the docent introduced spaces and key themes to visitors in each room, let them explore, and remained available for conversation or questions. Ultimately this style worked well, but it posed a unique set of problems because of ingrained tour etiquette for visitors, tour size, and docent availability. These problems left some docents wondering whether a self-guided tour should be offered.

At the beginning of the tour, MoRE docents explained and modeled the house's signature semiguided tour, a new tour experience where panels and interactives were coupled with a few well-chosen artifacts. Many in the HHM business remain committed to outdated tour design and structure despite data that suggests traditional tours are no longer the preferred form.[71] The semiguided tour injected guests spatially and temporally into the Wilson family's world "as the capital was rebuilt" and the city's Black residents "attempted to negotiate the difficult terrain of citizenship and free labor." Then docents let visitors wander.[72] The tour script and the MoRE docents' practice of encouraging guests to move ahead or linger behind violated the traditional norms of visitor etiquette by having them disengage from the docent and engage with the exhibit individually.[73] The experimental model replaced what Vagnone and Ryan call the "traditional passive operation model" of guided tours that offer guests a chance to peek inside "rooms in frozen tableaus" but bar entry or close inspection. The free movement of the MoRE tour created a "decentralized experience" that provided a variety of activities and means with which visitors could determine meaning for themselves.[74] Guests could inspect panels and artifacts, watch videos, explore an interactive map and family tree, dress up at a clothing station, and hold laminated art and recipes. An example of personalized meaning making was using the primary artifact of the house to allow guests to think about the Wilsons as first-time homeowners. The interpretive team felt this was a milestone for many modern-day Americans. Docents easily demonstrated the home as a showplace for the family by speaking to the preservation and how it expressed the family's growing socioeconomic status.[75] By connecting with visitors' experience of buying their first home, their aspiration to do so, or inequalities that prevent them from doing so, the MoRE engaged in *poetic preservation*, creating a moment where authentic, engaging stories of the house's past united with feelings visitors might have about their own lives.[76]

For each room of the home, the tour script required transition, room, and engagement statements that centered the Wilsons and Reconstruction and prompted visitors to explore. The engagement statement provided space for docents to pull back, a key component of the semiguided tour. Docents typically talk nonstop for thirty minutes to an hour on traditional HHM tours. To pull back, refrain from speaking, and let visitors explore was a skill that had to be developed and improved upon by all those conducting tours. Chapter 3 probes further into the pull-back technique and its challenges for the docent during training at the MoRE.

One of the most effective pull-back tools developed naturally in the formal parlor. Docents pushed play on a sound artifact, an early twentieth-century rendition of a song performed in Columbia during Reconstruction titled "Kathleen Mavourneen." Playing it created interpretive mood music, giving guests permission to delve deeper into the map or move toward panels and artifacts. The music generated space for the docent to step aside, wait for questions, or engage visitors one-on-one. This musical maneuver incorporated consultant Daniella Cook's suggestion that docents give verbal cues encouraging visitors to explore on their own.[77] Several other docents found this technique successful in encouraging self-exploration. Storm's visitors got a kick out of listening to the music after she joked, "Well, if you were partying at the time, then you would have listened to this music." Gunter wished there was more music.[78] The song not only encouraged visitors to play and explore, but it also aurally demonstrated music of the sort that most HHM docents only describe. The role of sound in shaping the cognitive and emotional experiences of museum visitors is less studied by public history scholars than it should be given the rise in multimedia exhibits, but sound can be used to reinforce an exhibit's message as well as affecting visitor mood, pace, and memory recall. Researchers conducted a study in 2010–11 of two types of music incorporated into an interpretive space at the Laiho Memorial Museum, which honors Lai Ho, a pioneering author of modern Taiwanese literature. They discovered that period music, even with lyrics that threatened to overload visitors with information, was more effective than light instrumental music from the modern era akin to that played in consumer spaces. Similar to consumers, most visitors found the light music relaxed them or made them comfortable, slowed their pace, and deepened their desire to explore the exhibit. But some of them thought the music should be from the historical era or promote the exhibit themes, if not actual music Lai Ho enjoyed or sounds he would have heard during his life. Even when they did not understand the lyrics (and some wanted the lyrics displayed for meaning), visitors that heard a contemporary piece of music from Lai Ho's generation felt like they were "stepping back in time" or felt nostalgia or connection to the era. The primary issue was listener fatigue generated from hearing the song repeatedly during an extended stay in the space. Thus the use of "Kathleen Mavourneen" produced results similar to both styles of music studied in the Lai Ho museum. Visitors received encouragement to explore via the historical ambiance of the music but had to physically push the button again to hear the song repeated.[79]

Playing "Kathleen Mavourneen" clearly orchestrated the new behavior docents were attempting to teach visitors about self-engagement, reflection, and exploration; but inventive options like this were not always available in every space. The rooms that most naturally sparked exploration were early stops on the tour: the spacious formal parlor with its map, the study's original Wilson artifacts, and the architecture of the butler's pantry.[80] Previous museum experiences taught conformity, an "unwritten and unquestioned code of conduct" in HHMs, which rendered some visitors immobile. The semiguided tour worked, but some guests could not abandon their docent for fear of violating preconceived notions of visitor etiquette: Do not move. Do not speak. Do not touch.[81] Numerous docents spoke of visitors that followed them, as one docent said, "like a puppy." To counter this, docents remained in a space rather than moving on to the next one to wait because otherwise visitors tended to follow them. Permission to explore mattered little to visitors once the docent exited a room. Storm confessed, "I would like them [visitors] to have more independence and to feel that they can walk around and look at things." But she ascribed this dependence to the traditional form of HHMs, noting, "They're almost always worried they're going to be left behind."[82]

Visitor response to the semiguided tour varied.[83] Size mattered significantly in determining if groups even split up at all. A small group of two or comprising a single family generally stuck close to the docents. But the pull-back worked well with larger groups, often made up of several different smaller groups.[84] With big groups, however, came "herding." Docents were reluctant to interrupt visitors engaged with the exhibit. One docent waited for questions in the doorway to the next room, hoping to draw visitors eventually to that area. Because the docent never had a group larger than ten and knew there was little time to backtrack, they tried to wait until everyone was ready to enter the next space.[85] Hogan took her cues from visitors. If a visitor moved quickly into the next space, she offered supplemental material not part of her regular transition statements. When half of the group moved into the next space, she would follow and deliver the transition. She repeated it quietly to those small groups that trickled in afterward. Her most difficult problem was when this technique didn't work because large groups of people with varying levels of interest finished rooms at different times. It could be a "real mess" when she wanted to show the informal parlor's exhibit film and move the group upstairs together.[86] Gunter's biggest tour included twenty-six visitors, half of whom disappeared regularly. The only effective way to draw most of them back together was resuming the narrative. It also proved challenging to move them through the house in ninety minutes, much less in seventy-five minutes, the standard length of the tour.[87]

The problem of steering exceptionally large groups through the semiguided tour illuminated other issues that arose giving this style of tour. Streakers are visitors who move fast through a museum or exhibit with only a few stops, while studiers spend more time looking at individual elements or the exhibit as a whole.[88] Both kinds toured the MoRE regularly.[89] Generally the semiguided tour provided just enough pace control for those who needed structure and enough space for those who liked to move at their own speed.[90] However, sometimes visitors moved so quickly that one docent could not catch them. Volunteer Pris Stickney sometimes left the main group to give the quicker visitors information, but her personal philosophy was that the people pacing themselves deserved docent accompaniment. Few groups split long enough to force her to make this decision, however. Other docents expressed the challenge posed by big groups that included both streakers and studiers. Accordingly one docent felt she and the tour were not equipped to handle larger groups.[91]

The freedom of the semiguided tour allowed visitors with varied learning styles to craft their own experience with the images, panels, and interactives. The panels appealed to the portion of people who preferred reading over interactives. The images and illustrations provided fodder for nonverbal learners.[92] Some visitors simply wanted the guide to talk. Others did not want to be coerced into participating. Gunter understood this sentiment, as she rarely enjoys guided tours. She preferred drawing her own conclusions, choosing her movements, and avoiding interaction. Then she contemplated her experience further after leaving a site.[93] Holmes worried the engagement model might make visitors feel forced to answer "led-by-the-nose discussion questions" that made her own college students "miserable."[94] Their distaste for participation was not unique, according to museum visitor participation expert Nina Simon.[95] When these learning styles collide, they can cause headaches for the docent and visitors. Volunteer docent Maria Schneider gave one tour where other guests grew frustrated with a gentleman's extensive interest in the home. She pulled him aside and let him know he could come back through and ask questions after the group tour. It was unclear whether he dominated her narrative by asking questions, rendering the pull-back ineffective, or if she was not instructing him to linger and continuing with her tour.[96]

Nonetheless, an advantage of the semiguided tour and the lingering docent was the one-on-one engagement opportunity. Some visitors approached Storm individually during the pull-back, more willing to speak to her than to a whole group of strangers. She learned from her guests during these engagement points as she imparted her own wisdom. Her actions generated decentralized, often individualized, conversations throughout the tour between docent and guest, as idealized by HHM reformers. Often guests who want to participate in a dialogue receive a monologue instead.[97] Stickney found she could "really interact with people" at the MoRE to a greater extent than the other houses Historic Columbia administered. This once culminated in a two-hour tour. The semiguided structure facilitated more discussion and created a relaxed atmosphere where she did not have to talk the entire time and her audience did not expect her to on many of her tours.[98]

A self-guided tour was not an option for visitors. Of 645 visitors who answered an evaluation question about whether they preferred the self-guided portions of the tour, such as rooms 4 and 5, only 51 people, or just under 8 percent, responded affirmatively. In late March 2015, the interpretive team added a survey question asking visitors if they wanted the tour to be self-guided. In the first month of responses, 32 people, or just over 91 percent of respondents, replied no.[99] But Historic Columbia's most consistent and largest conundrum was staffing the home, which made the self-guided tour appealing. Historic Columbia suffers from the larger issue in HHMs of volunteer recruitment declining along with attendance.[100] The organization relied on volunteer staff during the week and a paid, part-time weekend staff with docents that work a couple days a month. Staffing was an immediate concern because of the impending increase in spring visitation when attendance comes out of its winter lull, the heavier flow of guests expected on weekends, and the fact that tours for four HHMs left at the top of each hour.[101] Furthermore, of the volunteer docents who participated in the first round of training, few completed the process. Docents approved to conduct tours trickled through the training pipeline but not quickly enough to fill the schedule.[102] In the early months, staff filled numerous gaps in the weekday schedule, which ran Tuesday through Friday 10 A.M. to 4 P.M. Three of those days, I, as tour facilitator, conducted half of the six tours offered a day. Every day of the first full month that the site was open, there was at least one unfilled tour time.[103] On numerous days of the week, only one MoRE docent was available when two shifts were needed. Compounding this issue was the fact that docents typically worked three-hour shifts, only allowing coverage for two seventy-five-minute tours. As a result, staff filled in for the last tour of the day and frequently the first tour of the day.[104] Historic Columbia took measures to manage the homes more efficiently and ease the fatigue docents experienced after giving a tour that is both intellectually complicated and energetic and lasting more than an hour. The retirement of volunteer coordinator and frequent fallback docent Ann Posner resulted in more scheduling gaps as her replacement, Betsy Kleinfelder, underwent training. In the spring of 2015, Historic Columbia changed its tour times for all of its HHMs, staggering and offering tours of two houses every hour.[105]

The tour time changes relieved pressure, but MoRE docent fatigue remained a problem. Given the limited number of docents trained to conduct MoRE tours and the detailed exhibit itself, Doe thought the self-guided tour seemed a reasonable solution. Doe and Gunter supported a self-guided option, understanding there are pros and cons to both styles.[106] Gunter thought self-guided tours could spark an increase in visitation and allow visitors to take in information missed on the guided tour. The drawback was that some people need to be directed to specific information. For example, in the formal parlor, Gunter tried to make sure people read the demographics panel to comprehend how integrated the legislature was. Then she could demonstrate with the other panels the intelligence and power wielded by legislators, which was "part of what we whitewashed in the history."[107] The self-guided option also gave guests flexibility with time. They could take two hours or twenty minutes.[108]

Gunter's example illustrates that the written text of the exhibit more than any other factor worried docents about the self-guided tour. Bacon-Rogers too felt that the panel materials needed docents to make stronger connections. Such materials included mounted artifacts like the tissue ballot used to rig the 1876 election and information about Wilson's relationship with Thomas Dixon, his former college acquaintance who authored *The Clansman* and asked the president to watch D. W. Griffith's screen adaptation, *The Birth of a Nation*. However, docents were essential for other reasons. There was no one to pose a subject or question for exploration and no labels for the digital interactives and the stereoscopes to instruct visitors on use.[109] Docents answered questions that the panels sparked or did not address, which volunteer docent Doe almost always encountered on tours. In addition, the panels were too numerous. Their text extended beyond what could be consumed in a one-to-two-hour period. Furthermore, panels contained too much information, a common problem with exhibits codeveloped with historian consultants, who tend to write for their academic peers. Docents confirmed that panels, while well done, were excessive, containing more than they could cover.[110] On the opposite end of that spectrum, rhetorical questions on the panels written at a more remedial level confused some of Bacon-Rogers's visitors, who have asked her whether the questions were for school groups. While the self-guided tour had its merits in extending reading time, she could not envision a tour that was completely docent free. The language also prevented tours from being completely self-guided. She warned that the panels' advanced text played into the stereotype that museums are elite, white spaces and an "intellectual bore."[111] Lee understood that part of her purpose as a weekend docent was to accommodate people who are reluctant to read and aid visitors who did not yet know what a "museum of Reconstruction" was. Historic Columbia wanted "everyone to get at least something out of it," which may mean the docent giving some information in each room. Lee received some complaints from fellow public historians who did not want to be led around but also conceded they were specialists, or what visitor expert John Falk identified as the professional/hobbyists. These visitors will get something from a self-guided experience. Otherwise, both Lee and volunteer Westcott remained unconvinced how much a visitor would take away from the museum unaccompanied.[112]

The consensus from docents and visitor evaluation data was that docents remained essential to the experience. For Bacon-Rogers the guides were "the most valuable part of that house." Even a supporter of self-guided tours admitted that the docent dramatically increased the quality of the tour.[113] Data confirmed that nearly 46 percent of 556 evaluated visitors that were asked what information they found most interesting overwhelmingly selected what the tour guide had told them. The panels came in second at just over 23 percent, making docents critical to the visitor experience and the exhibit.[114] Only three visitors mentioned the panels specifically. One thought they were well done, and another thought there were too many. Two found the panels informative, but one of those wanted more time to read.[115] Docents stationed in the home may be a better solution than the self-guided tour, according to three docents. This approach would allow visitors to get their questions answered and offer docent engagement points. On "Dollar Sundays," Historic Columbia offered local residents one-dollar tours of one of its four houses each third Sunday of the month. Two docents who were stationed in the home for that event found the method effective. Bernadette Scott witnessed "people reading signage at their own pace and in so thoughtful a manner."[116] For stationing to work ideally, Bacon-Rogers argued, two or three docents would be positioned downstairs and upstairs at all times. This would accommodate those who were interested only in the house itself and some brief information as well as those who wanted extended time. She too had experienced visitors on Dollar Sundays spending two and half hours reading everything.[117] As of May 2023, the MoRE was the most popular house on these reduced-priced Sundays.[118]

The intellectual and emotional difficulty of challenging preconceived myths of Reconstruction and discussing white domestic terror, the text-panel-heavy exhibit that some docents and visitors found overwhelming, and the long tradition of docent-guided and -centered tours in HHMs dictated the need for a new docent experience at the MoRE. Its docents proved vital in presenting a provocative Reconstruction interpretation to HHM audiences. MoRE docents wove a small number of objects into a powerful narrative where visitors made meaningful connections with authentic objects related to the family and the time period of Reconstruction. Docents incorporated objects as they saw fit and spent more time in spaces where social objects generated more engagement. After seeing visitors embrace an unconventional house tour and express genuine interest in learning about the relatively little-known subject of Reconstruction, several docents came to favor museum interpretations that moved away from objects and were driven by thematic substance. Both docents and guests of the MoRE were in the midst of an HHM revolution, changing the way they thought about a century-old philosophy of ordering an abundance of nonessential objects into period rooms to tell the story of elite lives. While Historic Columbia successfully implemented a semiguided tour with a pull-back technique that facilitated visitor exploration and one-on-one engagement, there were drawbacks to this style of interpretation. It produced problems with tour management, particularly large groups, and there were only a handful of docents certified to conduct the tour. Some docents came to think that a self-guided or stationed tour should be offered. The semiguided tour was rewarding but experimental. And it would require special training on the topics of Wilson, Reconstruction, and inclusivity. The next chapter traces the development and implementation of the new docent training process for the MoRE, a best practice that helped docents and visitors unlearn state-sanctioned Lost Cause indoctrination and a white supremacist narrative of Reconstruction.

CHAPTER 3

Docent Training

Unlearning the Lost Cause and Reconstruction Memory

One of the first and most enduring changes in South Carolina made by the biracial, two-party system of Reconstruction-era government was Article 10 of the 1868 state constitution. It required compulsory public education for all children ages six to sixteen without a physical or mental disability. Article 10 also paved the way for the opening of an integrated State Normal School in 1873 at South Carolina College, now the University of South Carolina.[1] These revolutionary strides in education, a major theme of the Museum of the Reconstruction Era tour, appear in three different spaces.[2] The first discussion takes place in Joseph Wilson's study. Both Tommy Wilson's father and his maternal uncle, James Woodrow, worked for the Presbyterian Theological Seminary a block away. Today that site, now known as the Robert Mills House, is a historic house museum also administered by Historic Columbia. Tommy's local, private education as well as his college years are covered in his bedroom. Wilson and his father operated in the ivory tower of a Presbyterian world, and his all-white private school experience stood in stark opposition to the creation of South Carolina's integrated public school system, introduced in a bedroom near the end of the tour.[3]

This chapter explores the relationship between education, Reconstruction, and docent training. Reconstruction created public education in South Carolina, but that system evolved to indoctrinate generations of children, including docents, in the Lost Cause and a white supremacist narrative of Reconstruction. The docent script defined the Lost Cause for docents and visitors as "the rhetoric of southern nationalism" after Reconstruction that claimed the Civil War was fought for states' rights, not slavery. The script did not distinguish the Lost Cause from what Bruce Baker defines as a separate but interrelated white supremacist narrative of Reconstruction. Rather it expanded that a tenet of the Lost Cause was that Reconstruction was a failure. Central to that argument was that Black and white Republicans during Reconstruction were corrupt and incompetent and that white Democrats redeemed the South with election fraud and mob violence. In *Never Surrender,* W. Scott Poole defines the Lost Cause as "how southerners across the region celebrated the defeated Confederacy in the waning years of the nineteenth century." He uses the understudied South Carolina upcountry to challenge "two divergent interpretations" of the Lost Cause, by Charles

Reagan Wilson in *Baptized in Blood* and Gaines M. Foster in *Ghosts of the Confederacy*. Though there was a "Confederate religion" that bound the Lost Cause and religion together, the Lost Cause was not solely a self-conscious "civil religion" or a response to the "psychological anxiety" of Confederate defeat. It was an aesthetic defense of the New South and the "entrepreneurial values" of a young commercial class as well as a movement to advance a conservative southern ideology and shape public behavior. Its proponents crafted a "dream world" that came to fruition with Wade Hampton's 1876 gubernatorial campaign and conveyed the "boundaries of racial identity," antebellum gender norms, and "a new Confederate nationalism."[4] The power of the Lost Cause and white supremacist narrative of Reconstruction manifested itself during docent training, as docents unlearned century-old historical interpretations and thought deeply about how these narratives shaped their own education. Because of the close association of the Lost Cause with the white supremacist narrative of Reconstruction, many docents use Lost Cause language to describe both narratives.

Creating public education was a revolutionary act during Reconstruction-era South Carolina. Asking docents to not only eliminate any vestiges of white supremacist narratives of Reconstruction from their MoRE tours but also assess its impact on their lives felt revolutionary too. Historic Columbia's training facilitated the process via workshops on Reconstruction-era Columbia, Wilson's teenage years, language and adult learning practices, and the Lost Cause. The organization also evaluated and cleared each docent to conduct tours to ensure they modeled best practices of public history and would not default to an outdated interpretation. This approach did not come without dissent from white retirees who volunteered as docents, resulting in low retention rates in the pipeline from training to giving tours. For guides who completed training, most grappled with the Lost Cause and a white supremacist narrative of Reconstruction impacting their historical thinking and haunting their tours. By studying the modern historiography of Reconstruction and learning about this time in Columbia, docents often reversed the indoctrination from their childhood textbooks and the Confederate monuments on the public square. However, for those docents who struggled with or refused to participate in training or tours, the tedious training requirements of learning new material and inclusivity best practices, as well as a rigorous tour evaluation, illuminated weaknesses of twenty-first-century museums tackling complex histories that rely heavily on volunteer interpreters.

Designing the Training

The timeline for the first training program was a logistical nightmare. Six training sessions launched in November 2013 lasted three months because of breaks for the holiday season and uncharacteristic winter weather in Columbia. Training began as the tour and exhibit was finalized, leaving docents to engage with an incomplete exhibit and tour script.[5] To compensate, Historic Columbia circulated a fifty-page exhibit document for docents to reference. The organization also arranged a session with small groups to address general questions about the exhibit content and analyze exhibit images, such as a class of Black women attending USC's Normal School and Wilson's drawings from his childhood experiences during Reconstruction.[6] Training also devoted several days to an "open house" viewing of the ongoing installation and walkthroughs of MoRE demonstrating the tour. To accommodate the schedules of volunteers, Historic Columbia offered two days a week as options for each session. Volunteers could also attend the weekend staff sessions. Weekend staff, who had full-time jobs or were history graduate students at USC, had an alternate weekend schedule. Docents concluded training by presenting a tour to staff and friends. In total interpreters had to attend and complete ten active training requirements.[7]

The first sessions used academic lectures and preassigned reading material to tackle the subjects of both Reconstruction and Woodrow Wilson. Holding these paired sessions trained docents to meet the dual interpretive needs of the house. The first session on Reconstruction identified for docents the various timelines for the era, different Reconstruction plans among the executive and congressional branches, three new amendments to the US Constitution, the gains made by Black Americans, and the Lost Cause. Docents analyzed images from the exhibit and political data that challenged the Reconstruction myth of Black politicians' ineptness. These sources demonstrated an economically diverse, biracial coalition of Republican legislators.[8] A ninety-minute presentation and Q&A by two USC history professors in the second training session reinforced two key interpretive ideas of the MoRE: that Reconstruction could be taught through time and place, via a teenage Woodrow Wilson's experience in Columbia, and that the tour could speculate how the era shaped him. Long-time Historic Columbia consultant and MoRE scholarship committee member Dr. Thomas Brown spoke about Columbia during Wilson's teenage years—the zenith of Reconstruction. Tour docents walked away with content to define Reconstruction and its goals, achievements, and demise as well as why this history matters.[9] Fellow scholarship committee member and Wilson scholar Ken Clements argued that although Wilson never wrote a memoir or autobiography, docents could logically speculate whether Tommy Wilson wanted to emulate or compete with his father, his "first and most important teacher" who taught him the value of oration and leadership. Likewise, docent dialogue peppered through the tour could help visitors critically think about how Wilson's relationship to women shaped his views on the Nineteenth Amendment, ratified during his presidency. He was a self-described "momma's boy." He criticized his female students and opposed women's suffrage. Did he think of women as emotionally nurturing but intellectually inferior?[10]

Docent retention was an immediate problem. Twenty-six docents attended the first training session, but by the second session, attendance decreased by half. Some made up this work, while others in attendance began to drop the training program.[11] Docents understood the timing of training was unavoidable and that training takes time to do well but expressed their weariness of both the training length and break in continuity during the holiday season.[12] Volunteer docents were also far more likely to resist content in sessions on engagement and cultural sensitivity than weekend docents. This likely fueled the training exodus as well.

Volunteer docents interpreted the last two sessions on public engagement and cultural sensitivity by Dr. Daniella Cook, then assistant professor in the Department of Instruction and Teacher Education at USC, as more radical and less helpful than lectures or shadowing sessions. Cook was the only person of color who led training sessions, which were designed to encourage "thought and behavior that promotes greater interaction" between docent and the public.[13] While she included twenty-first-century language and scholarship about race, learning was the central thread. Cook's first session, "Engaging the Public," offered techniques to facilitate twenty-first-century learning goals, including critical thinking. She introduced docents to six points regarding adult learning theory:

1. Adults have a need to know why they should learn something.
2. Adults have a deep need to be self-directing.
3. Adults have more experience, and of a different quality, than young people.
4. Adults must see a need to know or be able to do.
5. Adults enter into a learning experience with a task-centered, problem-centered, or life-centered orientation.
6. Adults are motivated to learn by motivators both extrinsic (i.e., promotion) and intrinsic (i.e., self-esteem).[14]

Cook's presentation also included ideas on how docents could apply inquiry based learning and engagement theory strategies. Her coverage of Benjamin Bloom's revised taxonomy model gave staff and docents tasks and verbs to describe the higher order of thinking skills (creating, evaluating, analyzing) and the lower order of thinking skills (applying, understanding, and remembering). By applying effective questioning, docents could draft a tour that promoted both learning and higher order thinking. Effective questioning required docents give visitors time to think and a specific function for each question, such as listing and grouping. Below are a few examples of Cook's function questions:

1. Clarifying: Could you give me an example?
2. Refocusing: How does that refer to our earlier . . . ?
3. Summarizing: Can you put that into a single sentence?
4. Labeling: Can you suggest one or two words to label?
5. Interpretive: What are the differences between . . . ?[15]

Cook's session illuminated the larger debate within small and medium-sized intuitions, which historically and economically depend on volunteer frontline labor, about the value of a compensated and professionalized front line. In the case of Historic Columbia and the Wilson house, this conversation centered on the volunteers and paid weekend staff often trained in public history best practices. Weekend staff docent Halie Brazier found that the strategies presented improved her tours by providing training in visitor services she did not receive as a public history graduate student focused on exhibit and curatorial skills. She normally told guests about historical content "in an entertaining way" rather than asking visitors about an object or image. Yet these training sessions were the most unpopular for volunteer docents despite being centered on adult learning and inclusivity best practices. Only 43 percent of them found these small group discussions the most useful aspect of training. Two volunteers ranked this style of group work and interactive exercises as what they liked least. Pris Stickney claimed that she preferred "getting the facts" and did not have as much "baggage" about Reconstruction as other docents, implying that these sessions were designed for her volunteer peers who had been indoctrinated in the Lost Cause and myths of Reconstruction in their childhood and thus had inherited racism.[16] The session on language and cultural sensitivity, which dealt heavily with race and various forms of privilege, was one of the least meaningful for volunteer docents. The next chapter, on interpreting Black domestic workers, will address more fully these attitudes and how several white volunteer docents and visitors at MoRE updated historical traditions of whitewashing history within HHMs. They embraced what I call the *Downton Abbey* effect, which allowed them to use a popular British television show to erase unique racial circumstances that affected workers' lives beyond their economic and social status.

As the February 15, 2014, opening of the MoRE drew closer, the training sessions changed format and focused on the tour itself. Prepping tours proved as challenging as previous training sessions. Docents varied in their level of training completion, and weather delayed the evaluation process conducted by volunteer coordinator Ann Posner and myself, whom as tour facilitator would lead half of the tours.[17] In mid-January Historic Columbia held ninety-minute sample tours of each floor, led by members of the MoRE interpretive committee. The tours, to be followed by a Q&A period, accommodated twenty-five docents, but only eighteen signed up. Docent questions demonstrated the thematic challenges that lay ahead. They were fact oriented, concerning the price of the home, or logistical, concerning ticket sales and seating for guests, rather than expressing big picture ideas about Reconstruction as a civil rights movement or how the period might have shaped Wilson. Thirteen docents persevered, learning the tour in a less-than-ideal situation. Seven docents ultimately passed evaluation to become the original interpreters of the first museum of Reconstruction in the nation.[18]

Docent Response to Training

The debate among MoRE docents over more interactive training sessions based on best practices demonstrates that they responded differently and benefited more directly based on whether they were paid, public historians, though there were some exceptions among the volunteers. Volunteer docents generally preferred lecture-style workshops and reading on their own. Most felt prepared to conduct tours and found shadowing one of the interpretive team's tours essential to crafting a successful tour. Some embraced the structure of the tour, which limited putting too much of oneself into the delivery, while others found ways to make their tour their own. There were docents both paid and volunteer who found passing the training process and conducting tours incredibly gratifying. Other volunteer docents resisted training and the tour, covertly through conversation with one another and, to a lesser degree, overtly in their evaluations. This resistance bubbled under the surface despite the training program's simplification for the second round of training following the opening.

Historic Columbia took the concerns of docents seriously and sought docent feedback once the training process was underway. The results of these inquiries validated much of the training process among the majority of all docents. However, data among volunteer docents pointed to a preference for lecture and self-learning. The organization disseminated a survey to docents before training began and after it ended. Docents also evaluated each session in a corresponding survey. Over 70 percent of docents reported being "very satisfied" with training, with the remaining being "somewhat satisfied." Many docents who passed the training enjoyed the process, found it rewarding to learn a difficult tour, and were happy to learn about the lesser-known subject of Reconstruction.[19] The majority of docents reported learning from reading the material, large group lectures, and planned activities with the group. Fifty-seven percent deemed the large group lectures useful. The lectures filled gaps in knowledge or provided a refresher on Wilson and Reconstruction, specifically as those topics pertained to Columbia and social change.[20] Two volunteer docents cited they specifically prefer lectures over hands-on activities.[21] Others saw room for improvement, such as allowing more time for speakers. There were criticisms of the speakers, as a few docents expressed feeling elitism from one of the specialists and wanting fewer lectures.[22]

The vast majority of docents read recommended material and conducted research on their own to get a better grasp of Reconstruction and Woodrow Wilson. When asked about the most useful aspects of training across six categories ranging from lectures to small group discussions, 64 percent of docents selected "reviewing material on my own," the most popular response.[23] Volunteer Kathy Hogan immersed herself in Marion Lucas's *Sherman and the Burning of Columbia,* Richard Zuczek's South Carolina study *State of Rebellion,* Walter Edgar's *South Carolina: A History,* and Wilson's 1901 essay "The Reconstruction of the Southern States." Wilson biographies—especially A. Scott Berg's, which had been recently published at the time of MoRE's opening—were popular with volunteers. In addition to Wilson biographies, John Clark perused five recommended readings "to get a better feel for Reconstruction." Sitting at his computer after training sessions, he would gather his thoughts and seek additional information. Trainers and supervisors should note his use of fiction to illuminate the period. He highly recommended the novel *Freeman,* by Leonard Pitts Jr., about a formerly enslaved man who returns to Mississippi during Reconstruction to look for his family. Clark found that the novel provided a "different perspective than Columbia" and gave him greater clarity on early Reconstruction, particularly military government and the challenges faced by the Union soldiers. This supplemented the MoRE's focus on the socioeconomic and political developments between 1870 and 1874 during the Wilsons' time in Columbia.[24]

Training survey results showed that all docents felt prepared to some degree to lead tours and were more comfortable being challenged by visitors or talking about race by the end of their training. Over half felt completely unprepared before training commenced. However, training had not assuaged all fears. Two docents spoke of being "confident" going into their tours that they were "prepared" and ready to "deflect,"[25] but only 29 percent of docents surveyed felt "very prepared." Furthermore, the modest gains made in comfort levels with respect to discussing race demonstrated docent anxiety over race-related conversations and foreshadowed interpretive problems that will be discussed in the next two chapters.[26]

Docents agreed that shadowing an approved tour, a typical approach to training in HHMs, in order to see "how it is practically done in each room" was essential. Two volunteers considered it part of the training they liked most.[27] When giving shadow tours, trainers modeled techniques recommended by Daniella Cook and education programming consultant Annie Wright:

1. Use hand gestures.
2. Show rather than tell how the tour should unfold.
3. Avoid academic speech.
4. Ask visitors to "imagine for a moment" and then give them space to imagine.
5. Repeat visitor questions to answer clearly and concisely, expanding only if time allows.
6. Use previous and upcoming spaces to address questions and connect rooms and content.
7. Repeat new information to make it "stick."[28]

Some docents shadowed private and public tours more than twice to see a range of docent responses and techniques to incorporate. Volunteer Jean Morgan "split the difference between them all" and added her own signature interests.[29] Cook recommended Docent Doe's "stellar" tour as "a great model for guides." The docent wove "a clear, coherent story line between Reconstruction and the Wilsons," encouraged visitors to explore and answer questions, displayed a "strong grasp of the content," and used technology, such as the bird's-eye map of Columbia, proficiently. Docent Doe liked giving the tour first to potential docents because the first crop "didn't know what we were getting into" initially. The docent called leading those tours a "learning experience," because some of the shadowing docents would bring up topics that visitors had not.[30]

Docents practiced and crafted their tours in a variety of ways, illustrating diverse but successful techniques of value to HHM docents generally. Two docents wrote out their script by hand. Another rehearsed in front of a mirror. Two other docents, in contrast, avoided over-rehearsing. Volunteer Holly Westcott absorbed as much as she could and then spoke, hoping "something reasonable came out." Practicing tours with friends built confidence in learning to adapt them to visitor interest. Hogan reasoned practicing was the only way to learn how to give the tour and reduce nerves about presenting the material to "diehard" white southerners. Two of these diehard friends accompanied her on her practice tour and did not object to the interpretation that challenged the Lost Cause, praised Reconstruction, and identified white Democrats as domestic terrorists.[31]

HHMs undergoing interpretive and/or exhibit changes will need to revise and shorten training after opening and should seek docent feedback to expedite the process and maintain their support. The second training offered by Historic Columbia was a swifter and more rigid program. Nearly 40 percent of first round trainees thought the process took too long.[32] In addition expert faculty guests who had consulted on the interpretation and were eager to speak during the transitional first training would not be returning. As a result Historic Columbia streamlined the process into four sessions over two half-days.[33] The luxury of duplicate sessions disappeared. To accommodate docents who preferred to read materials, trainees received in advance a packet of materials with the adult tour script, Wilson frequently asked questions, panels and images, and lecture handouts. First, they attended a preview tour to showcase the format followed by two lectures given by interpretive staff, which provided an overview of Reconstruction and the Wilson family, President Wilson as a byproduct of the era, the home's restoration, and exhibit planning. The final session on audience engagement expanded training beyond the shadowing and lecture model. It covered controversial topics and race-related issues via small group activities and demonstrations led by Dr. Porchia Moore, who at that time was a doctoral student in library sciences at USC specializing in museum inclusivity. Finally, docents shadowed at least two tours with paying guests, one of which had to be with the tour facilitator, before entering the rigorous evaluation process. Docents who were not approved resumed shadowing, but if they failed a second time, they had to retake the entire Wilson training if they desired to continue.[34]

Evaluating the Docents

The traditional format of HHMs relies on a docent to do the majority of the speaking on an hour-long tour, a professional habit that is hard to break. Evaluations are standard in HHMs, but the requirements vary from site to site. Historic Columbia raised the bar for evaluations and required volunteers to master challenging material, a time-consuming process that risked scaring off the valuable volunteer base. Evaluations demonstrate that the greatest problems plaguing the Wilson docents as they began tours concerned pulling back their narrative as part of the semiguided tour and asking visitors engagement questions. But other issues with technology and choices in language manifested themselves as well. As a result staff evaluators remodeled the evaluation form to address specific benchmarks after the first wave of assessments. A successful evaluation required docents to hit content points on the Wilsons and Reconstruction and offer room statements, engagement questions, and transitions unique to each room. The new evaluation form included inclusivity and interactive checkpoints for certain spaces to ensure docents intertwined Black and white narratives of Reconstruction, incorporated gender, dealt with controversial topics effectively and comfortably, and displayed a level of ease working with interactives. Extra note-taking space allowed evaluators to list specific parts of tour content that needed attention. Annie Wright, a consultant for the reopening who created the original evaluation document, thought the revisions better monitored how docent training transferred to the tour and encouraged tour consistency.[35]

Evaluations also revealed that docents struggled to master the revised narrative and interactive exhibit components. Of the nineteen docents evaluated, seven had difficulty remembering the order of the rooms in the home or which information and themes went in each room. One docent performed the second-floor portion of the tour out of order. Other docents offered Wilson material in certain spaces that was better suited or assigned to other rooms.[36] Nine docents introduced incorrect content, mostly misstatements, or omitted critical information about Reconstruction, a requirement for each room.[37] Two volunteer docents actively resisted learning the new content that replaced the Wilson shrine narrative. In addition, over a quarter of docents ignored or seemed uncomfortable demonstrating the technology to visitors. This illuminated a generational ambivalence about twenty-first-century learning models for the HHM. Some retirement-age volunteer docents rushed visitors through the experience of digital play with the bird's-eye map. They failed to demonstrate its smart-touch features such as search by topic or abandoned visitors who needed assistance in order to have a richer experience.[38] Four docents, three of whom also struggled with the map, made no attempt to present the interactive pertaining to the Wilson family tree.[39] A few docents also avoided hands-on objects as well. One audience member had to ask a docent if the reproduction stereoscopes included for visitor interaction could be touched, and another guest fumbled to work it with no instruction from the guide. Some docents bypassed the stereoscopes altogether.[40]

The tour's attention to Reconstruction required precise language. Some docents excelled at this, while others slipped into coded language that reinforced an outdated interpretation of Reconstruction—which was noted and discussed by the evaluators. Coded language on race will be discussed in the next chapter, but negative, universalizing statements about carpetbaggers were the most common non-race-related example. Docents described carpetbaggers as "capitalizing on" Reconstruction and that they "took advantage" of the situation. Even after being corrected by evaluators on these myths, one docent replaced the language with problematic synonyms. Said docent referred to carpetbaggers as "white opportunists" and scalawags as "collaborationists." The docent replaced an incorrect reference to the Union presence during the Wilsons' time in Columbia as an "occupation" force with a "substantial" federal presence. In reality the largest number of troops stationed in South Carolina occurred before the passage of the 1868 state constitution. By late summer of that year, the army maintained only three posts in the state, in Columbia, Charleston, and Aiken.[41] But for every docent relying on ingrained Reconstruction language, there were others who used precise words to convey historically complex phenomena. One docent tackled the myth of the carpetbagger head-on in the political conversation sparked by the formal parlor. Other docents discussed the federal troop presence without using the word *occupation* and described Reconstruction as a "failed revolution" or situated it within the mindset of the New South.[42]

Notwithstanding language challenges, the most significant obstacle to mastering the semiguided tour was consistent inclusion of engagement questions. Most docents favored engagement questions designed to make audiences think critically about the exhibit or prompt exploration; however, two docents were uncomfortable with reflective questions, which they claimed resulted in awkward silences. Engagement required a common skill set cultivated by docents—distilling whether some visitors prefer active listening. Following their training, docents identified new skills—forming and asking engagement questions and giving time for visitor response. Inquiry-based learning required questions that moved beyond simple yes or no responses but were not so open-ended that they were overwhelming. One docent rightly observed that the home lends itself to asking questions in a way other HHMs do not, but docents have to gauge the best timing to ask a leading question and where to insert them in the tour. Weekend docent Halie Brazier found that people generally answered as she intended and was "pleasantly surprised" how the questions advanced her narrative. Volunteer Bernadette Scott found tailoring questions to the interests of the group strengthened her own tour. Another docent who gave a stellar evaluation tour modeled strong engagement techniques—repeating questions to make sure everyone heard and understood them and frequently inviting guests "to imagine" how Wilson felt as a teenager growing up and how (white) women felt about Black men voting when they could not.[43]

Even the most prepared docent struggled with full engagement. Nearly a dozen docents ran into some problem with posing engagement questions on their tours.[44] Of the eleven major engagement points existing in the exhibit rooms, three docents hit four or fewer of them.[45] Docents also reverted from opened-ended to yes or no questions. Similarly, others who heavily incorporated objects into their narrative or who had guests show great curiosity about an object missed opportunities to craft questions about material culture. Over a quarter of the docents performed only "fair" on the evaluation section or needed work on asking different levels of engagement questions—such as those that centered objects, invited guests to share from their own lives, or required deeper critical thinking based on the exhibit themes.[46]

Engagement evaluation results are partly a result of low visitor turnout during the workweek. Audiences trickled in, hindering the training program and its evaluation process. The lack of visitors limited docents' ability to practice engagement questions, which likely contributed to their struggles with this technique during their evaluations. Because of this problem, Robin Waites, the executive director of Historic Columbia, Cook, and other evaluators requested that full-time staff act as the visitor audience. Waites also invited employees at other museums to get a sneak preview and serve as tour guests. The most successful docent at encouraging participation had an audience of five, suggesting to the consultant that future training and practice should incorporate an audience "to connect with supported engagement."[47] For her evaluation Brazier brought in a half dozen coworkers who wanted to see the house. She thought it created a "more authentic" experience than awkwardly addressing the evaluator because she saw the reactions and fielded questions of uninformed people. When visitor attendance declined after opening, it also became difficult during shadow tours to demonstrate genuine engagement between docent and visitor and pull-back techniques that gave visitors time to explore. As such, when a small group tour was prearranged, volunteer coordinator Ann Posner contacted trainees.[48]

As troubling as the engagement questions predicament was mastering the techniques of a semiguided tour. A dozen docents could not sustain the semiguided tour throughout their evaluation, frequently giving too much exposition and running well over the tour's allotted seventy-five-minute time limit. Some added general knowledge about the home and the Wilsons and others brought friends on the tour, which may have extended the conversations. Either docents failed to encourage their audience to explore or talked so excessively that guests felt compelled to stay with them.[49] One docent never defined the semiguided tour but told guests to move "as you want to." Another docent's closing monologue segued from Wilson's passion for women to a recitation of a love letter he had written to his wife Ellen ten years into their marriage about a "storm of love making." On the opposite end of the spectrum, a single docent went "too far into the realm of self-guided," inviting guests to "take a look at" an artifact with no lead-in or description.

This was the only time during the nineteen evaluations that a docent was encouraged to add more to a "bare bones" tour.[50] Whether because of their nervousness, the compulsion to fill silences, or their struggles with historical content, some docents fell back on the information presented in the panels. This left no motivation for the visitor to read the panels or investigate the objects displayed. In one case a visitor wanted to use the stereoscopes, but the docent resumed their narrative and guided the visitor to a related panel.[51] Many of these same docents as well as a few others provided summaries of exhibit film content that were redundant, most often by detailing the Reconstruction amendments in the family parlor rather than letting the citizenship film do the work for them.[52]

Docents received tips and strategies to facilitate the self-guided design, such as looking for cues from guests. For example, one woman was about to explore the interactive Wilson family tree when a docent interrupted her to discuss the family picture. Evaluators encouraged docents to embrace rather than fight the silence that the semiguided tour generated. Docents were to show restraint after giving required thematic points, using their wide breadth of knowledge to supplement visitor interest on a case-by-case basis after inviting visitors to read panels and study objects. The volunteer coordinator scheduled those docents who were strong enough to pass the evaluation protocol but needed to improve their pull-back techniques for slower traffic days to give them time to practice in a low-pressure environment.[53] The most common concerns illuminated by the docent evaluations were failure to fully engage the audience; to maintain the semiguided style for over an hour; to demonstrate the interactive features of the twenty-first-century museum; to rely on panels appropriately; or to use precise, historically informed language. However, the most contentious training issue for docents was the evaluation process itself. Of the substantial portion of the volunteer docents who walked away from the process, a few did so because the interpretation challenged their negative view of Reconstruction and positive impression of Woodrow Wilson.

"You Cannot Please Everybody": Rejecting the Interpretation

The majority of volunteer docents eschewed the new tour and exhibit mostly because of the new evaluation process. However, some volunteer docents also held a negative view of Reconstruction and/or attachment to the previous Wilson interpretation. Only docents who gave MoRE tours consented to oral history interviews, though all docents were invited. Those who found the training or interpretation controversial quietly demonstrated their disapproval by not participating in interviews. As such, museums should expect to be challenged by their docents when stricter evaluation standards are implemented or the sites undertake a difficult or controversial exhibit or tour, especially one that dramatically revises history for white Americans or presents the nation's white supremacy. The backlash to these narratives is visible nearly every day in political discourse. Most recently the (limited) teaching of Critical Race Theory sparked imagined threats among Republican state legislators, and Governor Ron DeSantis proposed the erasure of Black American studies from Florida's history curriculum in January 2023.[54]

The issue of evaluations greatly divided the docents. Nevertheless, those who passed understood its purpose. This was the first time that formal evaluations, rather than a more casual approval process, had been required to conduct tours for one of Historic Columbia's four HHMs. Docents noted the lack of consistency in rigor and questioned whether the organization thought the MoRE was special or if the evaluations foreshadowed changes to come for the volunteer docent program. Stickney recalled that docents she spoke with did not like evaluation changes and perceived them as "very negative." For some docents the evaluation itself made them hesitant to participate.[55] Clark speculated that, with "people giving their own time" and not wanting to be "judged," the intimidation of an evaluation or defensiveness over "constructive criticism" could lead people to "walk away at any point." Evaluations of training and completion rates corroborate this conjecture. Only 14 percent of docents found "getting feedback on my practice tours from staff" useful, ranking the process last in most useful aspects of training alongside role playing in a group. Fifteen docents finished the first four training sessions, and four had one session to make up in the month before opening. Seven of them dropped the training before the evaluation process. In addition three more stopped training after failing their first evaluation.[56]

Some docents grew resentful of the Reconstruction-heavy script and evaluation demands and thereby minimized Reconstruction on their tours. The two docents most eager to give tours struggled the most with the evaluation process and made the tour about Wilson. They had both given specialty hard-hat tours of the Wilson home during its closure and renovation and desperately wanted to work opening weekend. Their devotion to the shrine themes of the previous tour made them a concern for staff, who ultimately decided that the opening with its staging of docents throughout the house would limit both docents' interpretive interactions with guests until they could pass the evaluation. Three volunteer docents in total ignored the new script and thematic organization of each room. Instead they relied on old tours with encyclopedic monologues about Wilson's education or the architecture of the home.[57] When volunteer coordinator Ann Posner retired, two of the three docents asked her replacement to add them to the Wilson schedule. Though they were encouraged to shadow more tours to learn the content and missed transitions, neither docent attempted another evaluation.[58]

One docent who was fixated on the Wilson shrine remained—an eager trainee who was evaluated four times. However, their evaluation failures went beyond being a Wilsonphile to open resistance to the new techniques. The docent expressed that the tour ventured "too deep in the weeds on Reconstruction" and, as a result, privileged Wilson and used some language rooted in a white supremacist narrative of Reconstruction.[59] They grew more disgruntled with each evaluation, unable to restrain the impulse to drift into long asides about Wilson's early life pulled from the old WWFH interpretation, biographies, and the Wilson boyhood home tour in Augusta, Georgia. They injected themselves into the narrative by sharing personal Wilson anecdotes. A particularly long one was about their visit to Wilson's birthplace in Staunton while driving a moving van. The presidential library staff feared the docent was retrieving Wilson's birth bed, on loan from Historic Columbia while its house was closed. The docent refused to explain the semiguided tour, wove a long narrative that stymied visitor self-exploration, and rarely used engagement questions. They offered basic thematic transitions with no complexity: "Now we're going to talk about . . ." and "I will meet you in the next room." They also made inappropriate jokes and refused to eliminate them. One was that the normal school was not teaching students how to be "normal." To reinforce that the constructive criticism stemmed from institutional policy, four different people evaluated the docent, and often teams of two or three people evaluated the same tour.[60] By the third evaluation the docent's body language was unfriendly and their tour half-hearted.[61] The docent presented their strongest performance for the fourth evaluation, though they still struggled with the semiguided nature of the tour.[62] Not long after passing, the docent stopped volunteering to pursue business interests.

In contrast to the docents committed to shrine interpretation, a few docents went too far in the opposite direction and lost the Wilson narrative on their tours. One volunteer, excited to talk about Reconstruction, failed the evaluation because the Wilson content was inaccurate or missing.[63] Post-approval, a weekend staff docent consciously chose to minimize the Wilson content. Docents deliver a room statement for each space that introduced its use for the Wilson family or a connection to their history as well as a theme related to Reconstruction. She pled guilty to omitting at times "what the room does for the family." She rejected the notion that the docent had to put Wilson in when Historic Columbia is "really getting at Reconstruction." For example, in the informal parlor, she bypassed the room statement on an after-dinner conversational setting for the Wilsons to explore citizenship.

Reconstruction was the most important part of Historic Columbia's work with the MoRE, she felt.[64]

The resistance of other docents ranged from indecisiveness to outright opposition because the requirements of the tour intimidated them or they were skeptical of the new dual interpretation of Wilson and Reconstruction. Education coordinator James Quint worried that Historic Columbia had erred in placing "this house tour on a pedestal" and, as a result, had "intimidated some folks, especially a number of the volunteers."[65] Three strong MoRE volunteer docents wanted to complete training but would not commit to giving tours initially. One of them felt that Historic Columbia assumed she would assist with the new tour. Similarly, new volunteer docents felt encouraged by Historic Columbia to learn the Wilson house first to meet the organization's scheduling needs. Holly Westcott sensed the lack of interest among seasoned docents upon her arrival as a volunteer.[66] For example, longtime volunteer Pris Stickney had no interest in giving Wilson tours before or after the reinterpretation. She presumed that "nobody wants to know about Reconstruction. . . . They come here to see Woodrow Wilson"—that is, the president. However, she decided that she owed herself and the organization the experience of training after serving on the MoRE committee in an early phase of reinterpretation. She was "won over" by learning Reconstruction history and used her change of heart to bring other reluctant docents along. The main complaint she heard was that the house was just "different." Volunteers had loved the house and its shrine tour.[67] Other volunteers, according to MoRE docent Jean Morgan, refused to do tours because they disagreed with viewing the house and Reconstruction through "twenty-first-century eyes."[68] Like Stickney, John Clark also urged reluctant volunteers to try the tour. He reassured those intimidated by the new semiguided tour and exhibit that he found the tour easier because of the panels.[69]

The encounters with other volunteers that Stickney, Morgan, and Clark described confirm that the combination of resistance to and the challenging nature of the tour led to low volunteer completion rates. Within three months of the February opening, Posner had lost hope for five docents. She continued to court ten partially trained docents, inviting them to come shadow on busier days and setting up makeup sessions designed to assist them through the process. Only three were approved in the next year.[70] Three successful long-term docents completed training but declined tours before the evaluation process. One of them pulled what Posner called the "volunteer trump card." The docent was so "out of sorts about the whole thing" that she warned she could always volunteer somewhere else. One new volunteer simply did not complete training due to time constraints, even though the "unique" and "thought-provoking" MoRE tour that he shadowed was "first class all around" and made him "proud to be a part of Historic Columbia."[71]

Docents with years of experience or attachments to previous interpretations that initially resisted tour changes will, with encouragement and continued exposure, come to embrace it. Teachable moments about restoration and preservation, according to Jennifer Pustz, can "help steer" docents "from the nostalgia to the interpretive benefits of the restoration."[72] Historic Columbia made valiant attempts to acknowledge and correct docent concerns. As a result of post-opening feedback sessions led by Cook, the organization circulated a revised script inspired by docent feedback and visitor evaluation results, created a virtual tour of the second floor for guests that physically could not go upstairs, and remade a controversial exhibit film about Wilson and the memory of Reconstruction, which is discussed in the final chapter. Docents appreciated the upgrades to the script and films, even if revisions did not meet everyone's individual requests. After seeing the revisions to the Wilson film, a reluctant docent commented that she was now interested in learning the tour. Historic Columbia debuted the revised film in April 2015 at a training session demonstrating the tour's evolution since opening. Existing volunteers who started Wilson training and some of the resisters were invited in hopes of bringing them on board.[73]

Despite concerns about the evaluation process, most of the MoRE docents, even if nervous or disapproving of evaluations in general, understood why this process was necessary for quality control and representing the site well. One docent felt compelled to make a good impression and believed the site needed docents "who really knew what they were talking about and were capable of giving the tours." As volunteer Kathy Hogan explained, the home was "not just about furniture" but "American values." Historic Columbia needed "to make sure that people understand that."[74] MoRE docents clearly recognized that the unique format and tour required deep knowledge of content and a strong delivery.

Who Makes the Best Docent?

The reopening of the Wilson home revealed that the majority of volunteer docents either refused to conduct or felt incapable of conducting the MoRE tour. Given this, public history professionals must consider whether volunteers make the best docents for distilling the complex narratives required for twenty-first-century museums. Administrators should expect to lose docents who are not paid and/or not trained as educators or historians. Mediocre HHM docents ruin a visitor's experience in stellar HHMs and may generate negative publicity. The best interpreters elevate the average HHM from forgettable to memorable. The primary problem stems from the fact that volunteers who provide tours or care for the home and collections are fiscally essential for many underfunded museums. Without them HHMs would have to close their doors. Half of Pustz's respondents in her study on interpreting domestic workers in HHMs had twenty or fewer part-time volunteers, but others had hundreds. Only a quarter of the HHMs paid all their guides. One third used all volunteers. The MoRE reflected a third of HHMs that used both volunteers and paid docents but relied mostly on volunteers.[75] Operating budgets aside, HHMs should consider if unpaid volunteers with limited public history training should be placed in frontline interpretive positions. If so, the MoRE interpreters illuminate key characteristics that define the successful docent, whether professional or volunteer, who is capable of giving complicated interpretations. In addition the training and tour forced these same docents, regardless of paid status or training, to come to terms with their own indoctrination in the Lost Cause and white supremacist narrative of Reconstruction.

In the context of learning and expressing complex ideas about race, gender, and politics, the most successful volunteer docents at the MoRE were history majors, educators, holders of advanced degrees, or a combination of these characteristics. A large majority of the sixteen docents who filled out the author's preliminary survey, eleven of which went on to participate in oral histories, were history majors and/or held advanced degrees. Five volunteer and four paid docents majored in history.[76] Despite previous exposure to Reconstruction, three specifically spoke of learning more about the subject in training, especially on the local level. Two strong volunteers believed they knew more about Reconstruction going in than others had.[77]

Most docents who excelled in giving the tour held advanced degrees. Two paid weekend staff docents were history PhD candidates at USC, exposing them to a large body of Reconstruction historiography.[78] Five weekend staff docents had or at one point were earning master's degrees in public history from USC. The visitor focus of Brazier's docent experience working for Historic Columbia brought her new frontline expertise, which differed from the heavy emphasis on research, exhibit design, and collections of her degree. Guiding tours required "translating all of that scholarship" into a performance and tapping into her customer service background.[79] Among the volunteers, one held a master's in US history and two earned PhDs, including one in English. John Clark's PhD in political science with an emphasis in international relations and work for a congressman and South Carolina governor Dick Riley gave him critical thinking and analytical skills related to historical and political events and the ability to handle a variety of audiences and inquiries diplomatically.[80] Five others held master-level degrees, including three related to teaching or school administration and one in library sciences and hospital administration.[81]

HHM experts agree, and MoRE docents confirm, that strong interpreters often have a relationship with education and performing. According to Jennifer Pustz, some of the best docents are retired teachers who transfer their classroom experience into public interpretation. In the case of the MoRE, two docents were librarians, but most were former teachers.[82] Among those docents taking the survey and conducting oral histories, five served as secondary teachers. Five also taught on the college level, including Clark, who spent a brief spell at Columbia's historically Black college, Benedict. Volunteer coordinator Ann Posner recruited retired principal and volunteer Bernadette Scott to undergo training because, as an educator, she "naturally" incorporated a "twenty-first-century learning model" on her tours. After retiring from teaching and a position as a school district social studies coordinator, Kathy Hogan saw the MoRE as a "wonderful opportunity" to use her professional talents to give back to the community. Jean Morgan, a French teacher who "always loved history," explained the "logical pairing" of teachers as volunteer docents was rooted in the "desire to inform people" about things they do not know. Morgan's need to "latch onto a thread and follow it and see where it leads to" stemmed from her teaching.[83]

Perhaps most significantly, the tour forced many white docents, regardless of age or paid status, to come to terms with their own indoctrination in the Lost Cause and white supremacist memory of Reconstruction in their homes and classrooms. Oral history evidence suggests a cathartic experience for many of the MoRE guides. Docent narrators hailing from South Carolina and the South were particularly cognizant of how states' rights and Confederate memorialization had crept into their education. Six spoke on the record, three of whom grew up in the upstate, a hotbed of Klan activity during Reconstruction and to some degree today. Five spoke openly about being taught the Lost Cause throughout their K-12 history curriculum.[84] It is important to note when speaking about Lost Cause and Reconstruction memory, docents conflated the two into the language of the Lost Cause.

Clark was the most vocal volunteer about his exposure to these Civil War and Reconstruction narratives. He grew up in Kingstree, South Carolina, between Florence and Charleston, in the same community as Michael Allen. At the time of MoRE's reopening, Allen, a community partnership specialist and three-decade veteran with the National Park Service, was working extensively in Beaufort on commemorating the Port Royal Experiment, South Carolina's unique Reconstruction experience. His job was inspired partially by an overgrown lot he had passed daily in Kingstree. He did not learn until adulthood that the property once belonged to Stephen Atkins Swails. Swails joined the famed Black regiment, the 54th Massachusetts, fought for equal pay with whites, and was the first Black line combat officer commissioned in the nation's military. Formerly employed by the Freedmen's Bureau, he was a multiple-term mayor in Kingstree during Reconstruction and a political and business boss in Williamsburg County. He helped pass the 1868 constitution and served six years as the first Black president pro tempore of the state senate. The state militia and Red Shirts made numerous threats on his life as he campaigned for Republicans in the 1878 election. As a result the native Pennsylvanian left South Carolina for the District of Columbia and worked as a clerk for the Department of the Interior, though he returned regularly until his death in 1890 to visit his family and attend to state Republican politics and his legal practice.[85] Kingstree ignored this remarkable local hero for more than a century, which is not surprising given what Clark revealed about how Reconstruction was taught to him.[86]

In 1957–58 Clark used the state history textbook by Mary C. Simms Oliphant as a student in his all-white eighth-grade history class. He learned that the "Yankees and the Carpetbaggers and freed slaves ran the government and it was corrupt." In this story corruption and excessive drinking plagued the state legislature. The "Ku Klux Klan was a good organization" and needed even if it was unsavory in the 1950s. The Klan rode with their white sheets and hoods and made "blacks think they were ghosts and scared them away from voting. And we all got chuckles out of that." The Klan and Red Shirts, the statewide paramilitary force that used fraud and violence to return white Democrats to power in 1876, bled together. According to Clark, "I don't remember a real clear distinction." He learned that Wade Hampton, aided by the Red Shirts, "saved South Carolina from the horrible Reconstruction when everything was corrupt and white people had basically lost their rights." He understood there was violence, but it was framed contextually as morally right.[87] Wade Hampton's stature has declined significantly from the days of being nationally recognized as "the most important figure in late nineteenth-century South Carolina." His biographer Rod Andrew Jr. argues that the hero worship produced by Hampton's amateur biographers and friends went too far, yet his villainy in the twenty-first century is also an oversimplification. The tragedy and humiliation in Hampton's lived experience led him to seek vindication, which played out in his contradictory rhetoric and actions during Reconstruction that pledged some measure of legal and civil protections for Black citizens. A paternalist at heart, Hampton believed it was both a privilege and duty for wealthy, educated men to rule and care for the inferior white women and Black people of South Carolina. He appointed Black citizens to state office and at times could check white South Carolinians' worst impulses. Nonetheless his moderate racial views, in comparison to some peers, were secondary to restoring and vindicating white leadership and a far cry from advocating for racial equality.[88] Commemorative efforts to remember Hampton via statues and the naming of buildings and streets began not long after his death on the twenty-fifth anniversary of taking formal control from Gov. Daniel Chamberlain on April 11, 1876. Not only did Hampton and his memory revive Confederate sentiment among veterans, but his Red Shirt campaign also fed the "the social memory of Reconstruction" and contributed to its white supremacist construction.[89] As Clark became "an inquiring adult" and avid reader, he explored Reconstruction further. Looking back at his segregated childhood, the interpretation he learned in that eighth-grade classroom made sense. Though at the time he was skeptical of the inequality around him and his all-white classroom, "we were taught colored people were happy the way things were." Fifty years later, he felt guilty that he "didn't think about it more" as a teenager.[90] The MoRE, Clark reflected, "conflict[s] with what I was taught then."[91]

In South Carolina in the twentieth century, Mary C. Simms Oliphant was arguably the single individual most responsible for spreading the tenets of the Lost Cause and a negative interpretation of Reconstruction.[92] Among the twenty books she penned on the state's history, her textbook *A Simms History of South Carolina*, first drafted by and named for her famous historian grandfather, was used in schools from the late 1930s until 1985. Upon her induction into the state's Hall of Fame in the early 1980s, Governor Dick Riley, whom Clark worked for, said, "We think of her as the lady that wrote our history book. We loved history because of her."[93] Oliphant's belief in the Lost Cause and the failure of Reconstruction never wavered, even if her overtly racist language became more coded after the 1960s civil rights movement and academics overturned the Dunning School that reinforced her interpretation. She could no longer write that Reconstruction was "the darkest and bitterest period the State has ever known," but that premise endured through her use of the textbook equivalent of dog whistles.[94]

Oliphant framed Reconstruction as "a tremendous problem" that unleashed an uneducated electorate and ruined race relations in the state. Reconstruction freed "thousands of uneducated and irresponsible slaves" (though the 1970 textbook edited out the word *irresponsible*).[95] Mostly illiterate and "unused to freedom" and citizenship, the formerly enslaved sought leadership from "the Union conquerors." As a result white leaders passed Black Codes to keep order and limit freed people's equality. Nonsoutherners and Republicans misconstrued these laws as an effort to "put the Negroes back into slavery" and politically seduced these new Black voters and potential officeholders. "Conservative white South Carolinians," Oliphant wrote, were held hostage by "an unlawful Assembly, maintained by federal bayonets." She villainized native white Republicans most, writing that the quiet nature and dignified behavior of Black politicians from South Carolina made them "men of better character than the white scalawags."[96] In Oliphant's 1970 textbook, the section "Feeling between whites and Negroes" noted that the "worst part of Radical rule" was dismantling the "old feeling of friendship and confidence" between Black and white South Carolinians. In the 1932 edition, she claimed that most of the enslaved demonstrated "their love for their masters by . . . loyally serving the wives and children of the absent soldiers" during the Civil War. The Freedmen's Bureau, carpetbaggers, and scalawags turned the "ignorant and child-like negroes" against white people.[97] In Oliphant's revised text, war hero Robert Smalls, who continued to hold office and political appointments through President Wilson's election, became the lens for the "Progress of the Negro." She praised "his kindness to the family of his former master when they were left destitute after the war." She ignored that Smalls purchased the home of his owner (and likely father) in an 1863 tax sale and that his descendants lived there ninety years.[98]

Oliphant and other textbook producers shaped generations of schoolchildren, including the MoRE volunteer docents, with their Lost Cause interpretation and white supremacist narrative of Reconstruction history. As baby boomers, docents grew up with these texts and their contents, which were reinforced in oral traditions in the home and community. Oliphant's success is akin to the United Daughters of the Confederacy, who decorated the public square with Confederate flags and monuments and filled museums and archives with Confederate culture.[99] Not until 1985, when state standards required the integration of Black history into the classroom, did the Board of Education replace Oliphant's eighth-grade textbook.[100] Bureaucratic state educators praised the enormous influence of her textbook when she died three years later.[101] Journalists of Clark's generation recalled reading it. Of all the authors and institutions that promoted the Lost Cause, Will Moredock called Oliphant "his favorite malefactor" in romanticizing the South and promoting white supremacy for generations of South Carolinians.[102] Oliphant's most prominent recent critic is her own granddaughter, Felicia Furman. In 2015 the historic preservationist rejected the textbooks as "racist to the core."[103] Bruce Baker, part of the last generation that used Oliphant's textbook, argues that the removal of her books represented the beginning of an ongoing transition to better public understanding of Reconstruction. Unlike Baker, most people who learned from textbooks like Oliphant's never receive a correction to these lessons or stories from family. MoRE docents such as Halie Brazier and Heather Bacon-Rogers are part of this transitional millennial generation, who received a trickle-down interpretation from Oliphant's textbooks last published the decade of their birth.[104]

Other volunteer docents recollected similar indoctrination in their homes and education. Decades earlier Holly Westcott conducted research on the Georgetown, South Carolina, planters club the Indigo Society. That was her introduction to the post–Civil War world as "a matter of reconstructing a society—of figuring out how life could be lived post-slavery." She realized the process "involved a lot more than I had been taught in history classes previously."[105] One docent from "an educated family" recalled that nearly all of them "believed in the memory that was created of the Lost Cause." The docent attended pep rallies in high school with the Confederate flag, where "we'd sing 'Dixie' all the time." The docent concluded, "The interpretation is exactly what we [white southerners] said it was." They created it, and a good many northerners accepted the idea that state's rights caused the Civil War and that Reconstruction failed because it was corrupt and the state was controlled by ignorant Black politicians. Thus the docent emphasized the new information they learned into the tour: the military "wasn't a real oppressive presence," there were massive rebuilding and municipal services offered, white children often did not attend public schools, and USC integrated its campus and normal school. The docent laughed, "And that's what makes it so exciting that it's here. This is the first place. And maybe that's the way it should be. That the South is the first place that has a museum dedicated to Reconstruction, the real facts about Reconstruction." For this docent Reconstruction was part of southern history, even if "it may be uncomfortable" to some. Reconstruction also was critical to the MoRE "if you want to talk about the house, the family and the era in which they lived and how that might have affected them." White southerners "would never admit" that they "are ashamed of the legacy," the docent chuckled. The MoRE's presentation of Reconstruction was not only vital to the tour and dismantling a white supremacist narrative, but it also showed potential in helping white southerners accept an uncomfortable legacy of white supremacy.[106]

The power of the Lost Cause and the white supremacist memory of Reconstruction extended beyond volunteers over fifty to millennial and generation X weekend staff docents who received less overt messaging in their education. Brazier still hears the Lost Cause narrative and people discounting slavery around her and in her hometown of Lexington, South Carolina. Just outside of Columbia, Lexington was also home to white teenager Dylann Roof, who spewed Lost Cause rhetoric in Mother Emanuel AME Church before he killed nine Black worshippers in the summer of 2015. Brazier still catches people saying the Civil War was about state's rights and not slavery. She remembered schools teaching, if not the Lost Cause, then "at least Lost Cause light" in the 1990s. Even in college she "wasn't really paying attention enough" to question interpretations. She continued, "This house definitely challenged those notions and made me really think about my own education and the way that we talk about [Reconstruction]." The tour was "something different" interpretively and "challenging to what I had grown up learning." She continued, "I got to stretch myself and learn something new or supplement what I knew."[107] It took time for her to process the new content and explain it to audiences, but once she did, the tour became her favorite to give.

Though decades separated them in age, two docents used the tour to come to terms with their own family's connection with white supremacy. In Heather Bacon-Rogers's asking of visitors to consider the possible racist actions of their ancestors rather than succumb to "white guilt," the tour and programs coordinator revealed, "this house makes me question too what my family was doing." She reflected, "I'm telling audiences about these horrible things that are going on. Do I have these horrible things in my past too?" Bacon-Rogers's miseducation on the history of Reconstruction was less egregious than previous generations or people she has had on the tour. As she recalled it, Black people were not portrayed as ignorant, but Reconstruction was framed as a "waste" with no positive outcomes and was violent for no reason. She grew up in Aiken County on the border of Edgefield County. She knew families that went back five generations in Edgefield, white families present during Reconstruction when white locals incited a violent riot against the Black community. She exclaimed, "Why did I not know this? The next county over." In her mind, "that [violence] was going on but not right next door." She learned this information from the tour. Realizing she had been taught misinformation in school, the tour mobilized her to engage "with the subject matter and to find out what I had missed out on by being educated in small-town South Carolina." While Bacon-Rogers wondered about her family's white supremacy, volunteer Walt Hall felt compelled to share and to some degree defend his Red Shirt family history. When transitioning to the Red Shirt campaign, he centered the Red Shirts intimidation of voters, though he believed the Klan to be more violent. He revealed that his Confederate veteran grandfather rode with Hampton from Edgefield to Columbia, forming an army by the time they arrived.[108] When he first shared this ancestry, he was encouraged to incorporate this personal element in his tour if he so desired. One staff member found that Hall's "family's history as an aside" in the room detailing political terrorism added to the tour.[109]

Three additional docents, two of whom were from Virginia, claimed the South as home.[110] Jean Morgan and other southern docents received a similarly biased education as their cohort from South Carolina. She laughed about how her textbooks said the enslaved were happy and well treated because they were property and masters did not mistreat property. She admitted in hindsight that that interpretation "now seems ridiculous." Lessons were "southern-centric" with a view that Reconstruction was "evil."[111]

Docents from outside the South suffered from a lack of information rather than a white supremacist narrative. Stickney, a "Midwesterner through and through," grew up in suburban Chicago and Milwaukee. She remembered "learning the term carpetbaggers and that's about it." She perceived that Reconstruction happened and was bad. After she listened in on a follow-up training meeting where docents talked about what they had learned in school, she concluded that bias had to have some impact. She said, "They had a lot of stuff thrown at them growing up that I didn't have. And I don't think you can totally leave that behind." When she delivered her practice tour to a good friend, Stickney could tell by her friend's physical response that she was hearing a different interpretation than the one learned in school. Rather than needing to overturn indoctrination, several non-southern docents learned Reconstruction for the first time (or the first with any depth) during training. Volunteer Anne Weir did not receive this content in Michigan, while Katy Menne grew up with no "strong opinion about the Civil War or Reconstruction." Only Wisconsin native Cyndy Storm spoke of learning Reconstruction from a northern perspective. In this narrative the federal government tried to rebuild the South and incorporate African Americans into the society and economy, but the effort was deeply resented by white southerners. But neither of Storm's two general survey college courses in US history spent much time on Reconstruction.[112]

Volunteer Kathy Hogan, a New Jersey native educated in Maryland before settling in South Carolina, was an exception to this trend of light Reconstruction coverage outside the South. The civil rights movement heavily influenced her Catholic schooling, which she credited with shaping her activism and profession as a social studies teacher. When she came to South Carolina, she waited fourteen years to enter a social studies classroom. She thought, "They won't be open to my understanding of history. I can't teach about the Civil War and Reconstruction the way that South Carolinians would expect." She was happy when she overcame this fear and returned to the classroom. It led to a position as social studies school district coordinator, where she and academic historians, including Valinda Littlefield of the USC history department, helped write the state's 2011 standards and select support documents for US history to ensure classrooms were historically up-to-date with scholarship.[113] State law requires that the Board of Education revise social studies standards every seven years. The 2011 standards apply to the time of the MoRE opening and docent interviews. Hogan, who retired in 2013 from Lexington/Richland School District Five in Irmo, South

Carolina,[114] "was delighted to see" that the MoRE's interpretation "reflected what the state is requiring students to be taught about the era." The 2011 standards covered Reconstruction in third-, fifth-, and eighth-grade US history as well as the eleventh-grade course United States History and the Constitution. Reconstruction themes in US history included presidential and congressional Reconstruction, the Freedmen's Bureau, economic impacts, successes and failures, and "subversive" or "discriminatory" groups. Third graders also were expected to understand "positive and negative effects of Reconstruction" in South Carolina, including the development of public education and sharecropping, rebuilding, and "racial advancements and tensions." Fifth graders received a positive interpretation of Reconstruction as an effort to rebuild and the "great hope" and incredible change it inspired. Students expanded their knowledge on the themes mentioned above, including the goals of Reconstruction and its constitutional amendments and white southern resistance, both initial resistance and the subversive groups that increased in prominence after the removal of federal troops in 1877. The eighth-grade course South Carolina: One of the United States packaged Reconstruction through the Progressive Era. Previous grade goals remained, though new language included Black Codes and emphasis on Black political, educational, and social opportunities. The role of state political leaders codifying Jim Crow and establishing "a system of racial segregation, intimidation, and violence" first appeared. The eleventh-grade Constitution course underscored the Reconstruction amendments, Reconstruction's effect on the South and federal government, and its end, including anti-Black factions, competing national interests that undermined it, removal of federal protection, and the disenfranchisement that followed during Jim Crow. Bloom's revised taxonomy heavily shaped the course, as it did Daniella Cook's training session for the MoRE.[115]

Hogan spoke of the "considerable controversy" over the Reconstruction interpretation in the classroom. She recalled that results of benchmark testing showed teachers were not meeting the standard and current interpretations. Teachers were not "purposely misinterpreting" Reconstruction but were instead teaching what they were wrongly taught with Dunning School–style education materials, thus demonstrating the long reach of Oliphant's textbooks and others like them.[116] The MoRE's mirroring of the state curriculum was no coincidence. Historic Columbia chose to interpret Reconstruction not just because of Wilson's light footprint in the home and the opportunity to interpret an often misunderstood part of American history but also because teachers expressed a need for this history.[117]

Hogan believed the 2011 standards to be a dramatic improvement, yet criticism of Reconstruction standards in both 2011 and 2018 endured, despite their more accurate telling of Reconstruction a century in the making. The primary issue was specificity. In his analysis of 2005 and 2011 standards, teacher Charles Vaughan surveyed twenty-one writers of the South Carolina standards to gauge respondents' opinions of Western historicism and political correctness. He also evaluated standards and required materials like textbooks and support documents. Vaughan calculated that 79 percent of the standards advanced a narrative of progress and exceptionalism at the expense of issues of race, gender, class, and sexuality. He blamed political correctness on both the left and right for creating a climate where teachers avoided historical controversy for fear of offending a particular group.[118] A report by the Southern Poverty Law Center analyzed South Carolina's state standards from 2011 and found eight "key concepts" missing, though slavery and Gullah culture were introduced in the third grade. Yet Chanda Robinson, a secondary social studies consultant in Richland County who worked on the 2011 standards with Hogan, received complaints from some teachers about the high level of specificity.[119] In a reversal seven years later, the 2018 standards came under scrutiny for lack of specificity, which the Board of Education countered with hundreds of pages of support documents. For example, key figures from the mid-twentieth-century civil rights movement were absent, as were nineteenth-century figures such as Robert Smalls. Michael Allen, by this time retired from the National Park Service, was concerned about Smalls's exclusion as a representative who helped bring public education to South Carolina. The lack of content was a response to a 2016 state law requiring that South Carolina graduates possess skills such as self-direction, global perspective, communication, and analysis.[120] Despite these critiques, much of the same thematic content from 2011 standards remained, such as the discussions of constitutional amendments and Black Codes and emphasizing how Reconstruction impacted a wide range of groups. Perhaps most important, new indicators stressed Reconstruction as a turning point foundational to civil rights as well as unique state elements, such as the Port Royal Experiment and the 1868 state constitution. In the high-school-level Constitution course, however, Reconstruction history was part of one standard focused on expansion and the natural rights of citizens from 1803 until 1877 and largely reduced to the response of legislative and judicial branches to sectional strife and reunion from 1830 through 1877.[121]

Volunteers and professional docents steeped in history, holding advanced degrees, and often working in education performed the tour effectively and used it to reconcile their misinformed Lost Cause and Reconstruction education. But the question remains whether volunteers are best suited to conduct a challenging interpretive tour. As tour and programs coordinator, Bacon-Rogers had total confidence in the "grade A" volunteers who could adapt to give each of the four HHM tours that Historic Columbia offered. Of the five dozen or so guides unwilling or unable to give the Wilson tour, only 25–30 percent retained her confidence in being able to conduct house tours in general. The MoRE training became a "litmus test" for Bacon-Rogers in determining docent excellence because it revealed which volunteers were exceptional in their ability to learn the information and handle controversial topics and conflict. She called for a more intense screening process to ensure quality and perhaps paying a small wage for the three-hour shifts volunteers worked.[122] Clark also suggested payment may be the key when he discussed volunteers' objections to the evaluation process. He said, "You're dealing with people giving their own time. They can walk away at any point. They can quit giving tours if they're not happy." For Clark volunteering should be "enjoyable and relaxing," not time intensive.[123] Although professional docents tend to be paid low wages, they work more frequently than volunteers, allowing them to hone their skills, and are more receptive to interpretive changes. They also require less supervision than volunteers but might have less availability if the position is not full time. Whether performed by a volunteer or paid docent, interpretation often requires extra, unpaid labor and an emotional, caretaking interpersonal connection with visitors that is simultaneously devalued for its feminine qualities.[124]

Professionalizing interpretive frontline staff would meet the need among public historians for placement on the job market. The service and knowledge economies began their boom a half century ago in the early 1970s, and interpreters teach the nuances of history to inform and engage the public, yet this work remains undervalued both intellectually and in its compensation by knowledge producers and management.[125] For example, Brazier worked weekends at Historic Columbia because she could not find full-time public history work after earning her master's degree. Many public historians excel as interpreters and provide valuable support to exhibition and curatorial staff. With museums strapped for cash, hiring new staff seems impossible, but institutions should consider the overall benefit, in terms of accuracy and productivity, in having two full-time staff versus ten volunteer docents. When snowstorms brought the evaluation process to a halt and left staff scrambling to conduct tours and evaluate docents under the stress of opening a museum, no member of the staff raised concerns that four weekend staffers conducted MoRE tours before being formally approved.[126] Bacon-Rogers, who managed weekend staff, explained that they could be fired if they presented an outdated narrative or lack professionalism. Furthermore, they were younger, between the ages of twenty-three and forty-five, and often in academia and thus constantly learning and educating themselves. They read and utilized the supplemental information circulated and conveyed Historic Columbia's approved research and information, which is not always assured with volunteers. They also shared information they encountered and sought permission to incorporate it. Bacon-Rogers thought weekend staff should be included in more workshops with the volunteers as a resource for helping docents answer complex questions and enhance their tours. Weekend staff docent Erin Holmes came to understand the necessity of training after listening to some of the older docents during the training process. Nonetheless, as a trained historian, she would have preferred to learn the content on her own.[127]

MoRE weekend staff in many respects reflected what Amy Tyson classified as a "new class of paraprofessionals." In her analysis of interpreters at Historic Fort Snelling, she defined paraprofessionals as service workers and cultural producers whose "work display" demands a more personalized, interactive style of service than, say, fast-food employees as part of a new Taylorized knowledge service economy, "wherein knowledge and services of all kinds (including emotions) are being subjected to a new kind of scientific management and oversight." These paraprofessionals often face a corporate culture that lauds the "customer service superstar," which relies on interpreters' belief that their work is important and a privilege, even if they at times feel underappreciated and underpaid. The superstar culture promoting a strong individual identity stymies a collective identity among interpreters, who struggle to create a class consciousness that demands professionalization, support, and fair pay in a saturated market with institutions marred by privatization, reduced state and federal support, and contingent labor. Tyson calls for retaining good cultural workers and treating them with dignity rather than as "disposable commodities." To do so institutions need to foster a culture of participatory democracy for frontline workers by providing training and identifying individual skills.[128]

Lastly, Historic Columbia suffers from the larger trend in HHMs of volunteer recruitment declining along with attendance. Staffing was an immediate concern and became the most consistent and largest logistical conundrum for the organization. As noted earlier, several docents felt pressure to learn the MoRE tour as a result. Bacon-Rogers argued that placing volunteers who did not agree with the interpretation or were incapable of learning such a complex tour into the MoRE defies the organization's mission. But turning guests away would be "equally bad for business."[129] Thus staff, including myself as tour facilitator conducting half of the tours each day, filled numerous gaps in the volunteer schedule during the week.[130] Historic Columbia eventually staggered its tour schedule, offering tours of two houses rather than four each hour. This somewhat eased docent fatigue.[131] However, Historic Columbia needed a small, reliable team of two to four full-time docents to professionalize tours and resolve scheduling conflicts.

The interpretive landscape of Historic Columbia evolved in the last decade, partly a reflection of the frontline training problems outlined here and partly a result of the COVID-19 pandemic. In May 2023 visitor experience manager Heather Bacon-Rogers, formerly the tour and program coordinator, counted on one hand the volunteers who currently gave Reconstruction tours. Bacon-Rogers, who managed, trained, and hired much of the frontline staff, including some volunteers, recalled that most MoRE volunteers were "originals," such as Cyndy Storm and Margie Richardson. Storm delivered her tour every Friday, the only MoRE tour slated that day. In the wake of COVID, Historic Columbia streamlined its tour schedule further, resulting in the need for less docents to cover the MoRE. The organization offered each of its four HHMs once a day and adopted an online reservation system.[132]

Covid was also a factor in the mass exodus of volunteers. Docents concerned about safety and exposure never returned, even after Historic Columbia implemented a mandatory masking policy. Katharine Allen, director of outreach and engagement, reasoned that long-term absences hurt retention because volunteers, many of them retired, were less likely to return and more likely to move on to other activities. Volunteers declined across the organization—not just in interpretation. However, Historic Columbia did not actively recruit to replace these volunteers. Post-COVID, Historic Columbia expanded its professional frontline staff to rely mostly on paid interpreters. Paid weekday guides, according to Bacon-Rogers, arrived with a working knowledge of history, a good grasp of Reconstruction, and confidence in discussing difficult topics. Historic Columbia simplified training again with the shift in interpretive labor. New docents shadowed the house three times, went through the house on their own once, and then gave the tour to Bacon-Rogers. She recalled this frontline staff was different than the volunteer docents of 2014, whose outdated education required a reeducation in modern interpretations of Reconstruction. Those volunteers "needed so much more background, so much more information."[133]

Lastly, volunteer docent fears that the MoRE foreshadowed a new interpretive mission at Historic Columbia were correct. In 2018, on the bicentennial of its construction, the Hampton-Preston Mansion reopened as a museum focused on urban enslavement and the groups of people who lived in the space throughout its history. The interpretation, which decentered the Hampton-Preston family and situated their success as enslavers and supporters of slavery, once again contributed to volunteers leaving the organization and demonstrated the strength of a professionalized frontline staff. Governor Hampton's grandfather, Wade Hampton I, believed by his contemporaries to be the largest slaveholder in South, purchased the home in

1823. The origin of the Hampton family's prestige originated with him, and by the time Wade Hampton II assumed control in 1840, there were over 12,000 acres of land and 460 enslaved people in their possession. Within a decade the number of enslaved skyrocketed to 3,000. Hampton was rumored to be far kinder to his "wards" than his father, who had a reputation for cruelty. In 1860 the family enslaved seventy-four men, women, and children on the mansion grounds in Columbia alone.[134] Historic Columbia adopted a training style similar to that for the MoRE, with outside experts as speakers and emphasis on how to discuss slavery and the Lost Cause. According to Allen, the tour dove deeper into the Lost Cause than did the MoRE. Allen explained that those volunteers who could not accept change or the work required to deliver a tour on slavery left. However, paid interpreters understood that "this is our mission. These are values. This is the type of tour we give." Professional docents wanted to be part of the interpretation. In some cases those docents and even one or two volunteers sought out Historic Columbia because of a tour experience.[135]

Strikingly, regardless of age or professional public historian status, docents walked away from MoRE training and tours with a profound sense of the impact of the Lost Cause and Reconstruction mythology in their own lives. Those from South Carolina and older docents who grew up with Jim Crow, both de facto and de jure, seemed most cognizant of these narratives' power. The MoRE is not just changing how visitors think about Reconstruction. It changed the way its docents thought about how history has been crafted and defended in their world to support white supremacy. Without a doubt, volunteers and paid professional staff are capable of giving complex HHM tours rich in social, gender, and racial history. But in the case of the MoRE, only a minority of volunteers were willing to attend the training required to learn this kind of tour and master its content. In Bacon-Rogers's experience, well-educated docents, regardless of professionalization, gave stronger than average MoRE tours and were more likely to remain volunteers. However, she believed the key characteristic was not education but rather an "openness to new study and to learning new material."[136] As the next chapter demonstrates, interpreting racial violence and oppression poses problems for everyone. However, the vocal and coded opposition to elements of language and cultural sensitivity training as well as an exhibit film interpreted by some as portraying Wilson as a racist came from retired white volunteer docents, indicating that age and white privilege pose problems on the front lines of interpretation.

PART II

Interpreting Silences, Violence, and Memories

CHAPTER 4

Aren't I a Citizen?

Interpreting the Lives of Black Women and Domestic Workers in Historic House Museums

In 1851 Sojourner Truth took the stage at the Ohio Women's Convention in Akron and delivered her famous speech that asked, "Aren't I a woman?" Except that she didn't. She did deliver a speech, but the presiding officer at the meeting, Frances Dana Gage, rewrote the speech twelve years later in an effort to dethrone Harriet Beecher Stowe as the white romantic writer who shaped Truth's identity for mass consumption. Gage's version continues to circulate as authentic and attributed to Truth.[1] Gage's question serves as a metaphor for the relationship between elite white women and Black women. There was little to no room for Black women on the white woman's pedestal or her public-facing "women's sphere." Even Sojourner Truth's story of freedom was not hers to tell. But Gage's question about womanhood was provocative and true, even if fraudulent. Nineteenth-century society expected the women's sphere to be occupied by ladies. Women performed the role of lady through participation in the "cult of true womanhood" and "cult of domesticity."[2] The *lady* was white, preferably educated, and wealthy, but also—most important—confined, obedient, and submissive to her family and God. These women were neither in control of their own destiny nor victims of social change; rather they networked within this sphere to create an identity, sisterhood, and public power that did not conflict with familial obligations such as education.[3]

The names of the Black women operating in the same space as matriarch Janet "Jessie" Wilson, Tommy Wilson's mother, are absent from primary sources. This absence threatened to diminish them on the Woodrow Wilson Family Home tour too; but to silence Black women negotiating their newfound citizenship and lived experiences during Reconstruction was not an option. The endeavor to convert the WWFH from a presidential shrine into the Museum of the Reconstruction Era led Historic Columbia to explain this deficiency in the historical record on the tour and implement a docent training session on language and cultural sensitivity. Outside consultants and Historic Columbia designed the session to help docents understand various forms of privilege, the social construction of race, interactions with diverse visitors, and the use of precise, inclusive language. While white, paid docents trained as public historians embraced the workshop, older white volunteer docents were divided about its effectiveness and utility. Historic Columbia envisioned that the training would prepare docents to discuss the Black experience during Reconstruction and venture into the turbulent waters of white violence against the Black community. Part of this discussion included the social and economic changes that the period ushered in for Black workers, including the unknown domestic laborers employed by the Wilson family. During the training process and in the first year of operation, a contentious debate emerged between docents and the interpretative team regarding how to frame the segregated spaces that domestic workers occupied in the Wilson home's pantries. The training also illuminated an interpretive weakness. Historic Columbia largely ignored sexual violence during Reconstruction in its training, and most certainly on its tour, leaving docents ill prepared to handle the subject should a visitor broach it.

In comparison to the three other historic house museums that Woodrow Wilson called home, the MoRE is the only site that has shed its origin as a Wilson shrine and presented a full narrative of Black lives during Reconstruction. At the time of the MoRE's reopening, the Woodrow Wilson Presidential Library and Museum, located at his birthplace in Staunton, Virginia, wove enslaved domestics into its tour and addressed slavery immediately. This approach made the WWPLM the next strongest tour incorporating the Black experience. Wilson's childhood home in Augusta, Georgia, and his final, post-presidency home in Washington, DC, both tacked on brief dialogues at the end of their tours. However, the WPPLM missed opportunities for a more racially inclusive narrative that addressed how the Wilsons' first introduction to slavery made them beneficiaries of the institution and shifted their opinions. The Woodrow Wilson Boyhood Home limited the role slavery and domestic servitude played in the Wilsons' lives after they moved to Augusta, when Tommy was only two years old, despite the fact that the institution's impact on the family dramatically increased. Conversations between all four Wilson HHMs would provide continuity and greater public knowledge about Black occupants that lived with Wilson much of his life and how they shaped his views on race.

The Problem of White Privilege: Language and Cultural Sensitivity Training

Inclusive museums require docents to speak to a multitude of audiences who do not approach history through the "heroic, white, male-dominated narrative."[4] Historic Columbia's attempt to prepare docents for this best practice resulted in the creation of an interactive training session on cultural and language sensitivity. Both the volunteer base and the weekend staff, often pulled from the ranks of public historians trained at the University of South

Carolina, attended. This training was necessary because Historic Columbia was a predominantly white institution. Of the eighty-six thousand nationally designated historic sites in the United States ca. 2015, just 3 percent "explicitly represent minority populations defined by race, ethnicity, gender, or sexual orientation."[5] The two women of color volunteering at the time of the MoRE reinterpretation embraced the exhibit and tour and participated in training. Outside obligations detoured them from becoming MoRE docents. Historic Columbia offered the hour-long inaugural workshop twice to accommodate docents' schedules. Eighteen volunteers and five paid docents completed the first sensitivity training before the museum reopened in February 2014. The organization ultimately extended the session to ninety minutes because the guided activities generated lengthy conversations that needed more time to finish. Thirteen volunteers, eight of them new inductees, and two paid docents attended the second workshop held in April.[6] In later sessions participation declined to a handful of recently recruited docents.

As a predominantly white institution, Historic Columbia sought Black voices to teach the cultural and language sensitivity workshops. That the MoRE's interpretation heavily emphasized the Black experience during Reconstruction required materials and discussion about interpreting Black history and white docents interacting with nonwhite visitors. However, the workshop also opened the opportunity for docents to consider audiences they may unknowingly exclude with their language. Daniella Cook, assistant professor in the Department of Instruction and Teacher Education at USC, crafted and led the first session two weeks before opening.[7] Cook specializes in understanding how students, teachers, and communities underserved in public education are affected by class, race, and power. The training and the tour explored these three themes, but inclusivity stretched beyond them to areas such as gender and disability. As preparation for the workshop, Cook assigned trainees "White Privilege: Unpacking the Invisible Knapsack" by Peggy McIntosh, a classic, introductory text that offers an accessible list of the ways McIntosh herself had benefited from her whiteness. Cook provided activities, readings, and handouts on normative language, the social construction of race, and tour tips for well-intentioned docents to make visitors feel included and welcomed. Tour tips ranged from not asking visitors to speak for their "race, ethnicity, religion, sexual orientation, or nationality" to not letting "racist, sexist, or homophobic language and comments go unnoticed." The tips also stressed the importance of body language, such as spreading "eye contact around" rather than primarily looking at women when addressing reproductive rights or Black visitors when discussing slavery.[8] Docents also challenged their assumptions by identifying normative language in a series of thirteen sentences. The exercise illuminated ageism, sexism, racism, and classism as well as biases against the disabled and non-Western cultures.[9]

For subsequent trainings the language and sensitivity workshop resumed under the leadership of Porchia Moore, who studies museum inclusivity. Moore continued to use the activities and handouts selected by Cook but brought her own insight as a public history practitioner and frequent visitor to museums.[10] She opened sessions with a twenty-minute presentation of her own research on museums and inclusivity. She generated complex conversations, particularly when she asked docents to identify appropriate terms for referring to enslaved people and people of color from a larger list. These issues surrounding language choice initially prompted Historic Columbia to develop the workshop. That several docents came of age during Jim Crow and were taught antiquated racial language that is inappropriate today concerned the organization.[11] Moore insisted that docents should know why they use a specific word and be able to explain that choice if asked by a visitor about it on the tour. She also introduced docents to the concept of the privilege walk, a visualization of privilege, in which they considered how their gender, class, sexuality and race benefited or hindered them by moving forward or backward based on a series of questions.[12]

The language and cultural sensitivity session combined with content training eased fears among docents related to the discussion of race. Before and after the first training program, Historic Columbia administered a survey to gauge docents' comfort level talking with museum visitors about historical issues related to race. After training, 6.5 percent of docents taking the survey that previously were "not comfortable at all" dropped to zero. Those "somewhat comfortable" remained nearly unchanged at just over 35 percent, but those "very comfortable" rose 6 percent to 64 percent. However, these statistics are not conclusive. Thirty-one docents completed the pretraining survey, but only fourteen of the twenty-three docents who completed all training took the post-training survey. Furthermore, three volunteers during their formal staff evaluation displayed obvious discomfort with talking about historical issues connected to race. They compensated by ignoring racial aspects of Reconstruction and focusing on Wilson content instead and did not pass those evaluation attempts.[13] However, of the 628 visitors who visited the MoRE in 2014 and completed a survey on their experience, nearly 84 percent thought docents handled sensitive issues "extremely well."[14] Survey results and the high standards set for the docent's tour evaluation that were built into the training process demonstrate that sensitivity programming is critical to a museum where docents interpret complex issues of race and create inclusive environments for all of its visitors. The training provides tools and language on the front end and identifies potential problems before placing docents on the front lines.

Although the training appeared to have correlations to positive feedback on visitor surveys and was thus a success, a docent survey and docent oral histories that I conducted around the MoRE's second anniversary reveal that older white volunteers were more likely to be critical of the sensitivity workshop than paid docents. Ten volunteers and six paid weekend staffers participated in the survey, and eleven gave oral histories. Sensitivity training divided volunteers. Some enjoyed and learned from the training, while others openly admitted disliking aspects of the session. Conversely the weekend staff welcomed and benefited from the training.

Four weekend docents praised exercises related to white privilege, with one calling the session their favorite. The discussion of privilege resonated most with them. They spoke specifically about being able to "see visually" privilege during the privilege walk. Docents worked through their preconceived associations of the word *privilege* from wealth by listening to incidents of discrimination experienced by leaders and attendees. For example, that a person of color would return clothes to a department store with a white friend to prevent accusations of theft had never occurred to one docent. After the session weekend staff member Halie Brazier described being hyperaware that she was a white docent telling the story of "terrible things that happened to Black people" as a result of Reconstruction-era violence, and that she was a "descendant" and "beneficiary of that system" in the present. Unpacking Peggy McIntosh's invisible knapsack drastically expanded Brazier's understanding of privilege but also made her overthink language and her presentation of Black history on her tour. One docent, however, suggested some activities and examples be "more directed" at the Wilson home rather than general ideas surrounding inclusion.[15]

There was no consensus among volunteers about the training session. They expressed a range of opinions, which also illuminated characteristics of their racial philosophies. Volunteer docents approved of and benefited from the session, were ambivalent about it, or openly admitted disliking it. Several spoke of the session's importance in both the training process and understanding white privilege. For the first time, some volunteers thought about privilege and considered the appropriateness of their word choices. Kathy Hogan wondered how much impact the training had on her tours. She believed language and behavior were "not conscious" and only had a few Black visitors to measure any language shifts against. Volunteers who dismissed the training did so because of their learning styles, their previous exposure to diversity training, or their belief that they possessed progressive or neutral views on race and racism. They argued that group work in general did little to facilitate their learning and labeled some exercises as too "touchy feely" or "silly." Pris Stickney explained she was a "facts person" and neutral on race, finding no language she should correct on her tour. She worried about political correctness, how "we have to be so conscious nowadays." Two volunteers claimed the session failed to add to their working knowledge of inclusivity from previous professional training. However, in their oral histories, both used the term "the Blacks" to refer to the Black community. This antiquated language suggests that their prior inclusivity training was outdated. Another volunteer used the same term on the formal tour evaluation required for clearance to conduct tours.[16] Weekend staff who trained with volunteers encountered older volunteers with ingrained racial views, who had not attended college in decades or given tours regularly. One weekend staffer noted that two volunteers were surprised to hear that docents should not single out Black visitors and ask about their experiences with racism. Another recalled that a white male volunteer "piped up" with a comment akin to how Black people can also be racist. She "figured he probably wasn't going to sit and marinate on his own white privilege."[17]

Volunteer Jean Morgan articulated the strongest objection to the training, which was rooted in a conversation that tested her racial and docent ideology. Morgan thought the session was not well prepared, citing a technical glitch and its quick pace, but that was not her primary complaint. She acknowledged institutional racism and the challenges of having white docents interpret Black history but found the workshop "one-sided." During the workshop Morgan shared a volunteer experience she had at the Mann-Simons property, another site administered by Historic Columbia devoted to the history of a Black entrepreneurial, middle-class family in the nineteenth- and twentieth-century South. A Black visitor argued that all white baby boomers of Morgan's generation were racists. Morgan thought her presence refuted this claim, but Cook countered that the visitor may have regarded Morgan as a "white do-gooder." The docent thought the comment contradicted an earlier session conversation that all people have biases but that racism is institutionalized prejudice. Both experiences reinforced for her that "maybe racism runs one way, but prejudice runs both ways." Morgan no longer volunteers at Jubilee, the long-running Black festival held each fall around the Mann-Simons site, because she does not want her presence to be misunderstood. She advocates for Historic Columbia finding a way to staff Jubilee with Black volunteers because Mann-Simons is considered by the Black community as "their" site, and "the presence of so many white faces is probably offensive to them."[18]

Regardless of the level of acceptance among volunteers, both volunteer and paid docents acknowledged that exposure to the concept of white privilege mattered and was a critical concept for the tour. However, the majority of paid docents had already been exposed to these ideas, because they attended university more recently. And while three weekend docents concluded that the training appealed to them on an intellectual level cultivated in graduate school, education level was not a factor in volunteers' ambivalence about the session.[19] Among the volunteers who spoke on record, five held master's degrees and two earned PhDs in a range of fields including history, English, political science, education, library sciences, and hospital administration.[20] Four docents, three of them volunteers, had previous exposure to diversity training as part of their professions. Survey data and the educational background of docents reinforce that language and cultural sensitivity are best practices. These practices keep an organization's cadre of well-educated, retired volunteer docents current with cultural sensitivity theory and trends even if they do not fully embrace the ideas. It also appeals to professional public historians on staff. As one weekend staffer surmised, "We can all use a little more training on sensitivity and language."[21]

A Labor of Love and Sorrow: Interpreting the Lives of Domestic Workers

Sensitivity and language training provided tools to tackle but not completely resolve the unique challenges of interpreting rooms that narrate the lives of Black individuals who occupied the Wilson home during Reconstruction. The pantries and dining room emerged as the central spaces for interpreting Black workers and their relationship with the Wilsons. Interpretations of middle- and upper-class homes struggle to expose the domestic complexities involved when people across racial and class lines occupy these spaces as laborers. Some HHMs omit these complexities or leave out controversial or potentially offensive information that traditional white museumgoers may not be prepared for or wish to learn. Nonetheless most sites are moving toward more inclusive narratives. In the mid-1980s and 1990s, HHMs began to address this important gap in their interpretation of domestic servants. A 2003 nationwide survey of 358 postbellum HHMs revealed domestic servant interpretation had been introduced in nearly three-quarters of house tours but still lacked proper racial and class contextualization vis-à-vis white elite occupants and domestics. Most tours limited discussion of racial and economic dynamics at play. Organizations wrestled with this interpretive turn. They believed that they lacked the material culture and primary sources to elucidate properly the lives of workers. To compensate, tours interpreted the architecture, original fixtures, and spaces associated with domestic service, such as the kitchen, servant stairs, and laundry room. Period tools rarely original to the home helped docents facilitate discussion with guests about tedious domestic tasks. This method explains why most HHM tours that interpreted domestics, according to public historian Jennifer Pustz, sidestepped uncomfortable subjects tied to race, class, and gender and instead focused tour attention on less contentious themes, such as the use of appliances/technology and working conditions.[22]

The goal of HHMs should be to present the servant narrative as central and not tacked on to an elite white story. Domestic workers were part of an inclusive "cast of characters," yet in the nearly two centuries of HHM history, tours rendered them invisible throughout the home and landscape. A multivocal HHM provides a richer, more holistic understanding of the past and domestic spaces. The four HHMs devoted to Woodrow Wilson vary in their levels of success incorporating servants and enslaved people. Pustz argued that the first step for HHMs in discussing domestic servants is to rethink the sites' previous history "as shrines, collections of antiques, and architectural masterpieces." The majority of America's shrines and museums are institutional spaces of white privilege dedicated to the history of white male conquest. The MoRE's new, inclusive interpretation erased its Wilson shrine origins, presented positive gains from the Reconstruction era, such as public education and voting rights, and centered Black South Carolinians in the narrative. Thus the discussion of domestic life in traditional workspaces that are considered segregated in other HHMs did not operate as a supplement to a white narrative. The Black experience is present throughout the exhibit and home. However, public historian and weekend docent Casey Lee believed that exhibiting the pantries, although "great," still "tacked on" Black domestics in a way similar to other HHMs. She concluded this might be unavoidable, since they were workspaces attached to more hospitable family spaces. The three other Wilson HHMs, like 85 percent of HHMs with publicly open spaces that would have been occupied by domestic workers, designed tours with tacked-on inclusivity. However, after the MoRE reopened, other Wilson sites were trying to maintain their relevance by challenging this lenticular logic and including nonwhites. Lenticular logic, as defined by Tara McPherson, is a fallacy in which one sees only one of two linked histories or images at a time, usually that of whiteness, when they are in fact bonded together.[23] While the birthplace of Woodrow Wilson was the most inclusive of the other three Wilson HHMs, by 2015 the other two had yet to incorporate fully a diverse racial narrative that includes the stories of Black occupants of these homes.

A decade ago the house tour at the WWPLM in Staunton, Virginia, retained its original interpretation highlighting the "virtues and sensibilities"

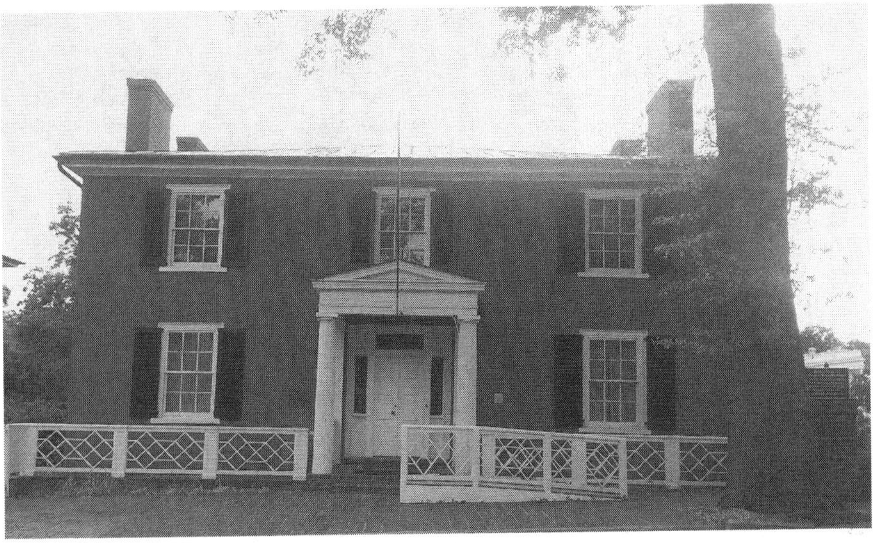

Figure 9. Woodrow Wilson was born in this Presbyterian manse in Staunton, Virginia. Today the Woodrow Wilson Presidential Library and Museum offers a house tour at the site. Photograph by author.

of America's Scotch-Irish Presbyterianism, but more recently it updated its coverage of those who performed labor in the home.[24] The tour started at the back entrance of the red-brick Greek revival manse, reflecting recent trends in moving tours through workspaces first rather than the front door. The scene was a typical breakfast in 1857. The first room unveiled the cook's world in the kitchen. She started her day at dawn, firing up her modern range stove, and likely had access to a few chickens, other livestock, and a garden on the property. Implicitly referring to the labor performed, the guide called this space the most important room in the house. Entering through the kitchen and addressing slavery immediately was a conscious choice to avoid stirring in slavery at the end of the tour. Staff changes in the curatorial department, script issues, and the recognition that Staunton was likely the setting for Tommy's first exposure to slavery prompted the revisions. The tour never clearly addressed the latter subject. The church where Joseph pastored leased one to three enslaved people under a strict contract with owners detailing specific provisions.

After passing through the family-centered sitting room, entry into the cook's private bedroom, a perk of her position, wove Black domestics back into the narrative. Other benefits awarded to the highly skilled enslaved cook included a nice bed, hand-me-down clothing, and a five-day Christmas break.[25] The interpretation in this final space of the floor painted the

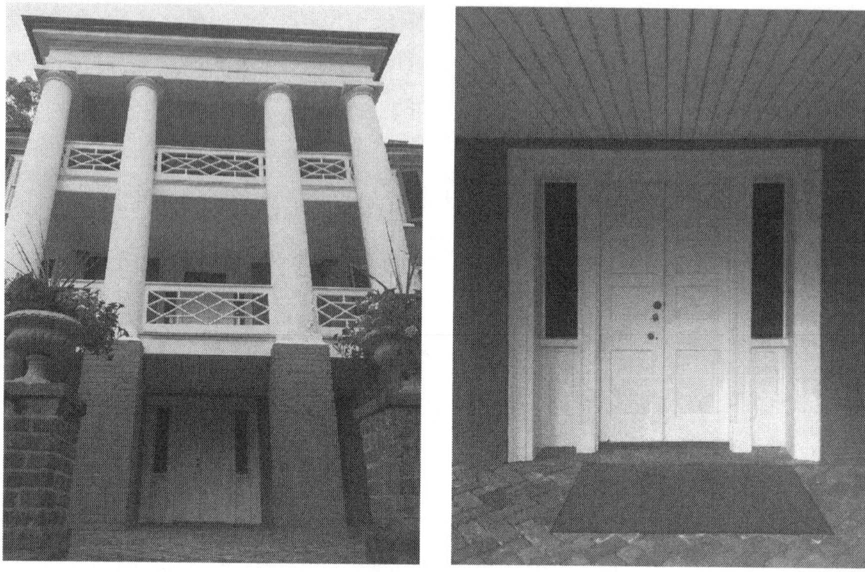

Figure 10. The back of the Staunton manse and the back door or servants' entrance, where the house tour began. Photographs by author.

Wilsons as benevolent paternalists who treated enslaved people well, even like family.

A racially segregated second floor removed enslaved workers from the remainder of the tour, though several opportunities for a more inclusive narrative exist within the script. The parlor transformed to a church room for weddings, church meetings, and evening devotionals. The image of enslaved individuals laboring during church-related services expanded the scope of the tour's primary theme: "a middle-class minister's family in antebellum Virginia and the household and *values* that produced a future President of the United States." The tour did not ask visitors to consider how enslaved labor in the manse where Tommy was born shaped the family as benefactors of slavery, which operated in conjunction with their values as Presbyterians, other than that they utilized it. In the dining room, a newspaper and scraps left on plates signal that the Wilsons just finished their quiet breakfast. The tour could have induced visitors to imagine the clearing of the table while the family enjoyed the leisure time that slavery produced for white families. Rather this space introduced Joseph's domestic life and career as a segue to his office. Cementing Wilson's status as southerner and Virginian, the tour concluded in the master bedchamber with Tommy's birth.[26]

Staunton introduced slavery upfront but did not weave the histories of Black lives throughout the entire tour. As such the home missed its potential to become what Jennifer Scott defines as a radical house museum that challenges biased power structures and "narrow histories" of white elites.[27] Over a decade ago, a study of plantation museums found that 60 percent "symbolically annihilated or erased" the lives of enslaved Americans, skewing the visitor's perceptions of antebellum society.[28] This magnolia-scented world erased the enslaved people who maintained the pristine gardens and produced agricultural goods, cooked and cleaned the big house, and lived onsite. Almost 30 percent depicted Black laborers as faithful and their enslavers as moral, hardworking people. Staunton's Presbyterian focus ensured the tour at times drifted into this second category. The remaining 10 percent of plantations fit in one or both of two categories: relative incorporation or segregated information such as irregularly offered or supplemental tours. The birthplace tour pushed the boundaries of relative incorporation but fell short of moving beyond the "add and stir" approach it wanted to avoid.[29] I argue that a bolder claim would build on the presidential library's assertion that the Wilsons were a "Northern-raised and educated couple" that "liked the Southern people and their way of life and remained in the South the rest of their lives." The tour could easily surmise that slavery was one of the things the Wilsons liked or easily accepted; after all, they remained in the region during the Civil War. Wilson biographer A. Scott Berg argues that Jessie Wilson was more conflicted over slavery than her husband, whose "ambivalence . . . would follow Tommy to the White House."[30] However, an 1857 letter Jessie wrote to her father on display in the WWPLM reveals the benefits and pleasant experience she had operating a slave household. Following her inquiry as to how her father was adjusting to his move to the slave state of Kentucky, she revealed, "My experience has taught me that there are some disadvantages connected with the peculiar institution, as well as advantages. The responsibility incurred by the housekeeper is so much greater than in a free state." Jessie performed less labor in Virginia, described her domestic sphere as "pleasant," and never feared Joseph's traveling because the two women and man sleeping beneath her in in the basement were "reliable good creatures." Jessie felt comfortable with the institution and her family's safety and appreciated the work and morality of the three individuals.[31]

Slavery continued to be an important force in the Wilsons' lives when they moved to Augusta, Georgia, in 1858, though the Woodrow Wilson Boyhood Home diminished the institution's impact on the family far more than the WWPLM. The WWBH's depiction of Black laborers and citizens rested between symbolic annihilation and the narrative of faithful Black workers and moral white employers. A detached two-story kitchen still stands on the property. However, the WWBH detached Black Augusta from the narrative just as the labor in this space was separated from the Wilson home during the Civil War and Reconstruction. The tour's most vivid description of a domestic was of Mitty, who, according to tradition, was famous for fruit pies. Also included on the tour was that domestics may have used a pump for running water. Because Augusta allowed free Black people to work, move, and worship freely and Joseph was not listed as a slaveholder in the 1860 census, Historic Augusta believes the family had two or three paid Black servants and that Mitty came with the family from Virginia. Again, according to tradition and Montgomery's research, one of them was an unknown man, most likely the butler, who supposedly said that "'Mr. Tommy was his father's boy outside the house but his momma's boy inside the house.'" Executive director Erick Montgomery took Staunton's older tour when it depicted the laborers as servants, which corroborated Augusta's traditional interpretation that Mitty was free. Augusta's interpretation is likely inaccurate given that the Staunton church leased enslaved people to work in the Wilsons' home. Montgomery rightly observed that the mystery may never be solved, but addressing this ambiguity exposes visitors to ideas about how Mitty and her peers reacted to emancipation and Reconstruction. Reconstruction brought an expanded labor market, voting rights, and more power in wage negotiation with employers if the laborers were free before the Civil War. If not, Reconstruction thrust these formerly enslaved people into the free labor system for the first time, making them dependent on Wilson's sporadic pay as a minister. Through the first year of Reconstruction, the church paid Joseph irregularly.[32]

Because the PWWH was Wilson's last home at S Street in Washington, DC, its tour need not address slavery; however, in 2015 the narrative tacked on domestic servitude at the end of the tour. The last spaces of the tour, like those in Staunton, privileged the functionality of rooms and technology that facilitated domestic labor but omitted an in-depth account of the Black laborers' lives. Visitors learned that the uppermost floor had more recently provided storage space but that originally the Black couple that worked for the Wilson family slept there. The home boasts a working elevator that aided staff in moving the frail former president through the home. The stairs to the butler's pantry, the pantry itself, and the dumbwaiter all could have been used to talk about non-elite people in the home and how they interacted in caring for the Wilsons, a glimpse of which visitors obtained in the nurse's room. The tour ended in the kitchen, which featured the original stove, toaster, and icebox used by the domestic couple and a series of pictures circulated to visitors. The docent, unaccustomed to being asked the names of Isaac and Mary Scott, could not recall them.[33]

A post-tour conversation I had with a PWWH docent, documents at Wilson's presidential library, and Wilson biographies demonstrate that a

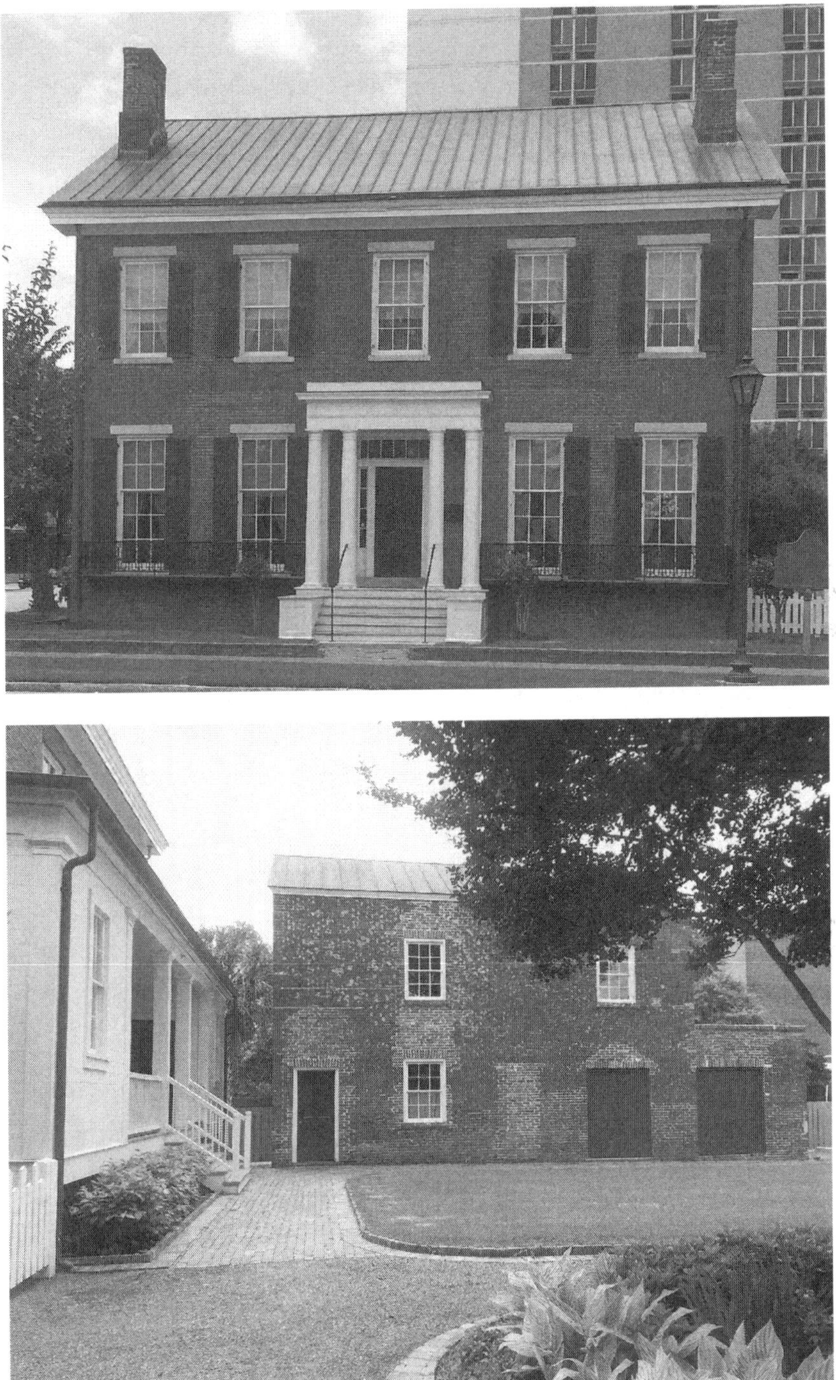

Figure 11. Tommy Wilson's second home was this manse maintained by the First Presbyterian Church of Augusta, Georgia. The family lived there from 1858 until 1871. The back has a detached kitchen where enslaved and recently freed Black Augustans labored. Photograph by author.

more open dialogue between Wilson sites expands our knowledge of the Scotts' and the Wilsons' most personal relationships with Black people. The paternalist relationship revealed offers greater context to Wilson's policies on race, such as allowing his cabinet to segregate the federal government. According to docent Betty van Iersel, a letter suggests that Isaac was a porter at Galt's Jewelry Store. The Scotts maintained a house, although they had no children and slept at S Street six days a week. They worked for Edith Galt Wilson, the president's second wife and widow, the rest of their lives.[34] Edith's relationship with the Scotts illuminates a paternalistic household reminiscent of the Old South. She called them "the best of the old-time coloured Virginia stock." Isaac "protected" the president in the hours before his passing after Edith requested that he shoo the press away from Wilson's death vigil.[35] In 1954 Edith described Isaac, once the president's valet, as "old—deaf now—but faithful as a watchdog." That year she brought Mary for an event at the Staunton museum and told its leader, Emily Smith, to "make use of" her maid of thirty-three years "if she can be of help in the kitchen or elsewhere."[36] Other than Edith, the Scotts occupied S Street longer than anyone else. They spent nearly all of their time at work. A tour that names them and discusses their lives crystalizes the privileges and power that the Wilsons enjoyed and how the president's life was filled with Black lives and their labor from his birth to his death. Far from the first, the Scotts were the last Black domestic workers to engage intimately with the dying southerner at his most vulnerable. In recent years the PWWH began to address "important issues of race, class, and wealth in 1920s America" with a seventy-five-minute tour, "Under One Roof: Living and Working in the Wilson House." Offered on Tuesdays only, the specialty tour, representing what Jennifer Scott labeled segregated information, includes the Scotts as well as Wilson's private secretary, chauffeur, and male nurse.[37]

The MoRE, similar to other Wilson HHMs, relied on architecture and room function to illuminate the lives of those laboring in the home and America's newest citizens. However, the MoRE's silence in naming and going in depth about specific workers lives was a product of the historical record rather than intentional omission. Those who staffed the Wilson's home in Columbia during Reconstruction do not appear in Wilson family documents or Columbia municipal records. As a result several MoRE docents used the built environment to illuminate their lives and labor. These guides also excelled in generating points of engagement and open-ended questions in two pantry spaces. Four MoRE docents emphasized the stark differences in workspaces from the rest of the home. Tour and program coordinator Heather Bacon-Rogers sarcastically introduces visitors to "a perfect lovely space just like the rest of the house." These docents build on the visual

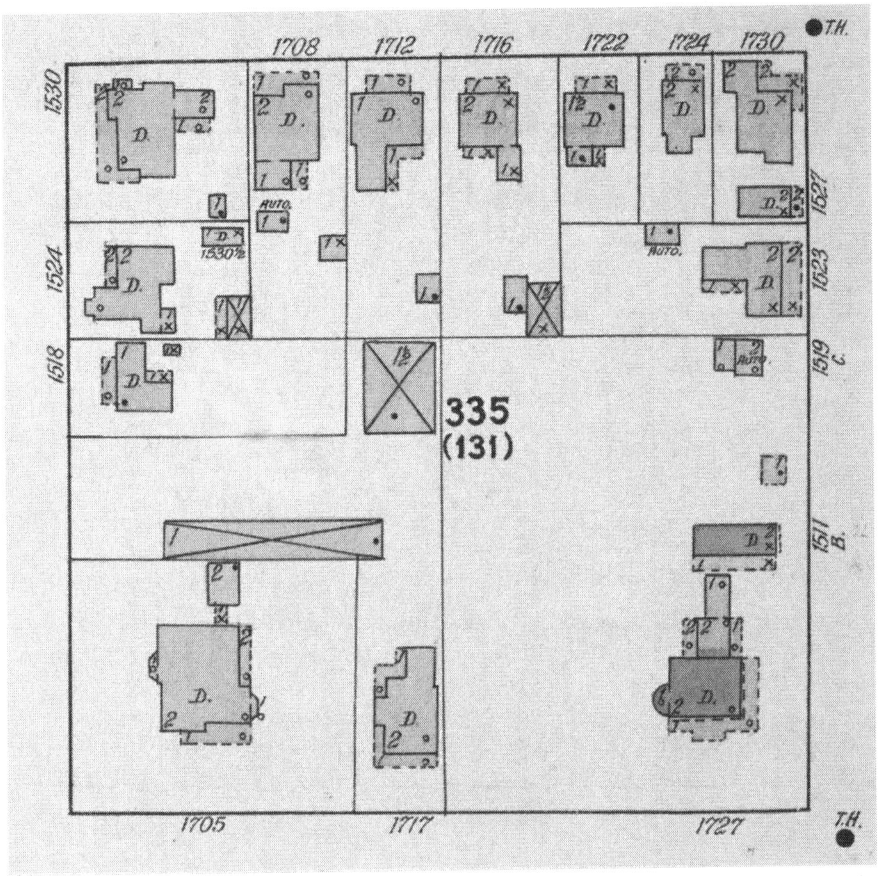

Figure 12. The Wilson Family Home, located in the bottom left corner of the image, shows the detached kitchen, which stood close to the two pantries. Detail from Sanborn Fire Insurance Map from Columbia, Richland County, South Carolina, 1919. Courtesy of the Library of Congress.

inconsistencies by asking questions about air conditioning, heat, insulation, and claustrophobia, the latter being effective with larger groups. The MoRE differs from most HHMs, which commonly interpret the kitchen, because the home's detached kitchen no longer stands.[38] However, Historic Columbia designed and constructed an accessibility ramp that corresponded to the kitchen's size and location. The ramp led to two segregated back porch doors and was visible through the pantry window. A panel from a Sanborn Fire Insurance Map from 1919 labeled "Domestic Servants" provided another visual reference. In the script's earliest version, visitors were to answer a question about the segregated architecture and locate the kitchen-turned-ramp. The first few months of tours demonstrated the butler's pantry provided docents

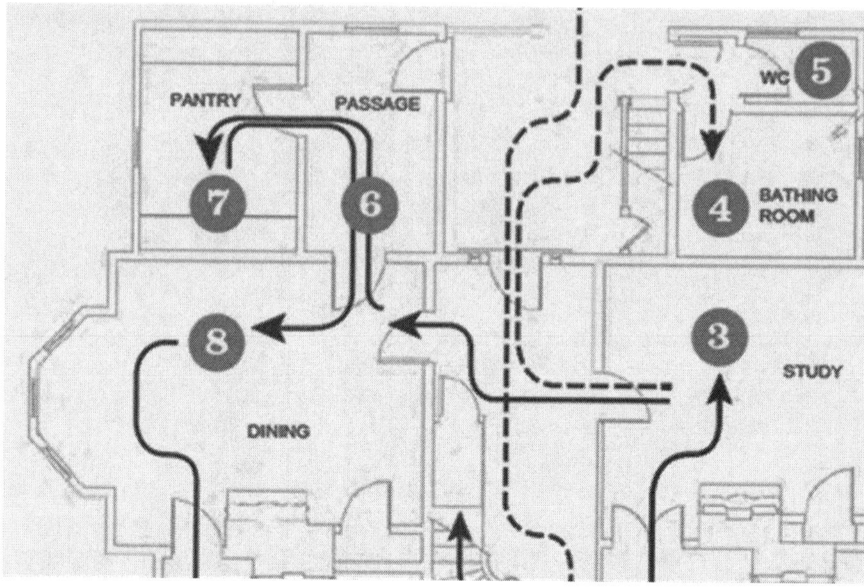

Figure 13. Rooms 6 and 7 of the MoRE tour map reflect the small size of the spaces and entryways from the detached kitchen. Courtesy of Historic Columbia.

the opportunity to ask a follow-up to an engagement question for visitors who showed great interest in the space. The final script set up the pantry, telling visitors that they had "passed through the dining room and are standing in spaces devoted to food storage and preparation." From there docents asked, "What is missing from the space?" Visitors generally responded correctly with "kitchen," which allowed docents to invite guests to view the ramp from the window, located next to a servant's entrance. Docents, if they chose to, followed up by asking how the architecture separated people by their staff position (and race).[39]

While discrete servant stairs traditionally are considered the most powerful architectural feature in an HHM to interpret domestic labor, MoRE docents relied less on these outside stairs and more on segregated entryways. Docents found that visitors easily imagined workers entering the space from the exterior door to plate meals for the adjacent dining room.[40] Because visitors forget that they just walked past a back door in the hallway, weekend docent Jennifer Gunter asked, "Why would you have this back door six feet away from the other back door?" The question unpacked the segregated racial dynamics of the household and Columbia. Erin Holmes, a weekend docent and historian who specializes in the built environment of elites and enslaved people, used the architecture to inspire complex conversations with her visitors. Some of them lingered after tours "to discuss how architecture expressed the ambitions of the middle class and was an instrumental part of the segregation of African Americans." She described those experiences as "always fantastic, especially when they [visitors] came in expecting (and wanting) a 'Woodrow Wilson: Future President' kind of tour."[41]

Despite the tight structure of the script, a highly popular BBC television program at the time of the reopening, *Downton Abbey,* frequently became a point of conversation between docents and visitors in the pantry. Depending on the docent, the show enhanced visitor understanding or reduced the conversation to one on class. Before programming like *Downton Abbey,* HHM guests had difficulty conceiving the experience of living with an employer while in a subordinate position.[42] Although English country estates began the shift to prominently interpreting servants' quarters in the late 1970s, by 2014 *Downton Abbey* served as the inspiration for renewed and increased visitation to sites that exposed the workers' world. Visitors spent more time exploring servant quarters than other rooms.[43] Similarly the program inspired both docents and visitors to make comparisons between the employees at the MoRE and the fictional show, a process that I call the *Downton Abbey* effect. Docents expressed strong reactions to this exchange. Bacon-Rogers felt the show stymied her narrative. She estimated that "50 percent of the time" visitors responded to Black inclusion with something akin to "just like *Downton Abbey.*" This posed a hindrance in explaining Tommy's domestic world. She wanted to get away from this association with the *Downton Abbey* and an earlier British series, *Upstairs Downstairs.* Domestic work in the South during Reconstruction was distinct from early twentieth-century Great Britain. She wished she could flatly reply, "No. These are former slaves who are finally able to make their own money, to make their own jobs. This is far more significant." She appreciated that visitors were connecting the tour to their personal pop culture experiences but wondered if "they're not getting the gravity of what work was like for these recently freed individuals."[44] Public historian Oliver Cox argued that English country homes faced a similar challenge in "how to use the quasi-historical shorthand of *Downton* as a way of enticing visitors into the longhand stories of the country house that can only emerge through detailed archival research and effective interpretation strategies."[45]

To dilute the *Downtown Abbey* effect, MoRE docents encouraged visitors to consider the transition to wage labor beyond abstract terms and the impact of citizenship, a conversation rooted in historical scholarship. Docents asked visitors about their economic worth. This became a stepping stone for discussing the excitement of women negotiating "this whole new system, a wage labor system."[46] Building on the work of Jacqueline Jones, historian Thavolia Glymph argues that in these early years of freedom, even when Black women were forced by economic necessity to take jobs in white homes, these women negotiated the terms of their employment and did not need to feign loyalty. Freedwomen capitalized on their knowledge of labor, calculating the time needed to perform tasks as free wage laborers rather than enslaved workers. They also resisted attempts by white employers to transform a skilled position into full-service domestic help, similar to what the Wilsons required of the Scotts at S Street. Black women chose part-time work for its flexibility, allowing time to build their own free homes and engage in household production to sustain their families and to sell at market.[47] Docents transformed Glymph's research into a question about skills and power. Gunter asked: "Are you worth ten cents for ten sets of sheets?" She also pointed out the recipes to demonstrate skill sets and asked, "How skillful do you have to be" to work in the Wilson home? Volunteer Cyndy Storm approached the subject from the perspective of employers, drawing on older, wealthier white southerners who remembered maids and cooks in their households that went home to their own families at the end of each day. She asked visitors to consider whether they would hire a sixteen-year-old girl or a more experienced older cook and what skills their budget afforded.[48] Choosing residency, commuting from home, or living on the second floor of the kitchen was another example of the considerations the script and exhibit offered to docents to convey the agency of African Americans and choices made possible by citizenship. The fire map became a popular panel image for docents to discuss workers' exercising autonomy in their choice of accommodations.[49] A revision of the script placed formerly supplemental statements about freedwomen, "rarely allowed to attend to their own families under slavery," into the required narration. The combined script, panels, and docent questions illustrated well the power that Black women wielded to negotiate wages and make financial choices with their families about sharecropping, part-time work in the home, and domestic work.[50] Starting in the pantries and culminating with a panel in the adjacent, family-centric dining room, docents were able to contrast the similar domestic work many Black Americans had performed while enslaved, such as taking care of white children, with their groundbreaking ability and attempts to reunite Black families and develop and keep their households intact for the first time.[51]

During training and on their own tours, a handful of volunteer docents gravitated to the *Downton Abbey* effect, which informed their opposition to early tour drafts that emphasized the household's racial divisions. The interpretive team worked to convey clearly that workers entered and used spaces differently than residents and guests. This opened a conversation between the team and docents about segregated architecture. From the beginning the script insisted that the Wilsons built a home that "reflected prevailing trends in domestic architecture that separated people according to their roles." The panel, however, acknowledged that while the middle and upper classes hired servants, in the South "domestic service usually intertwined with race relations."[52] Still, volunteer Jean Morgan interpreted early script versions as political because of their insistence that workspaces were segregated. For her and other likeminded volunteers, race only mattered in that the South relied heavily on Black workers because of demographics and the legacy of slavery. Segregated workspaces and staircases were "segregat[ed] by role," whether in the South, other parts of the US, Great Britain, or on television. Volunteer docent Pam Redfield noted that dishwashers and servers today often enter workplaces through a back door. Her great grandmother, a German immigrant and launderer, brought wealthy families' laundry out the back door.[53] As with the negative connotations surrounding the word *privilege*, semantics was the issue. Cook suggested that the pantry portion of the script should "talk about segregated architecture without using the word segregated." Volunteer docents favored a class-centered lens over one focused on race. They insisted the script acknowledge that, while architecture did separate southerners racially, it demonstrated the "segregated nature" of domestic labor both "before and after emancipation, regardless of region."[54] The MoRE docents who emphasized social and class segregation reflected trends in interpreting domestic workers at HHMs across the nation. Institutions in the southern Atlantic states, which had high Irish and Black servant populations, tended to rate discussing racial prejudice of high significance. But many HHMs privileged class prejudice more. Sites disclosed the race or ethnicity of domestic workers without contextualizing their status as immigrants or how their heritage and experience might have shaped the region or nation.[55]

In some ways the MoRE suffered from more problems in interpreting domestic workers than most HHMs. Not only did it lack any material culture that belonged to employees, but also none of the traditional primary sources identified their names. Over 56 percent of HMMs studied in 2003 conducted research on domestic servants, most commonly with census records and city directories. Historic Columbia did the same, also perusing the local resources available in Columbia's rich university and state archives, which can be overlooked by museums. But its research yielded only general information about domestic servitude at the time in Columbia. Although the people who worked for the Wilsons remained invisible, the butler pantry's panel presented two pie charts based on the 1880 federal census that show visitors that 90 percent of Richland County's washers, housekeepers, and butlers were Black and 75 percent Black women.[56] Bacon-Rogers wondered about the pair that worked for the Wilsons: "Was it a husband and wife?

Was it two women?" She was fascinated by these individuals more than the Wilson women and was embarrassed that Historic Columbia did not know more. Historic Columbia even struggled to identify Nannie and Minnie, two Black domestic workers employed by Wilson's older sister, Annie Wilson Howe. The dining room exhibit displays the circa 1892 Howe family portrait with both family and domestics posed on the front porch. Historic Columbia had a list of six possibilities based on city directories around the time of the photograph. Three laundry workers named Minnie, surnamed Clark, Sims, and Watts, were potential candidates. Records revealed only two women named Nannie: Chapple, a cook, and Antonio, occupation unknown.[57]

Though many HHM tours incorporate at least partial narratives of domestic work, they often ignore domestic conflict. This includes both the complexity of the relationships between domestic servants and their employers as well as familial clashes.[58] The MoRE struggled to interpret conflict as well. This can be seen in the interpretation of the Howe family portrait in the dining room and in the docents' lack of preparedness to address sexual violence against Black women, common in Reconstruction and domestic servitude. The portrait depicts Annie Howe's nuclear family on the porch of their Columbia home, along with her brothers Tommy and Joseph Jr. and father, Joseph Sr. The image became a popular engagement point with all but a handful of docents and visitors. When visitors did not broach the subject themselves, docents asked why Nannie and Minnie were included in the photograph and how those pictured felt about the workers' inclusion. Bacon-Rogers often experienced that one person would open the conversation by saying, "Oh, they thought of them as family," before another countered with "They don't look happy.'" This debate made the image "the best piece in that whole room." By contrast Morgan left the question open-ended, because cynics saw a display of wealth and status while others saw family.[59] The disparities between these two approaches reflect the tendency of HHMs to favor narratives of friendship or closeness between employers and employees over narratives of conflict. Stories of domestics who were like family survive because, like the best objects, positive tales and relationships are preserved rather than those of workers who came and went or experienced exploitation.[60]

Given that the social dynamics of the Howe household invited some interpretive division among docents, it was not surprising that the taboo subject of sexual violence in domestic spaces was ignored in the home and mostly absent from the training. This is partly fueled by the latent historiography of Reconstruction and sexual violence. Only recently have scholars explored the dynamic of sexual violence during Reconstruction. Just as the process of Reconstruction itself was not truly as radical as Americans remember, the

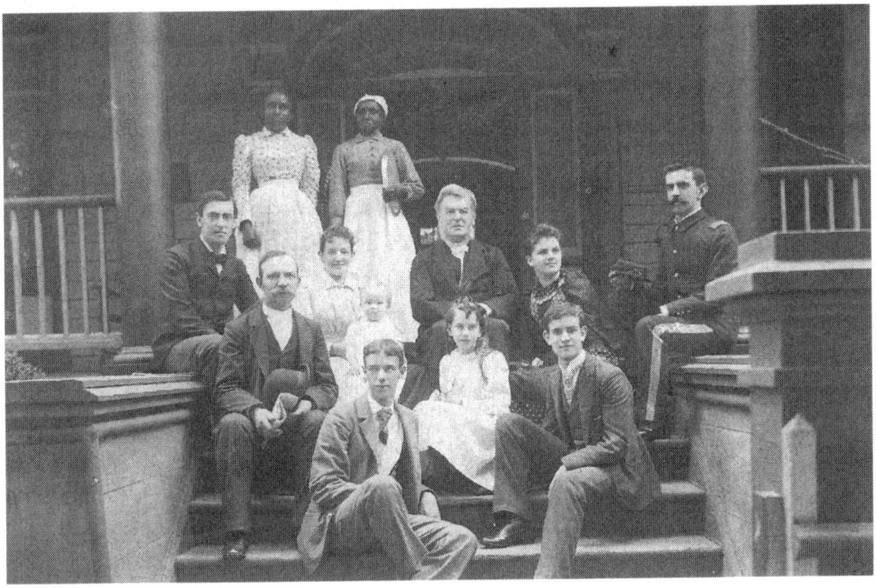

Figure 14. "Wilson Family," ca. 1892, courtesy of the Woodrow Wilson Presidential Library, Staunton, Virginia. In 1892 several members of the Wilson family joined the Howe family household for a formal portrait on the front steps of the Howe home in Columbia. Pictured left to right: first row, Joseph Wilson Howe; second row, George Howe III; third row, Dr. George Howe Jr., Jessie Howe Kennedy; fourth row, Thomas Woodrow Wilson, Annie Josephine Wilson Howe (holding daughter Annie Wilson Howe), Dr. Joseph Ruggles Wilson, Kate Wilson, husband Joseph Ruggles Wilson Jr.: fifth row, Nannie, Minnie (surnames unknown).

MoRE is not as radical as it could be because sexual violence is not interpreted in domestic spaces or discussed as a political tool used by white men to control Black bodies and intimidate Black citizens. There is no evidence that the men in the Wilson family perpetrated sexual violence, also making the conversation difficult to initiate.

While the pervasiveness of sexual violence perpetrated against Black women and exploitation of them during slavery has been established firmly by historians and Black feminist scholars, films such as *Twelve Years a Slave* (dir. Steve McQueen, 2013), *The Birth of a Nation* (dir. Nate Parker, 2016), and *Free State of Jones* (dir. Gary Ross, 2016) have contributed to solidifying this historiography in mainstream popular thought and culture.[61] The fact that white women also had a history of complicity in household violence is still a difficult subject for some to broach interpretively. Jealously and sexual repression inspired violence from white women. The masters' unchecked power over enslaved women brought into the center of the household a public violence that demeaned the women, while white women were protected against it.[62] Homes outside of the South were not immune to this violence. Domestics in the urban North, who MoRE volunteers insisted were no different from Black domestic workers, were also "at the mercy of lascivious masters and their teenaged son," just as their southern sisters were.[63]

Since the 1980s women's history has shown continuity between the rape and sexual coercion of the antebellum period and the late nineteenth century. In the 1990s Catherine Clinton exposed weaponized rape employed by soldiers on both sides during the Civil War, foreshadowing scholarship on its use as a political tactic to challenge Reconstruction.[64] Rape of Black women, which had no legal precedents established against it during slavery, became during Reconstruction a tool of political violence used to inflict both physical and psychological suffering. The tendency of night riders to strip women's clothing to their waists or pull it up to their necks before beating them were actions some of these same men may have performed as overseers or slaveowners. Scholarship on Ku Klux Klan and night rider violence as well as federal records suggest that the threat of sexual abuse escalated after the Civil War, even if it was underreported in other historical accounts and texts. White supremacists attacked women for their associations with Black Union troops and Black leaders or because their husbands or fathers had violated a southern white code of behavior, such as participating in politics or landowning. Despite the assaults on their bodies and denial of their attempts to claim full citizenship, Black women demanded dignity, which included withdrawing their labor from white households to escape sexual violence. But born out of this gendered violence was the myth of the Black rapist, which became the fuel for a turn-of-the-century lynching epidemic that eclipsed the real abuse conducted at the hands of white men who raped Black women.[65] In 1898 Alex Manly, a biracial newspaper editor in Wilmington, North Carolina, highlighted this hypocrisy when the state's Democrats weaponized the myth for their campaign. After Election Day the city erupted in white supremacist violence, ending the decaying experiment in Reconstruction with a coup d'état. The white mob killed dozens of Black residents, although the tally will never be known, and at least 1,400 permanently fled or were banished because of their economic success or political activities.[66]

Scholars have produced enough work on Reconstruction-era sexual exploitation to warrant its inclusion in the MoRE training materials to prepare docents for questions from visitors who may know this history or have seen films depicting the violence. Hannah Rosen's 2009 monograph *Terror in the Heart of Freedom: Citizenship, Sexual Violence, and the Meaning of Race in the Postemancipation South* uses federal records to argue that race, as it was being negotiated post-emancipation, was a battle fought on the "terrain of gender."

Sexual violence and racist rhetoric complemented one another in attempts by whites to create an atmosphere of terror for Black Americans negotiating citizenship. Between 1865 and 1871, according to historical records, white men raped or sexually assaulted forty-five Black women. Many rapes were not reported, not only because of fear but also because survivors' only options for lodging complaints were to the Freedman's Bureau, a federal prosecutor, or a congressional hearing, which were located in cities. In the summer of 1866, African Americans testified in Memphis before congressional investigating committees on the recent three-day-long massacre in the city as well as the rapes by rioters of women associated with Black troops. Five women dared to speak out on the record, and like Black women across the South, they demanded that the federal government protect them as citizens. Black women were not viewed as citizens, and white rapists participating in the Memphis massacre justified their sexual violence with the fantasy that lewd Black women were available for sex. White men first requested sex and then used force or threat to gain compliance. They also construed free Black homes and communities as spaces for their own pleasure, entering these familial dwellings as if they were brothels and choosing women to sexually exploit. Their assailants would generally separate the women from their families and domestic spaces within the women's sphere before raping them.[67]

As with the historiography of Reconstruction itself, public history is beginning to address the subject of sexual violence and coercion in domestic spaces. In May 2016 Memphis erected a marker commemorating the massacre that resulted in an estimated forty-six deaths and widespread property destruction, including all-Black churches and schools. The marker, unveiled on the 150th anniversary of the incident, acknowledges that several women were raped as part of the violence.[68] Five blocks from the Wilson home, on the grounds of the state capitol, stands a statue honoring former Dixiecrat governor and senator Strom Thurmond. In 2004 the name of Thurmond's biracial daughter was etched into the stone beneath the list of his four legally recognized white children previously engraved on the monument. The obvious replacement of the word *four* with an imperfect *five* chiseled on top and a less worn inscription of Essie Mae Washington-Williams's name in comparison to her siblings serve as jarring reminders of the hidden history of sexual assault in biracial households. In 1925, when Thurmond was twenty-two, his sixteen-year-old housekeeper, Carrie Butler, gave birth to their daughter. The social and economic power Thurmond exerted over Butler suggests that at best the affair was coerced rather than consensual.[69] While there is no evidence to suggest that the Wilsons were complicit in sexual abuse, the gendered, racial, and employment dynamics of the home make it similar to other elite white homes where this abuse took place. Thus the conversation, even if absent from the panel portions of the exhibit, can be raised by docents on MoRE tours with adult audiences.

The issue of sexual violence against women is part of a larger deficiency in HHMs. These institutions often address the roles women filled but not necessarily how womanhood and gender in the period affected their lives, a trend that historian and docent Jennifer Gunter feared would plague the MoRE. The Reconstruction lecture given during training touched briefly on sexual assault and rape as forms of terrorism utilized by whites during massacres in Memphis and New Orleans in 1866. Echoing the work of historians, consultant Daniella Cook also expressed to the interpretive team that the archives reveal relationships between white men and Black women, many of which were products of white violence. While the MoRE relayed stories of survival affiliated with the demise of slavery and the political unrest of Reconstruction, it stopped short of being an unapologetically radical HHM because of the interpretive challenges surrounding a discussion of rape.[70] At minimum guides should be prepared to address questions about this topic, both for communities aware of the historical violence and those who sense it was there but lack the tools to understand it fully. For example, one middle-aged white man exited the pantry and asked about the movie *The Butler* (dir. Lee Daniels, 2013). The visitor specifically mentioned the opening rape scene and was trying to ascertain the historical time period. He was unsure whether the setting of the cotton field was during slavery or the post-emancipation sharecropping era. This was a teaching moment that not all docents were equipped to embrace, that Black field labor and sexual violence continued from slavery into the twentieth century. Docents must be prepared to have these discussions, because visitors have questions about these difficult subjects. Additionally, by opening a discussion of sexual violence in domestic spaces, rape as a terror tactic used by the Ku Klux Klan in South Carolina's upstate and across the South during Reconstruction can be broached more effectively in the MoRE room exhibiting political terrorism, discussed in the next chapter.[71]

The homes Woodrow Wilson once occupied all interpret race, whiteness, and the Black experience but do so with varying levels of success in both representation and encouraging dialogue. Interpreting the labor of Black Americans for the Wilson family is the most common method linking these homes together. None are perfect as they traverse slavery, Civil War, intolerance, and political discord. In all four homes, sexual assault as a political tool and form of white terror remains a hidden topic. With the rise of popular television shows featuring domestic laborers in elite homes, the *Downton Abbey* effect further complicates conversations about spaces segregated along racial and class lines. But Historic Columbia's requiring white docents who interpret more inclusive narratives to attend language and cultural sensitivity training gave these frontline workers the education and skills needed for the task. Docents were not monolithic in their response to training or their approach to handling the racial themes demanded by the tour. In addition docents' varied interpretive choices, philosophies, and debates about segregated labor illuminate the challenges HHMs will likely face and provide a blueprint that can be explored and modified as more sites work toward greater inclusivity.[72] Lastly, a conversation centered around public history between the Wilson childhood homes in Staunton, Virginia, and Augusta, Georgia, would provide continuity and generate scholarship on the Wilson family's relationship with slavery and as beneficiaries and supporters of the institution. Likewise a dialogue between the MoRE and the president's final home in Washington, DC, would demonstrate Wilson's lifelong reliance on Black domestic labor and offer opportunities for conjecture on how that shaped his policies on race and segregation. Finally, knowledge of Mary and Isaac Scott's lives under a paternalistic Wilson household would expand if the President Woodrow Wilson House incorporated records from the Wilson Presidential Library about Edith Wilson's involvement in the founding of the site.

CHAPTER 5

Interpreting Domestic Terror

Reconstruction's Violent End in the Twenty-First Century

On January 13, 2021, during the US House of Representatives debate impeaching President Donald Trump for an extraordinary second time, Speaker of the House Nancy Pelosi called the insurrectionists who stormed the US Capitol on January 6 "domestic terrorists."[1] Thousands left Trump's fiery speech that morning embracing his final words to walk down Pennsylvania Avenue to give weak Republicans the encouragement needed "to take back our country." Some protestors exited believing he was accompanying them. He promised, after all, to "be there with you."[2] A force of two thousand police officers, most of whom lacked riot gear, unsuccessfully met the rally attendees turned insurrectionists, who penetrated the legislative chambers to disrupt the official count of the electoral votes for President-elect Joseph Biden. Paramilitary forces roamed the maze of hallways in search of Vice President Mike Pence and Speaker Pelosi. Among the weapons present that day were pipe bombs, zip ties, Molotov cocktails, and semiautomatic rifles. The mob, mostly unmasked due to COVID-19 conspiracy theories, stole electronics, trashed offices, and literally put their feet up, making themselves at home, while members of Congress hid or fled for their lives.[3] At the height of the violence, Capitol Police shot rioter Ashli Babbitt as she attempted to breach the House chamber.[4] Two other rioters died of separate medical emergencies. A total of five people lost their lives as a result of the infamous day's events.[5]

To meet this moment and address the homegrown domestic terror on display on January 6, the United States finally will be forced to reconcile its long history of militant white supremacy. How do we conduct this conversation? The Museum of the Reconstruction Era at the Woodrow Wilson Family Home and its interpretation of the end of Reconstruction in South Carolina and the violence of Red Shirts, the statewide paramilitary force that used fraud and violence to return white Democrats to power in 1876, illuminate one possible path. Combining white supremacist artifacts and images from Reconstruction with docent-guided open-ended questions can facilitate the dialogue. The bedroom exhibit in room 14 introduced Reconstruction-era violence to some white visitors for the first time. It also made others, including docents, assess their own personal connections to white supremacy. The home's interpretation of white domestic terror during Reconstruction can also help audiences better understand the larger paramilitary forces shaping modern white supremacy and right-wing militancy. The exhibit demonstrates continuity by offering concrete examples from history that are recognizable today, including federal and state responses that failed to stop white supremacist violence and political fraud.

A Brief History of White Supremacy and Its Paramilitary Forces

A brief history of modern white supremacy and the paramilitary movement leading up to the Capitol siege will provide the necessary twenty-first-century context to invite comparisons between Reconstruction and the present. Trump called his staunchest supporters to action at the January 6 rally. Embedded among them were paramilitary forces, strengthened by four decades of white domestic terrorism, that would transform a march on the Capitol into a violent attempted coup d'état. In *Bring the War Home,* a comprehensive study of the modern white power movement, Kathleen Belew argues that it stemmed from and was framed by the Vietnam War. It matured into an umbrella social movement, something new in the history of white supremacy, accepting a diverse range of white power symbols and ideology. Following Vietnam, disparate groups from different socioeconomic backgrounds and levels of education, both urban and rural, coalesced, united by economic hardship, institutional distrust, and a growing culture war. In this narrative of crisis and betrayal reminiscent of white southern Democrats during the Reconstruction era, military leaders and politicians betrayed soldiers who had fought a horrific war. This developing coalition rose above the country's military defeat and purported social and economic emasculation by embracing militant white masculinity. By the early 1980s, the white power movement successfully combined Cold War anticommunism, racism, and anti-Semitism into a rhetoric that a nonwhite globalist elite dominated government, banking, and the media. The violence this messaging incited resulted in assassinations and attacks on infrastructure, abortion clinics, synagogues, and federal sites. With stolen weapons and landmines from the military, members established militias and then paramilitary camps where they trained with discipline. On the fringe yet bigger than the John Birch Society, the movement made a distinct turn in 1983 toward apocalyptic revolution against the state, developing a successful leaderless strategy and cell-like structure. This strategy permitted covertly organized violence that would be difficult to link to either the larger movement or a particular leader. As the movement metastasized in the 1990s, it grew to the size of the revived Ku Klux Klan that spread across the nation a century prior. The federal response to two high-profile events incited the crescendo of the movement. The first was the standoff at the Weaver family's white separatist compound in Ruby Ridge, Idaho, in 1992, which resulted in the death of an officer and the family's mother and a son. The second was the loss of seventy-six Branch Davidians in a fire in Waco, Texas, the following year, which angered Timothy McVeigh and like-minded militants. Operating without leadership but within a cell comprising himself, Terry Nichols, and Michael Fortier, McVeigh killed 149 adults and 19 children and injured hundreds in the 1995 bombing of the Alfred P. Murrah Building in Oklahoma City. The largest mass casualty event between the Japanese bombing of Pearl Harbor in 1941 and Al-Qaida's terror attack on September 11, 2001, McVeigh's bombing temporarily inspired copycats and more white nationalist violence before a federal crackdown. The movement then retreated to its thriving internet community. The meek federal response, a public unaware of the threat that coordinated white power posed in the mid-1990s, and a failure to convict other white power activists invited future violence such as the 2021 Capitol insurrection.[6]

In the year leading up to the attack, congressional testimony from the Federal Bureau of Investigation, the Department of Homeland Security, the Southern Poverty Law Center, and the Global Project Against Hate and Extremism warned of the pervasiveness of white nationalism and the terror threat these groups posed. Empowered and emboldened by Trumpism, more hate groups proliferated in the United States than ever before. Right-wing extremists, most of whom are white power activists, committed two-thirds of all extremist-related killings, making 2020 the most lethal year for political extremism since Oklahoma City. The movement quickly escalated from a priority for DHS to the number-one terrorist threat, eclipsing radical Islamic and leftist extremism.[7] SPLC worried about the individuals such as Dylann Roof, perpetrator of the 2015 Charleston massacre, who was radicalized online at home yet served as a foot soldier of the nationwide white supremacist movement, according to Belew.[8]

Cultural bias, misinformation, zealous nationalism propagated by right-wing media to downplay the current threat, and historical misunderstanding about the topic cloud the nation's ability to see clearly the continuous danger posed by white domestic terror from Reconstruction to the present. Historic Columbia expected these same factors to complicate the task of delivering the interpretation to MoRE's visitors that political terrorism conducted by white Democrats in the 1860s and 1870s ultimately fostered Reconstruction's demise and violently ushered in Jim Crow. However, the organization felt confident that the facts and artifacts supported their interpretive claims.[9] The MoRE's northeast bedroom exhibit about the Red Shirt campaign and election of 1876 supports generations of historical scholarship that white South Carolinians continued to use extreme violence against Republicans and Black Americans to retain power after the Civil War and during Reconstruction. The space, likely the first HHM to do so in South Carolina, overturns what Bruce Baker, in his study of Reconstruction memory in South Carolina, called a "white supremacist narrative." It overshadowed a counternarrative created by and centered on Black citizens in the public sphere, helping to buttress Jim Crow and divide Black and white workers.[10] The interpretation also marks an example of vernacular challenging official cultural expression, which in the case of Reconstruction are both over a century old.[11]

Women, Public History, and White Supremacy

MoRE docents worked to topple the dominant white supremacist narrative that justified violence and terrorism. However, this powerful narrative, particularly the idea that Red Shirts were heroes, would not easily be unraveled. It had endured for more than a century, generationally passed down through white family history and prominently in South Carolina's public sphere. Textbooks, historic house museums, a federally funded tour guidebook, and other public history sites across the state cemented the white supremacist narrative of Red Shirt glory in print, stone, and brick. One MoRE docent initially proudly proclaimed his Red Shirt lineage but then grappled with it as a result of his training. This pride in Red Shirt heritage was made possible by the way public white supremacist spaces like Oakley Park glorified Red Shirts. The United Daughters of the Confederacy still maintain the rarely open and nearly forgotten HHM in Edgefield belonging to Confederate general Martin Gary. One of the key architects of the 1876 Red Shirt campaign, Gary rallied thousands of red-clad followers from the plantation home's balcony. Inside Oakley Park visitors can search for three authentic red shirts displayed among thousands of artifacts. Even the Red Shirt connection to contemporary right-wing militancy was not lost on Elizabeth Ready, local UDC president and part-time museum director. In 2014, after seeing a bit of the Red Shirts in Clive Bundy's standoff with federal officials over grazing fees on public land in Nevada, she proudly predicted that "pretty soon the Red Shirts are going to ride again."[12] Two years later jurors acquitted Bundy's son and other militants of charges related to their occupation and standoff at Malheur Wildlife Refuge in Oregon. Kathleen Belew compared this acquittal to another—the 1988 Fort Smith, Arkansas, sedition trial, the first and last serious attempt by the federal government to prosecute assorted white power groups for violent felonies and seditious conspiracy as a unified social movement.[13]

Historically, seemingly male-dominated white supremacy movements have depended on white women's public performance of virtue and support. As discussed in chapter 1, during the eras of the New South following

Reconstruction and the rise of Jim Crow, middle-class and elite white women in memorial associations launched public campaigns to vindicate and memorialize the Confederacy and Lost Cause narrative. The UDC, the largest women's club by World War I, proved the most successful Lost Cause defenders and preservers of white supremacy. Karen L. Cox contends the UDC won a cultural victory by creating a "Confederate culture" of ideas and symbols, most visible though monuments and flags displayed in public spaces such as courthouses and town squares. As part of their vision of Confederate motherhood, the UDC also indoctrinated children with textbooks and membership in the Children of the Confederacy. To vindicate the Confederacy and to interpret the central issue of the Civil War as a battle over states' rights and not slavery, the UDC gathered artifacts, manuscripts, and accounts from former Confederates to deposit in museums and archives. The UDC installed exhibits in government spaces, sponsored essay contests, and published historical fiction and nonfiction.[14] This concerted effort was part of what historian David Blight defined as a larger "reconciliationist vision" that over the course of a half-century allied itself with a "white supremacist vision," segregating and southernizing both Civil War and Reconstruction memory. This narrative reinforced the need for Jim Crow laws, the racist system born out of this national reconciliation that lawfully and culturally enforced segregation until the 1950s and 1960s. During this period most white women never defied traditional norms of race and gender. The racial contexts of their lives socially and legally forbade it. White women thus buttressed Jim Crow's apartheid system and permitted their presumed purity and the myth of the Black rapist to cement white supremacist rule. The mid-twentieth-century civil rights movement overturned Jim Crow and chipped away at the white supremacist narrative with its emphasis on white terror, which was no longer palatable as a response to activists.[15]

For the last half-century, white women have continued to strengthen and support modern white supremacy. The contemporary movement is nationwide and has directed its racism toward Jews and nonwhites (as well as Black Americans), similar to the nativist Ku Klux Klan revival of the 1920s. However, women's participation in white supremacy since the post-Vietnam era is less mainstream than at the peak of UDC and Women of the Ku Klux Klan membership in the 1920s. At that time conceivably half a million white Protestant women joined the Klan and were the majority of Klan members in some states. Membership in white supremacist organizations is difficult to track, but the performance of white supremacy for the public and press is not. From the antebellum period to the twenty-first century, white Protestant women launched their auxiliary organizations and fundraised. They performed vulnerable white womanhood and the need for protection from men of color. They were key players in violence and also enforced white supremacy through social networks and economic influence, including boycotts and fundraising. In the 1920s "poison squads" ruined reputations through rumor, and Women of the KKK adherents circulated their ideology at church and social engagements and among family. Modern white power groups thrive through marriage, which symbolically weds differing white power ideologies and white power groups. These activities also point to an enduring and evolving "cult of motherhood" within white supremacy. While the UDC created the Children of the Confederacy, more recently membership to white supremacist organizations required bearing and indoctrinating Aryan children, enough to one day populate a white homeland in the Pacific Northwest. An updated strategy to unite white women supremacists is a social network of sharing recipes and homeschool lessons. In addition, women's domestic support, including sexual service as wives, lends credibility to their partners as activists. Finally, in service to the modern war against the state, white supremacist women are recruited from and trained in nursing and survival prepping. They occupy, domesticate, and in some cases co-own paramilitary compounds.[16]

There is a long history of white Protestant women across the nation supporting white supremacy via their social, familial, and economic circles. In South Carolina two white women used their intellect and public-facing historical writing to enshrine and defend the activities of the state's Red Shirts. The Red Shirts were men who served as a paramilitary wing of the white Democratic Party during Reconstruction and used intimidation and violence to deter Black and Republican voting in the election of 1876. Similar to other racist women that publicly defended white supremacist narratives and actors, Mary Simms Oliphant and writer and editor Louise Jones DuBose upheld the memory of Red Shirts as heroes in the most important historical assessments produced in the state in the twentieth century. Chapter 3 demonstrated the notorious generational influence of Oliphant's textbook, *A Simms History of South Carolina*, particularly on volunteer MoRE docent John Clark. The chapter argued that many white docents at the MoRE used the tour's narrative, which challenged the myths about how Reconstruction failed and violently ended, to help overturn their own indoctrination in the Lost Cause and white supremacist narrative of Reconstruction. Clark recalled that Oliphant's textbook praised the terrorism of the Klan and Red Shirts as necessary and morally just in their efforts to restore the rights of white men, especially in the election of 1876.[17]

With state support, Oliphant indoctrinated generations of students. Her reach extended to South Carolina classrooms for a half-century, well into the 1980s. During the New Deal and less than a decade after Oliphant's first textbook appeared, however, the federal government vested Louise Jones DuBose with the power to draft a literal road map of Reconstruction-era sites that buttressed the white supremacist narrative of Reconstruction. These driving tours included public history sites similar to Oakley Park that celebrated the Red Shirts and the election of 1876. As assistant director of South Carolina's Federal Writer's Project, DuBose became the leading force in producing *South Carolina: The WPA Guide to the Palmetto State*, published in February 1941. The state guidebooks were an attempt to find an American homogenizing national identity and spirit while celebrating the country's cultural diversity across forty-eight individual states. The racial dynamics, poverty, and folk traditions associated with the South made the region both an asset and obstacle to these federal goals. In the first section of South Carolina's volume, essays on culture dominated, but others explored environmental issues, ethnic groups, economics, and education. Part II detailed cities and towns. A description of twenty-one-day trips rounded out the guide. Ideally the WPA guides would help safeguard historical relics and promote local preservation while simultaneously encouraging citizens to rediscover their nation.[18] By emphasizing whiteness and othering Black Americans, states like South Carolina got trapped in a nostalgic tourist mode, a problem still present at many of the South's HHMs today and one that the MoRE attempts to correct. By making Black and often white folkways "exotic and quaint" in the plantation tradition, the WPA guides revealed more about how white southerners wanted to depict the South than the region's reality. Thus the southern guides supplemented fictional works such as *The Birth of a Nation* and *Gone with the Wind* (dir. Victor Fleming, 1939) that supplied the "cultural beliefs that underwrote apartheid."[19] Washington officials criticized the South Carolina edition for offering local patriotism rather than truth and demanded multiple revisions of the essay "The Negro." In the preface director Mabel Montgomery and DuBose acknowledged the "disagreement of historians as to fact, and the argument between fact and fantasy." When poet and literary critic Sterling Brown claimed that South Carolina relied on simplistic and misleading sociological support, Montgomery reframed the issue as a battle between a "picturesque and interesting account" and a "sociological discourse carrying a Northern slant."[20]

Both Oliphant and DuBose described Reconstruction as the "darkest period" in that state's history. Their writings argued that the chaos of emancipation and Reconstruction warranted the violent and illegal efforts by the Ku Klux Klan and the Red Shirts to return South Carolina to white supremacist rule.[21] Oliphant claimed that Klansmen were the "best men" of the state, sworn protectors of property and white lives, especially that of white women threatened with "insults" on the street. She later explained away less than palatable violence by noting that disguises were sometimes adopted by the occasional carpetbagger, scalawag, and Klansman for "private vengeance."[22] DuBose shared KKK tales that ranged from benign to horrific. On highway 215 at West Springs, tour twelve provided a resting spot at the Confederate Holly. Also known as the Ku Klux Holly Tree, it stood as a reminder of the three Klansmen with arrest warrants who evaded soldiers overnight by hiding in its branches, even as the soldiers camped beneath them. Tour sixteen recounted the first KKK group organized in the state in 1868. The WPA guide's history of Rock Hill and York County in the upstate noted these communities were a hotbed of Klan activity and Reconstruction-era terror. DuBose advised readers to see tour sixteen of York County for further information on the Klan crackdown in the early 1870s by the federal government, a response to the group's growing control. DuBose insisted that corrupt officials arrested 195 citizens, many distinguished lawyers, doctors, and clergy, without warrant or evidence.[23] The MoRE works to correct this myth in room 14 as part of the discussion of domestic terror. A panel notes that the US Army arrested the Klansmen, and that their 1871 trial in Columbia, which would have taken place during Tommy Wilson's residency, was an attempt to "interpret" what citizenship and due process meant under the Fourteenth Amendment.[24]

The most persistent myths that Oliphant and Dubose perpetuated about the Klan were that it formed to protect white people from legally armed Black men and that the Republican government only allowed Black militias. In truth militias formed under Gov. Robert Scott in March 1869 after the Klan's appearance. Mostly comprising Black men since most white men feared serving, membership in militias swelled to one hundred thousand by fall 1870. Narratives by Democrats that Republican-backed militias intended to target and oppress whites generated fear in the white community; yet the militias, maintaining a difficult balance of respect and restraint to avoid "self-defeating violence," initially were successful in protecting the Black community and officeholders. But they too came under attack as part of a larger pattern of violence against Republicans and freed people.[25] When local Black citizens became "threatening," the Klan, argued Oliphant, righteously executed ten incarcerated Black militiamen accused of murdering a Confederate veteran. In later editions of her textbook, Black militias took on a less villainous role and were simply ill prepared to bear arms. Republicans in the state received the blame for inciting fear and suspicion.[26] Tour ten in the WPA guide included the National Guard Armory, the site of an 1870 Laurens riot by "armed Negroes, led by a 'scalawag.'" Historically a white mob fired on the armory after Black citizens of Laurensville came to the aid of a constable in a dispute with a local white constable. Nine Republicans, Black and white, perished, and Governor Scott ordered the Black militias to turn their weapons over.[27]

Similarly DuBose defended the 1870 Klan violence in Union County, for it quickly disarmed militias and inspired Scott to withdraw his support. She ignored, however, the larger and more dangerous conspiracy represented by the two extralegal jail raids, simply noting that the KKK retaliated against a Black militia by killing several of them. Politically the Republican coalition of Black voters and a few white scalawags in Union County was tenuous but powerful. Alex Walker, a Black trial justice and militia leader, was one of these Black leaders, along with three state representatives, two of the three county commissioners, and the school commissioner. Months of violence targeting trial justices both white and Black, Black ministers, and other Black citizens and politicians precipitated the violence that erupted on New Year's Eve 1870, which was, as Bruce Baker surmises, "fueled by a fatal combination of alcohol and nervous bravado, with a strong undercurrent of fear on both sides." That evening, in the absence of Alex Walker, Sylvanus Wright led his twenty-five-man militia as it guarded Budd Williams, a white constable and election commissioner, from Klan violence. The militia was one of two companies that intercepted Matt Stevens and Benjamin Robinson, two armed men moving illegal liquor cargo to a local hotel. Post-encounter rumors speculated that the militiamen wanted the whiskey to celebrate the new year, though it does appear some militia shot at the wagon. Under the influence, the bootleggers fled; Stevens, who DuBose described as a one-armed Confederate veteran, was captured and killed by members of the militia. What Elaine Frantz characterized as a white coalition of "respectable elites" and "violent, marginal men" responded the next day, ultimately seizing militia weapons and attacking a Black home with prominent Republicans and militiamen inside. Soon after the vigilantes arrested Walker for ordering the murder, pulling him from a train bound for the state's capital, where he was headed to inform Governor Scott of recent events. Thirty of Walker's militia attempted to rescue him, but they were told he would be executed immediately upon their assault. The first of two jail raids took place on January 5, 1871, ending with the murder of two of five Black Republicans being held there. Though W. J. Whipper and Robert Brown Elliott, two prominent Black state legislators, considered it an act of war warranting a strong response, Scott sent no reinforcements. The three men who escaped the mob returned to jail the next day and were murdered in a second raid a month later before they could be moved to Columbia to name and testify against their kidnappers. The masked mob, a substantial portion of which was on horseback, materialized in the rain on the night of February 12 and far exceeded the previous raid, numbering in the hundreds, perhaps as many as fifteen hundred. This time ten men were abducted, and no one survived. With the short-term goal of extinguishing the militia complete, the Klan was largely free to implement a six-month-long coup that forced local Republicans to resign. The lessons learned by those who implemented the Red Shirt campaign were that domestic terror was effective and that the federal government was slow to react, sending military companies and passing the Enforcement Acts too late. On the state level, Governor Scott made more Democratic appointments, demonstrating capitulation in the wake of white political violence.[28] DuBose's account reproduced the Klan's note defending their use of force against force and equating themselves with martyrs for Michael, the angel of justice. Historian Elaine Frantz argues that the long, "performatively literate" note, written after the grisly second raid, was an attempt to court national attention and convey that competent elites controlled a well-coordinated Klan in Union. As a result the press further disseminated the idea of the Klan nationwide, and the federal government launched an investigation. The 1871 Enforcement Act yielded arrests in Union County and across the South, but few ever entered a courtroom for trial.[29]

More recent work by Frantz and Bruce Baker has created a clearer picture of white domestic terror in Union County, South Carolina, during Reconstruction. Both provide thorough accounts of mob and Klan activity and underscore the importance of Klan and lynching narratives in shaping the response to the aftermath. Militias, mobs, and criminal vigilante groups formed in the early years of Reconstruction, often comprising members from the old antebellum slave patrols and Confederate home guard. The Union County Slickers, for example, emerged in December 1865. According to Frantz, political violence arose in Union County twice, once in 1868, which outsiders, rather than the local residents and perpetrators, labeled as Klan activity, and again in 1870 to challenge successful Black leadership and political power that threatened local criminal and vice activity. Using network analysis, she examines the social relationships that appear in the county's criminal indictment records to argue that social elites and small, violent criminal bands coalesced around William Faucett to conduct this organized political violence. Bootleggers Stevens and Robinson, for example, were landless white friends of Faucett. Newspapers provided misleading or partial accounts of the violence. National coverage of the Klan was a narrative for northern white audiences to reconcile the violence. These stories reminded readers of their own white supremacist beliefs and presented a performance of whiteness that demonstrated coordination, strength, and effectiveness. By the fall and winter of 1870–71, these men, many of them masked in recycled costume ball attire, adopted a culturally constructed concept of the Klan that validated their brutality and soothed local class tensions with a new coalition centered on whiteness. As it had become one the most violent and well-organized KKK groups during Reconstruction, the bloodshed left by the Union Klan's attacks rivaled the number of deaths in neighboring counties' riots. As a result, the Union County Klan's actions prompted federal investigations and legislation.[30] This Klan was but one of a number of white terror groups, such as the White League, whose members viewed themselves as part of the "revolutionary tradition," were unafraid of public association with their revolutionary performance of violence, and invoked the Second Amendment to defend that violence constitutionally.[31] As Carole Emberton astutely articulated, "Violence brought white supremacy into being, not the other way around."[32]

No story of white-led violence in South Carolina during the election of 1876 looms quite as large in public memory as the Hamburg Massacre in July. Oakley Park's Red Shirt shrine and the works of Oliphant and DuBose all justified this white violence. However, the MoRE's text on "The Red Shirt Campaign" panel in room 14 overturns this narrative. The panel clearly places responsibility on "Reconstruction opponents" who "executed six members of a militia unit that hesitated before permitting two whites to drive a wagon through the militia's Fourth of July parade."[33] Oliphant blamed the Black militia for refusing to apologize for the legal, armed policing of white citizens or to disarm after fortifying themselves in a building. Only in her last revisions did she concede that reports of the militia's threat to lynch two white citizens were not confirmed and that no one knew who shot first.[34] The narrative defending the massacre was so accepted among white South Carolinians that DuBose openly included in the guide that the executed men at Hamburg had surrendered.[35]

The plantation home Oakley Park displays the 1860 Springfield rifle that future South Carolina governor, US senator, and white supremacist "Pitchfork Ben" Tillman carried during his participation in the massacre.[36] Hamburg marked a turning point when, as the MoRE reminds visitors, Gen. Martin Gary, the same proprietor of Oakley Park that rallied the Red Shirts, could implement his strategy of "a 'straight-out' Democratic campaign of aggressive white supremacy," which used coordinated intimidation, economic coercion, and massacres. Violence escalated, culminating in the so-called Ellenton riot that September, which "resulted in the deaths of two whites and dozens of African Americans, including a state legislator shot in the head while praying for mercy."[37] The history of the city of Aiken that DuBose wrote for the WPA guide called the events in Hamburg and Ellenton "two of the bloodiest race riots of the period." She estimated that "three hundred whites led by rifle clubs massacred between thirty and fifty Blacks over a two-day period in Ellenton." These massacres, she argued, led to a "smoothly functioning" state government and community prosperity.[38]

Where the Klan had failed to restore native white supremacy, the Red Shirts succeeded. Both Oliphant and DuBose noted the central role white women and families played in the movement, including by perpetuating its memory as righteous. Oliphant viewed the campaign as a family affair, the support of which defined good citizenship. White women were complicit, sewing red shirts and abandoning farms and businesses to participate. By the 1970s Oliphant had removed her claim that "every decent white man went to work to deliver the State from its evil rulers."[39] Hero worship continued, however, as part of an assignment where students, presumed to be white, were asked to draft a story about a Reconstruction-era student whose father took part in the campaign.[40] DuBose vindicated the Red Shirts as well, on numerous occasions referencing their "flaming costumes." However, both the city sections and driving tours that she wrote did this most effectively by playing up violent Red Shirt roots and tracing the path of Wade Hampton's 1876 gubernatorial campaign.[41] In Anderson, Hampton delivered his first of forty speeches to six thousand enthusiastic people, a "highlight in the city's history." Bands played, banners flew, and long lines of cheering Democratic club representatives marched until the "mounted rifle club members, wearing brand new 'Red Shirt' uniforms, swelled the parade."[42] DuBose invited driving tourists to seek out the Hampton Oak in Sumter. The tree offered to visitors the same shelter that shaded Hampton, flanked by his Red Shirts, as he spoke to a crowd on October 7, 1876. DuBose also implied that white women's purity fueled the Red Shirts. She described a woman draped in funeral regalia and chains at this same event. As Hampton made his way to the platform, the woman's cloak fell away to reveal her white dress and golden crown, and the crowd supposedly yelled the famed battle cry "Hampton or Hell!"[43] DuBose's account is part of what W. Scott Poole describes as the "aesthetic of the Lost Cause," which during Reconstruction and the "Hampton Days of September and October 1876" ritualistically exhibited young, beautiful women's bodies to be read as "public texts" that validated the beliefs of southern Democrats.[44] The performance was political theater that framed the governor's race in religious terms as a battle between good and evil and played on white male southerners' anxiety about race and gender. Though Black men were not yet being branded rapists and beasts, the women represented purity and symbolic victims of Republican Reconstruction, a disease for which the only cure was Democratic power. The tableau also doubled as a response to Gov. Daniel Chamberlain's disbanding of rifle clubs.[45]

Of the twenty-one tours in the WPA guide, five include "points of interest" or history lessons related to Hampton's 1876 campaign for governor or the need for violent white supremacy to intimidate armed Black citizens. Tour nine moved through Columbia highlighting Hampton's long life there, including when the state summoned him to lead the Red Shirts and restore Democratic rule by bribery, intimidation, and voter fraud. Tour nineteen brought tourists to the courthouse where Hampton laid the cornerstone for his namesake county. A white community had recently formed Hampton County because Beaufort had been "overrun" with the usual villains of the white supremacist narrative of Reconstruction (northern soldiers, carpetbaggers, and scalawags).[46]

Both Oliphant and DuBose accepted voting fraud and violence as the price paid "to oust the Radicals at any cost" and proclaimed Hampton a defender of peace and moderate voice of reason. DuBose argued that Chamberlain, the last Republican governor, tried reform but simply could not compete with the "beloved" war hero Hampton and the organization, persuasion, and intimidation of his Democrats.[47] Two MoRE panels devoted to the election of 1876 explain further that, because of his moderation, Chamberlain was pursuing a fusionist ticket, under which Democrats would nominate him and his moderate wing of the Republican Party would support him. The straight-out Democratic ticket derailed this strategy with the support of the Red Shirt campaign and local rifle clubs. As the paramilitary wing of the Democratic Party, these forces dispersed Republican rallies and on Election Day ignited violence and fraud. For example, in Edgefield and Laurens Counties, there were more votes for Democrats than registered voters for both parties.[48] Oliphant emphasized Hampton's moderation over time, noting that he condemned violence to avoid federal intervention. But in her earlier text, eerily seeming to anticipate events 145 years later at the January 6 DC rally, Oliphant bragged that Hampton pleaded for peace and nonviolence "from the steps of the state house" in an attempt to mollify angry Democrats and "the excited and outraged people," who with "one word" from him would have killed federal troops and the Republican Coalition in the State House.[49] The Klan and mob violence in Union County at the beginning of the decade was central to ending Reconstruction in the state during the contested election of 1876, when both Democrats and Republicans claimed victory and maintained their own versions of the House. Judge William H. Wallace, who came to power in 1872 because of the 1871 Union coup, served as the interim Speaker of the House, which was run by Democrats. As Baker surmised, Wallace helped "carry off one of the great coups in the history of American politics, a political stunt that would shape the South and even the nation afterwards." Today the Wade Hampton statue still stands on the State House grounds. The equestrian design and battles engraved along the bottom as well as its funding by the state and Hampton chapters of the UDC and United Confederate Veterans suggest that the 1906 monument honors Hampton's Confederate service. However, drawing on Baker's analysis of the monument as a hybrid version of Hampton from the Civil War and Reconstruction, a MoRE caption notes that the hair and beard depict Hampton as he appeared during the Red Shirt campaign.[50]

Challenging White Supremacy through Material Culture: The Red Shirt and Tissue Ballot

Given the sustained hero worship of Wade Hampton and his Red Shirts via public history and white memory, docents must overturn decades of indoctrination in a matter of minutes. Two objects, a red shirt and a tissue ballot, are visitor favorites and vital artifacts in broaching these subjects.[51] Though the red shirt became the symbol of the campaign for redemption in 1876, its origin is unclear. One theory is that Martin Gary, who was an avid reader of European history, modeled it on Giuseppe Garibaldi's 1860 Red Shirts, who helped usher in Italian unification. During an 1892 speech in Anderson, Ben Tillman claimed that he was responsible for making the red shirt the movement's symbolic costume.[52] There are red shirts in collections across South Carolina, including the previously mentioned UDC-run Oakley Park and the South Carolina State Museum. The State Museum and the MoRE display red shirts to advance a conversation about white domestic terror. Oakley Park and the Sixteenth Regiment South Carolina Volunteers' Museum of Confederate History, run by Camp 36 of the Sons of Confederate Veterans in Greenville, present white supremacist interpretations of the shirt. The Museum of Confederate History possesses the shirt of Thomas Bissell Crews, a Confederate cavalry officer in Hampton's Legion, newspaper editor, and legislator from the upstate.[53]

Most docents head directly to the red shirt upon entry into the space for a discussion of domestic and political terrorism that began with the Klan.[54] Heather Bacon-Rogers witnessed the shirt's power to "drive home" the violence. When she opened the drawer holding an authentic red shirt, visitors realized someone wore it, and some asked, "What are those stains on it?" She too wondered, "Is it age? Is it blood? I don't know." She took her own discomfort with the brown stain on the object and directed it back on the visitor: "What does it look like to you?" Although Bacon-Rogers thought the reproduction red shirt in the sole glass exhibit case in the space looked "cheap" and added no value, weekend docent and public historian Halie Brazier preferred it. Clean and protected alongside a period rifle, it was "more

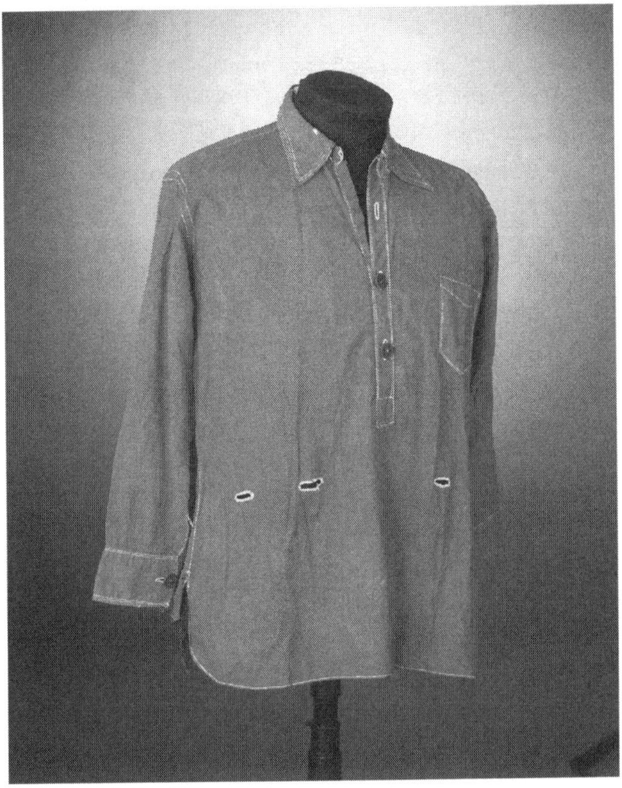

Figure 15. Unique features of this red shirt are that it is made on a sewing machine and has a few stains. Red shirt on loan from South Carolina State Museum and courtesy of Historic Columbia.

menacing" and "creepy." It offered a glimpse of the horror without going too far and putting off visitors. Bacon-Rogers also used the shirt to ask visitors about the difference between Klan and Red Shirt uniforms. Visitors had a strong reaction to realizing Red Shirts did not cover their faces. Some docents chose to privilege a gendered discussion of the shirt. Public historian Jennifer Gunter pointed out the shirt was a handmade garment and political terrorism was a "family affair." She reasoned that "this is not just the men getting together. Somebody's wife or domestic servant made this. This is the way a whole portion of society felt." Volunteer docent Cyndy Storm fused the gendered origin with technology, noting that a "new gadget," the sewing machine, was used to construct the shirt. As part of their participation in modern-day white supremacist cells, white women continue to prepare disguises as well as drive getaway cars, move people and weapons, and proofread important public documents.[55]

Though decades separated them in age, three docents used the tour to contemplate their own family's connection with white supremacy. Bacon-Rogers argued that familial connections to white supremacy hit "a little closer to home" with white visitors at the MoRE than with Historic Columbia's other house tours because they recognize that their ancestors were possible executors of this violence. "This house makes me question too what my family was doing," she revealed. "I'm telling audiences about these horrible things that are going on. Do I have these horrible things in my past too?" She grew up in Aiken County on the border of Edgefield County. She knew families that went back five generations in Edgefield, white families present during Reconstruction when locals incited a violent riot against their Black neighbors. She exclaimed, "Why did I not know this? The next county over. That [violence] was going on but not right next door." She learned this information from the tour. Likewise Brazier knew, by virtue of her "heritage," "history," and "blood," that the "violent perpetrators" could have been part of her family. While these two docents wondered whether their families had carried out Reconstruction-era violence, volunteer Walt Hall, a descendant of Red Shirts, struggled with whether he wanted to share this ancestry as a teaching tool.[56]

The tissue ballot, the straight Democratic ticket cast in the election of 1876, engaged visitors about how voter fraud was conducted but carried less emotional weight than the red shirt. The ballot drew people in because it was "proof" of fraud, a unique object not normally seen in house museums that allowed visitors to connect to their own familiarity with modern political corruption. Sometimes guests recalled George W. Bush's electoral victory over Al Gore in 2000 and contrasted that with the 1876 Rutherford B. Hayes–Samuel Tilden election.[57] But often visitors responded with laughter and chuckles rather than shock, as if they expect politics to be corrupt.[58] The false allegations of fraud in the 2020 election by former President Trump and his supporters will likely become a new reference point for visitors in the coming years. The new myth persists despite numerous federal agencies, a bipartisan group of government officials, and Supreme Courts on the state and federal level agreeing that there was no systemic fraud in 2020.[59]

To stress the severity of the situation, MoRE docents frequently asked visitors "to put themselves" in the election of 1876 and picture the violence. Docents instructed visitors to imagine the threats associated with open-air voting and risking their safety by asking for a Republican straight ticket. Visitors then considered whether they would vote their conscience with an armed Red Shirt present. Volunteer and former teacher Jean Morgan found that guests exclaimed, "No!" But Bacon-Rogers "stopped waiting for a response," even though that question "probes directly into what's important." She noticed body language that demonstrated visitors were "physically uncomfortable," so she spoke from her truth: "I'd love to think I'm brave and I'd march right up there and vote my conscience. But had I been a former

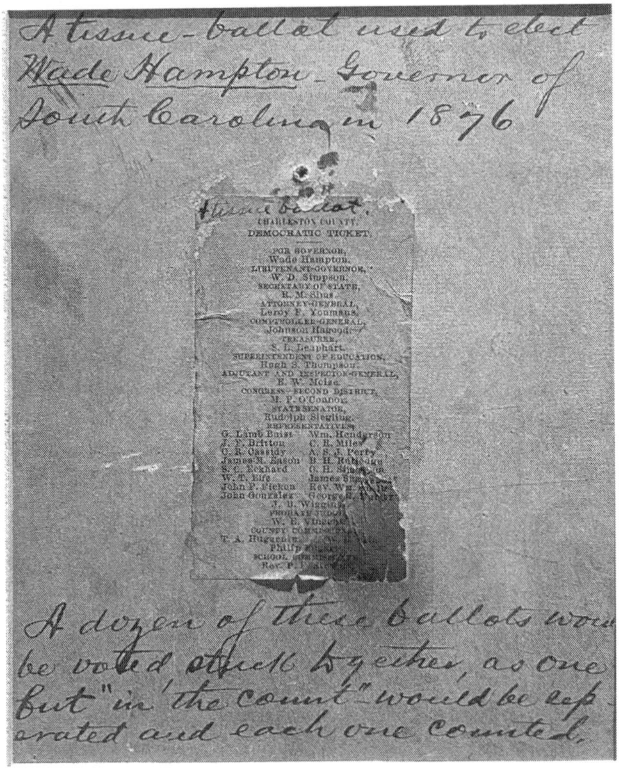

Figure 16. According to the handwriting found at the bottom of the 1876 ballot: "A dozen of these ballots would be voted, stuck together, as one but 'in the count' would be separated and each one counted." Tissue ballot, on loan from Confederate Relic Room and Military Museum and courtesy of Historic Columbia.

enslaved male, would I? I don't know. . . . I'm also a white female in the twenty-first century. Being brave now and being brave then are two different things." The question still left visitors with a level of discomfort while not opening them up to judgment from their peers. However, on smaller, more intimate tours, people felt comfortable enough to share their thoughts.[60]

Docents varied in how they presented Wilson's family in relationship to the violence. Some simply noted that the family had moved to Wilmington, North Carolina, by 1874.[61] Bacon-Rogers often referenced the 1926 historical account *Ousting the Carpetbagger from South Carolina*, which claimed Tommy Wilson's extended family frequently took food to Presbyterian Klan members imprisoned during the Klan trials in Columbia in the early 1870s. The future president's Aunt Felixina, wife of his Presbyterian minister uncle James Woodrow, and his sister Annie Wilson Howe's mother-in-law delivered food to incarcerated men like Dr. John A. Leland, an elder leader in the church. According to the book, Leland wrote fondly in his diary about witnessing an excellent sermon from Tommy's father, Rev. Joseph Wilson, during a temporary jail release. For Bacon-Rogers the story contradicted the impulse to paint presidents as coming from "wholesome backgrounds." She argued that while Wilson may have grown up within the seminary and Presbyterianism, that same institution leased enslaved people, including for work in the Wilson family household. According to the 1860 Slave Schedule for Richland County, George Howe, Annie's father-in-law, owned eleven women and eight men.[62]

The Howe family's slaveholding status was part of the research Historic Columbia presented to its docents as the museum approached its two-year anniversary. The new circumstantial evidence provided docents with tools to guide conversations with visitors about how Tommy Wilson might have responded to the rise of the Red Shirts. Two articles in the *State* newspaper in June 1946 and 1950 shared local Joseph Physioc's remembrances of Tommy and the election of 1876. Physioc attended Columbia Military Academy, two blocks north of the MoRE, and like Wilson was a student of a former Confederate officer. Wearing his red shirt and gray military pants, he stood with his honor guard at events for Hampton's gubernatorial campaign. He also played for the Alerts baseball team. Tommy, a decade older than Physioc, occasionally joined them as a "first rate first baseman, none better." Physioc also told friends about swimming with Wilson and their friends at a Congaree River swimming hole. He remembered Tommy as head of his class, a leader, and defender of white children attacked by "wild" freedmen. Implying that he was an honorary Red Shirt, Physioc recalled that Wilson proved his bravery "many times in those Reconstruction days before seventy-six." Tommy supposedly led his naked swimming buddies' defense "with sticks and stones and old discarded horse pistols" against attacks to steal the boys' clothes.[63]

MoRE docents expressed fears about interpreting violence and conflict in the Wilson house. Before opening, initial docent concerns were about reactions from guests, especially older South Carolinians, to descriptions of white on Black violence. They might object to vilifying the formerly revered Hampton and his Red Shirts, who went from heroes to terrorists over the course of the tour. One docent credited repetition of the domestic terror theme for being able to smoothly convey this history.[64] Three others made their discussions on violence brief to curb blowback. Bacon-Rogers attributed the interpretive success to not focusing on "specific violence, such as the Edgefield riots," partly due to the tour's pace.[65] Visitors attending BIPOC-centered history museums are generally given a celebratory, "insider" version of a story of "adversity, struggle, and triumph."[66] And while the MoRE celebrates accomplishments of the Reconstruction era, the violent and abrupt end of that era disrupts the traditional model of a happy or socially acceptable conclusion. For Brazier detailing the violence against Black people and Republicans was her "biggest interpretive challenge." She struggled to find a balance, wanting to avoid gore but worrying about being perceived as "glossing over it flippantly."[67]

As the MoRE exhibit on domestic terror demonstrates, identifying systemic violence and selecting appropriate representations bring interpretive conundrums for public historians. For instance, the community of Memphis disagreed on what constituted appropriate language for describing the violence that took place in July 1866 when a white mob, including police, raped several Black women and killed dozens of Black people over the course of three days. Beverly Robertson, former director of the National Civil Rights Museum and member of the Tennessee Historical Commission, argued that she and the NAACP ultimately endorsed a private marker for the Memphis massacre of 1866 after the commission insisted on describing the incident as a riot on a state-sanctioned marker. The language choice shielded white perpetrators of the violence by evoking twentieth-century images of Black riots in neighborhoods outside the South, such as those in Los Angeles, California, as the civil rights movement evolved to address the struggles of Black urban areas.[68] For MoRE docents the limit was graphic images of lynching. Volunteer docent Kathy Hogan, a former educator, objected in part because lynchings were more common during Jim Crow and because children attend the museum. She had firsthand experience working with a teacher who had shown a graphic lynching image to children. Children understand intimidation, bullying, and the constitutional rights of assembly and speech, Hogan argued; thus a lynching image does not advance the narrative. Conversely docents needed time to establish trust with their audience and contextualize the images. Thomas Nast's cartoon *One Vote Less*, with its less graphic depiction of the murder of an African American male voter, was a sufficient example from an exhibit panel that also engaged visitors. The story of Republican chairman Benjamin F. Randolph's assassination in 1868 and a lynching hidden in the background of Nast's cartoon *Worse Than Slavery* provided further evidence if needed. The panel about Randolph noted the "state legislature authorized a monument" at his grave in Columbia's Elmwood Cemetery in 1871, which prompted "prominent African Americans" to initiate a radical public response that endures today as a challenge to the white supremacist narrative of Reconstruction. They bought several acres from the cemetery to create Randolph Cemetery "as a community institution and tribute to black resilience."[69]

The authenticity of evidence presented at the MoRE gave its docents the confidence to discuss Reconstruction terrorism, which was once celebrated by white South Carolinians. Weekend docent and public historian Casey Lee had no qualms about using the word *terrorism*. In addition to being the correct terminology, as a graduate student Lee had a "firm grasp" on Reconstruction terrorism's history. Furthermore, the red shirt, rifle, and tissue ballot offered evidence that made it hard for visitors to dispute the MoRE's interpretation on terror. She "planted seeds" in the rest of the house, but her narrative fully bloomed in room 14. "You're not going to argue with me in that room," Lee said, followed by light laughter. She continued, "You don't have to like it. But you're going to accept it." Four docents never had a visitor contest the interpretation.[70] Docents also reported that most visitors were hearing the Red Shirt history for the first time and political terrorism held a high degree of interest for them.[71]

Evidentiary support did not ease all of the docents' fears and concerns, some of which were rooted in a lack of representation in the public history field. Brazier joked that visitors think far less about her failures than she does, but she still worried that her whiteness prevented her from understanding political and racial terrorism since she would "never have been the recipient" of that violence. She also was "very self-conscious" about describing the violence with the brevity required of a house tour but with proper respect for the victims who deserved to have their story told.[72] Brazier and other docents acknowledged how problematic it was to have white docents address white violence against Black bodies to overwhelming white audiences in white spaces. The white narratives and representation dissuaded most people of color from coming to museums, and when they visited the MoRE, they heard her, a white docent, narrating a "Black story to Black people." Gunter also questioned her role as both a docent and ally. Discussing race felt "strange," especially when she had a diverse audience. White visitors like herself, who could never fully grasp the violence, made Brazier feel as though she was "talking over everybody's heads a little bit." Gunter confirmed that explaining white on Black violence during Reconstruction to white people, often for the first time, when most Black visitors present were familiar with this history was "a weird situation to be in."[73]

Several docents embraced the opportunity to talk about race in general and felt confident in their abilities because of their academic training. Gunter earned bachelor's and master's degrees in southern studies, which placed great emphasis on sustained open dialogues about southern concepts of race. Lee thought more deeply about the racial elements of her MoRE narrative and honed her skills discussing race during a public history internship in Maine at the height of the Confederate flag debate in the summer of 2015. As a South Carolinian outside of the state, she learned to articulate how white South Carolinians regarded the flag and its history. For Lee tours were also cathartic. Visitors became surrogates for distant family members that she could not engage because it would "blow up." But her family gave her greater insight into how visitors who embraced the Lost Cause think and how far she could push visitors before those firmly committed to white supremacist narrative of Reconstruction dismissed her and a new narrative.[74]

One of the most successful but difficult interpretive spaces in the MoRE is the exhibit on political terror during Reconstruction. Docent experiences illuminate interpretive approaches to help sites discuss white supremacy and domestic terror with honest conversations and powerful artifacts. Yet volunteer Cyndy Storm wondered if "sometimes you can't talk about this stuff until everybody's dead." Gunter, however, suggested the site could push further, that museums bear more responsibility in making their sites more racially and ethnically inclusive beyond white southerners explaining systemic racism to white people.[75] Within a year of opening its doors, the MoRE hosted docents from the Columbia Museum of Art, who were preparing for an African American art exhibit. Could the site do more? Historic Columbia did not design the space devoted to white violence during Reconstruction to discuss the history of white domestic terror. However, the exhibit and narrative provide visitors with a starting point for understanding how white supremacy brutally brought an end to Reconstruction and continues into the present, with many of the same strategies. The exhibit and a comparative approach can also offer opportunities to better understand the connection between political and racial violence via paramilitary forces during Reconstruction and the era of Donald Trump.[76]

The Red Shirts and antidemocratic paramilitary forces in other reconstructed states arose because the federal government stopped intervening when white supremacist violence and political terrorism occurred. Similarly, for four decades the modern white power movement grew, successfully infiltrating the military, due to a lack of both consistency in federal regulations on white domestic terror and commitment to eradicating the problem. The Defense Department banned active participation in white supremacist groups in the late 1980s after active-duty Marines at Camp Lejeune, North Carolina, gave equipment and paramilitary training to the Klan. However, more "passive" activities, such as membership in these organizations, distributing racist propaganda, and listening to hate rock, continued among enlistees. Restrictions on extremist activities tightened again in 1995 following the Oklahoma City bombing.[77] Then a twenty-year War on Terror beginning in 2001 prompted lower recruiting standards and unclear regulations, which created an environment ripe for white power infiltration. The Defense Department refused to institute a zero-tolerance policy, rarely expelled extremists, and denied problems when members were publicly identified.[78] Not until 2009, under President Barack Obama's administration, did the military reinstate the ban on active participation in white supremacist organizations. Casting a wider net this time, active participation covered recruiting, fundraising, demonstrating, rallying, training, organizing, displaying associated tattoos, and distributing propaganda, including on the internet.[79]

Just two months before the Capitol siege, after the foiled plan to kidnap Michigan governor Gretchen Whitmer was uncovered, Belew warned, just as she had in her book, that more organized white power attacks would follow. A new generation of activists, with Trump serving as a figurehead, had reshaped the movement. Iraq and Afghanistan, like Vietnam, fueled this second generation, many of whom were ignored by the public until Trump's 2016 campaign. This ideological coalition of various white power groups, the militant right, tax resisters, and separatists produces paramilitary training camps, protestors like the "boogaloo boys," and mass shooters. For example, Trump instructed the Proud Boys, avid promoters of the white power guidebook *The Turner Diaries*, to "stand back and stand by" during a 2020 presidential debate—to which the group responded favorably. This group was also linked to the plot to burn Whitmer's summer home and bring her to a show trial, a step traditionally proceeding a lynching among white mobs. *The Birth of a Nation* depicts such a scene. The threats of violence, organized online, targeting Whitmer and politicians trapped in the Capitol were all coordinated efforts by white supremacists. Yet the public narrative, be it about the shooter at an El Paso Wal-Mart, a synagogue in Pittsburgh, or a Black church in Charleston, is one of a lone wolf or mentally ill attacker.[80] The only difference between Reconstruction-era terror and the militant movement today in its root causes is the medium of the internet. A powerful Black electorate, Black political leaders, toxic and racist rhetoric, extremist misinformation, and economic decline fueled both periods of domestic terror.[81]

Another lesson the MoRE's Red Shirt room can teach relates to the class dynamics of white domestic terrorists and insurrectionists. Active servicemembers and veterans, some of whom were using the crowd as cover for a violent assault, certainly made up part of the Capitol rioters. However, they also included "respectable," middle- and upper-class white people, leaders in business, and public servants in legislatures and law enforcement. There were stay-at-home moms and at least one stay-at-home dad.[82] Elite white southerners blamed mob violence of the Reconstruction era on the spontaneous actions of their poor counterparts when in fact it was often orchestrated from above.[83] The assumption then and now that modern white supremacy campaigns and right-wing political violence are products of poverty is erroneous, even if Trump did complain that the rioters looked "low class." Ideology drives the movement; thus "respectable" people plan and participate in this public violence. During Reconstruction, Wade Hampton and the Red Shirts as well as the rifle club equivalents in other states convinced elite planters, white middle-class professionals, the clergy, and skilled workers to join their paramilitary ranks or Black citizens and northern whites would steal the election. Mary Simms Oliphant and Louise Jones DuBose proudly asserted that Klansmen and Red Shirts were the "best men" of the state.[84]

In addition to the varied class composition of domestic terror and insurrection movements, politicians participating in or endorsing them use white supremacy and the violence it wields to boost their careers. Donald Trump and Senators Ted Cruz and Josh Hawley exploited the January 6 rally for their own political gain. Reconstruction's bloody end not only brought Hampton to power but also shaped the Jim Crow policies of Benjamin Tillman. He implemented "new centralized institutions of control and surveillance" via the codification of Jim Crow, most notably through the 1895 state constitution that erased the gains made from the 1868 version. These examples are stark reminders that domestic terror often yields gains for the perpetrators and their political agenda. Tillman was in his late twenties when he participated in the Ned Tennant riot of 1874 and the Hamburg massacre two years later. As captain of the Sweetwater Sabre Club, he helped execute seven Black Republican militiamen and reveled the next morning with celebratory breakfast. As a politician in the early twentieth century, he defended the attack on a legal militia, confiscation of arms, and executions of its members as part of the American revolutionary spirit. Even when his political opponents condemned his actions at Hamburg and his speaking engagements at Red Shirt reunions, Tillman praised Red Shirt violence as necessary, manly, and patriotic. Tillman praised Matthew C. Butler and Martin W. Gary as the real heroes and architects of 1876, not Hampton, who like other paternalist leaders had distanced himself from violent men like Tillman. Presenting his own white supremacist narrative of Reconstruction advanced Tillman's career and provided him legitimacy after he lost his eye to a cranial tumor and could not serve in the Civil War. Tillman was not alone as a white southern Democrat in his use of this memory. Others did so when it suited them, such as opposing the New Deal and referring to Franklin Roosevelt's allies as carpetbaggers.[85]

In addition, the MoRE's interpretation of domestic terror and docent-led conversation on white supremacy can be of service to the comprehensive strategy that experts have recommended to combat the current white power movement's public and military influence. Heidi Beirich, an expert on extremism, outlined eight requirements for the US military, two of which may also be applicable to the MoRE and similar historic sites. The MoRE most clearly meets Beirich's call to speak out forcefully against white supremacy. Moreover, the bedroom devoted to domestic terror and the election of 1876 can help explain to military officials, policymakers, and the general public the historic relationship between militias, white supremacy, and election fraud. The interpretation of paramilitary forces and rifle clubs like the

Ku Klux Klan and the Red Shirts reinforces Beirich's recommendation to close loopholes for militia members in the military who plan insurrections and attend white supremacist events like that in Charlottesville.[86] In the wake of the Capitol siege, Kathleen Belew endorsed actions similar to those Congress initiated during Reconstruction. She called for Trump's impeachment following the failure of Mike Pence and Trump's cabinet to invoke the Twenty-fifth Amendment for the president's role in inciting the insurrection. Most important, and reminiscent of the Ku Klux Klan Act of 1871, she advocated for updated statutes and policies to address legally the threat of white supremacy movements. The MoRE's interpretation of political terrorism as having been temporarily combatted and then ignored by the state supports the need for this legislation. Lastly Belew argued for more preventative measures and deradicalization efforts to combat white supremacy in general.[87] Learning the history of white supremacy during tours and workshops at the MoRE can educate the public as a preventative step and thereby help people identify, report, and avoid white nationalist propaganda and recruitment. With grant funding this program could be part of the process of deradicalizing white nationalists.

In the recent past, the nation's citizens, rather than use museums to process and learn from national trauma, instead use them to participate in a comfort culture and consumption of mass-produced goods, purchasing items like snow globes or teddy bears from site gift shops to shape memory. Here cultural memory, tourism, consumerism, paranoia, security, and kitsch meet as part of the public's deeper investment in the concept of innocent victimhood in American culture and a mediated depoliticization of the event. Marita Sturken labeled these visitors *tourists of history*. The process of creating innocence after the fact, as in the case of Oklahoma City when McVeigh was portrayed as a mentally unstable lone wolf, hides the role that empire and violence have had in shaping tragedy in the United States. For example, a narrative of innocence perpetuated by the media and the Oklahoma City National Memorial erased Timothy McVeigh's militia and military past and the recognition of the bombing as coordinated by homegrown terrorism. McVeigh's execution and the memorial, both sites of mourning that encouraged family members and survivors to grieve and offered little historical reflection, were the "twinned response" to the bombing itself.[88]

Another workshop could use *The Clansman*, the novel that inspired *The Birth of a Nation*, to introduce *The Turner Diaries*, the text driving the modern movement. Because Wilson knew the novel's author, Thomas Dixon, and watched the film in the White House, both works are featured in the space discussed in chapter 7. The modern white power movement retained a fondness for the film. As late as the 1970s, the Knights of the Ku Klux Klan, led by David Duke, held bicoastal screenings of *Birth* in North Carolina and California, prompting violent clashes with protesters. Just as the novel and film framed the violence of Reconstruction as a moral and political good, the 1970s novel *The Turner Diaries* has inspired the violence accompanying contemporary white power ideology. The book's plot centers on a coup d'état led by white-power paramilitary forces to exterminate non-whites and create a white nation. The Oklahoma City bombing bore striking similarities to events in the book, including the plan for the bomb McVeigh built with unidentified accomplices. He not only carried and read *The Turner Diaries* but also sold it on the gun show circuit.[89] Two events from the insurrection on January 6 mirror scenes depicted in the book. The mob erected a gallows, where people took selfies and assaulted journalists, and fashioned a noose from a television camera cord. Someone else scratched the words "Murder the media" on a door. These actions echo the novel's "Day of the Rope," a public hanging of "traitors," including congressmen, interracial couples, and journalists. Most alarming, *The Turner Diaries* includes a mortar attack on the Capitol to show not-yet-radicalized people the vulnerability of federal sites. The revolutionaries in the novel do not intend to orchestrate a mass casualty event. Militants symbolically replicating the mortar attack at the January 6 Capitol insurrection viewed their penetration as a similar victory. Those that invaded the Capitol forced legislators to hide or flee as they raided offices and effectively halted the official tallying of electoral votes.[90]

Trump's speech preceding the riot claimed that catching fraud during the 2020 election allowed for a "very different" set of rules. Red Shirts and white southern Democrats believed the same. He warned that without strength and further voter disenfranchisement, the crowd would lose their country and the Republican Party. He endorsed voter ID and specifically mentioned the threat posed by Stacey Abrams's success in voter mobilization and the election of two Democrat senators, one Black and the other Jewish, from the red state of Georgia.[91] As during Reconstruction, Black political power and voters posed a threat to white power. In an echo of the Red Shirt battle cry "Hampton or Hell!," Trump warned, "We fight like hell. And if you don't fight like hell, you're not going to have a country anymore." Then the mob exited the rally with the President's exhortation to walk down to Capitol, where violence, led by militias and white power activists, expectedly ensued.[92]

CHAPTER 6

Interpreting the Craft

Doing Reconstruction History

When MoRE weekend docent Halie Brazier broached the subject of crafting history, we were near the end of her interview at Speakeasy, a now defunct bar among a cluster of stores, restaurants, coffee shops, and bars called Five Points adjacent to the University of South Carolina. A popular spot for history graduate students to unwind, Speakeasy was not an ideal location for recording, but the familiar space and a cocktail were perfect for rapport building between two students who attended USC's public history program a few years apart. We had been the only customers when we began the interview, but people had trickled in slowly, and the jazz trio playing that evening was warming up. Reflecting on her public history training and giving tours, Halie mused that the MoRE "is really about the craft of history, which is what you don't get a lot of in museums where they just tell you what happened and that's the end." The MoRE is "a place," she continued, "where you could talk a lot about how historians can really do their craft and what it means to be a historian and what interpretation means." She laughed as she concluded, "I don't know how deep you can get into that in the tour itself, but you can get a little bit of those discussions going."[1]

This chapter builds on chapter 4's focus on domestic workers, where I discussed, first, the role of historical scholarship in filling historical gaps for visitors to the Museum of the Reconstruction Era and, second, popular culture's influence on HHM tours. I defined the *Downton Abbey* effect, whereby docent and visitor negotiated what domestic labor was like by building on their knowledge of the popular television program. This conversation risked reducing Black laborers in the Wilson home to wage workers only, without emphasis on how their Blackness shaped their experience. As chapter 4 demonstrated, in the absence of detailed information about domestics that worked for the Wilson family in Columbia, the scholarly literature on the history of Black women during Reconstruction proved invaluable in interpreting the two people who made up the Wilson staff. Thavolia Glymph's *Out of the House of Bondage* helped visitors better understand how Black women negotiated their labor and citizenship in the post–Civil War world. Ample scholarship on sexual assault as a Reconstruction-era political tool and form of terror also illuminated a gap in the MoRE's script and training.

The MoRE tour also benefited from drawing on the general and state historiography of Reconstruction in the difficult transition that MoRE docents faced coming from the "Red Shirt room," detailed in the previous chapter, to the final semiguided space in the home. This chapter addresses how docents and the interpretive team slowly constructed this transition. Literary house museums employ tragic narrative modes to create compelling interpretations that challenge the dominance of a traditional HHM tour.[2] The MoRE's interpretation also draws on tragedy and demonstrates the potential of adopting and adapting best practices from literary houses. Docents had the demanding task of bringing the visitor from a tragic narrative of election fraud and white violence to the final exhibit and tour space, which needed to explain Wilson the historian, his intellectual relationship with Reconstruction, and the impending era of Jim Crow. The most successful docents focused on how historians professionally produced Reconstruction history. Docents who earned public history degrees and volunteers with advanced degrees crafted a tragic narrative of Reconstruction literature for visitors whose understanding of the period was shaped by film and history books that distilled white supremacist interpretations. Most visitors arrive at the MoRE with no understanding of how history is constructed and revised or how the academic defense of Reconstruction, which was supported by Wilson as a historian, fused with popular culture. The decision to use docent and exhibit interpretation to teach the craft of Reconstruction history to visitors and overturn outdated scholarship serves as an example of Hilary Iris Lowe's call for HHMs to adopt the innovative interpretive techniques of literary house museums that create engagement points for visitors to make meaningful and enduring connections between authors and their books.

A Difficult Transition: From Political Terrorism to a White Supremacist Narrative of Reconstruction

Docents, the interpretive team, and consultants understood before opening that the last bedroom, devoted to historical memory, would be the most taxing for docents and visitors alike. Education consultant Daniella Cook warned that the space, centered on memories of Reconstruction and Wilson, required more than any of the other rooms on the tour a clear transition to explain artifacts and central themes. Many visitors, she cautioned Historic Columbia, would be both physically and intellectually fatigued, especially while still "processing the content and imagery" of racial violence shown in the Red Shirt room. She recommended "explicit staging directions." Standing near the mantle by Wilson's quote about Reconstruction would allow docents to speak of "Wilson's uniqueness as a president of firsts"—the first historian, the first doctorate holder, and the first southern president elected since James Buchanan—and how these firsts "shaped his understanding of Reconstruction."[3]

The previous bedroom devoted to the election of 1876 and the Red Shirts was both a blessing and a curse when it came to transitioning. Weekend docent Casey Lee believed the space to be the strongest in the home because it elicited the best responses from visitors. Conversation between the docent and guests often spilled into the last room on memory or resurfaced while the tour group walked back to the gift shop.[4] One interpretive challenge for docents was conveying the continuity between Reconstruction and Jim Crow. Heather Bacon-Rogers drew connections between Black Codes and Jim Crow and then let visitors explore.[5] Three docents reminded visitors that the antebellum white elites coordinated their violent revolt to resume power. Essentially, weekend docent Halie Brazier explained, "the South hadn't learned any lessons."[6] But volunteer John Clark thought the longer process of redemption, the term given to the period following Reconstruction when white Democrats returned to power, got lost. The "Black base" of the Republican Party did not disappear overnight. It took years to consolidate white control. Black congressmen such as Robert Smalls served as late as 1885. Furthermore, he wondered how active the Klan was and remained unsure of the extent of lynchings post-Reconstruction.[7]

For three trained public historians, the final space opened a dialogue about the craft of history to help visitors understand why interpretation changes over time, either because of new primary sources or asking new questions of the material. This conversation made the house special in Brazier's eyes. Other HHMs missed the opportunity to show "how historians can really do their craft and what it means to be a historian and what interpretation means." For Lee the transition was easy, because she framed it in terms of "who writes history, what narratives get passed along and why the legacy of Reconstruction" was initially viewed as an abuse of federal power and a disaster in granting the rights of Black citizenship. Jennifer Gunter introduced herself to visitors as a historian, which helped validate her tour narrative. She conveyed her love for the time period but could also cite historians from the Dunning School, who framed Reconstruction as a failure in the early twentieth century, through the current era.[8] These guided exchanges helped visitors understand both why they had learned Reconstruction was a fiasco and why modern historians framed the period as the first civil rights movement.

Prior to their arrival to the house, visitors knew little of Woodrow Wilson's life as an academic or that he wrote history akin to that produced by other white scholars interpreting Reconstruction as a colossal failure. Wilson wielded academic and political power that placed him at the center of this discussion. Nonetheless, a concise explanation of his role proved difficult for the interpretive team and for docents not trained in historiography. Wilson was among the first generation of southern students and historians "scientifically" trained in history and politics. A leader in the professionalization of history and a founding member of the American Historical Association, German-trained scholar Herbert Baxter Adams launched his seminar on historical and political science at the Johns Hopkins University in 1880. Wilson was one of Adams's students and received one of the university's first history doctorates. Professionalized history drew intellectual men that might have otherwise joined the ministry, certainly a fate that could have easily plucked Wilson from politics given his family's professional ties with the church. This cadre of well-respected, professionally trained historians, including Wilson's professor J. Franklin Jameson and the distinguished Frederick Jackson Turner, not only believed that national unity drove American history and the story of freedom but also drew on this unity to promote regional reconciliation following the Civil War. Wilson and his generation of historians, and white southerners in general, cemented the Lost Cause and a white supremacist narrative of Reconstruction during this era. Part of the work of the MoRE is overturning this narrative that professional history, with its scientific methodology, appropriated, canonizing Reconstruction as a catastrophe and depicting Black southerners as inferior. Part of this generation were John W. Burgess and his protégé William A. Dunning, founders of the Dunning School. Burgess helped found the field of political science, while Dunning established the fields of southern and Reconstruction history, drawing New South students to Columbia University.[9]

The history of Reconstruction scholarship is complex and difficult for MoRE docents to concisely and clearly deliver at the end of intricate tour. Both docents and visitors are in what Ed Ayers called "the Bermuda Triangle of American History, a place where we lose our bearings, where the usual American stories of progress and success simply do not work."[10] Seduced by the Lost Cause, Dunning and like-minded historians varied only by degrees. The Dunning School scholars were not unique in their belief in white superiority and social Darwinism. Their scholarship reflected attitudes about race and Jim Crow held by white academics and many in the white community, all of which were attempts to reconcile new immigration patterns, imperialism, and urbanization.[11] Similar to Adams, who pedagogically colonized colleges with the placement of his graduate students, the Dunning School transformed the popular memory of Reconstruction as a tragedy into scholarship, many tenets of which endure. Though the school is dismissed as racist today, it played a formidable role in professionalizing history on the graduate level in the United States.[12] With Dunning at the helm at Columbia, his followers and the state studies they produced warned of the dangers of Black men, controlled by Republican carpetbaggers and scalawags, who were ill prepared for citizenship. This alliance elevated racial discord and bred corruption until white political terrorism restored order. This interpretation fueled national reconciliation. According to Grace Hale, a "culture of segregation" first commandeered Reconstruction and its historiography to construct a "common whiteness" born out of the period's failures that could heal a fifty-year old-wound following the Civil War and promote a new American empire. For half a century, white southerners and historians considered the Dunning School gospel. The interpretation influenced Mary Simms Oliphant's South Carolina textbooks and Louise Jones DuBose's WPA South Carolina state guidebook, as discussed in chapters 3 and 5. The Dunning School's infiltration of public history and popular memory, via novels like Thomas Dixon's *The Clansman* and the blockbuster film adaptation *The Birth of a Nation*, ensured that Reconstruction would represent the "darkest days" of American history, not just in scholarship but also in the public's imagination as well. Marking the period as a deviation in the American experiment rather than the beginning of centralized, expanded government, citizenship for Black Americans, and the Republican Party, these narratives strengthened white supremacy and Jim Crow.[13] A newer historical turn argues that the Dunning School was not as impactful on shaping public memory as the field contends. It did not create the myths and tragedy of Reconstruction; rather it gave scholarly weight to an accepted white narrative and forged national consensus. Woodrow Wilson, a scholarly product of the same social and education system, gave the same weight and approval to *The Birth of a Nation* when he screened it in the White House, which had a far more lasting impact on the white supremacist memory of Reconstruction among white Americans than anything produced by the Dunning School.[14]

Five significant works that shaped Reconstruction in South Carolina historiography are on display in the final bedrooms of the home: James Shepherd Pike's *The Prostrate State* (1874), Thomas Dixon's *The Clansman* (1905), John S. Reynolds's *Reconstruction in South Carolina: 1865–1867* (1905), William Sinclair's *The Aftermath of Slavery* (1905), and Albert B. Williams's popular personal account *Hampton and His Red Shirts: South Carolina's Deliverance in 1876* (1935). All but *The Prostrate State* are in the Wilson bedroom. Before the 1890s Reconstruction historiography consisted only of partisan political writings. This was the case for Reconstruction historiography in South Carolina as well. The first was Pike's *The Prostrate State* in 1874, a contemporary account that originally appeared as a *New York Tribune* series. The MoRE panel "Politics and the Press" discusses the book, noting that Pike "spoke almost exclusively with Reconstruction opponents" in his

"Republican critique."[15] The second book, *Governor Chamberlain's Administration in South Carolina: A Chapter of Reconstruction in the Southern States*, was a defense of the governor's administration written by his friend Walter Allen. A 1901 essay Chamberlain penned for an *Atlantic Monthly* series on Reconstruction rebuked Republican rule for its corruption, ineptness, and dependence on Black votes. Though he denounced the methods of redemption, he sympathized with white southerners' responses to Republican rule.[16]

The Dunning School first established general facts about Reconstruction, emphasizing religious division and hardships. It also praised some aspects of Reconstruction, like education and rebuilding. Dunning approached Reconstruction generally with a national lens. He saw it as key to fostering reunion and accelerating nationalism, even if the federal government overreached, and cast corruption in a national framework. Dunning students, unlike their mentor, focused on local or sectional issues, which resulted in what revisionist historian Kenneth M. Stampp concluded in the 1960s was a tragic narrative with four acts. First, Radical Republicans abandoned President Abraham Lincoln's plans for a quick reunification in order to punish secessionists and maintain economic and political power. Second, though white southerners acknowledged the demise of slavery and the Confederacy, Radical Republicans refused to except President Andrew Johnson's Reconstruction and rejected new state governments and the southerners elected to Congress. Third, with control of Congress after the 1866 elections, Radical Republicans initiated their version of Reconstruction by vetoing Johnson and ultimately impeaching him and, during Ulysses S. Grant's two terms, militarily occupying the South and granting suffrage to freedmen while denying it to whites. This resulted in corrupt state governments run by scalawags and carpetbaggers. Lastly, Democrats brought redemption and the return of "honest government" in the 1870s legally or by force, which was cemented in the disputed election of 1876 that ended Reconstruction.[17]

In 1905 two academically trained historians from Johns Hopkins University, Thomas Dixon and John Porter Hollis, joined the conversation on Reconstruction in South Carolina. Dixon's contribution was the novel *The Clansman*, a copy of which is on display at the MoRE; Hollis's was his dissertation, *The Early Period of Reconstruction in South Carolina*, a work of the Dunning School. Hollis's interpretations of race relied less on sound evidentiary analysis and more on oral traditions. By contrast, John S. Reynolds's *Reconstruction in South Carolina: 1865–1867* (1905), first published in the *State* newspaper as a weekly series, moved away from narrative knowledge to scientific knowledge, minus footnotes and citations, as the first book to cover the period's entire chronology in a detailed manner. Though the tone of the book mirrored Dunning and exhibited some professional historical technique,

Reynolds was a South Carolina Supreme Court librarian with no direct association with the Dunning School. A copy of his book is also on exhibit in the MoRE.[18] One notable Dunning student, Paul Leland Haworth, did contest the arguments of his New South peers. An Indiana Quaker, Haworth's more moderate thoughts on Black citizenship and condemnation of violence and fraud thwarted his career and prestige. He denounced white South Carolinians' acceptance and use of brutal domestic terror, including the Hamburg and Ellenton massacres, and blamed Democratic fraud for South Carolina's 1876 election results, which had national implications in the federal election. He made an implicit argument to return Black Americans' rights by giving historical context to their present-day plight and exposing the culpability of white South Carolinians.[19]

Woodrow Wilson, before becoming president, also contributed to the scholarly literature on Reconstruction, which needed to be addressed by the MoRE. At the dawn of the twentieth century, Wilson published what was at that time a moderate, reconciliationist southern interpretation of the Civil War and Reconstruction. His *Division and Reunion* (1893), a supposedly unbiased war history that placed blame on both sides, and *A History of the American People* (1902) promoted a dominant, familiar narrative of carpetbagger villains, southern victims, and Klan rescuers, although the latter were not always righteous in their activities.[20] A MoRE panel contextualizes Wilson's place within the historiography. It includes a caption about his 1901 essay "The Reconstruction of the Southern States," which Wilson wrote for the same *Atlantic* series as Chamberlain's Republican rebuke. The panel notes that the essay "reflected the scholarship that prevailed at colleges throughout the nation during this time" and "focused primarily on the forging of a new nationalist spirit." Though Wilson was less reluctant than his predecessors to "glorify the violence of the time," he was guilty of presenting a "romanticized . . . relationship between the North and the South."[21] His interpretation was far more developed and derogatory with respect to Black citizenship than the panel could convey. He wrote that the Civil War made Americans fully conscious for the first time of a "national spirit" and unity that had been building. Thirty years after Reconstruction's end, he argued, the United States had moved on, "lost its passion, forgot its anxieties." Historians, without partisanship, could finally discuss this "dark chapter," which was constitutionally significant. First, the Union was legally indestructible. Only people seceded. More important, a "change of air" allowed a radical Republican Congress to usurp executive power by latching onto the failure of the first state constitutional conventions to protect the rights of recently freed people. Uncontrollable and devoid of a basic understanding of liberty and freedom, Black Americans "had the full advantage of the federal power" through the Freedman's Bureau, which promised education and property, and the forced ratification of the Reconstruction Amendments, which legally recognized the freedom, citizenship, and suffrage already being granted. The "dangerous intoxication of an absolute triumph" yielded generals who ruled the military districts. But far worse were Republican rule and "negro majorities" in states like South Carolina, made possible by disenfranchising the "better whites." Wilson wrote that thankfully the "traces of Reconstruction ha[d] worn away," allowing several southern states to reform education and suffrage laws in what became Jim Crow.[22]

Outside the Dunning School, white authors writing on Reconstruction in South Carolina spent three decades debating the merits and importance of Gen. Martin Gary to the 1876 campaign.[23] However, in the 1930s an economic turn in interpreting Reconstruction that also included Marxists like W. E. B Du Bois dramatically shifted the historiography and competed with the blockbuster book and movie *Gone with the Wind*. Within this economic turn, *South Carolina during Reconstruction* (1932) by Francis Butler Simkins and Robert Hilliard Woody was not only the first complete state study by professional historians but also the first book by white scholars to chip away at the Dunning School. In what could be considered an ironic turn, it won the American Historical Association's prestigious John H. Dunning Prize. Though not as sympathetic to freed people as historical assessments by Black scholars, the book penned by two white men from the Carolinas was a marked improvement for white academia. Simkins, who befriended a Brazilian historian and had some training with Dunning while at Columbia, demonstrated the changing nature of the field as new ideas on race and class emerged. The economic turn also included an intellectual field of radicals' Reconstruction, a component of the biracial Southern Popular Front, that marked the first effort to apply a biracial, class-based lens to the historical analysis of Reconstruction. Other radicals' Reconstruction interpretations were the commercially successful novel *Freedom Road* by Howard Fast, depicting a South Carolina plantation turned cooperative farm with white and Black workers, and James S. Allen's broader study *Reconstruction: The Battle for Democracy*, which like Du Bois's writing gave agency to freed people, who were a new addition to the proletariat and would be targeted by the industrial bourgeoisie.[24]

Although the revisionism was already underway, in 1947 the tragic narrative of the Dunning School came to an end with E. Merton Coulter's *The South during Reconstruction*, which failed to incorporate more recent scholarship from Simkins and Woody and Du Bois. What distinguished the Dunning School from revisionist historians who dismantled them was not so much the sources and methodology but their views not only on race but also class and state power. In fact, the revisionists used the primary sources identified and published by the Dunning School. Bruce Baker identifies Howard K. Beale's 1940 article "On Rewriting Reconstruction History" as "the clear beginning of a revisionist school of Reconstruction historiography," which was an acceleration of Simkins and Woody's work. In 1955 Beale's student C. Vann Woodward, an early member of Southern Front and an activist historian, published *The Strange Career of Jim Crow*, a takedown of Dunning that argued the contemporary mid-century civil rights movement, a second Reconstruction, would be more fruitful. The white supremacist narrative of Reconstruction, even if southern whites clung desperately to it, made no sense to others whose perceptions of racism changed.[25] Revisionists presented the merits of Radical Republican Reconstruction and argued that it remained, as Eric Foner would say, unfinished. Reconstruction historiography flourished for three decades following the publication of his synthetic "dominant narrative," *Reconstruction: America's Unfinished Revolution*.[26]

More recent scholarship by post-revisionists contends that Reconstruction was overturned, not incomplete, and failed. The mid-1990s brought women's history to Reconstruction, illuminating households and sexual violence. Historiography expanded knowledge of state-sanctioned violence in general and the centrality of sexual violence to terrorism. The first two decades of the twenty-first century significantly increased awareness of educational history, particularly for Black students and teachers. Economic questions about Reconstruction's place in merchant and industrial capitalism and workers as feudal peasants or wage laborers advanced the field until the early 1990s. Historians now have a better understanding of white coalition building among Republicans at the expense of Black members and physical and economic challenges faced by veterans of the United States Colored Troops during Reconstruction, who struggled to receive military pay, gain civilian unemployment, apply for pensions, and deal with disabilities.[27] The scholarship spread beyond the South's imagined borders to Indian Territory and abroad, though like memory and Reconstruction, far slower than the Civil War field; yet this turn improved our knowledge of American foreign policy, imperialism, and settler colonialism. Ayers warned that the global perception of the United States is that it is a "carpetbagger nation" that should heed the lessons of post–Civil War Reconstruction "as we look out upon a world we are tempted to remake." These lessons concern the South's size and varied geography, race, armed resistance and local power dynamics, religion, and how a popular opposition narrative can overwhelm an outside force. US policy in the age of New Imperialism determined that areas such as the Philippines inhabited by people of color, as with freed Black men and women, were incapable of running democratic governments. World War I provided Wilson and the United States with the opportunity to rebuild democracy and white civilization. For a brief moment in the Western Hemisphere, Reconstruction foreign policy implemented a new Monroe Doctrine to challenge empire and expel slavery. Brazilian abolitionists in the 1880s disseminated a "romantic narrative" of Reconstruction's success as part of its argument. The narrative served as a foil to both contemporary economic, social, and political problems in Brazil and planter narratives that warned of the further disorder emancipation would generate. However, colonizers in England, Canada, Brazil, South Africa, and Australia, like the Jim Crow South, employed a white supremacist narrative of Reconstruction to defend not only white supremacy but also their empires.[28]

Today Reconstruction historiography continues to grow, expanding the beginning and end of the era's chronology to the Civil War and Gilded Age and exploring multiple freedoms, both macro and micro, and multiple Reconstructions.[29] Digitization has provided primary sources, such as Freedmen's Bureau records, and new methodology, which has also benefited South Carolina's Reconstruction historiography. For example, Elaine Frantz's use of network analysis and legal records uncovered the origin and membership of the Klan in Union County, and the interactive digital humanities web and mobile site *Reconstruction 360* provides primary sources and concise engagement tools to teach the public.[30] Unfortunately, the public's knowledge of Reconstruction lags behind modern historical understanding. Historiography alone will not ignite a new revolution or finish a long civil rights movement that continues to fight for the enforcement of the Reconstruction Amendments. It will need public-facing sites and projects like the MoRE.[31]

That the second generation of post–World War II historians articulating Reconstruction fell short was not a new idea. The Black backlash to the white supremacist interpretation of Reconstruction in universities and popular culture was immediate and unremitting though less impactful in the academy. The MoRE thus curated the literature ignored by white scholars. Black journalists, historians, and filmmakers countered Dunning School narratives whenever they could. Excluded from white mainstream memory making in South Carolina, the progressive Black perspective emerged alongside the Dunning interpretation as a credible counternarrative that combined oral traditions with traditional documentary sources neglected by white historians.[32] A MoRE panel introduced visitors to William Sinclair, a former University of South Carolina student when it was temporarily integrated during Reconstruction, who protested Woodrow Wilson's support of racial segregation in federal workplaces. The exhibit also includes Sinclair's historical counternarrative *The Aftermath of Slavery* (1905), which he published while serving a foundational role in the NAACP and as a critical member of the

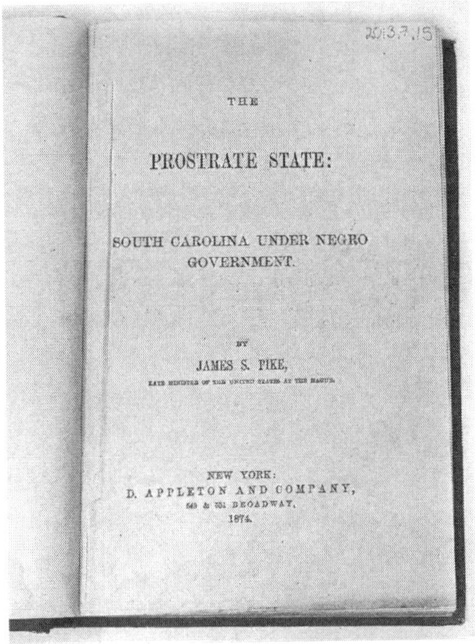

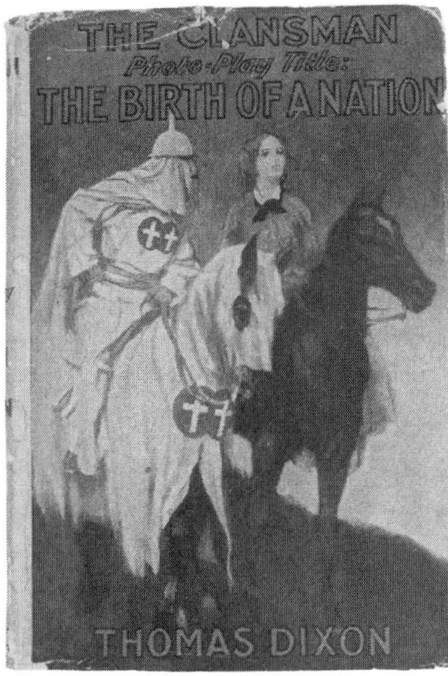

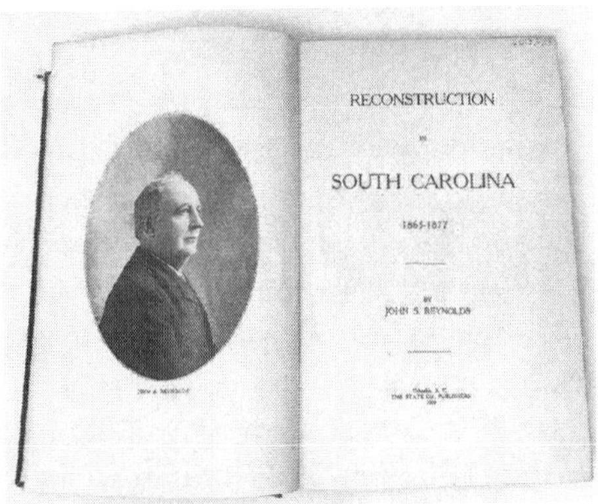

Figure 17. These early texts are significant works that shaped Reconstruction in South Carolina historiography and are on display in the final bedrooms of the Woodrow Wilson Family Home. Sinclair's book was a historical counternarrative that immediately answered Thomas Dixon's *The Clansman*.

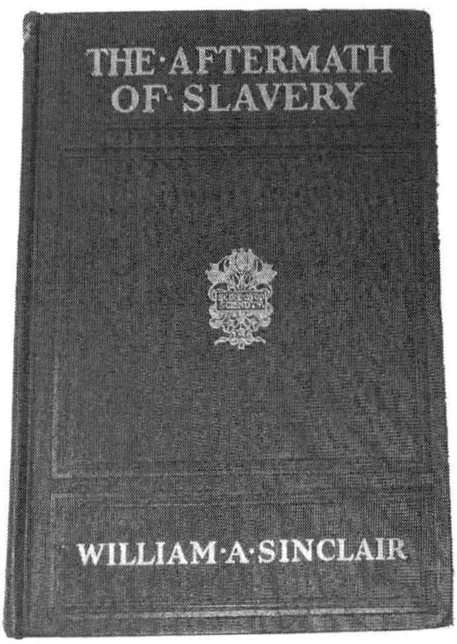

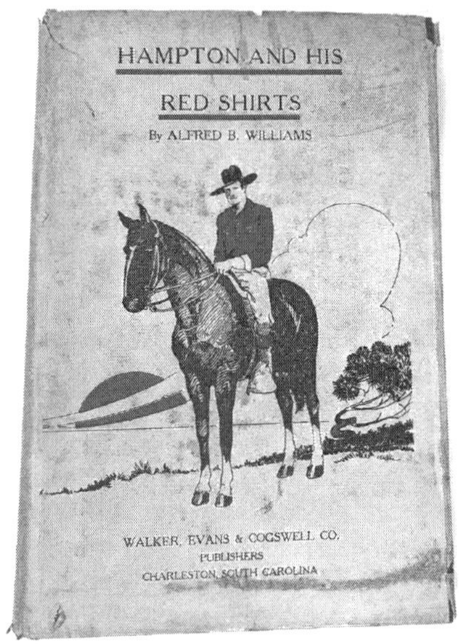

Niagara Movement. The book "answered" Dixon's depiction of Reconstruction and the racist rhetoric of his novels like *The Clansman*.[33] John Lynch's memoir *The Facts of Reconstruction*, published in 1913, the year Wilson took office, constructed a memory based on his experiences as a Reconstruction-era state legislator in Mississippi and US representative to counter biased accounts. Disputing the myth of "Negro domination," Lynch argued that the South created a biracial democracy and that Black suffrage and the Fifteenth Amendment were good for democracy. Furthermore, Republican control was a success, while white Democrats exacerbated racial tensions that led to Jim Crow. He directly countered the Dunning School and James Ford Rhodes, whose *History of the United States from the Compromise of 1850 to the Final Restoration of Home Rule at the South in 1877* influenced Burgess and Dunning. Lynch hoped that rectifying the historical record would lead to Black social and political gains. The Black press, including the *Chicago Defender* and the NAACP's *Crisis*, endorsed works like Lynch's. Carter G. Woodson and the newly founded *Journal of Negro History* continued publishing positive interpretations of Reconstruction. Woodson's Association for the Study of Negro Life and History hired Black scholar and social worker Alrutheus Ambush Taylor, whose research led to his publishing *The Negro in South Carolina during Reconstruction* in 1924. Part of the first generation of South Carolina–focused historians, Taylor centered Black Americans and emphasized the cooperation between both races in daily life and labor. Works like these, but particularly Taylor's, made contrasting memories available to the first white historians undermining the Dunning School in the 1930s, such as Woody and Simkins. However, W. E. B. Du Bois was the most well-known critic. He sustained an indictment of white historians of Reconstruction for over three decades.[34]

Black scholars like Taylor were outnumbered in academia until the civil rights movement, but Du Bois published extensively on the subject all the same. He penned an essay for the same 1901 *Atlantic Monthly* series that featured Wilson's and Chamberlain's essay and a restrained concluding essay by Dunning, and his *Souls of Black Folk* (1903) positively interpreted Reconstruction. In December 1909, at the AHA's annual meeting in New York City, Du Bois took up the gauntlet and challenged white historians' interpretations of Reconstruction, appearing at a session along with Dunning. White historians, Du Bois insisted, had overlooked how quickly freed people learned and engaged in citizenship with little support from the federal government. They were not bystanders. Black voters and legislators, via legislation and state constitutions, ushered in democratic government, free public schools, and revolutionary social legislation. Du Bois reported that Dunning praised the paper, which was later published in the *American Historical Review*. Though largely ignored by white historians, Du Bois's arguments culminated in the 1935 book *Black Reconstruction in America*, which synthesized the work of Taylor, Simkins, and Woody in his reinterpreted response.[35]

Though no tour could distill Reconstruction's historiographical turns to the extent detailed above, docents could draw from the historiographical well in the last room on the MoRE tour to contest the public's perception of Reconstruction shaped by education and popular culture. For example, Brazier pointed out Hillary Clinton's Reconstruction gaffe on the presidential campaign trail in January 2016. In response to a question, Clinton named Abraham Lincoln as the president she most admired. She then launched into a defense of her answer that could have come from Dixon, Dunning, or Wilson. Wilson speculated in "Reconstruction of the Southern States" that "had Mr. Lincoln lived, perhaps the whole of the delicate business might have been through with dignity, good temper, and simplicity of method." Lincoln and Johnson, had they remained architects of Reconstruction and not been thwarted by assassination and congressional obstruction, would have provided a smoother transition and kept white rule. Johnson simply lacked Lincoln's pragmatism, charm, and leadership skills.[36] For Wilson, in fashioning the memory of the executive and legislative branches pitted against one another for control of Reconstruction, Lincoln had to be right if congressional Reconstruction was to be remembered as so wrong. Furthermore, Reconstruction had to be wrong to defend Jim Crow. Wilson's interpretation lived on in Clinton's gaffe as well as comments MoRE visitors also made about Lincoln's untimely death. For Clinton, America might have been "a little less rancorous, a little more forgiving and tolerant," and reunited more quickly had Lincoln lived, she claimed. Instead the United States got Reconstruction, Jim Crow, and some "totally discouraged and defiant" southerners. She believed Lincoln "could have very well put us on a different path." The only difference between Clinton and Wilson was a negative connotation of Jim Crow. Her team quickly clarified that America might have been in a "better place" if the federal government had not abandoned Reconstruction before achieving "equality, justice, and reconciliation," paving the way for the "disgraceful era of Jim Crow." The legacy of "racist efforts against Reconstruction," her team explained, could still be seen in modern voter suppression.[37]

Wilson grew up in an environment hostile to Lincoln yet fashioned a positive historical interpretation as an academic to indict congressional Reconstruction. The MoRE does not detail this transformation of Lincoln from villain to martyr in its exhibit; however, a panel illustrating the city hall and opera house building and supplemental information in the script offer docents a local anecdote to explain the mythical Reconstruction narrative that

Lincoln's death ensured Reconstruction would fail and that white southerners believed he would have treated them fairly. *The Birth of a Nation* devoted an entire scene to this interpretation and Lincoln's assassination. White Democrats pointed to the opera house's construction as an example of lavish Republic spending, but this did not stop them from flocking to it in droves to catch a glimpse of the most popular Shakespearean actor in the nation.[38] As momentum was building among Democrats to overturn Reconstruction, Edwin Booth came to Columbia's opera house on January 26, 1876, for a one-day engagement of *Hamlet*. White Columbians, so excited to see the brother of the man who shot Lincoln, literally stampeded the ticket agent within several minutes of sales opening. The show sold out quickly, prompting locals' unsuccessful attempts to scalp tickets for five times their value. Booth privately confessed that he hoped to never return to the South, for his fanatical welcome stemmed as much from his brother John's infamy as his own critical fame.[39]

Public historians trained in historiography are comfortable discussing complex and conflicting interpretations of history in museum settings, making them incredibly valuable as frontline staff. Volunteer docents at Historic Columbia, however, demonstrate the need for institutions to clarify the nature of the historical discipline not only to visitors but also to guides less familiar with how history is crafted and its interpretive turns. Cook advised docents to set the stage immediately for framing the complexity of both Wilson's legacy and Reconstruction memory further explored in the exhibit film, panels, and exhibit cases.[40] The interpretive team continuously reworked the transition statement to bind the two memories of Reconstruction and Wilson together, to explain how both facilitated national reconciliation and acknowledge Wilson's racial views and discriminatory policies. This connected thematically to panel text on how "especially proud" white Democratic southerners were of Wilson. Not only was he the first southern president elected since the Civil War, but his "academic laurels and progressive policies" worked to combat "stereotypes of regional backwardness." The script countered that, though many white Americans thought like Wilson, some of his contemporaries worked to promote racial equality and fight discrimination. Some fatigued visitors who spent less time with the room's exhibit panels might miss that local Black citizens "vigorously protested" showings of *Birth* or that the "Columbia City Council asked a theatre to cancel" a World War I– era showing of the film "in recognition of black contributions" to the war effort.[41] Ultimately, months of giving tours revealed that the transition statement was better suited to conclude the tour. A basic transition statement emerged that empowered docents to select the evidence they wanted to use: "As we enter this next bedroom, we see that memories of Reconstruction and of Woodrow Wilson as President have been formulated and evolved over several generations."[42] Pinpointing a successful transition proved difficult, because it set up the last exhibit film. The film sparked the greatest interpretive battles in the room and the tour, which are discussed in the next chapter.

MoRE docents' attempts to transition from voter suppression and white violence to the historical memory of Reconstruction provide examples of how HHMs can employ both tragic narrative and the craft of history to make meaningful connections for visitors. In the May 2015 issue of the *Public Historian* that focused on the plight and future of HHMs, Hilary Iris Lowe called for more narrative storytelling in house museums and asked how they might incorporate method and historiography. These narrative-centered tours engage visitors with emotional content and strengthen historical interpretation, giving audiences the ability to make correlations between the tour, the past and the present, and their lives. Though Lowe disputes Hayden White's contention that, like all stories, historical narratives are fiction, she adopts his premise that historians depend on narratives and employ one of four plot categories: romance, satire, comedy, or tragedy. White's provocative argument emerged when Freeman Tilden's *Interpreting Our Heritage* (1957) was at its peak in terms of its impact on living history and HHM interpretation. Both insisted that crafting narrative is an artistic, not scientific, endeavor. Lowe analyzes tour narratives at four literary house museums and classifies each home based on White's four categories. Lowe claims public historians using storytelling driven by history and narrative will be cognizant of narrative modes influencing interpretation and "draw attention to the process, the choices, and . . . [the] historian's craft." The MoRE demonstrates this by asking audiences to complicate their understanding of Reconstruction and interpret the past like a modern historian does, to draw their own conclusions based on the tour narrative.[43]

Lowe makes a compelling case that the successful homes of literary giants not only provide visitors with space for reflection, speak to multigenerational audiences, maximize university and school partnerships, and address the history of race, gender, and sexuality, but also, most significantly, use fiction to present diverse perspectives of the past. She argues that the narrative modes of tragedy and satire work in academic monographs but remain off-putting to museums whose audience expect infotainment or that are not at sites of violence, such as the internment camp Manzanar, where the visitor anticipates a tragic narrative. The tragic narrative is one example of melodrama, which became a popular literary and theatrical form in the nineteenth century. Melodrama in theater studies also encompasses comedy, tragedy, and tragicomedy. By mid-century melodrama in the United States shifted toward sentimentality and courted middle-class audiences, though critics disparaged its important role in providing public discourse on cultural, political, and economic transformations ranging from gender to nationalism and imperialism. A "drama of excess," melodrama often included spectacular sets and settings, a complicated plot, and thrills. They were popular with women, a moral drama between good heroes and evil villains. The MoRE is a rare HHM that offers a tragic narrative, though literary house museums and artists' homes often do. Similarly public historians can employ tragic characters and their impending doom to illuminate limitations and the real conditions of the past. The MoRE, in abandoning its shrine to Woodrow Wilson, shattered the HHM's conventional romantic mode and prepared visitors to think judiciously about Reconstruction and contest their previous assumptions about the period framed by the Dunning School and popular culture.[44]

Lowe's research on literary house museums revealed that these sites surpassed HHMs in elucidating how complex the craft of composing history is, including methodology and constructing narrative. Historians take comfort in the idea that their analysis is scientific—a legacy of the professionalization of the field in the late nineteenth and early twentieth centuries. This process supposedly protected historians from bias and speculation. However, the work of the Dunning School and scholars such as Eric Foner, considered the preeminent contemporary Reconstruction expert, prove that language choices and the interpretation of the same primary sources result in different narrative modes and stories. Reconstruction failed, for sure, but not because it lacked promise or because freed people were not prepared for citizenship, as the Dunning School asserted. Foner argues that Reconstruction was a failure because as a civil rights movement it remains unrealized.[45] Literary houses use history as well as, and in some cases better than, HHMs. Literary historians devour historical monographs to situate close textual study of a writer's work within the context of cultural and historical forces in that writer's life.[46] HHMs too can incorporate historical monographs into their tours to demonstrate interpretive change over time.

Lowe's four literary house examples provide fodder for understanding how docents at the MoRE were able to use fiction, historical monographs, and memoir to unpack the scholarly literature on Reconstruction. The Amherst, Massachusetts, house of Emily Dickinson uses drafts of her poetry in an interactive to facilitate guest exploration of her poems and how they were constructed. Dickinson often drafted three different word choices at different times in her poetry drafts. The wall in her bedroom lets visitors play with these word variations to craft their own version of her poems and explore multiple meanings. The exercise reinforces the fluidity of her poetry, an interpretation of Dickinson scholars, and how historical understanding is framed by time, which can expand or revise knowledge. The invention of Emily

Dickinson in the classroom and by editors is not unlike the Reconstruction narrative constructed by the Dunning School, the textbooks of Mary Sims Oliphant discussed in chapter 3, and films like *The Birth of a Nation*. Both the MoRE and Dickinson home help visitors dismantle and reconstruct its most famous occupants. Both museums' interpretations benefited from a relationship between scholars, staff, and exhibit designers that extended beyond consultants to collaborators. Dickinson scholars and the University of South Carolina historians and educators helped their respective sites explain that the interpretation of historical figures and events evolve and are susceptible to myth. Dickinson's isolated life in popular culture often frames her story as a tragedy, but her HHM works to challenge this narrative by highlighting Dickinson's romantic feelings for her brother's wife, Susan Huntington Gilbert Dickinson, who lived next door. Most recently, the HHM screened composer Dana Kaufman's a cappella pop opera *Emily and Sue* (dir. Ron Bashford, 2022), which was filmed at the museum.[47] Though the end of Reconstruction is a tragedy similar to Dickinson's narrative, the limited triumphs of the Black community are presented so as to provide romance to balance the tragic mode. Notably, in her assessment Lowe too wondered why similar methods had not been implemented at presidential sites.[48]

Before visiting the House of the Seven Gables in Salem, Massachusetts, Lowe read Tami Christopher's analysis of eleven tour scripts from 1910–99 delivered at the HHM. Christopher's work offered me a framework for mining the drafts of the MoRE tour scripts for examples of HHM best practices.[49] The site had modified the home to convey elements of Nathaniel Hawthorne's novel *The House of the Seven Gables* but also remade its tours to meet the politics of the present, responding to immigration, civil rights, globalization, and its own economic power in the heritage tourism market. The evolving scripts also confirmed and nullified historical narratives the house told in the past.[50] Both the MoRE and the House of the Seven Gables illuminate once-popular artistic works for modern audiences and explain why each is significant to the house. Today Hawthorne's book and *The Birth of a Nation* need to be explained by docents to visitors unfamiliar with the work beyond name recognition.[51] The next and final chapter discusses how the MoRE tour explained the relationship of Griffith's film to Reconstruction and Woodrow Wilson. Other similarities between the MoRE and the House of the Seven Gables include providing space in the script for docents to tailor their tour to meet their own interests, to respond to visitor inquiries, and, most important, to incorporate updated research and thereby present new ideas, overturn misconceptions, and corroborate contemporary historical scholarship. However, Christopher cautions public historians that audiences must be receptive to new information, which in turn must be culturally relevant before being implemented into a tour.[52] The MoRE's subject of Reconstruction is culturally, socially, and politically relevant as the nation faces modern-day citizenship and equity issues that Michelle Alexander dubbed the New Jim Crow: the end of affirmative action, police brutality, mass incarceration, voter suppression, and ruinous student loans.[53] Though Historic Columbia worried there could be a backlash to new Reconstruction information, the responses of 645 visitors to a post-tour survey dispelled this concern. Eighty-eight percent of visitors indicated that they learned new information, and 87 percent were interested in the information being presented. Visitors' comments corroborate, month after month, what especially resonated with them was how much new, interesting history they were absorbing.[54]

Over two decades ago, the Mark Twain Boyhood Home and Museum changed its interpretation from one primarily focused on Tom Sawyer to expand on Clemens's life and Hannibal, Missouri, roots. Not unlike the MoRE, which weaves a Reconstruction narrative with one about the Wilson family, the Mark Twain site blends Clemens's history with his fictional works. Both homes ask how Wilson's and Clemens's childhood homes and communities shaped their professional lives. Lowe argued that the Mark Twain House interpretation forces visitors to question: "Whose house is this? Whose version of the past is on display? Which story is 'the truth'?" These same questions could be levied at the MoRE. Whose version of Reconstruction history is exhibited? What is the "truth" about Reconstruction? The MoRE's interpretation was more radical in that the Mark Twain House initially whitewashed slavery, including within Clemens's home. The attempt to share the story of an enslaved boy Sandy, who was leased to the family, fell flat. The effort improved on that of HHMs that erase Black labor, but the introductory museum panels and a floor pallet in both the museum and home were far less challenging interpretively than the Wilson tour offered in Staunton, Virginia, discussed in chapter 4. From the beginning and throughout the first floor, the tour of Wilson's birthplace incorporated enslaved people leased by the Presbyterian Church to provide domestic labor for the family. The Mark Twain Home's romantic and satiric interpretation included a range of voices, both historical and fictional. While the MoRE privileges Black voices during Reconstruction, fictional narratives of Reconstruction as a disaster are also addressed.[55]

Mark Twain's boyhood home and the Harriet Beecher Stowe Center provide settings that use the authors' novels for unconventional interpretations. Unfortunately, Mark Twain's house in Hartford, Connecticut, next door to Stowe's home, fell short of Clemens's boyhood HHM, which focused more on the beauty of restoration and furnishing period rooms. I started the Twain tour in 2019 while attending the National Council on

Public History's annual meeting. Having seen similar HHMs an uncountable number of times before, I left after the bottom floor. I jumped on the tour of the Harriet Beecher Stowe Center and discovered one of my favorite unconventional HHMs.

The Stowe Center scrapped the traditional HHM model to create a space for conversation about social justice and collaboration with educators and scholars. When Lowe visited the site while researching her 2015 essay, docents did not explain anything about Stowe's novels or *Uncle Tom's Cabin*, despite current exhibit cases filled with the novel published in dozens of languages.[56] I even stumbled on a VHS copy of a forgotten film adaption starring Phylicia Rashad, Samuel L Jackson, and Bruce Dern. Since a 2017 renovation, the Stowe Center uses her house, its collections, and her work to facilitate a dialogue on social justice and positive change. They warn on their website: "Don't expect a traditional historic house museum! Expect a conversational, interactive tour where you can participate along with your guide." The site uses *Uncle Tom's Cabin* and the historical moment that inspired Stowe to write the novel to connect past and present. Topics of discussion range from slavery, women's history, racism, mass incarceration, immigration, and equal pay to how the name "Uncle Tom" became a racial slur.[57] The center also packages its mission into a ninety-minute program for businesses, libraries, and community groups. Other programs, such as *Her Words Changed the World*, help participants take action on a contemporary issue. Modern audiences can also join a nineteenth-century salon to discuss bias, racism, and white privilege.[58] The Stowe Center also benefits from scholarly collaboration, as did the Emily Dickinson Museum and the MoRE. Over a third of the center's board are university scholars and college teachers. The board includes Jane Wald of the Emily Dickinson Museum, indicating a pattern of literary houses utilizing narrative modes that challenge the visitor to connect a writer's works with the present.[59] Both the Stowe Center and the MoRE ask visitors to consider how tragic fictional works like *Uncle Tom's Cabin* and *The Clansman* can impact the public's understanding of contemporary issues related to social justice. Similar to the Dickinson HHM and the Stowe Center, the MoRE's narrative provoking conversation with visitors about the modern legacy of Reconstruction and interaction with historical scholarship fuel the HHM's partnership with the scholarly community. Historic Columbia's director of research, Kat Allen, asserted that the MoRE was the "catalyst" that made the public and scholars at University of South Carolina see that the organization aspired to "do good stuff" and want to collaborate. Tom Brown, who led the first scholarly lecture on Reconstruction during the first training session, covered in chapter 3, continues to participate in programming.[60]

In addition to the literary houses' success in using narrative modes and engagement with authors' work, MoRE visitor evaluations also substantiate that HHMs need not shy away from subjects that are controversial or exclude tragic moments. MoRE docents facilitating the visitor's journey through a twenty-first-century exhibit filled with abundant panels but limited objects and a dual narrative introducing new information were vital to visitor reception. They held the full attention of more than two-thirds of evaluators and engaged nearly every visitor. As a result more than four-fifths of evaluators thought sensitive issues were handled extremely well. Arousing negative emotions such as anger, fear, and sadness promotes interest because they are vivid and easier to remember, particularly if positive emotions eventually supplant the negative ones. Take, for example, the traveling exhibit "Goose Bumps: The Science of Fear," designed to be an "emotionally arousing experience" for visitors. Facing common fears, from falling to bugs, appeared to improve visitors' short-term and long-term understanding of fear and promote reflection on their experience, phobias, and fears individually and in conversation with their loved ones.[61] If exposure to everyday fears elicits such a response, a crash course in the resilience displayed and tragedy experienced during Reconstruction may forever change the way the visitor to the MoRE remembers and talks about the most misunderstood period in American history.

Combined with the interpretation of domestics in the parlors described in chapter 4, unveiling how the historical sausage of Reconstruction scholarship is made in the final exhibit space of the MoRE demonstrates that illuminating the historical process and methodology is a best practice and critical to helping visitors understand modern scholarship and the period of Reconstruction. The conversation on how Reconstruction's memory was constructed can dismantle antiquated historical assessments that shape popular understanding of the period. Because this interpretation has been circulating for 150 years, built through the historical profession, HHM shrines, textbooks, films like *A Birth of a Nation*, and pro-Confederate monuments and markers across the landscape, it will take time and scholarly collaboration with the public to overturn and must be challenged in the same spaces that the outdated interpretation of Reconstruction was fabricated. Lastly, the interactive poetry and queer history at the Emily Dickinson Home and the MoRE demonstrate that public historians and HHMs have nothing to fear in incorporating the tragic mode of narrative in their interpretations to tell important and often absent stories in US history.

CHAPTER 7

(Re)Writing History with Lightning

Interpreting Memory and White Supremacy

In 2017 the film *Black Panther* reignited a decades-old debate among museum professionals about repatriation of colonial artifacts and thrust it into mainstream culture. The heist scene set in the Museum of Great Britain, a fictional version of the British Museum, situates antihero Erik Killmonger in the middle of an elitist, curatorial mini-tour of a collection from Africa. He informs the white curator of his intention to take a valuable artifact from Wakanda that she has misidentified. She rejects his effort to repatriate the item. As the gallery's museum guards eye his Black body, Killmonger asks, "How do you think your ancestors got these? You think they paid a fair price? Or did they take it, like they took everything else?"[1]

Although not a universally accepted ideological mission, an expectation exists that museums should address the evils of colonialism and capitalism. Tied to this legacy are the sins of white supremacist history in the United States, which has local, regional, national, and global repercussions. Appeasing both those who rightfully demand and fearfully oppose contextualizing America's racist and exploitative history requires nuance, constant revision, and an openness to inclusive discourse.[2] The Museum of the Reconstruction Era at the Woodrow Wilson Family Home's experiences crafting a discussion of white supremacy illuminate successful strategies for dialogue and approaches in public history institutions. The process of creating a narrative for the public also reveals the ways in which white supremacy hides itself in interpretive choices made by the exhibit staff and docents. The last interpretive space in the home, the bedroom devoted to the memory of Reconstruction and Woodrow Wilson, was the most challenging portion of the tour. Beyond mastering difficult script material and history, docents faced a daunting tour denouement for visitors, who like their guides were fatigued at the end of an approximately seventy-five-minute tour. Broaching white supremacy, the tremendous impact of *The Birth of a Nation*, and narratives that have challenged the film, both when it was released and today, proved more difficult than Historic Columbia imagined. But with a willingness to revise the interpretation well over a year after reopening, the organization resolved issues of clarity in a complicated interpretation of Griffith's film and President Wilson's relationship with it. Staff and docents also discovered a framework for continued conversations on white supremacy in which they interpretively converged.

Rewriting History with Lightning: Crafting the Legacy of Woodrow Wilson and Reconstruction

Docents expressed a host of concerns with the exhibit film *The Legacy of Woodrow Wilson and Reconstruction* (*Legacy*), which was played for visitors in the final bedroom at the end of the semiguided tour. The film attempted to reconcile the public memories of the president and the era with the silent blockbuster *The Birth of a Nation* (*Birth*). Docents expressed unease about the clarity, racist imagery, and negative tone of *Legacy*. They worried it misrepresented Wilson's feelings and ideas about *Birth* and minimized his achievements. Docents also thought a portion featuring the reworking of *Birth* by sound and visual artist DJ Spooky needed greater context. Less than a year after the MoRE opening, the docents' concerns ultimately resulted in Historic Columbia's approving a major in-house script revision in collaboration with the local production company that produced the original exhibit film. But in addressing docent concerns, the new version demonstrated how complicated interpreting *Birth* was and threatened to erase Black voices.

Legacy was one of the last exhibit pieces vetted by staff, film producers, and historians and finalized before the MoRE reopening.[3] It devoted the most time to contextualizing *Birth* for unfamiliar audiences. At that time none of the other HHMs devoted to Wilson in Virginia, Georgia, and Washington, DC, directly addressed Wilson's screening of the film in the White House in 1915 unless prompted. Although the exhibit at the WWPLM in Staunton includes Wilson's time at Johns Hopkins, there is no mention that he met Thomas Dixon there. On the centennial of *Birth*'s release, S Street in DC displayed a movie projector and screen to demonstrate that Wilson brought the first films to the White House, but none was mentioned by name.[4]

In the development of the exhibit film at MoRE, clarity was always a major concern to Historic Columbia's interpretive team. They hoped to explain Wilson's relationship with Reconstruction while avoiding academic jargon or vagueness. However, team members felt apprehension about other language and word choices. Scriptwriters corrected normative writing that specified the race of some people and groups but not others. DJ Spooky was described as Black, for example, while D. W. Griffith's race was never noted. The text referred to "Columbians" when it meant white Columbians. Daniella Cook, a professor who specializes in racially just and equitable schooling for communities traditionally underserved by public education, suggested avoiding the word *racist* because it might detract from white southern visitors' revising their Reconstruction interpretation. She cautioned there was "not a right or easy answer" to discussing race. However, scripts and training texts should offer explicit behaviors and specific quotes as evidence and be specific in naming the kinds of Black representation *Birth* promoted, such as Black men being "over-sexualized animals." As such the MoRE interpretive team included scenes from the film that directly addressed themes included in or myths of Reconstruction overturned on the tour: Black troops barring white citizens from voting, negative depictions of Black legislators, Gus grabbing Flora Cameron's arm, and two Ku Klux Klan scenes, one in which the riders drop Gus's lynched body on a porch and another of their fighting Black troops to regain control of the town.[5]

The most powerful imagery and persuasive evidence of white supremacy in the MoRE's exhibit film was archival footage of a 1926 Columbia parade commemorating the fiftieth anniversary of the Red Shirt campaign. William Esper Czarnitzki, a regional Boy Scout executive in South Carolina, shot the Wade Hampton Day parade as part of a larger collection of his home movies depicting his family, nature, and scout parades and camping. The parade itself was one of many parades and reunions celebrating the Red Shirts in the late nineteenth and early twentieth centuries. Though the reunions lost momentum after 1911, the fiftieth anniversary of Hampton's 1876 victory brought the Red Shirts back out of the closet. The celebration was a family affair, as demonstrated by Czarnitzki's extensive coverage of the scouts' involvement and his crowd footage. The fifteen-minute home movie captured a marching band, women dressed in white sitting atop floats, men on horses, and, of course, the Hampton statue at the State House.[6] The moving images were persuasive and haunting in visually conveying white supremacy and memory, taking pressure off of weekend docent Halie Brazier to tell it. She witnessed the footage commemorating the return of white rule physically jolt one of her visitors.[7] For Brazier the shocking nature of *Birth* and the parade were a "great way to hammer home" her tour narrative that white supremacy and its memory of Reconstruction endured, a topic she struggled to expand on with docent-guest dialogue alone. These primary sources backed her words with visual evidence to support current scholarship for people who had learned a different interpretation or silently dismissed the violence and racism she had discussed. Because *Birth* is fictional rather than an archival film, she favored the 1926 Red Shirt parade, as did another docent.[8] But the film was not fake to all of its early twentieth-century audiences. It did for mainstream cinematic Reconstruction memory what the Dunning School had for the history profession. Film critics and Hollywood were well aware that the film promoted negative stereotypes of Reconstruction and Black Americans. White Americans and recent immigrants who were negotiating their whiteness readily consumed these stereotypes when they watched the film. According to historian Karen Cox, by the end of World War II, Americans were three times more likely to see a film than read a periodical or newspaper.[9]

The revision process for *Legacy* was long and arduous with wide variations of drafts considered. The search for funding and script reviews began in the summer, only months after the 2014 President's Day reopening of MoRE. A small group of docents provided early feedback. After three revisions a draft circulated in mid-August for internal review. Historic Columbia began meeting with local director and documentarian Lee Ann Kornegay in the fall, but it would be well after the new year before a near final version of the script circulated.[10] The in-house scriptwriters, MoRE interpretive staff, Kornegay, and docents went back and forth on a number of issues, including a short-lived suggestion to cut the 1926 parade. This debate demonstrated both the popularity of the parade footage with docents and visitors and how tumultuous the exercise of revising a short exhibit film would be. A parade is an experience most visitors could relate to, and the film suggested the commemoration could be mistaken for a Fourth of July parade. Shots of men, women, and children, the "cross section of people" that attended the parade, were ultimately returned to the exhibit film with a new sensory experience of crowd sounds.[11] This was but a small skirmish in the battle over the film's interpretation. The real interpretive crusade was *The Birth of a Nation*.

The sheer complexity of *Birth* from historical and media studies perspectives and the need to keep the final exhibit film in MoRE brief were key interlocking issues. However, docent critiques of *Legacy* complicated this problem further. In addition to concerns about overall clarity, docents wanted more about Wilson's presidential policies beyond the Fourteen Points, the Nineteenth Amendment, and segregation. Historic Columbia scrapped an introduction rewrite, a fumbling attempt to recenter the Wilson family after they left Columbia, reconnect Wilson's presidency with Columbia, and link his Civil War and Reconstruction experience to his foreign policy in Latin America and during World War I.[12] The team added an excerpt from a new interview with Wilson biographer A. Scott Berg, who happened to be holding a book signing at Historic Columbia at the time of revisions. This allowed a Wilson expert to speculate about the impact Reconstruction had on the future president and his policies. Some team members and volunteers welcomed the addition, but a few public historians took issue with the echoes of an older Reconstruction interpretation in how Berg framed the period through Wilson's eyes as "potentially a good idea."[13] The interpretive team wanted to keep an audio recording of an excerpt from one of Wilson's speeches that opened *Legacy* originally, but even the most devoted proponents of the audio artifact acquiesced. The speech's focus on industry and monopolies felt out of a place with the needs of the film and required introducing additional context, including about Wilson's brand of progressivism and the 1912 presidential campaign.[14] Meanwhile, the revised conclusion lacked a cohesive, workable chronology for three events the team wanted to include: Wilson's death, the 1926 parade, and saving the home, all of which happened within a span of four years.[15] The team returned to the film's first conclusion and its critical thinking cues for visitors to explore "the legacy of Reconstruction and the impact it may have had on a fourteen-year-old boy named Tommy who later became president of the United States."[16] These would be the easy decisions.

Birth of a Problem

From the beginning, interpreting *Birth* was the greatest conundrum for Historic Columbia and its docents. Those working most directly with docents recognized the need to contextualize the scenes from the film effectively in both the tour script and exhibit film. After the tour a few visitors expressed confusion to the gift shop manager about why an offensive film would be privileged; however, this critique did not show up on visitor evaluations.[17] One volunteer was so concerned about the film that she requested a meeting about her reluctance to continue training after a sample training tour. She was uncomfortable conducting tours, especially because of the alarming images from the film of blackface actors, a dead body, and racist tropes. So distracting were these images that she missed the closing statements of the tour. Members of the interpretive team met with her and offered reassurances that revisions were coming both to the film and to a secondary background section of the script. She did not complete training.[18] Based on my conversation with her, the docent seemed trapped in her own personal connections to novelist Thomas Dixon. Several generations of men in her family had established and continued to serve in a Baptist church where Dixon's father was the first minister. She also recommended to me a chapter titled "Reconstruction and the Negroes" from the North Carolina edition of the WPA state guide that Louise Jones DuBose edited for South Carolina.[19] That work and its impact on cementing a white supremacist memory of Reconstruction via tourism is discussed in chapters 3 and 5.

Another problem for docents was a quote wrongly attributed to Woodrow Wilson that he endorsed *Birth of a Nation*. Dixon tapped Wilson to quell criticism of the film. They met for thirty minutes on February 3, 1915. Afterward Dixon coordinated with Wilson's daughter Margaret to schedule a private screening on February 18, 1915, attended by Wilson, his daughter, his doctor, Dixon, director Griffith, and cabinet members and their families. (The Wilsons had watched the first film in the White House, *Cabiria*, eight months earlier.) Dixon used the private screening to convince members of Congress and the Supreme Court to watch the film. Groups like the NAACP attempted to stop its general release by citing censorship laws that prohibited films or artistic productions that could incite public unrest or riots. Newspapers and critics also protested and condemned the film, citing its misrepresentation of Reconstruction and Black people, glorification of lynching, and promotion of bigotry against people of color. Wilson's implied political endorsements ended the censorship battle in New York City, setting a precedent to screen the film in other US cities.[20]

The question of how friendly Dixon and Wilson were gets to the heart of the interpretive and scholarly debate about Wilson's relationship with and endorsement of the film. The interpretive team even debated whether to refer to the two men as acquaintances or associates.[21] Wilson met Dixon during his brief stint at Johns Hopkins University. They both studied under German-trained scholar Herbert Baxter Adams and Richard T. Ely. Rooted in Hegelian theory, Adams's Teutonic germ theory that American democracy evolved from Germanic and Anglo-Saxon bloodlines gave the southerners a larger framework for their existing regional views. Wilson certainly came off as more subtle in his racism than Dixon did in his fictional works. In a 1905 curtain speech in Columbia for his stage version of *The Clansman*, Dixon proclaimed that he used Reconstruction and the white southern experience to unite the nation and spark a global movement to help colonial powers facing similar racial crises.[22]

Dixon and Wilson exchanged letters but did not correspond frequently. Dixon clearly admired Wilson, so much so that he convinced Wake Forest College to give his honorary degree to Wilson and later dedicated his novel *The Southerner: A Romance of the Real Lincoln* to the president. He also wrote to Wilson about politics. As a North Carolina legislator, Dixon shared news about a Confederate veterans' pension bill. He wrote in support of Wilson's governorship and presidential ambitions and as an advocate for white supremacy. He recommended a cabinet position for his friend Josephus Daniels. As young men in the early 1880s, the two had been members of Raleigh's Watauga Club, a group committed to an industrialized New South. As editor of the *Raleigh News and Observer*, Daniels was co-architect of the 1898 Democratic campaign in North Carolina that fueled the Wilmington massacre and coup d'état. Dixon used the events and historical figures as inspiration for *The Clansman* as well as his first novel, *The Leopard's Spots*. Glenda Gilmore, in her study of Jim Crow North Carolina, called Daniels "the New White Man's mouth" and Dixon "his libido." Wilson ultimately appointed Daniels, a key engineer in segregating federal offices, to the office of secretary of the navy. Wilson also appointed Walter Hines Page, Watauga Club member and Dixon's publisher, as ambassador to Great Britain. Daniels in fact arranged the meeting between Chief Justice of the United States Edward D. White and Dixon to convince the former Louisiana Klansman to host a screening of *Birth*. Dixon also wrote Wilson to encourage the withdrawal of a Black candidate for a Treasury Department position and received Wilson's assurances that there was no risk of interracial mixing.[23]

Wilson and Dixon certainly found themselves in some of the same white supremacist circles, but did Wilson endorse the most famous white supremacist film of all time? After the White House screening, Wilson reportedly said, "It is like writing history with lightning. And my only regret is that it is all so terribly true." Nine different variations of the infamous quote have appeared since 1915. Griffith told the *New York American* that Washington had praised the film, and "a man we all revere"—implicitly Wilson—said that it "teaches history by lightning." In December 1915 the *Atlanta Constitution* used the phrase "history written with lightning" twice in promoting the movie. Other publications hinted that the quote was from Wilson. The "terribly true" portion of the quote did not appear until journalist Milton MacKaye's 1937 piece in *Scribner's Magazine*. Mark Benbow speculated that Wilson, as a professor and president interested is using film as an educational and propaganda tool, spoke of the movie in terms of *teaching*, which quickly morphed into *writing* for advertising purposes.[24]

Twice the exhibit directly addressed the inauthentic quote, but some volunteer docents felt *Legacy* left visitors with the impression Wilson endorsed *Birth*. A panel included the quote but noted that it was "probably not authentic," because a journalist made the claim "much later." The exhibit film introduces it as an alleged quote. Yet a small number of docents viewed the presence of the quote itself as an indictment of Wilson. Scholars have done much to perpetuate the misquote, but it also endures because Wilson was vague in his public thoughts about the film. He never condemned *Birth of a Nation*, its message, or its use of his historical scholarship, possibly because he was engaged in a battle over segregation with William Trotter, a protestor of the film. Nor did Wilson cut off communication with Dixon, offering to consult on future historical or political films if time permitted. He once wrote, however, that the film was "a very unfortunate production" and that he wished it was not played, especially in communities with large Black populations. His administration publicly claimed that he was ignorant of the film's character before watching it. His screening was nothing more than a courtesy to an old college friend and certainly not an endorsement. Granted, Dixon was a notorious promoter of the movie, but that Wilson was unaware of the themes and mood of the film based on Dixon's well-known novels and plays is highly unlikely. In fact, *Birth* had originally been called *The Clansman*, after the novel that inspired the second half of the film, until Dixon convinced Griffith to change the title. The quote also persists because Griffith gave greater historical weight to his film by quoting Wilson's work as a scholar on various title cards, the narrative text that accompanies a silent film. Griffith misled his audiences by framing Wilson's interpretation of the Klan as a needed force to administer vigilante justice rather than a violent political reaction to the two-party and biracial system emerging during Reconstruction. A still of a title card quoting Wilson is included on a MoRE panel.[25]

Given the nuance required to explain the circumstantial evidence surrounding Wilson's endorsement, the revision to *Legacy* opted for simplicity. Wilson historians Arthur Link and Kendrick Clements (the latter was a MoRE exhibit team member) agreed that Dixon and the new medium of film duped the president. This was also the position of one member of the interpretive team and John Clark, the docent most vocally opposed to *Legacy*'s depiction of the quote. Prompted by his reading of John Milton Cooper's biography of Wilson, Clark expressed strong objections to the executive director and to the interpretive team when revisions and year-end reviews were announced. Clark viewed Wilson as "a naïve victim of his opportunistic college friend" rather than "a proactive host." He thought the exhibit film "a bit unfair" given that Wilson seemed "more guilty of incompetence than malice," and he considered it unwise to spread the popular misquote any further in light of the speculative evidence. He and the team remained in contact with updates on how the revision would interpret the controversy.[26] The team determined that the most definitive statement that could be made was that Wilson did not say what he thought of the film. That the "movie's producers capitalized on the White House connection" gave room for visitors to think about the various ways this process might work.[27] The team also decided to use the title cards quoting Wilson as a visual example of his implied endorsement of the film. By not crediting where he pulled the quote, Griffith implied that the president offered his historical assessment for the film. The caption text to the title card used in *Legacy* revealed it was "an excerpt from Wilson's 1902 monograph *A History of the American People*."[28] Additionally, one approach offered to docents was framing the "lightning" statement as a manufactured celebrity endorsement made possible by the screening and lack of public condemnation that appeared to sanction the message of the film.[29]

While the MoRE directly confronted Wilson's endorsement of *Birth*, Historic Columbia refused to let the endorsement question drive the entire exhibit film's interpretation. Rather the organization relocated the discussion of Wilson and the film back to Columbia and Reconstruction. Honing this interpretation resulted in fleeting suggestions that *Birth* be dropped entirely. Two interpretive team members began to wonder if Wilson's relationship with *Birth*, the whole purpose of the exhibit film, was reaching its goals.

Did visitors even care? Docents reported that some visitors had no frame of reference for Griffith's film, and those that did had rarely seen it. Scholars might associate Wilson with the film, but visitors thought of world war, the Nineteenth Amendment, the Federal Reserve, and segregation. An exhibit about *Birth* met the museum's goal to present new and challenging information, but the never-ending revisions suggested that the material was being forced. One team member feared Historic Columbia risked "overwhelmingly placing all our eggs in *The Birth of a Nation* basket." Maybe less of the film was the answer.[30] In the end looking at *Birth of a Nation* through a localized lens offered a new approach.

Reliving the Past and Nationalizing Columbia's Reconstruction History

In 1977 Marjorie Brown King told Wilson expert Arthur Link that she witnessed the president lost in thought during the screening of *Birth*. King, who was in attendance and married to one of Wilson's friends, also said that the president left without commenting. His wandering mind could have been caused by the recent death of his wife, Ellen, the stress of World War I, or the potential problems the film might cause. Or it may have been a fabrication to protect a long-deceased president in the post–civil rights era. Similarly, friend and physician Cary Grayson, who took excellent care of Wilson memorabilia, donated a crumpled program of the screening to Wilson's presidential library. The memory and artifact, if true, suggests two scenarios: either Wilson disapproved of the film, or he overidentified with it.[31] Either way, did he think of his teenage home in Columbia? And did his fellow Columbians have the same reaction? Griffith set *Birth* in the fictional South Carolina community of Piedmont. But once the viewer disregards the mythical South Carolina, the film not only presents Columbia but also nationalizes South Carolina's white memory of Reconstruction.[32] Evidence of historical South Carolina emerges, most clearly in the scene within Columbia's State House. Rather than solely focus on the Wilson endorsement, *Legacy* used the State House scene to ask visitors to consider if, while watching *Birth*, Wilson would have recalled his years in Columbia. This scene was one of the localized and regional connections binding Wilson, South Carolina, the nation, and Reconstruction together that the first interpretation of *Legacy* underplayed.[33] Griffith's derogatory representations of Black State House representatives eating chicken, not wearing shoes, and drinking alcohol were in the original version but not placed in the context of Wilson's memory of Reconstruction and place. In fact a team member suggested cutting some of the negative imagery, but the majority of the team wanted to keep the local representations.[34] The State House scene opened with Griffith's "historical facsimile" title card that informs the audience they are witnessing an authentic representation of the legislature based on a picture from Columbia's *State* newspaper. Griffith's depiction was contrasted with a *Frank Leslie's Illustrated* image of the dignified, newspaper-reading legislature awaiting results during the disputed 1876 election, used in the MoRE exhibit to demonstrate the director's inclination to misinterpret the past. Docents could choose to highlight this effective contrasting tool on the tour.[35]

Dixon did indeed strive for historical accuracy in the construction of the State House set, if not in the depiction of its legislators. Dixon wrote to the *State* publisher Ambrose Gonzales in Columbia asking for a local contact who could provide photographs of the House of Representatives chamber and serve as a fact-checker for the set. Gonzales, who had a decade-long feud with Dixon over the stage version of *The Clansman*, pushed the request off on a young journalist, Sam Latimer. Latimer hailed from York County, a community that inspired Dixon's novels and the fictional Piedmont setting of *Birth of a Nation*. Dixon visited family there frequently. In her WPA state guide, DuBose promoted the connection between York and *The Clansman* and also claimed that Dixon drew on the history of the Columbia Klan trials. Supposedly Klansman Dr. Rufus Bratton, whom federal officials "kidnapped" from Canada to stand trial, was the prototype for a character in *The Clansman*. Set designers in Los Angeles erected the chamber using Columbia photographer George V. Hennies's shots from thirteen angles. Although researchers in Columbia verified the authenticity, only the 1871 speaker stand was authentic. The chamber was contemporary. In 1871 the State House was just a year old and remained unfinished with a cheap tin roof. The *Leslie's* image with its granite walls, curtains, and gaslight fixtures, offers evidence of the mistake.[36]

Other manifestations of Columbia surface in *Birth*, even if these clips were too numerous and required too much context to include in the exhibit's truncated film clips.[37] Griffith dislocates the Cameron family plantation, the location of much of the action of the film, to an urban space. The front of the Cameron "big house" is accessible by a sidewalk decorated with a streetlamp and leading toward a church. A community bonfire is held on this same street. Behind the facade of the front porch and parlor, the audience catches glimpses of a cotton field and slave quarters; but otherwise the setting suggests an urban space.[38] This mise-en-scène likely invited residents of Columbia, and perhaps the entire state, to envision the city in their reading of the film. When watching Gen. William T. Sherman's fiery destruction of the city and the sacking of the Cameron home, South Carolinians most likely recalled the burning of Columbia on February 17, 1865. Griffith blamed

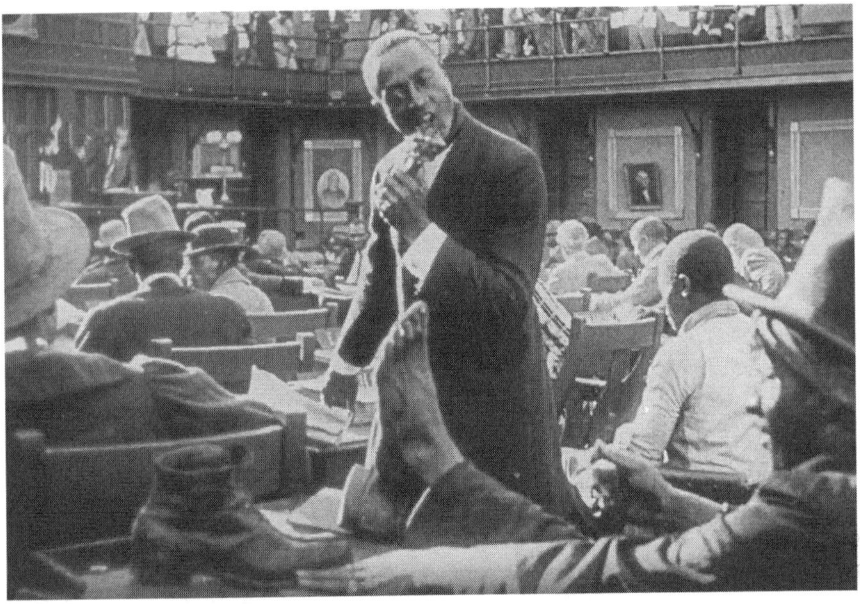

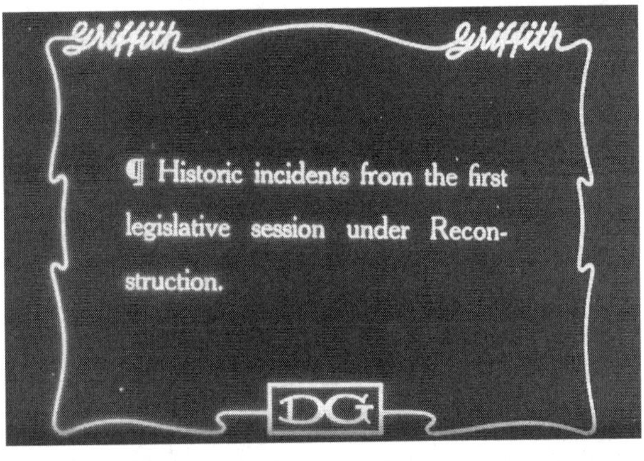

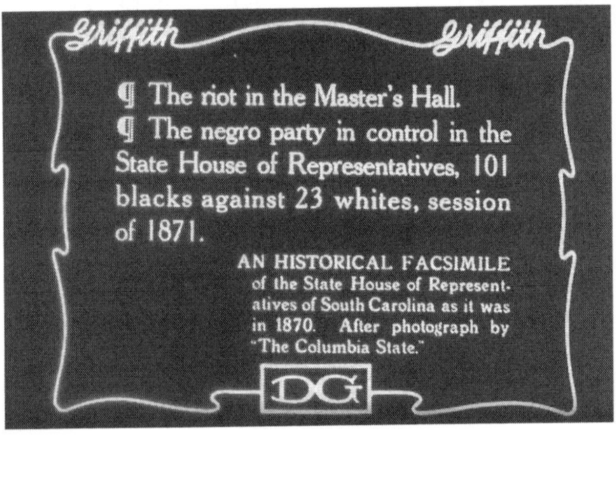

Figure 18. Griffith replicated Columbia's State House as the fictional Master's Hall and included a historical facsimile referencing an 1870 article in Columbia's *State* newspaper.

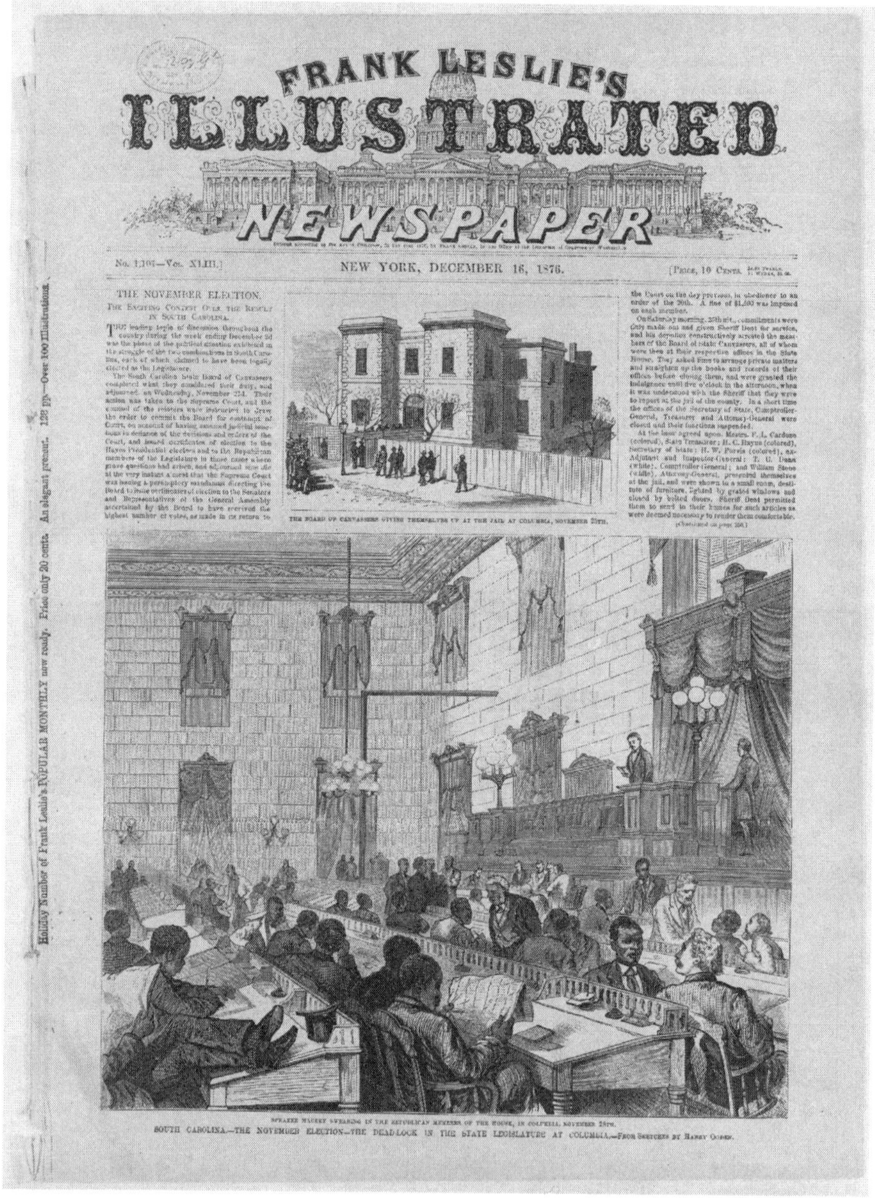

FRANK LESLIE'S ILLUSTRATED NEWSPAPER

No. 1,103—Vol. XLIII.] NEW YORK, DECEMBER 16, 1876. [Price, 10 Cents.

THE NOVEMBER ELECTION.

The Exciting Contest Over the Result in South Carolina.

THE BOARD OF CANVASSERS GIVING THEMSELVES UP AT THE JAIL AT COLUMBIA, NOVEMBER 25TH.

SPEAKER MACKEY SWEARING IN THE REPUBLICAN MEMBERS OF THE HOUSE, IN COLUMBIA, NOVEMBER 28TH.

SOUTH CAROLINA.—THE NOVEMBER ELECTION—THE DEADLOCK IN THE STATE LEGISLATURE AT COLUMBIA.—From Sketches by Harry Ogden.

Figure 19. Harry Ogden's sketch is a more accurate depiction of the Republican-controlled legislature. Here Speaker Edmund W. M. Mackey swears in the Republican House on November 28 during the disputed election of 1876. Democrats convened their own House. *Frank Leslie's Illustrated Newspaper*, December 15, 1876. Courtesy of Library of Congress, Prints and Photographs Online Catalog.

guerrillas. Columbians condemned Sherman, even though burning cotton stores, drunken, incapacitated soldiers, and wind provided fuel for fires that ultimately destroyed a third of the city.[39] A more subtle allusion to Columbia, the center of state and federal power for South Carolina, is Griffith's incorporation of a strong federal presence in Piedmont. Troops declined significantly after the passage of the 1868 state constitution. By late summer the army maintained only three posts in the state, in Columbia, Charleston, and Aiken. The frequent reoccurrence of federal troops, which could represent the Eighth Infantry stationed in Columbia, hails from one of these three cities. Additionally the short-lived Freedmen's Bureau, also featured in *Birth*, had its last headquarters in Columbia before it was abolished in 1869.[40]

The local connection to *Birth* that likely created the most emotional response from white audiences would have come from reading the Klan as the Red Shirts. Griffith's film offered a widely understood white supremacist narrative that would resonate with audiences and be easily understood. Given the Klan's spread across the South and into popular media of the Reconstruction era, the group offered a straightforward symbol recognizable to millions of Americans as the nation attempted to negotiate whiteness and middle-class values during the late nineteenth and twentieth centuries. In the film Black children frightened by two young white pranksters inspire Ben Cameron to create the Reconstruction-era terrorist group. Historically the Klan first appeared in Pulaski, Tennessee, in 1866. By 1868 the group infiltrated South Carolina, most notably in the upstate and York region. In the early 1870s, the group disbanded after federal legislation and trials, which rarely rendered convictions, made an example of the state.[41] In *Birth*'s closing scene, the Klan protects the ballot box. But anyone who knew local Reconstruction history, certainly Dixon, would be aware that while the Ku Klux Klan was the military arm of the Democratic Party in the early 1870s, by 1876 the party was supported by the terror of Red Shirts and rifle clubs.[42] The strategy led to the toppling of Republican-ruled Reconstruction by using intimidation and fraud at the ballot box. The Klan narrative in *Birth* would have made more sense to South Carolinians as a symbolic homage to the Red Shirts. To tell an authentic history of Reconstruction's end in South Carolina and establish who the Red Shirts were and their significance proved too complex for audiences outside of the state and thus unfit for national consumption.

White southerners, who at times rejected the stage version of *The Clansman* because it did not speak as effectively to Lost Cause ideology or have a documentary feel, embraced *Birth of a Nation*. Columbians so hated both Dixon and the play when it premiered in 1905 that locals attempted to mob a cast member and hissed at the author. *The Clansman*, and Dixon's presumption that he spoke for the South, was at the root of Gonzales's telegraph and press war with Dixon, part of a larger attack by the state's press. Gonzales called the play a "fairy tale." It glorified reprehensible acts of Klan violence, but most egregious, the group had disappeared five years before "the men who wore red shirts in broad light of day and the women who blessed them redeemed South Carolina from Negro rule." Gonzales cautioned against surrendering this legacy "for a tinsel setting to a sensational drama!"[43]

Despite objections to the play, white southern audiences had an intense connection to Griffith's melodrama. It better represented their manufactured historical version of the past and anxieties about the Black vote, crime, and sexuality than *The Clansman* had. The *State*'s review cited the State House scene as evidence of the film's authenticity and praised Griffith's work for tempering Dixon's racism. White South Carolina approved of *Birth*, many without reservation. Some saw it repeatedly. Others kept their viewing quiet, understanding the film's racial implications. For those of Dixon and Griffith's generation who did not remember or live through Reconstruction but had followed the white supremacy campaign of Governor Tillman, as historian John Hammond Moore notes, seeing *Birth* was "an unparalleled emotional experience. It was Christmas morning, circus day, and victory for the home team over its arch rival all rolled into one." Audiences at times suffered from "overidentification" with the characters. In Spartanburg, the first showing of the film in South Carolina, former Confederates and men who once donned "gray uniforms, white sheets, and red shirts wept, yelled, whooped, cheered," and shot the screen to protect white, virginal Flora Cameron from the Black rapist Gus.[44] In the first six months of 1916, *Birth* played in seven more cities across the state. Its popularity prompted railroads to offer reduced ticket prices for rural residents. Local papers heavily promoted the film, its accuracy, and its community connections. Rock Hill extended the film's engagement there by two days. The film returned to the state in 1921, and two years later it finally came "home" to York. Those residents, so drawn to *Birth* and their sometimes visitor Dixon, skipped a night of sleep to take the train to Charlotte in 1915.[45]

South Carolinians likely read the spectacle of Griffith's Klan as a glorification of the Red Shirts' role in overturning Reconstruction in 1876. Did Wilson also think of South Carolina when he watched *Birth of a Nation*? These questions, though unanswerable, gave MoRE visitors a way to consider the complicated and interwoven history of Wilson, South Carolina, and Reconstruction. As such the docent script's last revision acknowledged that *Birth*'s South Carolina setting had been downplayed in evaluations of the film and may "be just as important to why we show it in the house as

Wilson's connection to the film." The film was important not just for its artistic merits, which helped perpetuate an inaccurate history of Reconstruction, but also because it "captures the state's Reconstruction memory and nationalizes it."[46]

Rebirth of a Problem

A new interview with DJ Spooky helped resolve issues with clarity and corrected an imbalance in Black representation that emerged during the revision process of *Legacy*. The original version of the exhibit film featured DJ Spooky and clips from his *Rebirth of a Nation*, but the hip-hop-infused reedit of *Birth* confused audiences or failed to engage them. Without the scene the new version reduced Black representation to Griffith's negative depictions of corrupt and inept politicians in the State House. The team grappled with modifying DJ Spooky's portion or cutting it and focusing on a new subject, such as the Black community's fight against the film, against segregating federal offices, or against Wilson himself. The length of *Legacy* was a serious concern, but Black representation was not optional. I had worked with USC Media Arts faculty on projects related to Black representation and volunteered to explore options related to the themes of community resistance during the Wilson era. Fortunately an opportunity for an interview with DJ Spooky to elucidate his work emerged. It saved the material that was almost excised for its complexity.[47]

Given that his mother was a feminist historian and his father a lawyer who worked with Angela Davis, Paul Miller, aka DJ Spooky, expected to have a career in the Foreign Service. In the 1990s the teenager's love of music merged with a love of history. A good DJ scours music and thrift stores for "rare, cool stuff" to be different, and good sampling requires research. He eventually expanded his search from musical archives to repositories of history and film. He wanted artists to see a "living archive" rather than a "dead space." Although he sounded like a historian suffering from what Carolyn Steedman described as "archival fever," he understood his work to be different. An academic's archive, which required citation, differed from the DJ's archive of quoting by sampling.[48]

DJ Spooky, That Subliminal Kid, traveled the United States and the world showing *Rebirth* for a decade. In January 2015 the film brought him to the Nickelodeon theater in Columbia for a screening and director talkback with the audience. It was the first of six films in the theater's monthlong "Burn to Shine" program, part of the city's larger Burning of Columbia commemoration of the 150th anniversary of General Sherman's occupation. The event and Historic Columbia's interview with DJ Spooky offered much-needed context for *Legacy*'s revision. Historic Columbia gleaned valuable insight into *Rebirth*'s origin and significance and DJ Spooky's methodology. He found *Birth of a Nation* after developing an interest in visual sampling, using historical films as basic building blocks for visuals during his club shows. When he put images of the KKK on screen, the audience stopped dancing to stare. He was partly inspired by the disputed 2000 presidential election and the correlation between modern-day blue and red states with the Union and Confederacy. *Birth* provided a fantasy of Reconstruction, where Black people oppressed white, accepted as fact by white Americans. Believing that the art of sampling is "open-ended," DJ Spooky reimagined the fixed, white supremacist fantasy for modern audiences, who he hoped rejected the racist tropes and Civil War memory as their predecessors failed to a century ago. His added music and geometric shapes around various characters allowed him to highlight white supremacy, power, and class dynamics. He created electronic and ambient sounds based on blues riffs, writing music out note for note, sampling it, and reediting it back into the film. Editing was both thematic and practical. As a silent film a little more than three hours in length, *Birth* quickly generates fatigue for twenty-first-century viewers. Watching the entire film is "hell," DJ Spooky recalled. As he would with a song, he sampled the hook of the film, reducing it to one hour. Fond of the combat scenes, he kept those and cut much of Griffith's romanticism. Like early showings of *Birth, Rebirth* frequently played with live musical accompaniment, in the more recent case from DJ Spooky's laptop and sometimes a small orchestra. He placed the relevance of his work in the past and the present—recognizing he was screening his remix at the centennial of *Birth* and the sesquicentennial of the burning of Columbia but also on Martin Luther King Jr. Day as police brutality and Black incarceration debates were increasing. At that time #BlackLivesMatter was in its infancy.[49]

The interpretive team was pleased with the DJ Spooky edits, as were several docents. Two volunteers praised the artist's inclusion. One thought it one of the best and most important changes. Another appreciated placing Wilson and *Birth* "in the context of the time," in which Wilson was "moderate in his racial views." But this was not actually a point the artist made. In his interview excerpt, DJ Spooky argued *Birth* was a racist film that used fear to generate a "no holds bar indictment of the idea of Black political progress." But he encouraged understanding the context of time and place, saying, "Wilson at the time would have been facing the suffragist movement . . . agitation from people returning from WWI . . . economic upheaval." *Rebirth* was "holding up a mirror to society and showing them some things still need to change." Two public historians who gave tours thought DJ Spooky was giving context to the dilemmas facing Wilson, which was not the defense Wilson optimists posit.[50] DJ Spooky's interpretation of the Wilsonian era during his audience talkback at the Nickelodeon supported this interpretation. He understood the film peaked during a "series of upheavals"—those listed in the *Legacy* clip but also Prohibition, organized crime, suppression of Black rights, and the "appropriation of Black culture." He pointed to jazz's popularity and the use of blackface, commonplace in the stage performances and early film, as evidence of this appropriation. One hundred years later, DJ Spooky appropriated white supremacy from its loudest proponent. And his historical memory of Reconstruction, Woodrow Wilson, and *Birth* provides a strong counterpoint to the white memory of these same subjects. The president who screened *Birth* at the White House was the son of Confederate sympathizers. The Supreme Court viewed and essentially sanctioned the film. DJ Spooky speculated that there were "different Americas."[51]

The history of film and activism required to discuss *Birth of a Nation, Rebirth of a Nation,* and Black representation effectively guaranteed that a pithy exhibit film would suffer from issues of continuity and clarity. A long-standing debate existed between critics who valued the cinematic and technical importance of *Birth* and the detractors who opposed its racist message. *Birth* was the visual culmination of Dixon's literary attacks on Black people, augmenting white supremacy and assailing Black morale. With a greater fervor than ever, activists such as W. E. B. Du Bois and the NAACP contested the film. They joined forces with the Black press to coordinate and promote protests and encourage critical thinking about the film. The press proved vigilant in its decades-long protests at home and abroad, building on its campaigns against the derogatory roles Black actors were forced to play when not pushed out by white actors in blackface.[52]

DJ Spooky's *Rebirth* was a contemporary cinematic response that began with directors such as Oscar Micheaux and his 1920 film *Within our Gates.* Micheaux too promoted national reconciliation via a northern-southern marriage; but unlike Griffith, who matched a former Confederate soldier with a northern politician's daughter, Micheaux illuminated an urban Black courtship between a southern migrant, heroine Sylvia Landry, and Dr. Vivian, a cosmopolitan northern veteran. *Within Our Gates* made a case for full citizenship in light of the violent Black American experience while presenting a multitude of Black characters that were diverse, complex, and shaped by region. This included positive images of Black people, including Sylvia, a teacher raising funds for educating students, which mirrored a re-occurring theme at the MoRE of Black women's role in supporting education. Micheaux's films corrected Black misrepresentation that caused emotional trauma, violence, and political exclusion, but that did not always translate into box office success.[53] To dispel the myth of the Black rapist, Micheaux, through a flashback to the Reconstruction era, depicts Sylvia being attacked by her white father.[54] Mirroring the media and a segregated nation's propensity for double narratives, the director segregated the same event, juxtaposing an imagined white encounter with a more truthful Black rendition of the event. Dixon created and Griffith perpetuated a fantasy to conceal the unspoken truth, by whites at least, that biracial children where the product of white exploitation of Black women. Micheaux shattered this illusion via the incestuous attack on Sylvia in the Reconstruction South, the site of suffering for her and other Black characters.[55] Consultants suggested including Black cinematic responses to *Birth* such as Micheaux's in both versions of *Legacy*.[56] An attempt to reference generally through narration that "Black filmmakers and actors also created their own films to challenge Griffith's interpretation, although they never captured white America's interest as Griffith's film did," resulted in even greater confusion.[57] Micheaux's portrait and a newspaper advertising the film that accompanied the narration had no context. Another effort to resolve Black representational issues in *Legacy* failed.

DJ Spooky alone would serve as the counternarrative to *Birth* in the final *Legacy* film, but when combined with other edits, his inclusion dramatically improved the clarity and quality. Docents enthusiastically approved of the new interviews, B-roll (supplemental footage) of visitors in the home, design elements to showcase archival moving images, and helpful text and captions that allowed visitors to digest more information. The film gave visitors space to process important rhetorical questions, such as whether Wilson thought about Columbia when screening Griffith's film.[58] The substantial revisions warranted an introduction to prepare the guides and discuss the new interpretation centered more on Wilson's career and *Birth of a Nation*, its history, its critics, and its connections to South Carolina. Fourteen months after opening, Historic Columbia debuted the second version of *Legacy* for staff and docents in April 2015 during a demonstration of the tour's evolution.[59]

Racism in Degrees: Interpreting Wilson and White Supremacy

The concerns that docents had with *Legacy* illuminate that the interpretation's limit for them was the implicit claim that Wilson was a white supremacist. Cognizant that Wilson's racial views and discriminatory policies would need to be addressed up front, early script versions noted that Wilson was a product of his time and place. The script presented him as a complicated figure who was "considered moderate on race at the time but would be viewed as racist today," yet he won a Nobel Prize and "eventually endorsed suffrage for women."[60] Racial conservatives, like Wilson and Griffith, assumed that white supremacy was permanent and built on the Dunning School's concepts of racial superiority and Black inferiority, the key reason Reconstruction failed. Historian Joel Williamson identified three southern views toward race: liberal, conservative, and radical. The most optimistic about Reconstruction and Black progress was the southern white liberal intellectual, a rarity during Wilson's academic era because of the less-developed college system in the South. Wilson believed Black progress was possible in the *unforeseeable* future. Dixon was a radical white supremacist who believed emancipation was a step backward.[61]

Docents could admit that Wilson had a "mixed" record of successes and failures. Docents admired his progressivism, success in fighting World War I, and advocacy for the League of Nations.[62] When biographer A. Scott Berg came to Columbia, he said that "the Columbia years were definitely a turning point in Woodrow Wilson's life" and were "extremely formative intellectually, socially, spiritually."[63] Nonetheless docents disagreed about how much living in the South in his youth shaped Wilson, particularly his racial views. Most docents embraced that Augusta and Columbia made an impact on Tommy but resisted correlating this upbringing as the foundation for indicting Wilson as a white supremacist. Wilson expert Ken Clements asked docents to consider how, despite living in a community largely governed by African Americans, Wilson came to consider Black people "an ignorant and inferior race." How did his experiences in Columbia shape those racist opinions and his policies? Why did Wilson never reach the levels of racism displayed by his political contemporaries? Many volunteers were well-versed in South Carolina history and could use figures like Ben Tillman or Cotton Ed Smith to substantiate their claim that Wilson was a moderate product of the time.[64] Historian and exhibit consultant Thomas Brown, speaking to the fluidity of memory in his training lecture, unintentionally reinforced this idea when he noted that Smith, who had opposed federal anti-lynching legislation, celebrated his senatorial primary victory in a red shirt in front of Hampton's State House statue declaring that "we conquered in '76, and we conquered in '38."[65]

Living in Reconstruction era Columbia, most docents argued, would influence Wilson's life and his views on race. However, several docents had not known or thought of Wilson as a southerner or how his upbringing influenced his racial ideology before their training process. Clark thought people in general did not recognize Wilson as southern, but the MoRE made him a southerner. The exhibit illuminated those Wilsons that continued to live in Columbia and that the home was the only one the President's father owned. Until giving tours, two docents who knew he lived in the South still associated Wilson with New Jersey. Not until training did another begin to think about Wilson's "racial opinions" being shaped by that experience. He was "not a saint on a pedestal, which I think a lot of southerners have thought that he was." One volunteer disputed Wilson's southerness because his parents were not born in the South. Before moving to Columbia and conducting tours, another guide knew nothing of Wilson's upbringing or the segregating of federal offices. One docent suggested he used the experience to rationalize segregation as being good. Maria Schneider thought there was no debate that "he was prejudiced and that African American advancement economically and in civil rights was not his priority."[66]

Docents turned the ambiguity of Wilson's Southern upbringing and racism into an invitation for visitors to join them in thinking critically about these issues. When Kathy Hogan asked visitors their thoughts, they had no problem making the leap. Although she believed "we are the product of our upbringing, the product of our experiences," she, along with another docent, "had some reservations" about assuming how time and place might have impacted a young Tommy since he "left no memoir or other indication of what this time may have meant to him." That Historic Columbia avoided assumptions in favor of "asking visitors to come to their own conclusions" alleviated these concerns. Three volunteers believed the South had to influence Wilson because he was "an impressionable teenager." Two of them incorporated this into their tours. Pris Stickney accepted Reconstruction "certainly didn't make" Wilson "a more enlightened person" and had "a feeling he was a little bit more of a racist for that period than maybe others were." But rather than say his parents, the people of his time and his environment were racist, she encouraged visitors to explore these connections on their own. Volunteer Cyndy Storm framed the idea with how small Tommy's Presbyterian world was. She imagined family dinners, discussion about the seminary with a serious Presbyterian father, and local news. Volunteer docent Doe envisioned this world differently. While uncomfortable with attributing Wilson's racial views to his upbringing on the tour, Doe personally wondered what "things he might have heard at home" given the Confederate leanings of his father. It was "so disconcerting. And of course, he greatly admired his father."[67]

Another question which was tied to the larger issues of Wilson's racism and which docents expressed a range of responses was how much blame Wilson deserved for increased federal segregation during his administration. Three docents pointed to the power of southern Democrats, who Wilson appointed to cabinet positions and worked with in Congress. Southern cabinet members were the chief architects of segregation: Secretary of the Treasury and Wilson's son-in-law William McAdoo, Postmaster-General Albert Burleson, and Josephus Daniels. Conceding many Black workers lost their positions, Storm argued these southern congressmen wanted these individuals out of management positions and "pushing brooms." Clark viewed McAdoo and Burleson segregating their departments as a byproduct of Wilson delegating decision making to federal departments and agencies so that he could focus on macro issues. Similar to his "passive" support of *Birth*, Wilson's capitulation to segregationists was one of "active omission" or "inaction."[68] But Wilson, believing segregation a moderate position to avoid racial friction in these departments, knew about his cabinet head's policies. Segregation in the nation's capital where the Black community had made unparalleled gains united Black activists and white allies. They vigorously protested via public meetings, letter writing, petitions, and the press. One docent called it "difficult" to apologize, explain, or perform a good deed that can "make up for" Wilson allowing segregation in integrated federal offices. The docent had only recently come to terms with Wilson's racial views because of the tour. The docent confessed, "I suppose I should have assumed that." Given the docents' interpretation of the role of southern politicians, the script contextualized the flaws of Wilson's administration alongside his majority southern cabinet.[69] But one public historian sensed that explicit claims made Historic Columbia somewhat uncomfortable, a conservatism that stemmed from a lack of "definitive evidence." Weekend docent Casey Lee wanted the site to own the ties between Wilson's scholarship, presidential actions, and time in Columbia during Reconstruction and just go for explicit claims. Similar to new, more radical currents in HHM interpretation, Lee argued that historians are often required to craft interpretations without definitive evidence. The MoRE joins a growing list of museums that explore the importance of place and ask a variety of questions without providing clear answers. Guests understand ambiguity more than HHMs will concede, but the debate continues over how much conjecture is appropriate.[70]

Clark, a retired political scientist, was the most vocal about the danger of diminishing Wilson's achievements to overemphasize his racist ideology. Clark could not reduce Wilson to the second version of *Legacy*'s "insufficient" and "fairly modest list" of policies: the League of Nations, Federal Reserve System, signing the Nineteenth Amendment, and increased segregation. Clark argued people missed the nuances in the rush to portray presidents as "perfect or scoundrels." Clark likened the interpretation to how slaveholding had tarnished the image of the early Republic's Virginian presidents. Even Franklin Roosevelt commanded a segregated military and interred Japanese Americans. Wilson did "not move the country forward in better race relations," Clark acknowledged. But with "a good heart in many ways," Wilson attempted to "move the world forward" through self-determination and his peace plans. All white leaders were racist, but Wilson the progressive "was nowhere near" those "horrible right-wing racists" and "rabid" segregationists like Tillman or Smith who defended lynching. Clark wanted Wilson's actions placed in context with previous and subsequent presidents of the era and national trends among white Americans. He refused to buy into the myth of southern exceptionalism, exclaiming: "American society was horribly racist. Not just the South. It was worst." Clark wished Wilson had been more progressive and proactive, but Wilson did entertain Booker T. Washington while leading Princeton, a move that earned him derision. There are "valid reasons why people think he was a good president." Wilson was a "mixed bag," like other notable presidents.[71]

The interpretive problem for most volunteer docents was one of intention. *Legacy* was never envisioned as a highlight reel of Wilson's accomplishments but rather was meant to explain the public perception of his endorsement of *Birth* and "the film's role in the popular myth making of Reconstruction." There were fears among the interpretive team that *Legacy*'s revision could revert to the "presidential shrine interpretation." In addition to wanting Wilson's successes presented as part of *Legacy*, volunteer docents requested a biographical time line or other physical representation to trace Wilson's academic and political career. Jean Morgan thought this would help connect Wilson to Dixon and to those visitors who do not benefit from aural learning or think chronologically. Holly Westcott understood the MoRE was a museum of Reconstruction but thought the period got far more coverage than the "life and career of the President whom it represents."[72]

Docents may have been reluctant to delve too deeply into Wilson's white supremacy on their tours, but they had much to contemplate and plenty to say after a controversy in November 2015 at Princeton surrounding Wilson's memory. The campus's Black Justice League led a campaign that culminated with a walkout of two hundred students and a list of demands. It drew national attention to the complexity of national figures and racism in America, reminding the country that the way institutions simultaneously remember white men and forget white supremacy is open to scrutiny. At Princeton students took what historians have long known about Wilson and the contradictions of his progressivism out of the classroom and placed it directly into their protest. Only months prior, Randy Newman, professor of legal history at Harvard, wrote an op-ed piece in the *Washington Post* making a similar call to "expunge" Wilson's name in the wake of the Charleston massacre that led to the removal of the Confederate flag from the South Carolina State House in Columbia. In calls like that of the Black Justice League to rename buildings and awards that honor Wilson, questions emerged as to whether these campaigns risked erasing the memory, both positive and negative, of important yet controversial figures.[73] Morgan attributed the "intersection of attacks" on Wilson to his being "caught in the cross-hairs" of the Black community, who indict him as a racist for screening *Birth of a Nation*, and members of the political right, who condemn politicians affiliated with any progressive ideology. Another docent equated the Princeton debate with those objecting to Clemson University's close ties to Benjamin Tillman. The docent worried about an "overreaction to change everything" but understood the complaint. Wilson had an opportunity to make changes but "went a little backwards." Black voters supported him and expected change.[74]

Historic Columbia continued to explore the complexity of the Wilson family's time in the South within the context of the national debate about Wilson himself. Docents rarely addressed the controversy because visitors did not bring the subject up, although guides were prepared for the discussion. A workshop addressed current events and the Democratic and Confederate leanings of Tommy's father, Joseph Wilson. A few guests referenced the controversy as an aside after seeing *Legacy*.[75] One docent avoided the subject because she felt the students' requests were immature but did not discourage visitor conversation if it came up. But two docents exploited the controversy on their tours. They believed museums were designed for conversations about relevant current events, one calling the MoRE a "great opportunity to talk about flaws" of historical figures. Docents hosted a few visitors who knew about the controversy but primarily dismissed Wilson and his actions as a product of his times. Other guests wanted more information. Bacon-Rogers pulled up a *Washington Post* article on her phone for engaged nurses who were surprised they knew nothing about the controversy. The women launched a great conversation about public perception of historical figures and left with a passion to find out more about trends in museum communities and public arenas concerning famous figures.[76]

MoRE docents who favored a direct approach to the Wilson controversy attempted to meet more recent calls by public historians to confront contentious history. The more radical HHM can embrace the value of conjecture, which opens an opportunity to discuss events and stories about historical figures that illuminate human flaws. By challenging traditional heroic narratives, HHMs can make men like Wilson more relatable to visitors, who also make mistakes and are intellectually capable of discussing human complexity.[77] But several MoRE volunteer docents dismissed or warned against using contemporary values to evaluate people of the past and failing to contextualize the attitudes of the time period. Hogan broached the Princeton students' protest on her tours, thinking they had a valid concern worthy of discussion, but cautioned there was no white name on a building not stained by slavery or segregation. Stickney firmly opposed "trying to rewrite history" to the point "we're going to lose all of our history."[78] But this exclusive attitude is an ideological product of a century of interpretations produced by white public-history institutions and white-centered historical narratives. The rush to exempt Wilson by contextualizing his racism compared to his contemporaries misses that Wilson was protested in his time and that his memory continues to be contested. Still, the interpretive approach Historic Columbia has taken with Reconstruction and Wilson's memory marks its uniqueness given that many organizations were reticent in initiating or joining these kinds of conversations until Black Lives Matter and social equity protests reignited similar debates in 2020. Public historian Modupe Labode argued in the wake of the Charleston massacre that controversial monuments and memorials to flawed historical figures have to be evaluated on an individual basis and with the input of local and state history institutions. Only then can institutions consider common strategies for dealing with problematic history: "alteration, reinterpretation, creating new monuments, removal, and doing nothing."[79]

But What about *Gone with the Wind?* Conclusions and the Act of Letting Go

The second version of *Legacy* did not debut until April 2015. As such, for over a year the tour's conclusion remained a conundrum for the both the interpretive team and docents.[80] The key issue was succinctly conveying the big themes or ideas to audiences who were too fatigued from the tour and exhibit film to respond to engagement questions or interpreted them as rhetorical. Because of this fatigue that I and other docents witnessed, the revised docent tour script removed references to the abstract concepts of the Lost Cause and national reconciliation, although docents could broach the subjects at their discretion. The script also converted a "big theme" engagement question into a definitive concluding statement on memory that ended the tour positively. It reminded visitors that the MoRE was a site of healing, initially dedicated to the "first strong Southern president since Reconstruction at a time when the South was viewed as having a negative impact on the nation in the 1930s. Today the home helps heal old wounds and address the myths of Reconstruction that became accepted as truth."[81] The MoRE sparked historical questions that had no easy, definitive answers: Did Wilson look to his post–Civil War experience in framing his understanding of World War I and the League of Nations? Did the equality brought by Reconstruction influence Wilson's decision to allow federal offices to be segregated? Did Wilson and his European counterparts' racial attitudes determine which peoples deserved national sovereignty in the wake of the Great War?[82] The challenge for tour and program coordinator Heather Bacon-Rogers was that there were a "lot of conclusions you're asking people to draw on their own." To leave a lasting impression on tired visitors, Lee chose two big ideas: that Reconstruction was not a southern phenomenon and that people are afraid to confront Reconstruction.[83]

After the opening, Samuel L. Schaffer's 2017 essay confirmed some of the answers that docents had drawn from the expertise they had regarding the teenage Wilson's world. Wilson's presidential goals had been domestic, so when World War I ignited, he drew upon his Civil War experiences and domestic agenda to help frame his neutrality policy. Schaffer argues that Reconstruction influenced the president's postwar philosophy, though he never explicitly stated so. The idealism of his League of Nations aside, Wilson hoped for a stalemate or "peace without victory" to avoid dividing the postwar world into victors and losers. He feared that harsh treaty terms, when combined with a toppled political and social order, would yield disastrous results. This argument and his "emotional language of 'humiliation' and 'resentment'" could have been lifted from his and others' Reconstruction scholarship during the time. Schaffer notes that Wilson left few recollections of Columbia or reflections about how much his real experiences and the "manufactured memory of Reconstruction" inspired his foreign policy. The MoRE cannot definitively quantify that influence, either, but it can make Wilson's time in Columbia clearer and deepen our understanding of Reconstruction's impact. Schaffer juxtaposes Wilson's "absorbing the myths of Negro Reconstruction in Georgia and South Carolina" with Georges Clemenceau, who spent the first four years of Reconstruction in New York City writing positively about it. But Wilson's few short years in Columbia directly contradicted these myths. This moment, when the family's district was represented by businessman and state senator W. B. Nash, who had been enslaved by Wade Hampton III's in-laws mere blocks away, was the pinnacle of his father's financial and professional success. Schaffer argues that the League of Nations brought order "rooted in racial hierarchy" and southern-style white democracy to a global stage, offering former colonies paternalistic self-determination "with restrictions." How countries within the League's established mandate system were assessed in terms of stage of development, with nation-states of the old Ottoman Empire being fast-tracked but Brown or Black colonies, especially in Africa, receiving only the promise of eventual freedom, "derived in part from Wilson's graduate training in Germanic racial theories." Similarly, Wilson recoiled at a Japanese representative's call at Versailles for a racial equality amendment.[84]

The difficulty in ending the tour represented the struggle in discussing contentious issues surrounding Reconstruction and memory in general. Above the mantel in the final bedroom, a partial quote from Wilson's essay on Reconstruction encapsulated this problem: "*Reconstruction is still revolutionary matter. Those who delve in it find it like a banked fire,* still hot and fiery within, for all it has lain under the ashes a whole generation."[85] Hogan best explained why the narrative of the home felt unresolved. She wanted more on how the return of a southerner to the executive branch helped bridge the divide created by the Civil War and promote nationalism. Given that Reconstruction was a civil rights revolution that failed with Jim Crow, she asked, "Who was it a reconciliation for? It certainly wasn't a reconciliation for African Americans. Because then they wound up moving to the North, the Great Migration. You can't tell that whole story." She even saw the possibility of linking World War I with the Great Migration. "It's such a big complicated story. You have to stop it somewhere." Just where to stop was difficult for some docents who saw this much larger picture. One, in fact took, their conclusion all the way to the 1963 March on Washington during an early evaluation.[86]

Truly, the tour could speak to many moments in twentieth-century US history. Cinematic, presidential, Reconstruction, and Great Migration history were woven together in a complicated tapestry. *Birth* sparked controversy and challenges, but an even more popular film, *Gone with the Wind,* succeeded it in the interpretation of Reconstruction memory. If the South was a "media colony, an elsewhere for the American majority's amusement or negative example," *Gone with the Wind* and its nostalgic Old South fascinated the colonizers most.[87] This white fantasy and its "idealized race relations" not only stalled racial progress in the nation but also bred a segregated tourist industry where visitors hoped "to see the Dixie they witnessed on film," with "blacks working in the cotton fields next to grand, white-columned mansions."[88] Storm believed that HHM narratives about rich people and the notion that "this is how people in *Gone with the Wind* lived" still drive much of the tourism of northerners and a large number of tourists who do not want to see or be reminded of slave labor.[89] The familiarity of visitors with *Gone with the Wind* convinced several docents that it should be included as part of the discussion on Reconstruction memory. Jennifer Gunter, who has nostalgic but conflicting attitudes toward the book and film, gave a tour to a woman who professed her love for it and defended its realism. Because *Gone with the Wind* was a "part of that genre that lives on," Gunter thought it warranted inclusion in the exhibit film. It revived "all of those same tropes," such as the "scary black man," and had a global impact that surpassed *Birth of a Nation.* People in Japan reenact the film.[90] Halie Brazier, who until recently watched *Gone with the Wind* annually, agreed that visitor familiarity with themes or plots made it a useful interpretive tool, especially given *Birth* was less known. Docents even disagreed on whether *Birth* or *Gone with the Wind* was worse. Brazier found the latter's "detrimental" Lost Cause narrative "quite cringe worthy" and "bad enough"; but it was moderate compared to *Birth,* which was "way more overtly racist and awful" and "much more visceral."[91] But Morgan and an artist on her tour disagreed that *Birth* was the most racist of the two films. *Gone with the Wind* was "so offensive," Morgan argued, yet *Birth* was "singled out as being the most prejudiced piece of filmmaking ever committed to celluloid."[92] *Gone with the Wind* is an example of how complicated interpretations veer down important rabbit holes, not all of which can be included in the narrative.

The memory of Reconstruction and Woodrow Wilson created long-term problems for the MoRE. Contextualizing it precisely and concisely for the conclusion of the tour was a major interpretive issue. But Wilson's presidency, both its successes and flaws, also proved difficult material for docents. Despite its strengths, the exhibit film *The Legacy of Woodrow Wilson and Reconstruction* was the most controversial element of the tour, culminating in a revision within the first year of the reopening. The chief complaint among docents was that it misrepresented Wilson's opinion of *Birth of a Nation* and diminished his accomplishments while emphasizing the failings of his racial ideology. This issue was not unique to MoRE docents. A docent at Wilson's DC home also confessed upon my provocation that Wilson was a product of the South but the term *racist* was misleading.[93] No exhibit film or scripted conclusion could ever address everyone's concerns. But the multiple revisions and debates in service to achieving the best interpretation possible and answering contemporary questions about Wilson's racist legacy proved instrumental in demonstrating to docents how to have conversations with visitors about the legacy of Wilson and Reconstruction.

Conclusion

The Public's Response to the MoRE

The Museum of the Reconstruction Era tour opens with a simple question: "When I say the word *Reconstruction*, what comes to mind?" The inquiry is a best practice in interpretive questioning, because it allows for a variety of answers, asks the visitor to draw on their own knowledge and personal experience, opens opportunities for dialogue among visitors, and provides useful information to the docent, namely the visitors' working knowledge about the period. Most visitors knew that Reconstruction followed the Civil War, but few, according to docents, seemed to know much more than the term *carpetbagger*. When the Buffalo Bill Historical Center in Wyoming evaluated visitors to determine what reinterpretation content would interest them, nearly half associated "Buffalo Bill" Cody with his Wild West Show even though it was not mentioned by evaluators. Visitors possess strong attachments to the history lessons they learn in popular culture, even after a tour. However, the MoRE's introductory exchange established that the visitor takeaway would be "a better understanding of this misunderstood period when the South rebuilt itself economically, socially and physically."[1] This precise language conveyed the wide reach of Reconstruction in the postwar South and planted the seed for a conversation about memory, where visitors learned neither history nor their own education were immune from bias. MoRE visitors stepped onto the porch not as "blank slates" but with an "entry narrative" composed of their own experiences and memories, "like baggage," which the MoRE tried to unpack.[2]

Historic Columbia designed MoRE at the WWFH to convey a narrative about the importance of time and place. The biracial space the Wilsons and their employees occupied became a lens to explore the biracial democracy and labor system created by Reconstruction. This approach sought to correct the historical amnesia surrounding Reconstruction, which public history reviewers of the site thought successful. Visitor evaluations and docent oral histories demonstrate that the vast majority of visitors approved of dismantling the shrine and learned from the reinterpretation, primarily because they knew so little about Reconstruction. Like the MoRE docents reconciling the white supremacist narrative of Reconstruction that they were taught with the new information of the tour, a significant portion of visitors changed their thinking and gained a new appreciation for others. A reviewer for the *Public Historian* praised in particular the domestic servant space in the pantries built on historiography, census records, and architecture. Similarly, the reviewer for the *Journal of American History* commended the Red Shirt room exhibit for explaining the political demise of Reconstruction and white violence, bolstering docents' assertions that they thrived in the space. The digitized 1872 map of Columbia and exhibit films were popular based on docents' experiences and reviews. However, some constructive criticism emerged about the limited number of artifacts, timing, the Wilson family tree interactive, and the amount of Woodrow Wilson information on the tour. The dual narrative divided the MoRE's two formal reviewers and received minimal complaints from visitors. Despite these critiques, evaluation data and docent experiences prove that the majority of museumgoers are, as one visitor put it, "hungry" for Reconstruction history and open to a modern thematic historic house museum.[3]

Consultant Annie Wright professionally designed the MoRE visitor evaluation. She looked to other institutions' evaluations for inspiration, including the Smithsonian Institution and the National Endowment of the Arts. Docents administered the final Survey Monkey evaluation on a tablet at the end of the tour, but paper options were also offered on two clipboards. Wright constructed the evaluation to capture audience engagement and the information the interpretive team thought the audience should receive. Stellar evaluations measure three visitor responses to interpretation: *cognitive*, related to learning and processing information; *affective*, reflecting attitude and emotions; and *behavioral* actions. The MoRE evaluation measured behavioral responses to the guide, cognitive responses about changing one's thinking, and affective responses such as gaining empathy for different people. Two small changes could improve the evaluation responses: incorporating questions that offer a range between two opposing statements, such as whether the presentations were enjoyable/unenjoyable, and ranking on a scale of one to five whether the content made visitors angry, which would determine how much of the interpretation violated their preconceived notions of Reconstruction.[4] Docents appreciated receiving visitor evaluation data, and the results reinforced best practices. Docents corrected deficiencies as data changed month to month and worked to convert acceptable results into the best categories, such as moving visitors from being engaged at many points to being fully engaged.[5]

The first two chapters of the present study established that the MoRE, preserved in the 1920s as part of a larger white women's club movement, shed its shrine origins and showcased the WWFH as the primary artifact, opening the door for a place- and period-centered interpretation of Reconstruction-era Columbia. MoRE visitor evaluations overwhelmingly indicated that the vast majority of visitors were engaged and welcomed the dismantling of the shrine, its period vignettes, and the fully guided tour. Nearly 3,000 people, 85 percent of them adults, came to the MoRE within its first year of opening. A quarter of visitors, or 648 individuals, submitted evaluations.[6] Nearly everyone who visited the MoRE approved of the overall quality and were engaged.[7] A quarter of the 324 evaluation comments reinforced the high quality of the museum and tour and the positive experience it yielded.[8] Over a dozen visitors commented on the preservation efforts, including the beauty of the home and how the restoration helped them understand historical events of the 1870s.[9] The most important attraction for visitors to historic or heritage buildings is the building itself, which arouses emotion. In one study of two HHMs, "the perception of the building" was one factor in visitors feeling "happy, pleasant, and stimulated."[10]

Visitor evaluations also confirm that the training process discussed in chapter 3 was successful: MoRE docents, and their handling of the information in an engaging and respectful way, were the most important component of the tour. The mandatory tour evaluation that followed workshops on history, public history best practices, and racial and cultural sensitivity ensured that capable and knowledgeable docents delivered the MoRE tour. The training proved that docents need not be professional public historians but that paid docents, often public history graduate students, and well-educated volunteers, primarily with careers in education or the humanities, were best suited to convey the complex, narratively rich tour. Cecelia Moore, who reviewed the exhibit for the *Journal of American History,* noted that the semi-guided tours by trained volunteers and paid staff were important to keeping visitors following the narrative. And in commending everyone's work, she also correctly imagined "that there were a number of difficult conversations among curators, board members, and volunteers—some of whom must have an emotional stake in the previous, non-Reconstruction-based interpretation of the house."[11] Research suggests that visitors have positive feelings toward a heritage site if they have positive employee-visitor interactions, especially when seeking help or information. Cognitive and emotional interest theories indicate that museum components, such as texts and objects, are more interesting when the visitor understands them. These components also become more enjoyable when they encourage positive emotions, especially when supplemented with "humor, remarkable stories, or surprise." Docents are critical not only in providing the supplemental anecdotes but also in nurturing a fleeting interest into an experience that connects with the visitors' motives or values.[12]

MoRE docents had the full attention of more than two-thirds of evaluators on the tour. Visitors also ranked "what the tour guide told" them as the most interesting type of information, more than double its closest competitor, the panels.[13] Visitors praised docents in the evaluation's comments section, most commonly describing them as knowledgeable. Guests stressed their docents were extremely educated and well informed.[14] Several visitors left detailed commentary that spoke to how docents were engaged and demonstrated superior quality. Docents created an informal space to answer questions and encourage dialogue and displayed enthusiasm and confidence when sharing knowledge. One visitor wrote that the docent educated them "on the difference between the past and 'history,'" offered a new perspective, and inspired future research into the topics.[15]

Despite stellar evaluations in general, visitor feedback also demonstrated the contradictions and varied preferences of those who experience twenty-first-century HHM exhibit elements, namely limited artifacts, panels, question-driven conversations, and interactives. After docents, the text and photographs in the panels were the second most popular form of information for visitors, closely followed by artifacts. However, the docents were twice as popular as panels and preferences toward the three choices of artifacts, panels, and interactives fluctuated dramatically, representing the "participatory power" of visitors to allow content and interactives to pull them toward what they find interesting and to retrieve the interpretation.[16] In the comments section of the evaluations, over twice as many visitors wanted more artifacts than those who liked the restrained use of objects.[17] Guests needed these objects to balance the thirty-eight panels and wanted more time to read them. Tour and program coordinator Heather Bacon-Rogers claimed that the sheer number of panels and their college sophomore reading level overloaded 75 percent of visitors on her tour. Other docents had difficulty gauging how much time visitors wanted to spend with the panels but encouraged them to read panels even if docents were speaking.[18] Docent and visitor comments suggested that asking how much time visitors desired would be helpful on the visitor evaluation.[19]

One surprise from the visitor evaluations was that questions, at 10 percent, underperformed as a source of visitor engagement, as did interactives, defined as hands-on reproductions and digitized technology.[20] Visitor comments and docent testimony validate that some interactives, especially the digitized 1872 map of Columbia, were incredibly popular, but the family tree failed to engage audiences.[21] That the MoRE docents' demonstration of the family tree and encouragement to explore did not result in prolonged visitor engagement speaks to the interactive's design. Studies on active recruitment reveal that visitors spend significantly more time with interactive exhibits when invited and observed by personnel. Docents blamed the sometimes unresponsive touch screen, unfriendly user design and format, and the lengthy text descriptions of family members. One visitor suggested it needed "color."[22] The lower results for questions was unexpected given that a common problem visitors have with museums is that these spaces do not inspire dialogue between friends and strangers about content. The MoRE's semi-guided presentation designed for questions and conversation reflected Nina Simon's participatory five-stage "me-to-we" design. By the end of the MoRE tour, a skilled docent could guide members of the group into feeling like a "close-knit team," where they have moved from consuming and asking questions about content to interacting with the docent and their fellow visitors socially about content and interests.[23] Docents admitted that some visitors preferred to listen rather than ask questions. Whether the visitors preferred this learning style, lacked interest, were committed to a white supremacist narrative of Reconstruction, or opposed the interpretive approach was less clear. However, popular points for audience questions occurred during discussions of the political parties, elections, the Klan, and Jim Crow's rise, including voting restrictions and poll taxes.[24]

Chapter 3 also argues that the training process helped MoRE docents come to terms with their own exposure to a white supremacist narrative of Reconstruction and unlearn it. Subsequently their tours often educated visitors on the power of this narrative and, in some cases, the audiences' own indoctrination. Docent experiences and evaluations illustrate that most visitors had no idea about the promise of Reconstruction and the violent white Democratic response.[25] Although John Falk argued that prior interest and knowledge were vital predictors of what and how much knowledge a visitor walked away with, evaluations of MoRE visitors refuted this. Most visitors exited the tour thinking it was excellent and that they had learned a great deal of new information. These results confirm a previous study that found prior knowledge and interest had little direct effect on what exhibits fascinated visitors. What mattered most was cognitive accessibility, and to a lesser degree a pleasant emotional response. Visitors were more likely to enjoy and find interest in an exhibit if they understood the content.[26] Docents described the thrill of giving the tours when, as weekend docent Casey Lee labeled them, these "A-ha!" or "light bulb" moments occurred. Docents clarified for visitors how to correct an outdated Reconstruction narrative, that the Democrats and Republicans of Reconstruction were not the same parties of today, and how the Red Shirts' violence was commemorated.[27] For those horrified visitors who were open and attentive to the narrative, weekend docent Jennifer Gunter explained, "you've just undone . . . what they've known their entire life and all of sudden you're telling them they were wrong, their parents were wrong, their teachers were wrong. That's a lot to grasp."[28] Like MoRE docents, visitors Black and white also began to consider their own family history and their ancestors who lived in the state during Reconstruction.[29] Non-southerners made connections with Klan and segregation material, often overturning the myth of southern exceptionalism in their own minds. Volunteers met visitors who lived in a Klan stronghold like Indiana, had been in a sundown town, or had worked in law enforcement that infiltrated klaverns.[30] Docents reported non-southerners began to see de facto Jim Crow segregation in their own communities, realizing segregation was "not just a southern phenomenon."[31]

"Aren't I a Citizen?," the chapter devoted to interpretation techniques that illuminated the lives of unknown domestic workers, argues that historiography, census records, architecture, image analysis, and docent training were essential. Lauren Safranek, who published her MoRE review in a special issue of *Public Historian* devoted to HHMs, cited the pantries as "one of the most memorable and poignant sections" of the tour. Even though information was lacking in this space about employees, the space produced a "textured" experience driven by the "home as an artifact" that highlighted the "larger experiences in Columbia during Reconstruction."[32] Her assessment reflects an interpretation produced by numerous debates between docents and staff about how best to represent the lives of domestic workers. The *Downton Abbey* effect was one manifestation of the interpretive tension between class and race.

MoRE docents excelled in producing a compelling narrative of domestic terrorism in the Red Shirt bedroom, a process detailed in chapter 5, and used the tragic narrative to question their own privilege as white docents discussing violence. They described the space as the most compelling in the home and the one in which they felt most confident because of the overwhelming evidence of Reconstruction's brutal end via voter intimidation, mob violence, and fraud by white Democrats. Reviewer Cecilia Moore thought the MoRE did an "admirable job" helping visitors understand the political complexity of how conservative forces resisted federal changes and used violence to intimidate Black voters.[33]

As chapter 6 on the historian's craft discussed, visitor evaluations overwhelmingly showed that guests learned interesting new information and that a significant portion changed their perceptions. However, by presenting multiple narratives and voices with complexity and tension that spanned Reconstruction through the Great War, the tour allowed visitors to contextualize their experience within a larger, diverse story of America and come to understand themselves and others better.[34] One quarter of visitors had their beliefs or thoughts challenged or changed and gained appreciation for people not like themselves. These results are especially important given that 88 percent of visitors were white and the exhibit was equally devoted to the Black experience during Reconstruction.[35] Visitors also gained insight into Woodrow Wilson and his influence beyond World War I and the League of Nations. A few walked away with a diminished respect for the president because of his racism.[36] Evaluations and docent oral histories revealed that visitors came to the MoRE with open minds and walked away thinking about Reconstruction and its memory. The large number of visitors with open minds was the most pleasant surprise for docents. These open minds were the product of a lack of information not misinformation. If anything, giving an unusual but pleasant tour to more than a dozen bikers taught weekend docent Halie Brazier to overcome her own bias about who constitutes an open-minded visitor.[37]

The final chapter examines the revision of the exhibit film *The Legacy of Woodrow Wilson and Reconstruction* and connections it made between D. W. Griffith's film *The Birth of a Nation* and Wilson's presidency and Reconstruction memory. The tour and docents faced significant challenges in effectively discussing white supremacy in the final space, especially when associated with a well-memorialized figure, with primarily white audiences. Time constraints, visitor fatigue, difficulties discussing racialized violence, the complexity of concepts such as the Lost Cause, and the complicated intersection of history and media involved in discussions of *Birth of a Nation* converged to present unique challenges and imperfect solutions. Nonetheless, exhibit films were the most popularly mentioned interactives by visitors.[38] Cecelia Moore praised the films for conveying that a "major theme" of the MoRE was that, after the Civil War, Americans fought to define their country and themselves locally, regionally, and nationally. The battle shaped subsequent movements in the twentieth century and today.[39] Where Moore embraced the rhetorical question of how Reconstruction "might have influenced the world view of the future president," Safranek believed the MoRE's greatest flaw was no "clear connection between Tommy Wilson and Reconstruction." Given the dual narrative, its "absence" was "too big to ignore," even if "reliable documentation" was lacking. She left with unanswered questions about the Wilson family's politics during Reconstruction and how his teenage experience shaped his politics and leadership. The case and exhibit film on the legacy of *Birth* hinted at this but left the visitor "in the dark" with "too much unsaid."[40] The artifact that best represents Safranek's criticism of the dual narrative is Tommy's birth bed. Even Moore called the bed the "most glaring inconsistency" in the home. The review continued: "It dominates the room, yet remains mostly uncurated, while arrayed around it are displays about carpetbaggers, *Birth of a Nation*, and Wilson's presidency."[41]

As the first Reconstruction museum in the nation, the MoRE offers a blueprint of the challenges and rich rewards that will accompany commemorating Reconstruction in public spaces. Both exhibit reviewers understood that the reinterpretation was daring given institutional size, available artifacts, and diverse exhibit elements. For Safranek the exhibit presented "provocative ideas" and was "trying to accomplish laudable and worthy interpretive goals." Moore called the attempt to convey the "nuance and complexity" of Reconstruction as well as its promise "a bold undertaking" and a "mostly successful endeavor."[42] While all docents, staff, and consultants made significant contributions to this intrepid enterprise, executive director Robin Waites and her leadership made the interpretive turn possible. Waites retired in 2024, choosing to leave "on a high note" after twenty years at the helm of Historic Columbia. She departed on her own terms, having checked everything off her list of personal goals and creating new ones she never imagined. She left a far more inclusive organization behind than the one that wealthy white Columbians founded to frame their own narratives. She had no executive experience managing human resources, budgets, or boards yet grew the organization dramatically. She inherited six full-time staff, a $300,000 budget, six historic buildings, and fourteen acres of poorly maintained grounds. She more than tripled the staff and increased the budget to $2.5 million. She oversaw the rehabilitation of all property gardens to both provide educational opportunities, increase revenue, and offer green space downtown. In addition to the groundbreaking and award-winning interpretation at the MoRE, Waites lead the reinterpretation of every building except the Robert Mills House and Gardens and expanded the website, which also includes collections. The Waites era boosted Historic Columbia's preservation profile, garnering the support of the once-reluctant Chamber of Commerce, and included a vast array of progressive projects often part of partnerships that amplified multivocal local history: collecting and preserving Columbia's Jewish and queer history, documenting of the South Carolina Lunatic Asylum, and placing the Black public high school Lakeview on the National Register of Historic Places. Waites also cofounded City of Women, an annual event honoring women from the past and the present, and the Columbia SC 63 Project, which focuses on the civil rights movement in Columbia. Cofounder Bobby Donaldson, historian of southern and Black history at the University of South Carolina, used the language of Reconstruction to describe her work, "reconstructing" how Columbians view slavery and civil rights for marginalized people. Her vision ultimately prepared Historic Columbia to join national dialogues on the Confederate flag and Black Lives Matter with its expertise. Because of her, the MoRE changed what visitors and docents knew about Reconstruction and, to some degree, themselves.[43]

This will ripple into the community as these individuals continue conversations with friends, family, and acquaintances.

The Political Road to Reconstruction in the HHM and Where to Go from Here

Edith Galt Wilson's efforts to preserve shrines at Woodrow Wilson's birthplace and their home in Washington, DC, serve as a reminder that HHMs' engaging political and social issues as part of a new turn in the HHM movement is not new. The message is. For Patricia West, who traced the first century of HHMs, these homes were always political, shaped first by the period politics of their origin and then the public role they perform, such as exemplifying patriotism, loyalty, and good citizenship. Sometimes founders hid the politics of the house beneath a "creation myth" of shrines and "romantic patriotism"; but even the establishment of the HHM movement itself was political, because both conservative and activist women, "enmeshed in the 'cult of domesticity,'" were highly visibly practicing "domestic religion" as applied to the HHM in the male public sphere. This made HHMs "documents of political history."[44]

Journal of American History reviewer Cecelia Moore noted that the MoRE was "ahead of the trend" in Reconstruction commemoration, since the National Park Service took several years to get its Beaufort site off the ground.[45] However, national recognition of Beaufort could be the tipping point in correcting disparities between Reconstruction scholarship and public knowledge. Although few know Beaufort's foundational role in Reconstruction, the other major problem is that white violence and national complicity were always center to an accurate telling of Reconstruction. White Americans have yet to come to terms with this. As Kate Masur and Gregory Downs forewarned, commemorating Reconstruction meant "remembering how frequently white Americans resorted to violence and corruption to disenfranchise black voters and passed discriminatory laws to block African American economic and social equality, while the U.S. government stood by passively."[46]

Patricia West has called for "administrative history" to acknowledge the political tensions and historical context that shaped the evolution of HHMs. Professionals have both "the right and responsibility" to engage "new scholarship, new communities, and new agendas."[47] And hopefully the context of those endeavors would be evaluated in the future. The MoRE answered this call. Like all political HHMs, the MoRE was founded for political reasons. But the MoRE reinvented the "culture of reconciliation," using cultural tourism to change the memory of Reconstruction and narrative about the reconciliationist President Wilson. Reconciliation through disruption is one way HHMs can heal old wounds of national tragedy and promote greater equity. The Matilda Joslyn Gage home discussed in the introduction and Pauli Murray Center for History and Social Justice in Durham, North Carolina, are part of the International Coalition of Sites of Conscience, a global network nearly two hundred strong in over four dozen countries. Similar to the MoRE, these two homes and fellow coalition site the Centro Cultural y Museum de la Memoria in Uruguay all have an "uncomfortable relationship" with their houses. In the latter, fear is an emotion welcomed, and "dangerous memory" is employed as a "new weapon" to transform the structural artifact into "safe containers" for community discussion and navigating social issues and rights. The country house of late nineteenth-century dictator Máximo Santos claims to be a "memory museum, not a history museum." A space of political power, in this case a dictator's home rather than a president's teenage home, is used to process the modern struggle for democracy and the legacy of authoritarianism in Uruguay. Although the MoRE keeps Wilson in view, the Centro Cultural substitutes a 1973–84 dictatorship for Santos's reign. Like the MoRE, it devotes a room to the memory of state terrorism. Less structured than the semiguided Wilson tour, Centro Cultural visitors can begin their tour in any room.[48] Masur and Downs argued that the Beaufort NPS designation would show the world "how important it is that we continue talking about the fundamental questions of democracy, race and citizenship that trouble our politics to this day."[49] The future of the MoRE's reinterpretation is bound by these same contemporary political and social issues as well. Currently it is slowly revising the memory of Reconstruction for its docents and audience, giving them a new historical perspective on America's promise and shortcomings. All South Carolinians and Americans would benefit from this exchange.

Exhibit reviewers to various degrees understood the contemporary social issues that the MoRE's reinterpretation addressed. While Safranek hinted at the political implications and climate the MoRE operated in, Moore was more sympathetic to the undertaking. Moore saw both the short and long game the MoRE was playing. She submitted her review before the Charleston massacre yet situated her review as the United States approached the precipice of that historical moment. The events in Ferguson following Michael Brown's death had yet to play out fully, but they were national news. Using Wilson's words, she remarked that Reconstruction remained a "'banked fire' in Columbia," as evidenced by the Confederate flag flying at the capitol—yet to be lowered in the wake of the Charleston shooting at Mother Emanuel AME. But Moore was encouraged as a historian that the public was willing to engage in conversation about our divisions. Social tension combined with the growing popularity of films placing race front and center suggested to her that the public was prepared to learn how central race was to American history and contextualize contemporary problems within that past. Public historians were in unique positions to offer this lesson. The MoRE provided such a space, which could also show historians how dialogues about Reconstruction operate in public settings.[50]

Annette Gordon-Reed once asked a question about Sally Hemings's relationship with Thomas Jefferson so profound that her answer became the catalyst that spurred Monticello toward an narrative that includes Jefferson-Hemings descendants. In the wake of racially charged events in 2015 engulfing the nation, Gordon-Reed wondered, "What if Reconstruction hadn't failed?" Freed people may have become landowners and voters. Black and white students might have been educated together. Further, "what if American historians during the aftermath of Reconstruction had not been white supremacists?" Maybe those same integrated students would have learned "another narrative about black people's place in America." Reconstruction would never have become a "tragedy" that harmed "the good and innocent white people of the South." Furthermore, Gordon-Reed argued, D. W. Griffith would never have visually presented the literary and historic Lost Cause and white supremacist Reconstruction interpretations in *Birth of a Nation,* such as the State House scene of Black legislators "with their bare feet up on their desks during sessions, eating chicken and watermelon while taking the occasional swig of alcohol." Instead the Dunning School "echoed his sentiments," substituting "faux scholarly detachment for the director's cinematic pyrotechnics on the race question." This led to "disfranchisement, Jim Crow, and, for extremists, lynching." The ripple effect of these losses reverberated in the struggles for equality today.[51] What if HHMs had not been born of this same ideology? It might not have taken 150 years to present an interpretation that offered what reviewer Cecelia Moore called a picture of Reconstruction's "promise and opportunity" instead of the narrative of "defeat and despair" given by the victors of the political and cultural battle to destroy Reconstruction. Visitors to the MoRE see the era as "still open to possibility" and can imagine a different outcome where the Klan and Red Shirts did not win with violence and Jim Crow never existed. This was a far "different picture" of Reconstruction than most visitors would "recall from high school history class."[52]

The MoRE can treat national scars by serving as a resource for learning about the first civil rights movement and contemplating the first expressions of African American political, economic, and social independence following emancipation. Watching Black successes in politics, business, and the legal system and then bearing witness to these rights being stripped away in blood and with terror make the path from white supremacy during Reconstruction to its current state in the twenty-first century clearer and more familiar.

The devastation unleashed by Dylann Roof in Charleston or the murder of Heather Heyer by James Alex Fields Jr. during the white nationalist violence incited over monuments in Charlottesville, Virginia, in 2017 transform from shocking, isolated incidents to an absurd pattern that reminds the nation Reconstruction remains unfinished.

It took over a century to build and entrench a white supremacist narrative of Reconstruction. Even as historians began to chip away at the narrative, the memory continued to endure in textbooks, monuments, historic sites, and popular culture, especially film. Filmmakers persist in their engagement with *Birth of a Nation*—not just DJ Spooky and his *Rebirth of a Nation* featured in the MoRE exhibit. Robert Zemeckis, "simulating Griffith's simulations," gave Tom Hanks a cameo as Nathan Bedford Forrest in the reproduction of *Birth of a Nation* that begins *Forrest Gump*.[53] Quentin Tarantino confessed to Henry Louis Gates Jr. his obsession with and desire to "deconstruct" *Birth of a Nation*. Both scholar and director found Thomas Dixon's influence, via his original work *The Clansman*, to be "evil." Tarantino opined that it compares only to "*Mein Kampf* when it comes to its ugly imagery." The director blamed *Birth* not just for rebirthing the Klan but for "all the blood that was spilled" until the early 1960s. He argued that if Dixon and Griffith were "held by Nuremberg Laws, they would be guilty of war crimes" for their creation.[54] Nate Parker attempted to reset *Birth of a Nation* by giving his film about Nat Turner's rebellion the same name.[55] Reconstruction-era films in Hollywood are unicorns, but the 2016 summer blockbuster season brought *Free State of Jones*. While the film was panned by some for its reliance on the "white savior" trope, the director Gary Ross consulted historical monographs and historians, including Victoria Bynam, David Blight, and Eric Foner. Ross even footnoted the film.[56] However, it would be nice to see a Reconstruction film not told through a white male lens.

The white supremacist narrative that inspired *Birth*'s depiction of Reconstruction in South Carolina saved Wilson's home, kept the Confederate flag flying at the State House over fifty years, motivated the gunman in Charleston, and killed the first NPS attempt to create a Reconstruction monument in 2002. As Woodrow Wilson wrote in his 1901 essay on Reconstruction: "It is a wonder that historians who take their business seriously can sleep at night."[57] The MoRE can facilitate the hard conversations about white supremacy and its myths that shape the modern era. It can guide the dialogues about white supremacist symbols and important historical figures and presidents with inexcusable flaws and what place they should have in public spaces that define what it means to be an American, southern or otherwise.

The MoRE is a start in shattering the white supremacist narrative of Reconstruction once and for all and mainstreaming positive images of Reconstruction that have circulated since its destruction. One of the most visible presentations of a Black countermemory of Reconstruction was the Southern Negro Youth Congress major convention in Columbia, October 18–20, 1946. Reconstruction permeated much of the meeting. Over one thousand delegates of the congress, part of the larger Southern Popular Front, filled Township Auditorium, the building that almost resulted in the demolition of the MoRE and ultimately led to its preservation. On the auditorium's walls hung photographs of Black Reconstruction-era politicians. A biracial crowd of seven hundred listened to W. E. B. Du Bois give his speech "Behold the Land" at Benedict, one of Columbia's Reconstruction-era historical Black colleges. The speech looked backward to Reconstruction at the moment a modern civil rights movement was gaining greater traction but also looked to a future that still may not fulfill America's democratic promise. Du Bois's speech praised the power of young people, which historian Patricia Sullivan saw reflected in Black Lives Matter. The convention was largely forgotten until USC's History Center, as part of their loftier goal to present public programming on Reconstruction's legacy, and the Center for Civil Rights History and Research organized a seventieth anniversary event. In the same chapel Du Bois spoke in, his Pulitzer Prize–winning biographer David Levering Lewis delivered "Our Exceptionalist Quagmire: Is There a Way Forward," a speech reflecting on "Behold the Land" in light of contemporary racial and political issues.[58] Commemorative events for the next decade, such as those shaped by a new national monument in Beaufort or those celebrating countermemories of Reconstruction, will build on this momentum.

Historic Columbia continues to provide programming and collaborate with local institutions, such as USC, to commemorate Reconstruction's sesquicentennial. It perseveres in promoting Reconstruction narratives with expert speakers, like Neil Kinghan, author of *A Brief Moment in the Sun: Francis Cardozo and Reconstruction in South Carolina*, and walking tours of Reconstruction sites. The most exciting development is that Historic Columbia secured a Reconstruction-era ballot box from South Carolina. It came with a handwritten note revealing that the donor's great-grandfather blew on the ballots to separate extra votes while he counted. With the South Carolina State Museum, Historic Columbia built a vitrine to display the box with the existing tissue ballot in the Red Shirt room and designed a new double panel on voter suppression.[59]

Historic Columbia updates the MoRE regularly as well to meet the interpretive needs of visitors. The organization revised the citizenship video in the family parlor and hired Black contractors for the work. Visitors and docents complained that a young boy's narration, meant to represent a child-like Tommy, was difficult to understand. A few visitors complained there

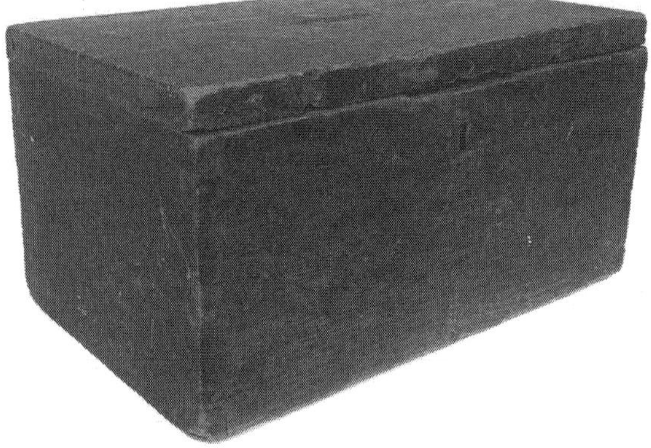

Figure 20. A newly acquired ballot box from Sumter County used in the 1876 election joined the tissue ballot and red shirt in 2024 on display in the bedroom devoted to domestic violence and election fraud. Ballot box, 1876. Courtesy of Historic Columbia.

were misleading images of civil rights and LGBTQ issues today being linked to the Reconstruction's Fourteenth Amendment and issues of citizenship. The critique demonstrates the challenges facing queer-centered HHMs.[60] A Proposition 8 protest sign against a ban on same-sex marriage in California, which was struck down in federal district court in 2010, provoked backlash from two visitors who refused to frame LGBTQ rights within the perimeters of this amendment and thought it unrelated to South Carolina.[61] Two HHMs that masterfully broach conversations about the LGBTQ community through innovative interpretations are the Matilda Joslyn Gage Home and the Pauli Murray Center. Gage's home ingeniously managed to create a dialogue about transsexuality using a single image of the parlor in which L. Frank Baum married Gage's daughter. The image's placement in the only restored room in the home conveys that Gage helped inspire the Oz series, which had a transgendered character. The Murray Center presents the "classic hero narrative" through Murray's achievements as a writer, educator, lawyer, feminist, poet, and the first Black female Episcopal priest. Her representation as a queer woman of color "feels like a revolutionary act" and heals wounds through an intersectional historic home demonstrating her philosophy that the lived experience is not defined by one social construct. The center provides a safe space to discuss Murray's story and contemporary issues rather than a traditional guided tour of period rooms.[62]

Other MoRE revisions include removing the final exhibit film prominently featuring DJ Spooky and *The Birth of Nation* and replacing it with a new film. Intended to facilitate the transition from the Red Shirt bedroom into the final space and ease visitor fatigue, the film will offer a clear narrative on the historical continuity of Reconstruction to the present.[63] The film will link Reconstruction and the long civil rights movement by plugging the multimedia exhibit *An Advocate of the People* on display at the Modjeska

Monteith Simkins House, also administered by Historic Columbia. The late nineteenth-century, one-story cottage was home to Simkins, a premier human rights advocate in South Carolina from the New Deal until her death in 1992. Whether any *Birth of a Nation* footage or analysis will be included in the film is not yet clear, though the parts of the exhibit that discuss the film will remain. New content will include information about the Wilson administration's firing of federal employees like Civil War hero Robert Smalls, who served five terms in the US House of Representatives during and after Reconstruction before becoming collector of the Port of Beaufort.[64]

The most important modification Historic Columbia made to the MoRE was the name change from the Woodrow Wilson Family Home. A persistent criticism of the HHM was that it was perpetrating a bait and switch, replacing a Woodrow Wilson shrine with a Reconstruction exhibit. Moore somewhat agreed in her review but argued that visitors who came knowingly to a presidential site still received a narrative about Wilson's youth and "genteel white southern society." In exchange they also had "to consider uncomfortable information about how the nation has somewhat failed to live up to its promise." Moore and Safranek disagreed on how effective the dual narrative was. Moore felt the Wilson study used it well to illuminate the role the Wilson men played in Presbyterianism at the time and a larger theme that religion influenced public debates about race and citizenship. While she believed the dual narrative worked well in the pantries, overall, Safranek found it an "imperfect method." The character of Tommy Wilson gave the home and curators a "safety net" to present a "strong and positive stance" on South Carolina's Reconstruction history and provide "guard against the potential for visitors to reject completely" an unexpected experience. A Wilson home and Reconstruction museum occupying one space, essentially two different museums with "dueling messages," was a recipe to confuse and cloud visitor expectations, especially those that came expecting a period home or extensive Wilson family history.[65] Visitors' reactions to the dual narrative were mixed in the evaluation comments. Those that mentioned the importance of a museum devoted to the Reconstruction history praised the home for the "intelligent, thoughtful manner" in which it presented a complicated, conflicted, progressive, and emotional time period and its lingering impact today. The comments also commended the dual narrative and contextualized the interpretation with other presidential homes.[66] The dual narrative left some visitors wanting a better flow, more information, and answers to unresolved questions. After more artifacts or furnishings, the second most recorded criticism in the comments section of the visitor evaluation was wanting more material about Wilson's family and presidency, including their relationship with Black servants, the segregation of federal offices in Washington, DC, and how his childhood in the Reconstruction South impacted his "social or political thinking."[67]

Historic Columbia changed the name of the Woodrow Wilson Family Home to the Museum of the Reconstruction Era to ensure guests understand the home is no longer a shrine to Wilson before they purchase the tour tickets.[68] In 2014 the organization's staff and docents initially feared a political backlash or potential confrontations over the facts of Reconstruction with visitors familiar with the white supremacist narrative or who supported the "Heritage, Not Hate" movement.[69] A hostile response never manifested itself, because state and county appropriations emphasized the need for preserving the home and archeological research on the grounds. Hidden beneath the so-called bait of Wilson's name, funding in the years leading up to the relaunch and afterward placed little emphasis on Reconstruction.[70] Nonetheless most docents experienced the discomfort of a rare encounter with unapologetic Lost Causers or defenders of Redemption who rejected the material.[71] In these cases docents established authority through their confidence in the facts and remained cool. They did not let these inaccurate responses go unnoticed, sometimes asking where the guest got their information or offering a correction and suggestions for reading material.[72] The vast majority of evaluations corroborated that docent fears of pushback were mostly unfounded.

Visitors thought sensitive or controversial issues were treated extremely well, and a small but significant portion of visitors entered the museum believing Reconstruction and issues of race, gender, and violence were appropriate topics for discussion and not controversial.[73] Only four people dismissed the tour as too "political" or "politically correct," three on the evaluations and one in the press. One wrote, "Negative. Disappointing. An unfortunate social experiment. Waste of an opportunity to have something good. The museum house deserves a finer tour, and the people who visit deserve better, too." Another visitor wrote a letter to the editor published in the *State* newspaper expressing upset that the interpretation was "an excuse to glorify the days of Reconstruction following the War Between the States, which were probably the darkest days that this state has ever experienced."[74] Volunteer Jean Morgan encountered two guests who seemed to be on a fishing expedition to prove Historic Columbia was misappropriating government funds to advance a progressive agenda or at worst posed a security threat. One woman politely explored the exhibit, but her companion wrote in a notebook throughout the tour, including copying exhibit text. She asked questions about the restoration funding, whether a staff member was always present on site, whether visitors could visit the home unaccompanied, and why Morgan gave tours.[75]

The challenge for the MoRE and other Reconstruction sites will be reaching audiences of the same size and influence as groups like the United Daughters of the Confederacy did in the late nineteenth and early twentieth century. Attendance, rather than the quality of the MoRE content, director of research Kat Allen argued, remains a problem. Nonetheless, Allen and tour and program coordinator Bacon-Rogers believe the MoRE is the biggest draw of Historic Columbia's four houses for out-of-town visitors and that the name change lures more people to the site. When the Richland County Council unanimously approved the name change, a Black member, Joyce Dickerson, reconsidered taking a tour, where previously she had bypassed the site when it centered on Wilson's formative years.[76] The site also competes with other institutions such as the local zoo and Columbia Museum of Art. However, MoRE visitor evaluations suggest that another factor is generational. Millennials desire a different interpretive experience than previous generations and a less traditional guided tour. They favor interactives and questions at higher rates than average, are more open-minded, and often prefer the self-guided portions.[77]

The battle for a new memory of Reconstruction must be waged in the public sphere, for this is where the dominant white supremacist narrative was so successfully crafted and maintained. Public historians and their peers in academia may have to accept that it could take another century to dismantle the indoctrination that our professional ancestors and cultural makers created. But the work must be done. MoRE reviewer Cecelia Moore suspected that Wilson the historian "would have been fascinated by how Reconstruction . . . continues to dictate how Americans think about individual rights, citizenship, and nationhood." In his Reconstruction essay, Wilson asked, "How deep did the revolution go?"[78] That would make for a great engagement question on the MoRE tour.

Notes

Introduction

1. Amanda Seim, Sydney Yates, and Deanna Berryman, three graduate assistants assigned to me from 2017 until 2023 at Duquesne University, performed a Google and research database deep dive to locate new literature or information on pre-2014 Reconstruction museums to confirm my original findings.
2. National Park Service, "Discover the Reconstruction Era National Historic Network." The page appears to be maintained by the American Association for State and Local History, because the MoRE received its 2015 Award of Merit. American Association for State and Local History, "Woodrow Wilson Family Home."
3. Burns, *From Storefront to Monument*, 10; Dagbovie, "Black Public History," in *Radical Roots*, 538.
4. C. S. Coleman, "African American Museums," 151–56; Burns, *From Storefront to Monument*, 7–8; Dagbovie, "Black Public History," 529.
5. Ruffins, "Building Homes for Black History," 14–15.
6. Ruffins, "Building Homes for Black History," 14–16, 18–21, 23, 26, 29, 33; Burns, *From Storefront to Monument*, 3–4, 8, 10; Dagbovie, "Black Public History," 525, 534–35; Hayward and Larouche, "Emergence of the Field," 165.
7. By the 1960s, Black expositions and fairs that created a public space to present knowledge about the Black community and its legacy no longer provided the racial uplift they once did for early twentieth-century race activists like W. E. B. Du Bois and Carter Woodson. During this time museums were established in Boston and DC's Anacostia neighborhood. Margaret Burroughs and Charles Wright founded the Ebony Museum of Negro History and Art in Chicago (now the DuSable Black History Museum and Education Center) and the International Afro-American Museum in Detroit (now the Charles H. Wright Museum of African American History). An institution committed to the global fight for freedom and equality, the International Afro-American Museum created the Mobile Museum, a mobile trailer, inspired by African art and history, that hailed earlier Black expositions claiming a temporary public space. M. O. Wilson, *Negro Building*, 244–45, 252–54, 258, 261–63, 274–80, 295, 304, 311; Burns, *From Storefront to Monument*, 5–6, 9, 11, 13; Ruffins, "Building Homes for Black History," 25, 38; Hayward and Larouche, "Emergence of the Field," 164; Dagbovie, "Black Public History," 533.
8. For example, the African American Museum of Philadelphia opened in 1976 as a direct response to American bicentennial celebrations, though it was plagued by controversy. The International Afro-American Museum formed the Association of African American Museums in 1978. Black museums were heavily dependent on volunteers and operated with limited hours. While they lacked professional training, these public historians demonstrated best practices, drafting institutional missions, housing exhibits, though often temporary, and providing educational programming. Nonetheless these institutions struggled to

conduct research and properly manage collections, largely supplied by neighbors or donated by cultural institutions. Wilson, *Negro Building*, 302; Burns, *From Storefront to Monument*, 3–4, 11–13; Ruffins, "Building Homes for Black History," 14, 25–26, 28–29, 31, 33–34, 39–40.

9. Wilson, *Negro Building*, 304, 306–7; Burns, *From Storefront to Monument*, 7, 10, 12; Ruffins, "Building Homes for Black History," 26, 40–41; Dagbovie, "Black Public History," 532–33.
10. C. S. Coleman, "African American Museums," 151–56; Upton, *What Can and Can't Be Said*, 2, 4, 18, 21–24.
11. In the 1960s Wright and the International Afro-American Museum forcefully opposed an early version because of distrust of the government and usurping Black museum work. Anacostia director John Kinard continued the fight in the 1980s. Until 1991 the Smithsonian did not want to separate Black history, and Margaret Burroughs fought any Smithsonian control at all. Fath Ruffins, a historian at Smithsonian, argues that Jesse Helms blocked the bill for a national Black museum because it openly disputed the Lost Cause. Wilson, *Negro Building*, 254, 283–84, 288–89, 297, 302, 306–9; Burns, *From Storefront to Monument*, 13–14.
12. In 1988 the estimated number of local Black museums was over 200. That year the African American Museums Association surveyed 52 Black museums, mostly located in cities across 23 states and Canada. In 2003 the National Museum of African American History and Culture Plan for Action Presidential Commission sent 237 surveys to Black museums in 37 states and Canada. Thirty percent responded. Hayward and Larouche identified 221 museums in 2018. Wilson, *Negro Building*, 307; Hayward and Larouche, "Emergence of the Field," 164–65, 167; Burns, *From Storefront to Monument*, 9–10.
13. Like the MoRE, the North Carolina History Center added *Reconstruction* to its name by the time it broke ground in 2018. In November 2022 it added *Emancipation*. National Constitution Center, "Civil War and Reconstruction"; NC History Center on the Civil War, "Community Foundation Announces $500,000 Grant Investment"; NC Civil War Center, "Groundbreaking Ceremony Speeches"; Healy, "November 2022 Year End Update."
14. National Park Service, "Guided Tours," Andrew Johnson National Historic Site Tennessee, http://www.nps.gov; National Park Service, "History and Culture," Andrew Johnson National Historic Site Tennessee, http://www.nps.gov; National Park Service, "Go to Kansas," Nicodemus National Historic Site Kansas, http://www.nps.gov; National Park Service, "The Five Historic Buildings," http://www.nps.gov; *Sites of Cold War; Sites in Beaufort; McLoughlin house; or, Boundary of Glen; and River Watershed on S. 452 S. 500 S. 601 S. 621 S. 630 H.R. 519 H.R. 733 H.R. 788, Before the*, 26 (2003), statement on behalf of the American Historical Association, Organization of American Historians, and the National Coalition for History, ProQuest Congressional.
15. Of early interest was a George Washington Carver memorial to ease racial tension and draw more southern Democrats into the New Deal coalition. Though the NPS first rejected incorporation in favor of a future (yet unplanned) site at Tuskegee, Booker T. Washington's birthplace became part of the NPS system in 1957. Likewise the NPS rejected Frederick Douglass's home because his role as abolitionist was not of "outstanding national significance." It would finally join the NPS in 1962. West, *Domesticating History*, xii, 50, 129–30, 136–39, 143, 145, 153–57; National Park Service, "Cedar Hill," https://www.nps.gov.

16. C. S. Coleman, "African American Museums," 151–56.
17. Jennifer Schuessler, "Taking Another Look at the Reconstruction Era," *New York Times*, August 24, 2015; Gregory P. Downs and Kate Masur, "The Perfect Spot for a Reckoning with Reconstruction," *Washington Post*, October 7, 2016; Emma Dumain, "Just Under the Wire, Obama Establishes National Monument to Reconstruction Era in Beaufort County," *Post and Courier*, January 12, 2017; Taylor and Miller, "Reconstructing Memory"; Downs and Masur, "Era of Reconstruction."
18. In 1988 Fish Haul Archaeological Site, now Mitchelville, joined the National Register of Historic Places. The local effort to preserve and commemorate Mitchelville began in 2005. In 2010 the Historic Mitchelville Freedom Park was formed. See the "About Us" and "Mitchelville Today" pages at Explore Mitchelville.
19. SC Department of Archives and History, "South Carolina's Reconstruction."
20. South Carolina ETV, "40 Acres and a Mule"; "Seat at the Table." The first full length and definitive study of the Port Royal Experiment in Beaufort County is Rose's book. Willie Lee Rose, *Rehearsal for Reconstruction: The Port Royal Experiment* (New York: Vintage Books, 1964).
21. South Carolina State Museum, "Fourth Floor Galleries"; Tom Mack, "Reevaluating History: Reconstruction Gets a More Nuanced Treatment in State Museum Exhibit," *Free Times*, May 23, 2018; South Carolina State Museum, "South Carolina and Reconstruction."
22. Falk, *Identity and the Museum Visitor Experience*, 50–51, 73, 80; Simon, *Participatory Museum*, ii; Davidson and Sibley, "Audiences at the 'New' Museum," 177.
23. Strategies vary from the architectural style, setting, and signage outside to interior variables such as color schemes, lighting, and the comfort of the space. Atmospherics also consider the exhibition design, including décor, case displays, images, interpretive signage, and object and interactive labels. Spaces of commercial consumption like ticketing and food, crowding, and interactions with staff and visitors are also factors. Forrest, "Museum Atmospherics," 202–3, 205–6.
24. Falk, *Identity and the Museum Visitor Experience*, 64; Stylianou-Lambert, "Re-conceptualizing Museum Audiences," 135; Dawson and Jensen, "Towards a Contextual Turn," 128–29, 131, 136–37.
25. Coxall, "Open Minds," 139–40; Falk, *Identity and the Museum Visitor Experience*, 29, 64; Dawson and Jensen, "Towards a Contextual Turn," 128–29, 131–34, 136–38, 159; Stylianou-Lambert, "Re-conceptualizing Museum Audiences," 134–35; Davidson and Sibley, "Audiences at the 'New' Museum," 178.
26. C. S. Coleman, "African American Museums," 157; Bennett, *Birth of the Museum*, 10–11.
27. From a Foucauldian perspective of knowledge and regulation, public museums should have audiences that match the diversity in these institutions' collecting, conservation, and exhibit practices. This diversity, though, is meant to promote social betterment through hegemonic messages rather than inclusion for inclusivity's sake. Bennett, *Birth of the Museum*, 7, 8–9.
28. Bleick, "Volunteer in Art Education"; Jones, "Volunteer-Guides and Classroom Teachers," 32, 35–35. In an interview with ten art museum docents, interpreters revealed they joined the museum to contribute to their community, become involved with museum programs and other like-minded docents, and expand their mental capabilities.

29. Pattison and Dierking, "Staff-Mediated Learning in Museums," 118.
30. Tamura, "Ethnic Museums in Hawai'i," 69–71, 73; Johnson et al., *Museum Educator's Manual*, 2–3, 16, 20.
31. Interpretively, the site is positioned to discuss early but short-lived Reconstruction land partition that temporarily divided the McLeod plantation into forty-acre plots for freedmen before returning ownership to the family in 1870. The site also expanded its time frame to 1851–1990 and took a thematic approach, distinguishing it from other plantations nearby, such as Middleton Place, Drayton Hall, Magnolia Plantation, and Boone Hall. Halifax, "McLeod Planation Historic Site," 256–57, 260–61, 264–65, 269, 276.
32. As of 2018 Shawn Halifax offered a workshop titled "Ethical Interpretation of Slavery and Its Legacy" to fill the training gap. It stresses interpreter identity, presenting corrective narratives and recognizing emotional and cognitive disruption for learners, and responds to "dissonance" respectfully while offering emotional protection for the docent. Halifax, "McLeod Planation Historic Site," 266–68, 270.
33. Designers titled the exhibit *An Invisible Life*. Crane, "Memory, Distortion, and History," 50–51.
34. The new script incorporated Howard Gardner's multiple intelligence theory that stressed critical thinking through music, physical activity, speaking, and both interpersonal and intrapersonal practices. Rutherford and Shay, "Peopling the Age of Elegance," 32–33, 35–36, 40, 42, 45–46.
35. Pyatt, Rosser, and Powell, "Undergraduates as Science Museum Docents," 16.
36. Conn, *Do Museums Still Need Objects?* Conn's book claims we are in a second golden age of museum building and museum studies that is not object centered. Rutherford and Shay, "Peopling the Age of Elegance," 32–33, 35–36, 40, 42, 45–46; Crane, "Memory, Distortion, and History," 50–51.
37. For more, see Olsen, "Are Guided Tours at Historic Houses Dead?"; Graham, "Great Historic House"; Lopez, "Open House"; Lee, "'Anarchist's' Plan"; Vagnone and Ryan, *Anarchist's Guide to Historic House Museums*.
38. A far from exhaustive list includes Hale, *Woodrow Wilson*; R. S. Baker, *Youth*; Link, *Road to the White House*; Link, *Wilson* Vol. I-VI; Link, *Wilson the Diplomatist*; Link, *Revolution, War, and Peace*; Clements, *World Statesman*; Clements, *Presidency of Woodrow*; Knock, *To End All Wars*; Cooper, *Breaking the Heart*; Cooper, *Biography*.
39. Jennifer Scott, former vice-director and director of research at the Weeksville Center, argued that the question was not whether there were too many HHMs "but rather, are they useful?" For Lisa Lopez, HHMs are more like "mausoleums . . . petrified and lifeless" in their guided presentations of daily routines, "the domiciliary equivalent of sticking a pin through an insect and calling it an exhibition." J. Scott, "Reimagining," 74, 88; Lopez, "Open House," 10–11.
40. Lopez, "Open House," 10; Pharaon et al., "Safe Containers," 62–63, 71; J. Scott, "Reimagining Freedom," 75, 77; West, *Domesticating History*, xii, 47–48, 95.
41. Scott, "Reimagining Freedom," 73-75, 77–78.
42. Gunter interview.
43. Scott, "Reimagining Freedom," 82.
44. Pharaon et al., "Safe Containers," 62–64.

45. Bennett, *Birth of the Museum*, 1–7, 10, 19, 25, 28, 33, 48, 55, 59, 61. Bennett traces the origins of the modern museum primarily through a Foucauldian lens of the heterotopia. *The Birth of a Nation* was part of the culture produced for this larger bourgeois public sphere and was designed to civilize the masses by modeling and performing white middle-class values. Stylianou-Lambert, "Re-conceptualizing Museum Audiences," 131, 133; Simon, *Participatory Museum*, ii.
46. Vivian assesses seventy-six estates in the Lowcountry. Vivian, *New Plantation World*, 1–3, 8–10, 13, 16–17, 20, 22, 28, 207, 209, 249, 278; McPherson, *Reconstructing Dixie*, 40.
47. McPherson, *Reconstructing Dixie*, 42–44, quote 43.
48. Halifax, "McLeod Planation Historic Site," 253.
49. In 1999 retired trial attorney John Cummings purchased Whitney Plantation for $8.5 million. The new interpretation is partly based on work of Ibrahima Seck, a member of the history department of Chikh Anta Diop University (also known as the University of Dakar) in Senegal, who now serves as Whitney's head of research. Commander, "Plantation Counternarratives," 34; Golanska, "Against the 'Moonlight and Magnolia' Myth," 142, 144–45, 150; Harnay, "Slavery and Plantation Tourism in Louisiana," 1–3, 7, 10, 12–13; J. Rose, "Collective Memories."
50. Golanska, "Against the 'Moonlight and Magnolia' Myth," 140, 146–47.
51. Harnay, "Slavery and Plantation Tourism in Louisiana," 10; Commander, "Plantation Counternarratives," 35–36, 40–41.
52. Like any site, Whitney Plantation has flaws. It relies greatly on the rich but highly problematic WPA interviews, rendering them as more authentic than they may be. The intense sculpture memorials can be potentially triggering, and *Children of Whitney* could be construed as playing into the trope of the infantile slave. In addition the counternarrative, though desperately needed in an unbalanced plantation tourism market, is too niche and erases the radical act of living spiritually, building communities, and creating Black joy. Commander, "Plantation Counternarratives," 29, 35–38, 40–42; Golanska, "Against the 'Moonlight and Magnolia' Myth," 137, 146–47, 150–52, 155; Berry and Gross, *Black Women's History*, 75.
53. B. E. Baker, *What Reconstruction Meant*, 6, 11–12, 87, 89, 108–9, 145, 147, 158–60, 162; Brundage, "Introduction," 3–4, 6, 8.
54. Bennett, *Birth of the Museum*, 8, 47, 55; Stylianou-Lambert, "Re-conceptualizing Museum Audiences," 135–36; Dawson and Jensen, "Towards a Contextual Turn," 128.
55. The Sons of Confederate Veterans successfully blocked the theme study by convincing the original bill's sponsor, SCV member Rep. Joe Wilson, to kill it by not moving it forward. See Taylor and Miller, "Reconstructing Memory."
56. Jason Horowitz, Shaila Dewan, and Frances Robles, "Dylann Roof, Suspect in Charleston Shooting, Flew the Flags of White Power," *New York Times*, June 18, 2015.
57. "Gov. Nikki Haley Calls for Removal of Confederate Flag from State House Grounds," WIS-TV, June 22, 2015.
58. In response to this "desecration" of the site, McLeod leadership offered additional support and training for interpreters to discuss their feelings and racist comments or questions from visitors. The creation of a shared journal allowed for one-on-one coaching following an encounter. The training expanded to provide layers of protection via mandatory active shooter training, two-way

radio silent alarms, and education on white terrorist groups' symbols. Halifax, "McLeod Planation Historic Site," 268–70; Frances Robles, "Dylann Roof Photos and a Manifesto Are Posted on Website," *New York Times*, June 20, 2015; "FBI: Dylann Roof Displaying Racist Symbols Even During His Trial," *Chicago Tribune*, January 6, 2017; Cynthia Roldán and John Monk, "Roof Gets Death Penalty after Telling Jury 'I Still Feel That I Had to Do It,'" *The State*, January 10, 2017.

59. Jess Bidgood et al., "Confederate Monuments Are Coming Down Across the United States. Here's a List," *New York Times*, August 28, 2017; Jay Reeves, "Report: 110 Confederate Monuments Removed in US Since 2015," *AP News*, June 4, 2018; K. L. Cox, *No Common Ground*, 3–5, 151, 157, 159–60, 172.
60. "James Alex Fields, Driver in Deadly Car Attack at Charlottesville Rally, Sentenced to Life in Prison," NBC News, June 28, 2019; "The People, Groups and Symbols at Charlottesville," Southern Poverty Law Center, August 15, 2017, https://www.splcenter.org/.
61. Launched following George Zimmerman's lethal assault on seventeen-year-old Trayvon Martin in 2013, Black Lives Matter became a mainstream social movement in the summer of 2020. Brakkton Booker et al., "Violence Erupts As Outrage Over George Floyd's Death Spills Into A New Week," NPR, June 1, 2020; Nicole Dungca et al., "A Dozen High-Profile Fatal Encounters that Have Galvanized Protests Nationwide," *Washington Post*, June 8, 2020; Jason Silverstein, "The Global Impact of George Floyd: How Black Lives Matter Protests Shaped Movements Around the World," CBS News, June 4, 2021; Dylan Lovan and Piper Hudspeth Blackburn, "Jury Selection Starts in Lone Trial Over Breonna Taylor Raid," *AP News*, January 28, 2022; Liz Baker, "A Jury Finds Ahmaud Arbery's 3 Killers Guilty of Federal Hate Crimes," NPR, February 22, 2022; Cox, *No Common Ground*, 6, 158–59, 169.
62. Cox, *No Common Ground*, 6–7, 164, 169–71.
63. Jan Wolfe, "Democracy Under Siege: An Hour-by-Hour Look at the Assault on the U.S. Capitol," *Reuters*, January 4, 2022; Jacques Billeaud, "Jan. 6 Rioter Who Carried Spear, Wore Horns, Draws 41 Months," *AP News*, November 17, 2021; Dorany Pineda, "'The Turner Diaries' Didn't Just Inspire the Capitol Attack. It Warns Us What Might Be Next," *Los Angeles Times*, January 8, 2021.
64. Democratic candidate Wade Hampton led incumbent governor Daniel Chamberlain by 1,134 votes, though in two counties Hampton received more votes than registered voters. With the governor's race thrown into the State Assembly, the state supreme court certified those county's Democratic legislative representatives, while the Republican-controlled state election commission certified their party's candidates. After Chamberlain convinced the local federal military to station two companies at the State House and honor the election commission's ruling, a mob materialized. The Republicans remained in the State House, and the Democrats left to form their own official state government. Both Chamberlain and Hampton took the oath of office, and both houses operated for four months, though only the Democrats had tax revenue, produced by their supporters. Edgar, *South Carolina*, 404–6.
65. Coxall, "Open Minds," 139.
66. King, "Taking What Action?," 6; Hein, "Assuming Responsibility," 5–6; Luke, "Museum," 22–24.

67. Benfield et al., "'Honest Visionary,'" 56–57, 70.
68. Falk, *Identity and the Museum Visitor Experience*, 35; Jensen, Dawson, and Falk, "Dialogue and Synthesis," 160.
69. Bennett, *Birth of the Museum*, 1, 6, 61; Stylianou-Lambert, "Re-conceptualizing Museum Audiences," 131, 133, 136–38, 140–41; Simon, *Participatory Museum*, iii; Hein, "Assuming Responsibility," 4.
70. Bennett, *Birth of the Museum*, 8, 47, 55; Stylianou-Lambert, "Re-conceptualizing Museum Audiences," 135–36; Dawson and Jensen, "Towards a Contextual Turn," 128.
71. Shopes, "Legal and Ethical Issues," 127–28, 132; Ritchie, *Doing Oral History*, 75–76, 126–27.
72. Department of History, "Public History."
73. Tyson, *Wages of History*, 3, 6, 8–9.
74. Lowe, "Dwelling in Possibility," 45, 47, 54, 60.
75. Vagnone and Ryan wrote *The Anarchist's Guide to Historic House Museums* in 2015 to answer the HHM debate via "equal parts manifesto, guidebook, and laboratory of ideas." The authors lay out five critiques of house museums: (1) they reflect political and social propaganda, often telling partial truths to their communities; (2) they have nothing relevant to contribute to conversations; (3) they are boring; (4) they have been narrowly curated and do not reflect real-life use; (5) they are too expensive to preserve and engage in deceptive conservation practices. Vagnone and Ryan, *Anarchist's Guide to Historic House Museums*, 11, 16, 40–41, 142.
76. Docent Doe interview, February 17, 2016.

Chapter 1: Building Shrines

1. John Randolph Bolling to Mrs. E. Henry Cappelmann, February 14, 1930, Woodrow Wilson Boyhood Home, 14 April 1930–24 April 1932, South Caroliniana Library, University of South Carolina (hereafter cited as SCL); John Randolph Bolling to Mrs. E. Henry Cappelman, January 8, 1929, Woodrow Wilson Boyhood Home, Records, 8 January 1929–31 January 1929, SCL.
2. American Legion Auxiliary, "History"; Lewis, "Curation of American Patriotism," 79, 82.
3. Brundage, *Southern Past*, 13–20, 24–25, 41, 48–49.
4. An example of commemoration not centered on the Civil War is the Nashville Ladies' Hermitage Association, which preserved Andrew Jackson's home. Some of the organizations modified their mission and focus following changes brought by modernity and suffrage. The DAR, for example, transformed into a nationalist organization that loudly protested radicalism and communism and purged members that supported social reforms once acceptable to the organization. Brundage, *Southern Past*, 13–18, 20, 23–24, 29, 36–37, 41, 48–51, 53.
5. George Washington's legacy drove the early HHM movement. By the end of the Reconstruction era, three of the first five HHMs were George Washington sites. The first was Hasbrouck House, his headquarters in Newburgh, which opened on Independence Day in 1850. The State of New York continues to own and operate the site. In 1860 Ann Pamela Cunningham and her Mount Vernon Ladies' Association preserved the most significant site, Mount Vernon. The Kansas-Nebraska Act and the caning of Charles Sumner by South Carolinian Preston

Brooks fueled sectional tension. Edward Everett raised a quarter of the Mount Vernon purchase price by giving 137 speeches titled "The Character of Washington." During the fundraising campaign, he contextualized the movement as an example of the moderation needed to avoid civil war. Similarly Anna Morris Holstein founded the Centennial and Memorial Association of Valley Forge to purchase and restore Washington's headquarters there in 1878. In 1893 Valley Forge became Pennsylvania's first state park, though the National Park Service administers the site today. Egner, "Ann Pamela Cunningham"; West, *Domesticating History*, xi, 6–11, 13–14, 16, 18–28, 29, 37; New York State Parks, Recreation and Historic Preservation, "Washington's Headquarters State Historic Site"; National Park Service, "Washington's Headquarters"; "Famous Army Nurse Dead," *Allentown Leader*, January 2, 1901; Pennsylvania Conservation Heritage Project, "Anna Morris Holstein."

6. A group of New York lawyers and businessmen turned "museum men" formed the Thomas Jefferson Memorial Foundation and purchased the home in 1923. The organization was highly visible at the 1924 Democratic Convention, and members were divided over their support for Wilson's segregationist son-in-law, William Gibbs McAdoo; Al Smith; and foundation charter member John W. Davis, who received the nomination. Grantham, "Southern Historiography," 267; West, *Domesticating History*, 99–105, 107–9, 112–13; K. L. Cox, *Dreaming of Dixie*, 1–2, 131–32.
7. New Deal projects preserved and promoted places critical to US history or of national significance. The National Park Service more than doubled the size of the areas it administered, the Civilization Conservation Corps improved sites, and WPA state guidebooks highlighted important locations to visit and preserve. L. V. Coleman, *Historic House Museums*, 18; West, *Domesticating History*, 4, 43, 130; Pustz, *Voices from the Back Stairs*, 15–16; Bodnar, *Remaking America*, 41, 249.
8. There is a historiographical gap on the legion and its auxiliary, according to Lewis's 2023 essay. Lewis, "Curation of American Patriotism," 79–82, 84, 87–90, 92, 94–96, 98, 101–4.
9. L. V. Coleman, *Historic House Museums*, 17.
10. Pustz, *Voices from the Back Stairs*, 14–15.
11. Pustz, 19; "Slavery,"; "Plantation and Slavery," Thomas Jefferson's Monticello; Whitney Plantation, "Tours of Whitney Plantation Museum"; "Guided Tours," Tenement Museum; C. S. Coleman, "African American Museums," 155.
12. Vagnone and Ryan, Anarchist's Guide to Historic House Museums, 45.
13. Ashley Halsey, "Trust to Be Accepted at July Meeting," April 24, 1932, Woodrow Wilson Memorial 14 MPs, 1929-1969, SCL, USC.
14. Reese, "Agreement between J. M. VanMetre and American Legion and American Legion Auxiliary," Columbia, SC, 25 August 1928, Records, 25 August 1928–4 December 1928 and c. 1928, Woodrow Wilson Boyhood Home, South Caroliniana Library, University of South Carolina (hereafter cited as WWBH); quote from Mary R. Forbes to American Legion Auxiliary Unit Presidents, "To the Units of the American Legion Auxiliary, Department of South Carolina," January 17, 1929, Records, 8 Jan. 1929–31 Jan. 1929, WWBH.
15. American Legion Auxiliary Richland Post No. 6, "Resolution," Columbia, SC, 28 September 1928, Records, 25 Aug. 1928–4 Dec. 1928 and c. 1928, WWBH;

"Woodrow Wilson Home Bed-Room" 1956, 13 backside, Records, 1952–29 December 1956 and 1956, WWBH.

16. American Legion Columbia Post no. 6, "Resolution," Columbia, SC, October 4, 1928, Records, 25 Aug. 1928–4 Dec. 1928 and c. 1928, WWBH; M. S. Whaley, "Auditorium Trustees Meeting Announcement," Columbia, SC, October 6, 1928, Records, 25 Aug. 1928–4 Dec. 1928 and ca. 1928, WWBH.
17. For the first comprehensive book on the women's club movement, see Scott, *Natural Allies*. The definitive work on the Daughters of the Confederacy and their role in preserving Confederate culture and the Lost Cause is K. L. Cox, *Dixie's Daughters*; see chap. 6, "Frances's Sex," for a synthesis of the Black women's club movement and the importance of the National Association of Colored Women. Berry and Gross, *Black Women's History*.
18. These sites were the Joseph Manigault House, Market Hall, Miles Brewton House, Old Exchange, Old Powder Magazine, Thomas Heyward House, and Wilson House. L. V. Coleman, *Historic House Museums*, 152.
19. The Chester, Rock Hill, Sumter, Darlington, Greenville, Charleston, and Spartanburg ALA chapters sent resolutions. "Full Text of Resolutions Adopted by 95 Various Organizations in South Carolina as to the Proposal That the Woodrow Wilson Home in Columbia Be Preserved," October 1928, 1–22, Woodrow Wilson Memorial MS vol. bd., 1928, SCL; "Similar Resolutions Have Been Passed by the Following Organizations since the Preceding Ones Were Made Up," 1928, Woodrow Wilson Memorial 2 MSS, 1928 and 16 Jan. 1929, SCL; O. A. Alexander to Mrs. Henry Cappelmann, November 7, 1928, Records, 25 Aug. 1928–4 Dec. 1928 and c. 1928, WWBH; American Legion Darlington Post No. 13, "Be It Resolved by the Executive Committee, Darlington Post No. 13, American Legion," November 7, 1928, Records, 25 Aug. 1928–4 Dec. 1928 and ca. 1928, WWBH.
20. Marie Jones served as chair of the Wilson home from 1941 until 1943. Her husband was Curran Jones. Eunice Leonard served as president of the Shandon Parent Teacher Association and first vice president of the Central Parent Teacher Council of Columbia. Jessie Mercer served as secretary for the latter and as president of the Shandon Mother's Club, another supporter. The Council of Farm Women were in Richland and Marlboro Counties. "Full Text of Resolutions Adopted by 95," 2–22; "Similar Resolutions," 1; Whaley, "Auditorium Trustees Meeting Announcement"; "Woodrow Wilson Home Bed-Room,", Records, 1952–29 December 1956 and 1956, WWBH, 13 backside; Mrs. Percy Crown, Mrs. W. F. Fiertick, and Mrs. Theron Woodward, "Be It Resolved That We, the Members of the Afternoon Music Club" (Columbia, SC, October 5, 1928), Records, 25 Aug. 1928–4 Dec. 1928 and c. 1928, WWBH.
21. War-related supporters included five ALA units, the American Legion's Sumter post, and two DAR chapters. While seven groups showed sympathy for the auditorium committee's goals, they hoped the committee would move the location of the auditorium to save the home. Five groups noted the historical value of the house, but two in particular stressed the importance of monuments and memorialization. Both the Mary Ann Buie chapter of the UDC and the Apollo Music Club of Johnston specifically feared a "land without history." Four groups, including one chapter of the DAR, UDC, and American Legion each, mentioned the benefit for future generations. Recognition of Wilson as a southerner and

southern Democrat motivated three resolutions, while two others conveyed that the site was key to supporting Americanism. "Full Text of Resolutions Adopted by 95," 2, 4–6, 8–9, 11–12, 14–22.

22. Courson, Jackson, and Hembree, "Senate Education Oversight Subcommittee Summary Report," 2.
23. Forbes to American Legion Auxiliary Unit Presidents, "To the Units of the American Legion Auxiliary, Department of South Carolina"; "Summary of Provisions of the Act to Preserve the Woodrow Wilson Home in Columbia as a Memorial and Shrine," January 17, 1929, Records, 8 Jan. 1929–31 Jan. 1929, WWBH; "S. 52 A Bill to Provide for the Purchase of the Premises and Buildings Thereon Situate at the Corner of Hampton and Henderson Streets in the City of Columbia, South Carolina, Being the Boyhood Home of the Late President Woodrow Wilson," January 16, 1929, 1–2, Records, 8 Jan. 1929–31 Jan. 1929, WWBH; "A Bill to Provide for the Purchase of the Premises and Buildings Thereon Situate at the Corner of Hampton and Henderson Streets in the City of Columbia, South Carolina, Being the Boyhood Home of the Late President Woodrow Wilson," draft, January 16, 1929, 2–3, Records, 8 Jan. 1929–31 Jan. 1929, WWBH.
24. The State Department commander, George Levy, himself "happily sent" fifteen telegrams to senators upon request of Cappelmann's husband. "S. 52 A Bill," 1; "Help Save the Woodrow Wilson Home," March 1929, Records, 14 Mar. 1929–13 Apr. 1929, WWBH; Halsey, "Trust to Be Accepted at July Meeting"; "Legion Men and Women at Woodrow Wilson Home," *Columbia (SC) Record*, March 8, 1929, Records, 4 Feb. 1929–13 Mar. 1929, WWBH; Eutalie Salley to James H. Hammond, February 12, 1929, Records, 4 Feb. 1929–13 Mar. 1929, WWBH; F. C. Robinson to George D. Levy, February 27, 1929, Records, 4 Feb. 1929–13 Mar. 1929, WWBH; George D. Levy to Mrs. E. Henry Cappelmann, February 28, 1929, Records, 4 Feb. 1929–13 Mar. 1929, WWBH.
25. "Minutes of the Woodrow Wilson Home Purchase Fund Committee, 6 March-11 May," 1929, 1–18, Records, 4 Feb. 1929–13 Mar. 1929, WWBH.
26. Fitz Hugh McMaster, R. K. Wise, and Henry Johnson served as chairman, vice chairman, and treasurer, respectively. "Minutes of the Woodrow Wilson Home," 1–2; "The Executive Committee" (1929), 2, Records, 14 Apr. 1930–24 Apr. 1932, WWBH.
27. The Colonial Dames president was Nathalie Fitzsimmons. The League of Women Voters president was Caroline Swaffield. "Minutes of the Woodrow Wilson Home," 6; "Executive Committee," 1; Woodrow Wilson Memorial, April 1929, Records, 16 Apr. 1929–28 June 1929, WWBH.
28. Hall, *Sisters and Rebels*, 39–41, 43, 55, 102, 106–7, 118–19, 148, 179–80, 447, 449.
29. "Minutes of the Woodrow Wilson Home," 2, 5, 14. Lumpkin also donated to the house a handmade crochet spread and dozens of china plates and cups for teas. "Woodrow Wilson Home Bed-Room," 4, 11, 13.
30. Delegates met Cathcart's suggestion by hiring a field agent for the Lions Club with the last name Ormsby, but R. E. McCaslan became the state organizer. "Minutes of the Woodrow Wilson Home," 6–7, 9–10; "Executive Committee," 2 backside.
31. Founding WWPF member W. P. Blackwell headed up the men's team. "Executive Committee," 2; "Minutes of the Woodrow Wilson Home," 2, 11.
32. More than three hundred women filled the streets armed with thousands of colored tags labeled "Woodrow Wilson Memorial." Anyone who contributed to

the fundraiser received a tag. "Minutes of the Woodrow Wilson Home," 8–9; Halsey, "Trust to Be Accepted at July Meeting"; "Observe Tag Day on Wednesday," *American Legion Auxiliary Scrapbook, 1925–1929*, n.d., 126, Jennie Clarkson Dreher Papers, SCL.

33. Three days after Tag Day, the treasurer reported that $16,915.43 sat in the WWPF account with a prospect of $2,000 more from the city and county. Woodrow Wilson Memorial, April 1929; Unknown to Sir, "Fundraising Letter," April 1929, Records, 16 Apr. 1929–28 June 1929, WWBH.
34. "Executive Committee," 2; "Minutes of the Woodrow Wilson Home," 7, 14–15; Mrs. Henry Cappelmann, *Wilson Home Committee Meeting Notes*, May 11, 1929, 1, Records, 16 Apr. 1929–28 June 1929, WWBH; Mrs. Henry Cappelmann, *A Garden Party and Sale of Plants from Historic Gardens*, program, Edgefield, SC, May 17, 1929, 1–4, Records, 16 Apr. 1929–28 June 1929, WWBH.
35. "Minutes of the Woodrow Wilson Home," 8–9; Halsey, "Trust to Be Accepted at July Meeting."
36. "Woodrow Wilson Bed Acquired for Memorial; Put in Room War President Occupied Here," *Columbia (SC) State*, April 14, 1930, 14 Apr. 1930–24 April 1932, WWBH; "Minutes of the Woodrow Wilson Home," 17; "Woodrow Wilson Home Bed-Room," 1, 4; Cappelmann, *Wilson Home Committee Meeting Notes*, 2.
37. "Whereas It Is a Recognized Fact," July 24, 1930, Records, 14 Apr. 1930–24 Apr. 1932, WWBH.
38. Stanley Llewellyn to Mrs. E. Henry Cappelmann, March 13, 1931, 14 Apr. 1930–24 Apr. 1932, WWBH; "Auxiliary Proposes to Preserve Wilson Home," March 1932, Records, 14 Apr. 1930–24 Apr. 1932, WWBH; "Legion to Take Charge of Wilson's Early Home Here," April 24, 1932, Records, 14 Apr. 1930–24 Apr. 1932, WWBH; Halsey, "Trust to Be Accepted at July Meeting"; "Woodrow Wilson Home Bed-Room," 15.
39. *Charter Members Honored by Garden Club*, newspaper photograph, 1961, Records of the Crape Myrtle Garden Club (Columbia, SC), box 2, 3Ps, 25th and 30th Anniversary, SCL; "Crape Myrtle Garden Club Year Book, 1937–1938" (Columbia, SC), 1–2, 6, 8, Records of the Crape Myrtle Garden Club (Columbia, SC), box 2, Yearbook, 1937–1949, SCL; "Crape Myrtle Garden Club Year Book, 1938–1939" (Columbia, SC), 3, 7–8, Records of the Crape Myrtle Garden Club (Columbia, SC), box 2, Yearbook, 1937–1949, SCL; "Crape Myrtle Garden Club Year Book, 1939–1940" (Columbia, SC), 3; Rose E. Dye, *April 1939 Minutes* (Columbia, SC, April 12, 1939), 57, Records of the Crape Myrtle Garden Club (Columbia, SC), Records (1936–2001), box 1, SCL; Ester Matheson, *November 1939 Minutes* (Columbia, SC), November 1939, 62–64, Records of the Crape Myrtle Garden Club (Columbia, SC), Records (1936–2001), box 1, SCL.
40. Centennial invitations went out to officials across the state, leaders of patriotic organizations, and, of course, all legion and auxiliary members who helped save the home thirty years earlier. "Woodrow Wilson Home Bed-Room," 5 front, 14–15 backsides; *Whereas the Am. Leg. Aux. of S.C. Is Deeply Concerned about the Preservation & Care of the Boyhood Home in Columbia of Our World War I President Woodrow Wilson*, statement (1965), Records, 28 Sept. 1961–16 Nov. 1969 and n.d., WWBH.
41. Ruth Cappelmann, "Woodrow Wilson Boyhood Home," n.d., 1–2, Records, 28 Sept. 1961–16 Nov. 1969 and n.d., WWBH.

42. J. A. Cathcart to Mrs. E. Henry Cappelmann, January 26, 1929, Records, 8 Jan. 1929–31 Jan. 1929, WWBH; John Randolph Bolling to Mrs. E. Henry Cappelmann, January 31, 1929, Records, 8 Jan. 1929–31 Jan. 1929, WWBH; Mrs. Henry Cappelmann to Ray Stannard Baker, February 12, 1929, Records, 4 Feb. 1929–13 Mar. 1929, WWBH.
43. Ray Stannard Baker to Mrs. Henry Cappelmann, February 13, 1929, Records, 4 Feb. 1929–13 Mar. 1929, WWBH.
44. Giorgio Bertellini, *The Divo and the Duce: Promoting Film Stardom and Political Leadership in 1920s America* (Oakland: University of California Press, 2019), 35, https://www.ucpress.edu/books/the-divo-and-the-duce/paper.
45. H. F. Drugan to Col. Fitz Hugh McMaster, January 19, 1929, Records, 8 Jan. 1929–31 Jan. 1929, WWBH; H. F. Drugan to Mrs. Henry Cappelmann, March 16, 1929, Records, 14 Mar. 1929–13 Apr. 1929, WWBH; John Randolph Bolling to Mrs. E. Henry Cappelmann, March 19, 1929, Records, 14 Mar. 1929–13 Apr. 1929, WWBH; H. F. Drugan to Mrs. Henry Cappelmann, March 30, 1929, Records, 14 Mar. 1929–13 Apr. 1929, WWBH; H. F. Drugan to Hon. Richard I. Manning, April 3, 1929, Records, 14 Mar. 1929–13 Apr. 1929, WWBH; H. F. Drugan to Col. Fitz Hugh McMaster, April 9, 1929, 1–2, Records, 14 Mar. 1929–13 Apr. 1929, WWBH; H. F. Drugan to Mrs. Henry Cappelmann, April 9, 1929, Records, 14 Mar. 1929–13 Apr. 1929, WWBH; H. F. Drugan to Mrs. Henry Cappelmann, April 12, 1929, Records, 14 Mar. 1929–13 Apr. 1929, WWBH; H. F. Drugan to Mrs. Henry Cappelmann, April 13, 1929, Records, 14 Mar. 1929–13 Apr. 1929, WWBH; H. F. Drugan to Mrs. Henry Cappelmann, June 6, 1929, Records, 16 Apr. 1929–28 June 1929, WWBH.
46. John Randolph Bolling to Mrs. E. Henry Cappelmann, February 14, 1930, Records, 14 Apr. 1930–24 Apr. 1932, WWBH; "Minutes of the Woodrow Wilson Home," 18; Cappelmann, *Wilson Home Committee Meeting Notes*, 3; "Feby 5, 1930," February 5, 1930, Records, 14 Apr. 1930–24 Apr. 1932, WWBH.
47. Yuhl, *Golden Haze of Memory*, 127, 130–34, 179, 182.
48. Six Woodrow women graduated from the seminary between 1869 and 1885. Link, *Road to the White House*, 1, 3n11; Montgomery, *Thomas Woodrow Wilson*, 13, 18; R. S. Baker, *Youth*, 26; Berg, *Wilson*, 30; Brown, *Woodrow Wilson Presidential Library*, 20.
49. Link, *Road to the White House*, 4n11; Brown, *Woodrow Wilson Presidential Library*, 6, 20; Berg, *Wilson*, 356, 359.
50. Arthur S. Link and Katherine E. Brand, "Edith Bolling Wilson: Tributes Given at a Memorial Service at the Woodrow Wilson Birthplace," January 28, 1962, 11, Edith Bolling Wilson Papers (hereafter cited as EBWP), folder 37, Miscellaneous, Woodrow Wilson Presidential Library, Staunton, VA (hereafter cited as WWPL).
51. Smith served as director of the Garden Club of America. Her service of two terms on Mary Baldwin College's board resulted in an alumnae award in her honor in 1965. In addition to her volunteer work, she possessed social prestige through her marriage to Herbert McKelden Smith, one-time mayor of Staunton and member of the Virginia House of Delegates. James S. Wamsley, "Staunton's Indomitable Mrs. Herbert McK. Smith," *Commonwealth*, April 1973, Chairman of the Board-Incoming Correspondence-S-1960, box 6, folder 12, 5 Feb. 1959–Apr. 1973 Miscellaneous Typed or Printed Tributes to Emily Smith, Papers of Emily P. Smith, WWPL (hereafter PEPS); "Mrs. Herbert McKelden Smith,"

n.d., Chairman of the Board-Incoming Correspondence-S-1960, box 6, folder 12, 5 Feb. 1959–Apr. 1973 Miscellaneous Typed or Printed Tributes to Emily Smith, PEPS; Mary Baldwin College, "Announcing The Emily Smith Citation," 1965 1964, Chairman of the Board-Incoming Correspondence-S-1960, box 6, folder 12, 5 Feb. 1959–Apr. 1973 Miscellaneous Typed or Printed Tributes to Emily Smith, PEPS.

52. "Mrs. Herbert McKelden Smith," n.d., Incoming Correspondence-S-1960, box 6, folder 12, 5 Feb. 1959–Apr. 1973 Miscellaneous Typed or Printed Tributes to Emily Smith, PEPS; Mary Baldwin College, "Announcing the Emily Smith Citation," 1965 1964, Incoming Correspondence-S-1960, box 6, folder 12, 5 Feb. 1959–Apr. 1973 Miscellaneous Typed or Printed Tributes to Emily Smith, PEPS; Woodrow Wilson Birthplace Foundation, "Resolved, by the Woodrow Wilson Birthplace Foundation . . . Retirement of Mrs. Emily P. Smith," February 19, 1973, 2, Incoming Correspondence-S-1960, box 6, folder 13, 6 June 1968–19 Feb. 1973 Tributes to Emily Smith, PEPS; Emily P. Smith, "Report of Woodrow Wilson Garden," Staunton, Virginia, February 20, 1934, 1, 3, Outgoing Correspondence 1934–1964, February 1934-December 1939, folder 1, PEPS; Brown, *Presidential Library and Museum,* 20.
53. Wilson also met Smith's husband. Edith Bolling Wilson (EBW) to Mrs. H. McK. Smith, October 8, 1931, folder 9, 1931, EBWP; EBW to Charles Catlett, January 8, 1932, folder 10, 1932–1933, EBWP; L. V. Coleman, *Historic House Museums,* 157.
54. EBW to Emily P. Smith (EPS), July 28, 1939, folder 14, 1939, EBWP; EBW to D. L. Groner, July 29, 1939, folder 14, 1939, EBWP.
55. EBW to EPS, October 12, 1933, folder 10, 1932–1933, EBWP.
56. EBW to EPS, November 18, 1939, folder 14, 1939, EBWP; EPS to Mrs. Cordell Hull, July 3, 1939, Outgoing Correspondence 1934–1964, February 1934–December 1939, folder 1, PEPS (quote).
57. EBW to EPS, May 30, 1935, folder 11, 1934–1935, EBWP; EBW to Michael Kibligan, May 30, 1935, folder 11, 1934–1935, EBWP.
58. John Randolph Bolling to Mrs. H. McK. Smith, January 28, 1939, folder 14, 1939, EBWP.
59. Brown, Woodrow Wilson Presidential Library, 20.
60. The WWBF elected Admiral Grayson as its first president, but he died soon thereafter. Emily P. Smith to Justice D. Lawrence Groner, April 8, 1939, Outgoing Correspondence 1934–1964, February 1934–December 1939, folder 1, PEPS. The language of "national shrine" was used in the following two documents: "Memorandum," February 12, 1940, folder 37, Miscellaneous, EBWP; EPS to Jesse H. Jones, April 20, 1939, Outgoing Correspondence 1934–1964, February 1934–December 1939, folder 1, PEPS.
61. EPS to Mrs. Ambrose Ford, July 1, 1939, Outgoing Correspondence 1934–1964, February 1934–December 1939, folder 1, PEPS; Brown, *Woodrow Wilson Presidential Library,* 22.
62. EBW to EPS, June 26, 1939, folder 14, 1939, EBWP; EBW to D. L. Groner, July 29, 1939; "Memorandum."
63. EBW to EPS, July 28, 1939.
64. EPS to Jesse H. Jones, January 23, 1939, Outgoing Correspondence 1934–1964, February 1934–December 1939, folder 1, PEPS; EPS to Jones, April 20, 1939; EPS to Jones, May 1, 1939, Outgoing Correspondence 1934–1964, February 1934–

December 1939, folder 1, PEPS; EPS to Mrs. Cordell Hull, May 1, 1939, 1, Outgoing Correspondence 1934–1964, February 1934–December 1939, folder 1, PEPS.

65. The team Smith selected served as a model for other states, and she approved each state's chairman. EBW to EPS, July 28, 1939, folder 14, 1939, EBWP; EBW to D. L. Groner, July 29, 1939, folder 14, 1939, EBWP; EPS to Hull, May 1, 1939, 2; EBW to EPS, June 26, 1939, folder 14, 1939, EBWP. The legion lent some support over the course of the next year and half, as they are referenced briefly in the following letter. EBW to EPS, October 27, 1940, folder 15, 1940, EBWP.

66. Edith also worried about Smith's low estimated budget of $12,000 for restoration. EBW to EPS, August 19, 1939, folder 14, 1939, EBWP; EBW to EPS, August 30, 1939, folder 14, 1939, EBWP.

67. The Philadelphia's Democratic Luncheon Club furnished the dining room, and Smith's DAR chapter outfitted the nursery. Edith Wilson sent a wardrobe, table, bookcase, trunk, and vest set. She also gave several desks and chairs, including an oak rolltop desk, a large mahogany desk chair, and an oak typewriter desk and chair. She retained the right to withdraw the items at any time and stipulated that unused items would be returned. The artwork included portraits of George Washington, Thomas Jefferson, Robert E. Lee, William Gladstone, the Wilson family, and Wilson's father, an old map, an Italian scroll, three images of Wilson, and various images of his alma maters Princeton and Johns Hopkins University. EBW to EPS, October 8, 1931; EBW to D. L. Groner, June 30, 1938, folder 13, 1938, EBWP; EBW to Groner, June 18, 1938, folder 13, 1938, EBWP; EBW to EPS, November 28, 1938, folder 13, 1938, EBWP; EBW to EPS, August 12, 1940, folder 15, 1940, EBWP; EBW to EPS, January 29, 1941, folder 16, 1941, EBWP; EBW to EPS, March 4, 1941, folder 16, 1941, EBWP; John Randolph Bolling to EPS, November 7, 1940, folder 15, 1940, EBWP; Bolling to EPS, November 15, 1940, folder 15, 1940, EBWP; EBW to EPS, January 29, 1941; EBW to EPS, March 28, 1941, folder 16, 1941, EBWP; EBW to Mrs. Cordell Hull, April 7, 1941, folder 16, 1941, EBWP; EBW to Smith, April 23, 1943, folder 18, 1943, EBWP; Brown, *Woodrow Wilson Presidential Library*.

68. EBW to EPS, October 8, 1931; EBW to EPS, August 30, 1939; EBW to EPS, April 29, 1940, folder 15, 1940, EBWP; EBW to EPS, August 12, 1940; EBW to EPS, October 27, 1940; EBW to EPS, November 3, 1940, folder 15, 1940, EBWP; EBW to EPS, November 14, 1940, folder 15, 1940, EBWP.

69. EBW to EPS, October 27, 1940; Brown, *Woodrow Wilson Presidential Library*, 21; EBW to EPS, March 28, 1941; EBW to EPS, May 5, 1941, folder 16, 1941, EBWP (quote).

70. EBW to EPS, August 19, 1939, folder 14, 1939, EBWP; EBW to EPS, August 30, 1939, folder 14, 1939, EBWP; EBW to EPS, April 13, 1942, folder 17, 1942, EBWP; EBW to EPS, July 20, 1942, folder 17, 1942, EBWP; EBW to EPS, September 3, 1943, folder 18, 1943, EBWP.

71. EBW to EPS, August 8, 1942, folder 17, 1942, EBWP; EBW to EPS, December 19, 1942, folder 17, 1942, EBWP; EBW to EPS, September 3, 1943.

72. Commercialization quote from EBW to EPS, July 25, 1944, folder 19, 1944, EBWP; train quote from EBW to EPS, September 12, 1944, folder 19, 1944, EBWP; EBW to Colonel Opie, September 14, 1944, folder 19, 1944, EBWP. In early 1961 Edith still hoped the endowment would reach the $100,000 mark. EBW to EPS, January 3, 1961, folder 35, 1961, EBWP.

73. EBW to EPS, November 22, 1945, folder 20, 1945, EBWP; EBW to EPS, September 7, 1948, folder 23, 1948, EBWP; EBW to EPS, December 1, 1948, folder 23, 1948, EBWP; EBW to EPS, December 1948, folder 23, 1948, EBWP; EBW to EPS, February 1, 1949, folder 24, 1949, EBWP. One of Edith's closest friends, Louise Pennington, made a sizable donation to the endowment "out of the blue." EBW to EPS, August 21, 1949, folder 24, 1949, EBWP; EBW to EPS, August 27, 1949, folder 24, 1949, EBWP; EBW to EPS, July 19, 1950, folder 25, 1950, EBWP; Rockefeller quote from EBW to EPS, July 29, 1950, folder 25, 1950; EBW to EPS, October 22, 1952, folder 26, 1952, EBWP; EBW to EPS, November 5, 1952, folder 26, 1952, EBWP; EBW, "Prospect List Given by Mrs. Wilson," November 5, 1952, folder 26, 1952, EBWP; EBW to General Opie, October 29, 1952, folder 26, 1952, EBWP; EBW to EPS, April 24, 1953, folder 27, 1953, EBWP; EBW to EPS, October 9, 1954, folder 28, 1954, EBWP; Joseph M. Hartfield to EBW, September 8, 1955, Folder 29, 1955, EBWP; EBW to EPS, Sunday 1955, folder 29, 1955, EBWP; EBW to EPS, December 22, 1959, folder 33, 1959, EBWP.
74. E. W. Opie and Harry F. Byrd to EBW, November 19, 1954, folder 28, 1954, EBWP; EBW to EPS, April 24, 1953; EBW to EPS, October 9, 1954; EBW to EPS, June 25, 1955, Folder 29, 1955, EBWP; EBW to EPS, June 30, 1956, folder 30, 1956, EBWP; EBW to EPS, November 17, 1960, folder 34, 1960, EBWP.
75. Wamsley, "Staunton's Indomitable Mrs. Herbert McK. Smith"; quote from EBW to Mary Jones, January 30, 1956, folder 30, 1956, EBWP (quote); EBW to EPS, November 16, 1959, folder 33, 1959, EBWP; EBW to EPS, March 7, 1960, folder 34, 1960, EBWP. A curator in 2015 joked that the manse could burn to the ground, but if anything happened to the car, he would be in major trouble. Phillips, "Behind-the-Scenes Tour."
76. EBW to EPS, October 30, 1954, folder 28, 1954, EBWP; WWBF, "Resolved," 1; Brown, *Woodrow Wilson Presidential Library*, 21; Wamsley, "Staunton's Indomitable Mrs. Herbert McK. Smith." The fact that Smith had declined the presidency until the last decade of her public service was circulated in written accounts celebrating her tenure.
77. EBW to EPS, October 11, 1960, folder 34, 1960, EBWP.
78. Wilson knew Kennedy personally and knew that he admired her husband. She wrote to Mrs. Kennedy, whom, in the expert estimation of the former First Lady, was cultivated, charming, and a real "asset to her husband." Through the Associated Press, the WWBF learned that President Kennedy verbally accepted the invitation during a meeting. EBW to EPS, November 17, 1960; EBW to EPS, November 25, 1960, folder 34, 1960, EBWP; EBW to EPS, February 27, 1961, folder 35, 1961, EBWP; Geoge M. Cochran to EBW, March 23, 1961, folder 35, 1961, EBWP; EBW to EPS, October 16, 1961, folder 35, 1961, EBWP; EBW to EPS, November 2, 1961, folder 35, 1961, EBWP; EBW to EPS, November 9, 1961, folder 35, 1961, EBWP; EBW to EPS, November 1961, folder 35, 1961, EBWP; Mrs. H. McKay Smith, December 7, 1961, Outgoing Correspondence 1965–1974, Selected, Wilson, Edith B., PEPS.
79. EBW to EPS, November 17, 1960; EBW to EPS, November 25, 1960; EBW to EPS, January 3, 1961; Dale D. Drain to Woodrow Wilson Birthplace Foundation, "Estate of Edith Bolling Wilson, Deceased," December 7, 1962, folder 37, Miscellaneous, EBWP; US District Court for the District of Columbia, "Estate

of Edith Bolling Wilson, Deceased, Receipt of the Legatee," n.d., folder 37, Miscellaneous, EBWP; Link and Brand, "Edith Bolling Wilson," 3.

80. WWBF, "Resolved," 1–2.
81. Smith kept Link informed of meetings and developments and arranged staggered visits. Arthur S. Link to Mrs. Herbert McK. Smith, December 5, 1960, Incoming Correspondence-Link, Arthur S., PEPS; Link to EPS, January 16, 1962, Incoming Correspondence-Link, Arthur S., PEPS; Link to EPS, February 19, 1962, Incoming Correspondence-Link, Arthur S., PEPS; Link to EPS, November 1, 1963, Incoming Correspondence-Link, Arthur S., PEPS.
82. Link to EPS, March 26, 1964, Incoming Correspondence-Link, Arthur S., PEPS (quote); Link to EPS, December 4, 1968, Incoming Correspondence-Link, Arthur S., PEPS; Link to EPS, September 28, 1966, Incoming Correspondence-Link, Arthur S., PEPS; Link to Mrs. Herbert McK. Smith, March 30, 1970, Incoming Correspondence-Link, Arthur S., PEPS; Daniel Martinez, "Former U.S. Archivist to Step into Wilson's Shoes," *Harrisonburg (VA) Daily News-Record*, June 17, 2009.
83. Virginia Travel Council, "Meritorious Service Award Presented to Mrs. H. McKelden Smith," June 5, 1968, Incoming Correspondence-S-1960, box 6, folder 11 10 May 1968–24 Jul. 1968, Undated Correspondence Relating to the Tributes Dinner Given for Emily Smith, PEPS (hereafter Tributes Dinner); quote from Virginia Travel Council, "A Recognition from the Board of Directors of the Virginia Travel Council," March 26, 1968, Tributes Dinner; Richard S. Gillis Jr. to Mrs. George M. Cochran, June 3, 1968, Tributes Dinner; W. C. "Dan" Daniel, "The Virginia State Chamber of Commerce Send Greetings to Mrs. Herbert McKelden Smith," 1968, Tributes Dinner.
84. William T. Alderson to Mrs. H. McKay. Smith, May 30, 1968, Tributes Dinner; Richard Nixon to Mrs. H. McKay Smith, March 17, 1973, Incoming Correspondence-S-1960, box 6, folder 12 5 Feb. 1959–Apr. 1973 Miscellaneous Typed or Printed Tributes to Emily Smith, PEPS.
85. Smith claimed that she shared her dreams with the trustees. Delores Lescure, who directed the Augusta County Historical Society and Historic Staunton Foundation, proved a worthy successor to Smith. During her twenty-year presidential term, Lescure moved the WWBF closer to Smith's mission of a museum and library. Smith's fundraising and leadership expertise honed at the birthplace improved her community as well. She served eight years as hospital board president, running a $2.5 million fundraising campaign. Emily P. Smith, "Mr. Toastmaster, Mr. Darden and Friends," 1968, 2, Tributes Dinner; WWBF, "Resolved," 2; "Mrs. Herbert Mck. Smith Retires as Birthplace Foundation President," *Staunton (VA) Leader*, February 19, 1973, Incoming Correspondence-S-1960, box 6, folder 13, 6 June 1968–19 Feb. 1973 Apr. 1973 Tributes to Emily Smith, PEPS; Wamsley, "Staunton's Indomitable Mrs. Herbert McK. Smith"; "Mrs. Herbert McKelden Smith."
86. Calvin R. Trice, "Woodrow Wilson Library Planned," *Richmond Times-Dispatch*, March 29, 2004, city edition; Bob Stuart, "Wilson Library Plans Revealed—Staunton Facility to Become Nation's 14th Presidential Library," *Richmond Times-Dispatch*, August 26, 2004, One Star edition; Chris Kahn, "Virginia City Plans Wilson Library for Its (Briefly) Native Son," *Times* (Trenton, NJ), August 29, 2004; Bob Stuart, "Wilson Library Has Big Plans for Exploration—It

Hopes to Examine His Presidency and the Period's Way of Life," *Richmond Times-Dispatch*, December 26, 2006, final edition; Alicia Wotring Sisk, "Wilson Library Looking for Boost-Lawmakers Propose Grant Legislation for Expansion," *Harrisonburg (VA) Daily News-Record*, August 2, 2007; *The Woodrow Wilson Museum*, digital video (Staunton, Virginia, n.d.), accessed June 22, 2015.

87. The PWWH is commonly called *S Street*. I did not research any archival materials related to the National Trust transaction. The PWWH entered the Wilson HHM canon in the 1960s, making the shrine formation of Staunton and Columbia by Emily Smith and Ruth Cappelmann most alike.
88. In 2015 the PWWH general tour did briefly celebrate the Wilson's Virginia roots in the Solarium, where the couple ate breakfast. The silver Virginia cup represents the Wilson's place of birth and that two Virginians resided in the White House. Sometime between 2015 and 2021, the mission changed. See the "About Us" page at the PWWH website, http://www.woodrowwilsonhouse.org; Toegel, guided tour.
89. Toegel, guided tour.
90. Berg, *Wilson*, 738–39. Wilson's modernization of Princeton with a new graduate college, common meals, and dormitories replacing socially exclusive eating clubs and residential houses angered the administration, trustees, faculty, and alumni. Ambar, "Woodrow Wilson."
91. Lopez, "Open House," 10.
92. Taylor, notes from meeting with Betty van Iersel, PWWH, Washington, DC, June 20, 2015.
93. Toegel, guided tour.
94. Joseph Wilson was from Ohio and of Scotch-Irish descent. His wife, Jessie, daughter of a Presbyterian minister, was born in Carlisle, England. Wilson moved the burgeoning family from Ohio to Hampton-Sydney, Virginia, before taking his position in Staunton in 1855. Link, *Road to the White House*, 1.
95. Link notes that almost all of Wilson's biographers testify that he was "essentially a Southerner." See Link, *Road to the White House*, xi, 3–4n11; R. S. Baker, *Youth*, 26.
96. Link, Road to the White House, 2–3.
97. Woodrow Wilson, *Robert E. Lee: An Interpretation*, v–vi.
98. "Woodrow Wilson: President in a New Era," panel; "Washington Welcomes a Democrat to the White House, panel," *Woodrow Wilson: His Life and Times*, WWPLM, June 19, 2015. For additional information on the violent overturn of Reconstruction, see the following: Zuczek, *State of Rebellion;* Lemann, *Redemption;* Foner, *Reconstruction*. For a discussion of the New South and national reunion, see Woodward, *Origins of the New South;* Lears, *Rebirth of a Nation;* Blight, *Race and Reunion*.
99. Link, *Road to the White House*, 1; Ayers, *What Caused the Civil War?*, 55, 58–59.
100. Blight, *Race and Reunion*, 7–9, 11.
101. K. L. Cox, *Dixie's Daughters*, 5–6, 69–71, 112–13, 148.
102. Montgomery's book was not peer-reviewed, but I consulted its original primary source material if I used it in my own research and found much of Montgomery's evidence sound. Montgomery, *Thomas Woodrow Wilson*, 148–52.
103. A brief tour of the manse with Erick Montgomery for CSPAN can be found here: *Woodrow Wilson's Boyhood Home*, https://archive.org/details/CSPAN3_20150802_181200_Woodrow_Wilsons_Boyhood_Home.

104. A 1901 Colonial Revival remodeling changed the front of the home, removing the small portico and iron balconies under the windows. Montgomery, *Thomas Woodrow Wilson*, 38, 128, 130, 137.
105. Herzberg, guided tour. In 1860 the church, eager to keep Wilson, gave him a five-hundred-dollar raise and built a new manse for ten thousand dollars to replace the deteriorating one. Montgomery, *Thomas Woodrow Wilson*, 24–26, 31.
106. Montgomery, *Thomas Woodrow Wilson*, 141–45, 147. The executive committee included President Nancy Bowers, Vice President Herb Upton, and Treasurer Dean Childress.
107. The researchers for the study were architect Normal Davenport; archaeologist Dr. David Collin Crass; Montgomery, who researched the history; and landscape consultants Mary Palmer and Hugh Dargan. Montgomery, *Thomas Woodrow Wilson*, 148–52; Herzberg, guided tour.
108. When I attended a tour, the guide never used the word *Reconstruction* to describe the time period after the Civil War. Herzberg, guided tour.
109. Wilson shared the story of his first memory in a 1909 speech on Abraham Lincoln. Montgomery, *Thomas Woodrow Wilson*, 2, 44; Parlor quote from Herzberg, guided tour; Polhill, guided tour.
110. W. B. Hale, Woodrow Wilson, 30; Montgomery, Thomas Woodrow Wilson, 55–56; Corley, Confederate City, 97.
111. Tommy Wilson's love of baseball is a theme interpreted both in Augusta and Columbia. The Clark brothers, who attended school in New Jersey, introduced baseball to the community. Wilson, one of the Clark brothers, and his friends set up the baseball club. Tommy drew the picture of the balloons and lineup on the inside cover of his *Elements of Physical Geography* textbook. According to Montgomery, Prof. S. A. King charged twenty-one cents to see the balloon *Hyperion* lift off behind the Opera House on its journey to Beaufort, South Carolina. Montgomery, *Thomas Woodrow Wilson*, 70–73; Herzberg, guided tour.
112. Herzberg, guided tour; Montgomery, *Thomas Woodrow Wilson*, 69, 75, 77, 79 (quotes).
113. Montgomery, *Thomas Woodrow Wilson*, 19–20, 41, 43 (quote).
114. W. B. Hale, Woodrow Wilson, 36; Montgomery, Thomas Woodrow Wilson, 80.
115. W. B. Hale, Woodrow Wilson, 34–35.
116. Montgomery, *Thomas Woodrow Wilson*, 56–59, 67, 69; W. B. Hale, *Woodrow Wilson*, 38–39.
117. Wilson, "Robert E. Lee," 68–69; Montgomery, *Thomas Woodrow Wilson*, 71, 82.
118. Wilson, "Young People," 478, 480; Link, *Road to the White House*, 2.
119. Montgomery, *Thomas Woodrow Wilson*, 4, 153–54 (quotes).
120. Herzberg, guided tour.
121. Montgomery, *Thomas Woodrow Wilson*, 18, 22, 41.
122. Montgomery, *Thomas Woodrow Wilson*, 47–50, 52–53, 61, 63–64; Corley, *Confederate City*, 4.
123. Poole, *Never Surrender*, 47–48; Montgomery, *Thomas Woodrow Wilson*, 51–52, 44 (quotes), 46–47; Corley, *Confederate City*, 39–40, 46–49, 51, 60.
124. Montgomery, *Thomas Woodrow Wilson*, 65, 82; Joseph R. Wilson to Thomas Woodrow, October 22, 1866, Woodrow Wilson Papers, S. 2 P. 4.
125. Montgomery, *Thomas Woodrow Wilson*, 83–85, 103–4, 108.
126. Montgomery, 36, 73, 75, 138–40, 138–39 (quote); Herzberg, guided tour, "Tour of Boyhood Home."

127. "Staunton Welcomes Its Native Son," panel, *Woodrow Wilson: His Life and Times*, June 19, 2015, WWPLM; Stuart, "Wilson Library Has Big Plans for Exploration."
128. This Wilson quote appears in Wilson biographies by Hale and Montgomery and the exhibit film within Staunton's Woodrow Wilson Museum W. B. Hale, *Woodrow Wilson*, 7–22; Montgomery, *Thomas Woodrow Wilson*, 12; *The Woodrow Wilson Museum*, digital video (Staunton, Virginia, n.d.), accessed June 22, 2015.

Chapter 2: The Rebirth

1. Taylor, "Woodrow Wilson Family Home Adult Tour Script," 1–3.
2. Steven Conn, *Do Museums Still Need Objects?* (University of Pennsylvania Press, 2010), 5, 40–41, 46-47, 50, 56-57, 94.
3. Brazier interview; Morgan interview; Taylor, email message to Heather Bacon-Rogers, "Practice Tour of WWFH," July 30, 2014; Vagnone and Ryan, *Anarchist's Guide to Historic House Museums*, 95.
4. "The Woodrow Wilson Family Home," panel, *Woodrow Wilson Family Home*, 2014. Evidence showing how the interpretation and tour evolved comes from the tour script evolution. I circulated numerous drafts of the script to the interpretive team in the months before opening as part of my job as tour facilitator. See Taylor, "WWFH Interpretation Adult Tour 01 31 14 Working Draft," 4; "WWFH Interpretation Adult Tour 02 06 14 Working Draft," 4; "WWFH Interpretation Adult Tour Second Training Version," 4.
5. Local filmmaker Lee Ann Kornegay produced the film in collaboration with Historic Columbia. She also directed the final exhibit films discussed in the last chapter of the present book.
6. Only Tommy's room and his parents' are identified. The Wilsons' bedroom is the tour's denouement.
7. Vagnone and Ryan, *Anarchist's Guide to Historic House Museums*, 121.
8. Taylor, "WWFH Interpretation," 1.
9. Taylor, "WWFH Script," 1; Blackwell, "Tour-SAB Edits," 1.
10. Link, Road to the White House, 2–3.
11. This path also allowed visitors to learn about the origins of saving the home. The tour passed Township Auditorium, which was to be built where the Wilson house stands. See chapter 1 on shrine building. Blackwell, "Tour-SAB Edits," 3; Waites, "WWFH," 1; Taylor, "WWFH Interpretation," 1; Waites, Sherrer, and Taylor, "WWFH Adult Tour," 1.
12. Waites, "WWFH-Tour Review"; Vagnone and Ryan, *Anarchist's Guide to Historic House Museums*, 85, 116.
13. Gunter; Morgan interview.
14. Redfield, "Thoughts on the Scrip[t]"; Taylor, "Adult Tour Script," 6; Taylor, "WWFH Interpretation," 1; Waites, Sherrer, and Taylor, "Marking Changes RW JMS," 1.
15. Taylor, "Adult Tour January 2nd Draft," 1.
16. Taylor, "WWFH Script," December 10, 2013, 1; Waites, "Revision 2 Dec 16 RW Notes," 1; Taylor, "Tour 01 31 14 Working Draft," 4; Taylor, "Tour 02 06 14," 4; Waites, Sherrer, and Taylor, "Marking Changes RW JMS," 2.
17. Annie Wright, email message to Waites, "Feedback on the WWFH Tour," March 18, 2014.
18. Vagnone and Ryan argue historic house museums ignore a vast cast of characters and groups connected to their homes in favor of one or two significant

individuals, which stymies a multi-vocal and diverse interpretation. Vagnone and Ryan, *Anarchist's Guide to Historic House Museums*, 138.

19. Gunter interview.
20. Vagnone and Ryan, *Anarchist's Guide to Historic House Museums*, 130.
21. Docent Doe interview.
22. Vagnone and Ryan, *Anarchist's Guide to Historic House Museums*, 44, 89.
23. Brazier interview.
24. "Woodrow Wilson Family Home" panel.
25. Hogan, "Historic Columbia Docent Survey."
26. Hogan interview.
27. Segregating federal offices united Black activists who had been divided on other racial issues. They aligned with anti-segregation white people to protest the policy through public meetings, letter writing, petitions, and stories in the press. Wolgemuth, "Woodrow Wilson and Federal Segregation," 158–59, 163–68, 170.
28. According to Trygve Throntveit, the language of national self-determination, much less the idea of ethnic nation-states, was not a key feature of Wilson's peace plan. Wilson lacked clarity as to how the process would work outside Europe. The level of freedom, if any, was contingent on local conditions. Erez Manela argues that, rather than ushering in the Wilsonian century as previous Eurocentric historians have contended, the president's rhetoric sparked an international Wilsonian moment. This moment began with US entry into World War I in April 1917. Although European leaders had articulated the concept of self-determination as a path to peace earlier, Wilson's postwar vision circulated among a global audience on an unprecedented level, including to colonized peoples in Egypt, India, China, and Korea, who interpreted his rhetoric as an endorsement of universal self-determination. China's May Fourth movement, Mahatma Gandhi's nonviolent resistance movement in India, revolution in Egypt, and Korea's March First movement are 1919 campaigns contextualized in each state's national history but rarely placed in an international one. All four emerging nations had long-established social, economic, and political histories as well as educated elites, which allowed nationalist ideology to flourish. These nationalists were not radicals but rather shrewd politicians who used the Wilsonian moment to legitimize their demands for sovereignty within a new international order. More influential than V. I. Lenin, Wilson became an international symbol for self-determination, a temporary protagonist and icon for anticolonial nationalists. They seized his message, quoting his Fourteen Points and speeches, and worked within the negotiation process to challenge imperialism on an international stage. The Wilsonian moment peaked between fall 1918 and spring 1919 during the Treaty of Versailles negotiations. Throntveit, "Fable of the Fourteen Points," 446–48, 451, 476; Manela, *Wilsonian Moment*, x, xii, 3–13.
29. "State Government," panel, *Woodrow Wilson Family Home*, 2014.
30. L. V. Coleman, *Historic House Museums*, 17; D'Oney, "Louisiana's Old State Capitol," 78–79; Conn, *Do Museums Still Need Objects?*, 11.
31. Toegel, guided tour; National Trust for Historic Preservation, "President Woodrow Wilson House"; Olga Oksman, "The Unusual Gifts Given to U.S. Presidents," *The Atlantic*, February 15, 2016, https://www.theatlantic.com.
32. Bennett, *Birth of the Museum*, 2; Coxall, "Open Minds," 140.

33. Vagnone and Ryan, *Anarchist's Guide to Historic House Museums*, 35, 45, 130–31, 134; Conn, *Do Museums Still Need Objects?*, 7, 21–23, 26, 175.
34. Conn, *Do Museums Still Need Objects?*, 20, 23.
35. Vagnone and Ryan, *Anarchist's Guide to Historic House Museums*, 36. The objects were painted white as part of the new interpretation following a major restoration at the turn of the twenty-first century. Олександр Удовенко, "Mikhail Bulgakov Museum," Museums of Kyiv History, http://www.kyivhistorymuseum.org (accessed August 9, 2022).
36. Bacon-Rogers interview.
37. Morgan interview.
38. Taylor, "WWFH Script,"; Waites, "Revision 2 Dec 16 RW Notes," 2; Taylor, "Tour Jen's Dec. 30 Revision," 3; Taylor, "Woodrow Wilson Family Home Adult Tour Script," 6.
39. Hogan interview; Storm interview; Clark second interview; Scott, "Historic Columbia Docent Survey."
40. Docent Doe interview; Morgan interview; Storm interview; Hogan, "Historic Columbia Docent Survey."
41. Bacon-Rogers interview.
42. Hogan, "Historic Columbia Docent Survey"; Morgan interview; Storm interview.
43. Storm interview (quote); Morgan interview; Hogan interview.
44. Bacon-Rogers interview.
45. Docent Doe interview; Brazier interview; Clark second interview; Gunter interview.
46. Docent Doe interview; Bacon-Rogers interview.
47. Hogan interview; Stickney interview; Westcott interview; Clark second interview; Serrell, *Exhibit Labels*, 38.
48. Bacon-Rogers, "Historic Columbia Docent Survey"; Bacon-Rogers interview (quotes); Hogan interview; Holmes, "Historic Columbia Docent Survey."
49. Docent Doe interview; Brazier interview. In 2018, on the two-hundredth anniversary of the site, Historic Columbia initiated a "holistic rehabilitation" with new interpretation, interactive exhibits, and renovations. The Hampton-Preston family's role as slaveholders and secessionists as well as the lives of those enslaved at the urban mansion were central to the changes. Coincidentally the Preston family enslaved future state senator W. B. Nash. Historic Columbia, "Hampton-Preston Mansion and Gardens."
50. Lee interview; Bacon-Rogers interview.
51. Simon, *Participatory Museum*, 127–28, 130; Gunter interview; Bacon-Rogers interview; Clark second interview.
52. Lee interview; Simon, *Participatory Museum*, 131.
53. Bacon-Rogers interview.
54. Gunter interview.
55. Storm interview (first quote); Storm, "Historic Columbia Docent Survey" (second quote); Gunter interview; Clark second interview; Bacon-Rogers interview.
56. Storm interview.
57. Westcott interview; Docent Doe interview; Stickney interview; Gunter interview.
58. Morgan interview; Hogan interview.
59. Bacon-Rogers interview.

60. I evaluated the visitor evaluation data for 2014. Taylor, "Woodrow Wilson Family Home Trends"; "WWFH Visitor Evaluation 2014 Summary," Survey Monkey, January 8, 2015, 5, Historic Columbia.
61. "Copy of Wilson Survey Monkey Download Feb 2014–Jan 2015," Survey Monkey, February 2015, Historic Columbia.
62. Docent Doe interview; Bacon-Rogers interview; Clark second interview.
63. Bacon-Rogers interview.
64. Bacon-Rogers, interview; Bacon-Rogers, "Historic Columbia Docent Survey."
65. Stickney interview; Bacon-Rogers interview.
66. Clark second interview; Bacon-Rogers interview.
67. Bacon-Rogers interview.
68. Conn, *Do Museums Still Need Objects?*, 40–41, 56–57.
69. Conn, *Do Museums Still Need Objects?*, 5, 46–47, 50, 94.
70. Taylor, "Tour 01 31 14 Working Draft," 2; Waites, "Tour Review First Floor."
71. Vagnone and Ryan, *Anarchist's Guide to Historic House Museums*, 12. According to Olsen, only 45 percent of participants in a 2010 Connecticut Cultural Consumers study liked guided tours. Because of visitor and nonvisitor feedback, the Charles Lindbergh Historic Site moved away from lecture-style tours in favor of a conversational tour. Cindy Olsen, "Are Guided Tours at Historic Houses Dead?"
72. Taylor, "Tour Jen's Dec. 30 Revision," 2; Taylor, "Adult Tour January 2nd Draft," 2.
73. Taylor, "WWFH Script," December 10, 2013, 1; Blackwell, "Tour-SAB Edits," 1; Waites, "Revision 2 Dec 16 RW Notes," 1; Taylor, "Tour 01 31 14 Working Draft," 4; Taylor, "WWFH Script," June 13, 2014, 5. However, these instructions appeared in the earliest drafts of the script.
74. Vagnone and Ryan, *Anarchist's Guide to Historic House Museums*, 12–14, 26, 45, 115, 117.
75. Waites, Sherrer, and Taylor, "Marking Changes RW JMS," 4; Taylor, "WWFH Script," June 13, 2014, 4.
76. Vagnone and Ryan, *Anarchist's Guide to Historic House Museums*, 35.
77. Taylor, "WWFH Script," June 13, 2014, 6; Waites, "Tour Review First Floor."
78. Storm interview; Gunter interview.
79. Vagnone and Ryan, *Anarchist's Guide to Historic House Museums*, 112, 127; Chen and Tsai, "Influence of Background Music."
80. Hogan interview; Brazier interview; Westcott interview.
81. Vagnone and Ryan, *Anarchist's Guide to Historic House Museums*, 18; Storm interview; Brazier interview; Hogan interview; Lee interview.
82. Brazier interview; Storm interview; Lee interview.
83. Gunter interview; Clark second interview; Docent Doe interview.
84. Clark second interview; Gunter interview; Hogan interview.
85. Docent Doe interview.
86. Hogan interview; Hogan, "Historic Columbia Docent Survey."
87. Gunter interview.
88. Serrell, *Exhibit Labels*, 41.
89. Lee interview; Stickney interview; Gunter interview; Docent Doe interview.
90. Serrell, *Exhibit Labels*, 54.
91. Gunter interview; Stickney interview; Bacon-Rogers interview; Lee interview.
92. Serrell, *Exhibit Labels*, 57–58.
93. Stickney interview; Gunter interview.

94. Holmes, "Historic Columbia Docent Survey."
95. Simon, *Participatory Museum*, 4.
96. Schneider, "Historic Columbia Docent Survey."
97. Storm interview; Vagnone and Ryan, *Anarchist's Guide to Historic House Museums*, 81, 107.
98. Stickney interview.
99. Taylor, "WWFH Trends"; "Evaluation 2014 Summary," 2; James Quint, email message to Taylor, "Question Added to Wilson Survey," March 31, 2015; Taylor, "WWFH April 2015 Survey Monkey Stats," Historic Columbia, May 2015, 13.
100. Vagnone and Ryan, *Anarchist's Guide to Historic House Museums*, 97.
101. Waites, email message to interpretive team, "WWFH Follow Up," December 7, 2013.
102. Posner, email message to interpretive team, "Staff WW Tours for March," February 27, 2014; Posner, email message to interpretive team, "April Staff Tours," March 26, 2014.
103. Posner, "March WW 2014 Calendar," Historic Columbia, February 27, 2014.
104. Posner, "April Woodrow Wilson Tours Calendar," Historic Columbia, March 26, 2014; Posner, "May 2014 Woodrow Wilson Tours Calendar," Historic Columbia, April 2014; Posner, "June 2014 Woodrow Wilson Tours Calendar," Historic Columbia, May 13, 2014; Posner, "July 2014 Woodrow Wilson Tours Calendar," Historic Columbia, June 2014; Posner, "September WW 2014 Calendar," Historic Columbia, August 2014.
105. Posner, "September WW 2014 Calendar"; Betsy Kleinfelder, email message to interpretive team, "October Woodrow Wilson Schedule," September 24, 2014; Kleinfelder, email message to interpretive team, "November WW Schedule," October 17, 2014; Kleinfelder, "November 2014– WWFH Calendar," Historic Columbia, October 2014; Kleinfelder, email message to interpretive team, "January WWFH Schedule," December 19, 2014; Kleinfelder, email message to interpretive team, "February WWFH Schedule," January 23, 2015; Kleinfelder, email message to interpretive team, "March Woodrow Wilson Schedule," March 3, 2015; Kleinfelder, email message to interpretive team, "April WWFH Schedule," March 17, 2015; Heather Bacon-Rogers, email message to weekend staff, "Weekend Updates 6/27–6/28," June 25, 2015. The new tour schedule launched April 7, 2015. "New Tour Times," April 2015, Historic Columbia.
106. Gunter interview; Docent Doe interview.
107. Gunter interview.
108. Bacon-Rogers interview.
109. Serrell, *Exhibit Labels*, 165, 174.
110. Docent Doe interview; Bacon-Rogers interview; Serrell, *Exhibit Labels*, 75, 127; Menne, "Historic Columbia Docent Survey"; Clark second interview.
111. Bacon-Rogers interview; Vagnone and Ryan, *Anarchist's Guide to Historic House Museums*, 47.
112. Lee interview; Westcott interview; Falk, *Identity and the Museum Visitor Experience*, 64.
113. Bacon-Rogers interview; Docent Doe interview.
114. I evaluated the visitor evaluation data for 2014. Taylor, "WWFH Trends"; "Evaluation 2014 Summary," 5.
115. "Survey Monkey Download."
116. Gunter interview; Scott, "Historic Columbia Docent Survey"; Lee interview.

117. Bacon-Rogers interview.
118. Heather Bacon-Rogers and Katharine Allen, interview by Jennifer Whitmer Taylor, Zoom recording, May 11, 2023.

Chapter 3: Docent Training

1. Constitutional Convention, Article 10, S 131081, 1868, 42–44, South Carolina Department of Archives and History, Columbia.
2. Edgar, *South Carolina*, 390–91; Williams, *Self-Taught*, 4, 193–94.
3. The occupant of the public education bedroom is unknown, but it was not Tommy or his parents. See the relevant panels at the MoRE: "A Religious Posting"; "A Center for Religious Thought"; "Tommy Grows Up"; "Public Schools"; "The University of South Carolina"; "Training New Leaders."
4. Taylor, "Home Adult Tour Script," 26; B. E. Baker, *What Reconstruction Meant*, 6, 9, 11–12, 22, 24, 34, 69, 149; Poole, *Never Surrender*, 1–3, 121.
5. Waites, "WWFH Tour Training Opening 1.8.14," Historic Columbia, January 8, 2014; document sent by Waites, email message to interpretative team, "WWFH General Calendar," January 13, 2014. This was also the deadline for school, garden, and preservation tours, which took less precedence during the relaunch.
6. Robin Waites, "Exhibit Content Training Session 3," Historic Columbia, December 12, 2013, Historic Columbia Collection; Waites, email message to Posner and Quint, "WWFH Session 3," December 12, 2013. Images from an unlabeled file folder in Historic Columbia's collection.
7. Waites, "WWFH Tour Training Opening 1.8.14"; Waites, email message to interpretive team, "Dialoging about Race," November 15, 2013; James Quint, email message, "WWFH Training-Final Schedule," January 13, 2014; Sarah Blackwell, "Wilson Training Update," March 19, 2014, Historic Columbia Collection. Blackwell circulated this document via email.
8. Two charts presented during the session listed the occupations, literacy rates, and servitude status before the Civil War of South Carolina's Black legislators during Reconstruction. A third broke down the state legislature by party and race. Jennifer Taylor, "General Overview of Reconstruction Lecture and Questions to Consider," presentation, Historic Columbia, November 2013; Quint, email message to Ann Posner, "Woodrow Wilson Family Home Training Session 1 Reconstruction Era," November 13, 2013. I used charts 1–3 from Thomas Holt, *Black over White*, 39, 52, 97.
9. Brown has an extensive list of authored publications related to the Civil War and Reconstruction, including *Civil War Canon: Sites of Confederate Memory in South Carolina* (University of North Carolina Press, 2015) and, most recently, *Civil War Monuments and the Militarization of America* (University of North Carolina Press, 2019), which received the Tom Watson Brown Book Award of the Society of Civil War Historians. He has edited several books, including the coedited work *Hope and Glory: Essays on the Legacy of the 54th Massachusetts Regiment* (University of Massachusetts Press, 2001); *Reconstructions: New Perspectives on the Postbellum United States* (Oxford University Press, 2006), which includes his essay "Civil War Remembrance as Reconstruction"; and *Remixing the Civil War: Meditations on the Sesquicentennial* (Johns Hopkins University Press, 2011). According to Brown's lecture, Reconstruction was "the renewal of nationhood" and the "destruction of slavery" through the "reconstitution of a financial system"

and citizenship. To achieve these goals, the Republican Party, which controlled the federal government and initially was committed to Black rights, introduced a two-party system to the South and allowed federal courts "to determine and enforce" citizenship for Black Americans as well as for women, immigrants, veterans, and former Confederates. Reconstruction was both "an open-ended process" and a "historical period." Waites, "WWFH Tour Training Opening 1.8.14"; Waites, email message to interpretive team, "Dialoging about Race," November 15, 2013; Thomas J. Brown, "Main Points for Training of WWFH Volunteers," November 12, 2013, Historic Columbia Collection; Fielding Freed, email message to Waites, "WWFH Materials for Ken and Tom," December 4, 2013.

10. Clements, "Discussion Questions about Woodrow Wilson in Columbia," December 2013, Historic Columbia Collection; Freed, email message to Waites, "Ken and Tom," December 4, 2013.
11. Posner, email message to Taylor, "Woodrow Wilson Training," November 14, 2013; Posner, "WW Volunteer Training Attendance," Historic Columbia, December 10, 2013, Historic Columbia Collection.
12. The discussion took place during a meeting held after the New Year between the interpretive committee and select long-term or elite volunteer docents to discuss the Wilson home's script. Annie Wright, "Results of WWFH Volunteer Training," slide 15, PowerPoint, Historic Columbia, March 10, 2014, Historic Columbia Collection; Docent Doe interview; Richardson, "Historic Columbia Docent Survey."
13. Vagnone and Ryan would likely identify Cook's session as offering examples of N.U.D.E. traits of interpretation (Non-linear, Unorthodox, Dactylic, and Experimental). Rather than training, they call for encouragement of thought and behavior that promotes greater interaction. Vagnone and Ryan, *Anarchist's Guide to Historic House Museums*, 93. Waites, email message to Taylor, "WWFH Staff Engagement Training," November 12, 2013; Waites, "WWFH Tour Training Opening 1.8.14"; Waites, email message to interpretive team, "Dialoging about Race," November 15, 2013.
14. "Volunteer Training," Historic Columbia, 2013, author's personal files; "WWFH Training Session Planning," Historic Columbia, November 13, 2013, Historic Columbia Collection; Daniella Cook, "Application of Adult Learning Theory," n.d., Historic Columbia Collection. The handout was adapted from M. Knowles's "Adult Learning" in the ASTD Training and Development Handbook.
15. *Taxonomy for Learning, Teaching, and Assessing: A Revision of Bloom's Taxonomy of Educational Objectives* revised Benjamin Bloom's 1956 book. Daniella Cook, "Support HCF Staff Prepare Volunteer Trainings," PowerPoint, slides 1, 4–5, 9, Columbia, SC, December 9, 2013.
16. Brazier interview; Wright, "Results of WWFH Volunteer Training," slide 6; Stickney, "Historic Columbia Docent Survey"; Clark, "Historic Columbia Docent Survey."
17. Delays in installation and a rare snowstorm derailed plans to give docents a week to practice tours and another week to be evaluated.
18. The second week of January was devoted to the first floor and the following week to the second floor. Five sessions each week meant that the number of participants in each group was limited to five or fewer for questions. Posner, email message to Volunteer Docents, "Upcoming Woodrow Wilson Training," January 9, 2014;

Waites, "WWFH Tour Training Opening 1.8.14"; document sent by Waites, email message to interpretive team, "WWFH General Calendar," January 13, 2014; Posner, "First and Second Floor Training Sessions Sign-Up Sheet," January 21, 2014, Historic Columbia Collection; Posner, "Questions and Suggestions from WW Training Session First Floor," January 21, 2014; Quint, email message to Taylor and Sherrer, "Tour Notes," January 24, 2014; Posner, "February WW 2014 Calendar," Historic Columbia, February 2014; Daniella Cook, "Historic Columbia Foundation WWFH Tour Observation Report," March 13, 2014, 1; Clark second interview.

19. Wright, "Results of WWFH Volunteer Training," slide 4; Gunter interview; Brazier interview; Bacon-Rogers interview; Docent Doe interview; Hogan, "Historic Columbia Docent Survey"; Menne, "Historic Columbia Docent Survey."
20. Blackwell, "Wilson Training Update"; Wright, "Results of WWFH Volunteer Training," slide 6; Gunter interview; Brazier, "Historic Columbia Docent Survey."
21. Scott, "Historic Columbia Docent Survey"; Richardson, "Historic Columbia Docent Survey"; Docent Doe interview; Stickney interview.
22. Morgan interview; Hogan interview; Hogan, "Historic Columbia Docent Survey"; Wright, "Results of WWFH Volunteer Training," slide 14.
23. Storm interview; Docent Doe interview; Schneider, "Historic Columbia Docent Survey"; Weir, "Historic Columbia Docent Survey"; Wright, "Results of WWFH Volunteer Training," slide 6.
24. Hogan interview; Storm interview; Scott, "Historic Columbia Docent Survey"; Clark second interview.
25. Bacon-Rogers interview ("prepared"); Stickney interview ("deflect").
26. Wright, "Results of WWFH Volunteer Training," slides 2, 9 (charts), 10. Wright cautioned that post-evaluations were a smaller sample size. Thirty-four docents completed pretraining surveys, but only fourteen completed the post-evaluations.
27. Storm interview; Gunter interview; Westcott interview; Morgan interview; Clark second interview; Stickney interview; Hogan interview; Hogan, "Historic Columbia Docent Survey"; Brazier interview (quote).
28. Waites, email message to Taylor, "Technique Recommendations for WWFH," January 21, 2014 (imagine quote); Cook, "Tour Observation," 3 (stick quote); Annie Wright, email message to Waites, "Feedback on the WWFH Tour," March 18, 201.
29. Lee interview; Storm interview; Stickney interview; Morgan interview.
30. Cook, "Tour Observation," 1; Docent Doe interview.
31. Gunter interview; Brazier interview; Docent Doe interview; Westcott interview; Storm interview; Hogan interview.
32. Twenty-three percent of first-round trainees wanted more time. Two docents wished the more sensible form of training finalized by Historic Columbia had been possible the first time. Wright, "Results of WWFH Volunteer Training," slide 5; Brazier interview; Docent Doe interview.
33. A lunch break separated the two sessions each day. Weekend staff adopted this format too.
34. Historic Columbia used the new model for its April, July, and September 2014 training programs. The interpretive team lectures replaced those of University of South Carolina faculty Ken Clements and Tom Brown. Porchia Moore offered different content but supported the sessions originally conducted by Daniella

Cook. Historic Columbia also removed the expectation that docents should initially colead a tour with a small group, which offered the real environment of a tour but with staff support. Posner, email message to interpretive team, "April Staff Tours," March 26, 2014; Taylor, email message to Posner and Quint, "April 7th-Training Session 1," April 3, 2014; Taylor, email message to Posner, "June 2014 Volunteer Training Class," June 24, 2014; Waites, email message to interpretive team, "WWFH Action Items," May 21, 2014; Taylor, email message to Docent P and Jean Morgan, "WWFH June Follow-Up," August 6, 2014; Waites, email message to volunteers, "WWFH June Follow-Up," June 13, 2014; Posner, email message to Taylor and Quint, "Monday Afternoon Presentation with Portia," April 9, 2014; Ann Posner, "Woodrow Wilson Family Home Training Schedule July 21 and 28," Historic Columbia, July 15, 2014, Historic Columbia Collection; Blackwell, "Wilson Training Update"; Waites, email message to interpretive team, "WWFH Volunteer Feedback," May 6, 2014; Wright, "Results of WWFH Volunteer Training," slide 5; Bacon-Rogers interview; Taylor, email message to Bacon-Rogers, "Evaluations," August 29, 2014; Betsy Kleinfelder, email message to volunteer docents, "Tour Coverage Needed and Training," September 17, 2014.

35. Taylor, email message to interpretive team and Cook, "Revised Tour Review," January 23, 2014; Sarah Blackwell, email message to Posner, Quint, and Taylor, "Volunteer Survey Review from Annie," April 4, 2014.
36. This data is based on twenty-eight total evaluations of nineteen docents. Fifteen were volunteers, two were staff, and two were weekend staff. Sixteen passed the evaluation process. Additionally Daniella Cook evaluated two of those docents as well as one staff member and Docent U (a volunteer who did not pass the tour evaluation). She did not use the formal evaluation form, so her reflections on those evaluated are included but not factored into statistical analysis. I intentionally use gender-neutral plural pronouns to promote anonymity in the evaluation process. Jennifer Whitmer Taylor, "Docent B Tour Review," Historic Columbia, February 20, 2014; James Quint, "Docent C Tour Review," Historic Columbia, February 20, 2014; Ann Posner, "Docent F Tour Review," Historic Columbia, March 4, 2014; Posner, "Docent G Tour Review," Historic Columbia, March 6, 2014; Taylor, "Docent H Tour Review," Historic Columbia, March 12, 2014; Posner, "Docent O Tour Review," Historic Columbia, n.d.; Taylor, "Docent S Informal Tour Review," Historic Columbia, June 18, 2014; J Taylor, "Docent S Tour Review," Historic Columbia, July 18, 2014.
37. Posner, "Docent H Tour Review," Historic Columbia, March 12, 2014; Taylor, "Docent I Tour Review," Historic Columbia, March 17, 2014; Taylor, "Docent J Tour Review," Historic Columbia, April 2, 2014; Taylor, "Docent K Tour Review," Historic Columbia, October 30, 2014; Taylor, "Docent L Tour Review," Historic Columbia, June 6, 2014; Posner, "Docent O Tour Review"; J Taylor, "Docent R Tour Review," Historic Columbia, July 24, 2014; Taylor, "Docent S Informal Tour Review"; Cook, "Tour Observation," 1.
38. Taylor, "Docent M Tour Review," Historic Columbia, August 21, 2014; Posner, "Docent N Tour Review," Historic Columbia, October 30, 2014, Historic Columbia; Posner and Taylor, "Docent P Tour Review," Historic Columbia, February 11, 2014; Taylor, "Docent S Tour Review."
39. Taylor, "Docent K Tour Review"; Posner, "Docent N Tour Review"; Posner and Taylor, "Docent P Tour Review"; Taylor, "Docent P Tour Review," Historic

Columbia, March 26, 2014; John Sherrer, "Docent P Tour Review," Historic Columbia, June 4, 2014; Taylor, "Docent S Tour Review."

40. A stereoscope viewer creates a three-dimensional image from two different images at angles representing the left- and right-eye views. Taylor, "Docent I Tour Review"; Taylor, "Docent P Tour Review," Historic Columbia, June 4, 2014; Taylor, "Docent M Tour Review"; J Taylor, "Docent G Tour Review," Historic Columbia, March 20, 2014.

41. Posner and Taylor, "Docent P Tour Review"; Taylor, "Docent K Tour Review"; Taylor, "Docent P Tour Review"; Zuczek, *State of Rebellion*, 50; Edgar, *South Carolina*, 397.

42. Taylor, "Docent R Tour Review"; Taylor, "Docent L Tour Review" (quote); Taylor, "Docent S Tour Review."

43. Posner, "Docent D Tour Review," Historic Columbia, February 24, 2014; Wright, email message to Waites, "Feedback on the WWFH Tour"; Allison Marsh, email message to Waites, "Questions on Panels @ WWFH," December 17, 2013; Docent Doe interview; Brazier interview; Bernadette Scott, email message to Taylor, "March Results," May 1, 2015; Celia Galens, email message to Taylor, "Walt's Tour," June 12, 2014; Clark second interview.

44. Taylor, "Docent A Tour Review," Historic Columbia, February 10, 2014; Taylor, "Docent G Tour Review"; Taylor, "Docent L Tour Review"; Taylor, "Docent M Tour Review"; Posner, "Docent N Tour Review"; Posner, email message to Taylor, "Jean Morgan," August 21, 2014; Taylor, "Docent Q Tour Review," Historic Columbia, October 1, 2014.

45. Taylor, "Docent K Tour Review"; Taylor, "Docent R Tour Review"; Taylor, "Docent S Informal Tour Review."

46. Posner, "Docent B Tour Review," Historic Columbia, February 20, 2014; Quint, "Docent C Tour Review"; Taylor, "Docent P Tour Review," March 26, 2014; Taylor, "Docent R Tour Review"; Taylor, "Docent S Tour Review."

47. Waites, email message to interpretive staff, "WWFH Trial Tours," February 4, 2014; Waites, email message to interpretive team, "Guide Evaluations," January 16, 2014; Cook, "Tour Observation," 1; Posner, email message to Historic Columbia staff, "Please Be a 'Audience Member,'" February 21, 2014.

48. Brazier interview; Taylor, email message to Posner, "Maria Schneider," May 14, 2014; Posner, email message to Taylor, "Group Tour at Woodrow Wilson," May 15, 2014; Kleinfelder, email message to Taylor and Posner, "Shadowing at WW," August 14, 2014.

49. Taylor, "Docent A Tour Review"; Posner, "Docent B Tour Review"; Taylor, "Docent E Tour Review," Historic Columbia, February 28, 2014; Posner, "Docent F Tour Review"; Posner, "Docent G Tour Review"; Taylor, "Docent G Tour Review"; Taylor, "Docent H Tour Review"; Posner, "Docent H Tour Review"; Taylor, "Docent I Tour Review"; Taylor, "Docent J Tour Review"; Taylor, "Docent K Tour Review"; Taylor, "Docent L Tour Review"; Taylor, "Docent M Tour Review"; Taylor, "Docent S Informal Tour Review"; Taylor, email message to Kleinfelder and Holly Westcott, "Holly's Evaluation," October 30, 2014.

50. Taylor, "Docent K Tour Review"; Taylor, "Docent I Tour Review"; Posner, "Docent N Tour Review"; Posner, email message to Taylor, "Jean Morgan," August 21, 2014.

51. Taylor, "Docent B Tour Review"; Taylor, "Docent E Tour Review"; Posner, "Docent G Tour Review"; Taylor, "Docent G Tour Review"; Taylor, "Docent H Tour Review"; Posner and Taylor, "Docent P Tour Review"; Freed, "Docent P Tour Review," Historic Columbia, June 4, 2014; Taylor, "Docent P Tour Review," June 4, 2014; Cook, "Tour Observation," 2; Taylor, email message to Posner, "Docent P's Evaluation," March 14, 2014.
52. Posner, "Docent G Tour Review"; Taylor, "Docent G Tour Review"; Taylor, "Docent H Tour Review"; Posner, "Docent H Tour Review"; Taylor, "Docent M Tour Review"; Taylor, "Docent S Informal Tour Review."
53. Posner, email message to Taylor, "Walt's Evaluation 3/20/2014," March 21, 2014; Taylor, email message to Posner, "Docent U," March 5, 2014; Docent U, email message to Posner, "Woodrow Wilson Tour," March 6, 2014; Posner, email message to Docent U, "WW Tour," March 11, 2014; Cook, "Tour Observation," 2; Taylor, email message to Posner, "Docent P's Evaluation."
54. As of February 2023, legislators in twenty-five states considered laws or other maneuvers to control how teachers teach race and racism. Eight Republican-controlled states banned or reduced the teaching of legal theories such as Critical Race Theory. Anthony Izaguirre, "Florida Gov. DeSantis Pushes Ban on Diversity Programs in State Colleges," PBS NewsHour, January 31, 2023; "Florida Teachers Move to Block DeSantis Questions on CRT," *AP News*, January 11, 2023.
55. At the time of the MoRE's opening, Historic Columbia administered three other homes: the Mann-Simons Site, the Robert Mills House and Gardens, and Hampton-Preston Mansion and Gardens. Mills and Hampton-Preston were the most popular HHMs and focused on the household's occupants and decorative arts, the more traditional style of HHM interpretation. The volunteer coordinator trained and approved volunteer docents, who shadowed tours and received a tour manual. New weekend docent hires shadowed weekend staff on tours and were evaluated by the weekend staff manager or director of education. In 2018 Historic Columbia reinterpreted its Hampton-Preston Mansion to center urban slavery within the household. This exhibit style and training resembles the MoRE. Historic Columbia, "Hampton-Preston Turns 200"; Historic Columbia, "House Tours."
56. Clark second interview; Wright, "Results of WWFH Volunteer Training," slide 6; Posner, email message to interpretive team, "WW Attendance Record," January 15, 2014; Posner, "WW Volunteer Training Nov. 2013 Session 4," January 15, 2014, Historic Columbia Collection.
57. Wilson's home was so important to Docent U that they offered their schedule before passing the evaluation process and volunteered to work non-tour-related events at the home. Posner, email message to Waites, "WW Schedule," January 31, 2014; Waites, email message to Posner, "WW Schedule," January 31, 2014; Docent U, email message to Posner, "March Schedule," February 18, 2014.
58. Kleinfelder, email message to Taylor, "Tour Coverage," September 8, 2014; Kleinfelder, email message to Taylor, "WWFH Tour," October 16, 2014; Taylor, email message to Kleinfelder, "WWFH Tour," October 21, 2014; Taylor, email message to Posner, "Donna Stokes," February 26, 2014; Kleinfelder, email message to Taylor, "Volunteers for WW Book Signing," September 4, 2014.

59. Docent P, email message to Posner and Docent U, "Meeting with Ann," March 25, 2014; Posner, forwarded email message to Taylor, "Meeting with Ann," March 25, 2014.
60. Docent P needed tremendous support with content and themes and omitted half of the room statements. The second evaluation brought only slight improvement and only in selecting Wilson evidence. Taylor, email message to Posner, "Shadow Volunteers," February 4, 2014; Posner and Taylor, "Docent P Tour Review"; Taylor, "Docent P Tour Review," March 26, 2014; Fielding Freed, "Docent P Tour Review," Historic Columbia, April 18, 2014; Freed, "Docent P Tour Review," June 4, 2014; Sherrer, "Docent P Tour Review"; Taylor, "Docent P Tour Review," June 4, 2014; Augusta tour information from Montgomery, *Thomas Woodrow Wilson*, 72–73; Herzberg, guided tour.
61. The docent's progress declined to fair and/or needs support across the board on presentation and content, audience engagement, and to some degree procedures. Freed, "Docent P Tour Review."
62. In most areas of content, timing, engagement, assessing the audience, and self-exploration, the docent ranked fair or between fair and good from all three evaluators. Drawn to controversial Reconstruction topics on previous evaluation tours, the docent spoke extensively on Sherman and the burning of Columbia. Freed, "Docent P Tour Review," June 4, 2014; Sherrer, "Docent P Tour Review"; Taylor, "Docent P Tour Review," June 4, 2014.
63. Taylor, email message to Posner, "Make Up Sessions," May 14, 2014; Kleinfelder, email message to Taylor, "Tour Coverage," September 8, 2014.
64. Lee interview.
65. Quint, email message to Erin Holmes, Jennifer Thraikill, and Halie Brazier, "WWFH Tours This Weekend," February 18, 2014.
66. Posner, email message to Waites, "WW Volunteers," December 19, 2013; Richardson, "Historic Columbia Docent Survey"; Scott, "Historic Columbia Docent Survey"; Pris Stickney, email message to Waites, "WWFH," June 25, 2014; Westcott interview; Holly Westcott, "Historic Columbia Docent Survey"; Schneider, "Historic Columbia Docent Survey."
67. Stickney interview.
68. Morgan interview.
69. Clark first interview.
70. Posner, email message to Taylor and Quint, "WW Sample Tours," February 26, 2014; Posner, email message to Taylor, "Make Up for Volunteers," May 7, 2014; Posner, email message to Taylor, "Shadowing Jen Taylor's Tours," April 23, 2014; Posner, email message to Anne Weir et al., "Woodrow Wilson Training Session Make-Up," May 14, 2014; Ray Hopkins, email message to Ann Posner, "Woodrow Wilson Training Session Make-Up," May 14, 2014; Kleinfelder, email message to Taylor, "WWFH Tour," October 16, 2014; Posner, email message to Vicki Cannon, "Vicki Cannon," June 3, 2014.
71. Posner, email message to interpretive team, "July WW Schedule," June 19, 2014; Posner, email message to Taylor, "Jean and Jeanette," March 18, 2014; Jim Staskowski, email message, to Posner, "Tomorrow," June 12, 2014.
72. Pustz, *Voices from the Back Stairs*, 44; Vagnone and Ryan, *Anarchist's Guide to Historic House Museums*, 97.
73. Waites, "WWFH Tour Training Opening 1.8.14"; document sent by Waites, email message to interpretive team, "WWFH General Calendar"; Cook, email

message to Waites, "Follow Up from Training and Next Steps," February 4, 2014; Waites, email message to interpretive team, "Volunteer/Staff Feedback Sessions," April 17, 2014; Waites, email message to volunteers, "WWFH June Follow-Up"; Stickney, email message to Waites, "WWFH"; Clark second interview; Docent Doe interview; Kleinfelder, email message to Waites, "March Volunteer Meeting Notes," March 5, 2015.

74. Clark second interview; Docent Doe interview; Hogan interview; Brazier interview.
75. Vagnone and Ryan, *Anarchist's Guide to Historic House Museums*, 92; Pustz, *Voices from the Back Stairs*, 43–45.
76. Stickney interview; Hogan interview; Storm, "Historic Columbia Docent Survey"; Storm interview; Clark first interview; Richardson, "Historic Columbia Docent Survey"; Docent Doe interview; Holmes, "Historic Columbia Docent Survey"; Brazier, "Historic Columbia Docent Survey"; Menne, "Historic Columbia Docent Survey"; Bacon-Rogers interview.
77. Gunter, "Historic Columbia Docent Survey"; Clark first interview; Docent Doe interview. Gunter wrote her undergraduate thesis on Reconstruction in Mississippi.
78. Holmes, "Historic Columbia Docent Survey"; Gunter interview.
79. Lee interview; Brazier interview.
80. Hogan interview; Westcott, "Historic Columbia Docent Survey"; Clark first interview.
81. Scott, "Historic Columbia Docent Survey"; Weir, "Historic Columbia Docent Survey"; Menne, "Historic Columbia Docent Survey"; Richardson, "Historic Columbia Docent Survey"; Stickney, "Historic Columbia Docent Survey."
82. Franklin Vagnone and Deborah Ryan argue that traditionally the majority of docents lack training as educators or performers. Vagnone and Ryan, *Anarchist's Guide to Historic House Museums*, 112; Pustz, *Voices from the Back Stairs*, 44; Posner, email message to Waites, "WW Volunteers," December 19, 2013; Richardson, "Historic Columbia Docent Survey."
83. Morgan interview; Hogan, "Historic Columbia Docent Survey"; Scott, "Historic Columbia Docent Survey"; Westcott, "Historic Columbia Docent Survey"; Weir, "Historic Columbia Docent Survey"; Posner, email message to Waites, "WW Volunteers," December 19, 2013; Clark first interview.
84. Westcott interview; Lee interview; Bacon-Rogers interview; Clark first interview; Clark second interview; Docent Doe interview; Morgan interview; Brazier interview; Zuczek, *State of Rebellion*, 62; Kimberly Johnson, "Ku Klux Klan Recruitment Drive Raises Old Fears in South Carolina," *Aljazeera America*, August 1, 2014, http://america.aljazeera.com/; "KKK Drops Recruitment Candy Bags in Oconee Co. Neighborhood," July 14, 2014, http://www.foxcarolina.com/; Carla Field, "Group Announces KKK Rally at Upstate 'Headquarters,'" WYFF4, May 8, 2014, http://www.wyff4.com/; Andrew Reeser, "Klan Member Rides Across Two Upstate Towns Promoting Rebel Flag," July 2, 2015, http://www.foxcarolina.com/.
85. Rhea, *Stephen A. Swails*, xii–xiii, 107–9, 128–31, 138–39, 142–44, 147–48, 150–51.
86. Clark first interview; Gina Smith, "Reconstruction History Long Ignored, Neglected: Are We Finally Ready to Talk?," *Island Packet*, June 12, 2015; Jennifer Schuessler, "Taking Another Look at the Reconstruction Era," *New York Times*, August 24, 2015.

87. Clark first interview.
88. Andrew, *Wade Hampton*, xiii, xi–xv, 500, 503–4.
89. Andrew, 499, 503; B. E. Baker, *What Reconstruction Meant*, 38–39; Poole, *Never Surrender*, 123.
90. Clark first interview.
91. Clark second interview.
92. Multiple authors reference the generations of students who read Oliphant's textbooks. "Mary Oliphant, Author of S.C. History Text, Dies," *Columbia (SC) State*, July 28, 1988, final edition, sec. Metro/Region; "Mary Simms Oliphant," *Columbia (SC) State*, August 9, 1988, final edition; Will Moredock, "Palmetto State Mistaught Its Own History for Decades," *Columbia (SC) State*, May 30, 2003, final edition, sec. editorial; Farmer, "Playing Rebels," 57; Clark first interview.
93. Farmer, "Playing Rebels," 57; B. E. Baker, *What Reconstruction Meant*, 168; Riley's quote appeared in Oliphant's obituaries. Associated Press, "Mary Simms Oliphant, 97, Author of S.C. Histories," *Charlotte Observer*, July 28, 1988, six edition, sec. Metro; "Mary Oliphant, Author of S.C. History Text, Dies"; "Mary Simms Oliphant"; Moredock, "Palmetto State Mistaught Its Own History."
94. Oliphant, Furman, and Oliphant, *History of South Carolina*, 375; Oliphant, *Simms History of South Carolina*, 244 (quote); B. E. Baker, *What Reconstruction Meant*, 168.
95. Oliphant, *Simms History of South Carolina*, 241; Oliphant, Furman, and Oliphant, *History of South Carolina*, 285.
96. Oliphant, Furman, and Oliphant, *History of South Carolina*, 283–91.
97. Oliphant, *Simms History of South Carolina*,240, 243; Oliphant, Furman, and Oliphant, *History of South Carolina*, 284, 291 (quote).
98. Oliphant, Furman, and Oliphant, *History of South Carolina*, 290, 299, 305; "Robert Smalls House," n.d., http://www.nationalregister.sc.gov.
99. The UDC also indoctrinated children with textbooks and membership in the Children of the Confederacy. Cox, *Dixie's Daughters*, 1–5, 26, 29, 65, 95–99, 120–23.
100. Henry Eichel, "A Very Different S.C. History Textbook," *Charlotte Observer*, December 1, 1985, sec. Viewpoint. #B; Michael Sponhour, "Professor Has Flair for History Flashy New Textbook Gains Teachers' Favor," State, August 18, 1991, sec. Metro/Region, 1A; Paul Tosto, "The History We Don't Teach Confederate Flag an Invisible Issue in Most Schools," State, January 26, 1997, sec. Front, A1; "Confederate Flag Isn't an S.C. Classroom Issue," *Charlotte Observer*, January 27, 1997, sec. Metro, 5C; Paul Tosto, "History Learns a Lesson: Blacks Also Built S.C.," State, February 1, 1997, sec. Front, A1; Adam Parker, "Link to the Past - Perennial Debate Over Black History Month Is Considered Afresh," *Post and Courier*, February 22, 2009, sec. Faith and Values, F1.
101. "Mary Simms Oliphant," 8A; Bruce Smith, "S.C. Novelist Coker Is Honored Grand Lady and Writer Simms Inducted into Hall of Fame," *Charlotte Observer*, February 8, 1992, 1C; "Mary Simms Oliphant, 97," Associated Press, 5C; For quotes, see "Mary Oliphant, Author," 1A.
102. Eichel, "Different S.C. History Textbook"; Moredock, "Palmetto State Mistaught Its Own History"; Will Moredock, "Mary C. Simms Oliphant's Troubling History of South Carolina," *Charleston City Paper*, May 9, 2012, sec. Opinion.

103. Cindy Sutter, "A Complex Relationship - Boulder Filmmaker Explores History of Slaveowners and Slaves on Her Ancestors' Plantation," *Daily Camera*, February 16, 2006, sec. Living and Arts, D01; Issac Bailey, "Textbooks Were 'Racist to the Core' - How S.C. Schools Taught History," *State*, September 14, 2015, sec. Palmetto Voices, 17. Sutter, "Complex Relationship-Boulder"; Quote from Bailey, "Textbooks Were 'Racist,'" 17 (quote).
104. B. E. Baker, *What Reconstruction Meant*, 168; B. E. Baker, "Whom Is Reconstruction For?," 20–21.
105. Westcott interview; Westcott, "Historic Columbia Docent Survey."
106. Docent Doe interview.
107. Brazier interview; Robles, "Dylann Roof."
108. Bacon-Rogers interview; Posner, email message to Taylor, "Friday," November 14, 2013; Ann Posner, "Docent F Tour Review," Historic Columbia, March 4, 2014; Galens, email message to Taylor, "Walt's Tour," June 12, 2014.
109. Celia Galens, email message to Jennifer Taylor, "Walt's Tour," June 12, 2014.
110. Gunter interview; Holmes, "Historic Columbia Docent Survey"; Morgan, "Historic Columbia Docent Survey."
111. Morgan interview; Morgan, "Historic Columbia Docent Survey."
112. Stickney interview; Weir, "Historic Columbia Docent Survey"; Menne, "Historic Columbia Docent Survey"; Storm, "Historic Columbia Docent Survey."
113. Littlefield also consulted on the 2018–19 standards. Zais, "South Carolina Social Studies Academic Standards," iii, iv; Spearman, "South Carolina Social Studies College-and Career-Ready Standards," 164.
114. Shireese Bell, "District 5 Announces New Social Studies Coordinator," Irmo-Seven Oaks, SC Patch, May 2, 2013, 5, https://patch.com/south-carolina/irmo/.
115. *Taxonomy for Learning*; Zais, "South Carolina Social Studies Academic Standards," iii, 26, 36–37, 61, 66, 99, 103, 136–39; Vaughan, "Official Social Studies," 120, https://scholarcommons.sc.edu.
116. Hogan, "Historic Columbia Docent Survey" ("considerable controversy"); Hogan interview.
117. "WWFH Training Session Planning," Historic Columbia Collection.
118. Vaughan, "Studies Curriculum Standards," viii, 205–6, 122.
119. Paul Bowers, "Proposed S.C. Social Studies Standards Don't Mention MLK, Rosa Parks or John C. Calhoun," *Post and Courier*, February 2, 2018.
120. Charges the standards ignored the Holocaust and Nazism prompted revision. Bowers.
121. Spearman, "South Carolina Social Studies College-and Career-Ready Standards," 28, 36–37, 73, 79–81, 111–14, 164.
122. Bacon-Rogers interview.
123. Clark second interview.
124. Pustz, *Voices from the Back Stairs*, 43–44; Tyson, *Wages of History*, 5–6.
125. Tyson, *Wages of History*, 24, 172, 174.
126. Brazier interview; Posner, email message to Sherrer and Freed, "Make Up Tours," February 18, 2014; Blackwell, email message to Waites, "Make Up Tours," February 18, 2014; Quint, email message to Blackwell, "WWFH-Weekends," March 14, 2014.
127. Bacon-Rogers interview; Holmes, "Historic Columbia Docent Survey."
128. Tyson, *Wages of History*, 3–6, 8–9, 11, 14, 17, 19–20, 23–24, 172, 174–77.

129. Vagnone and Ryan, *Anarchist's Guide to Historic House Museums*, 97; Waites, email message to interpretive team, "WWFH Follow Up," December 7, 2013; Bacon-Rogers interview.
130. Posner, "March WW 2014 Calendar"; Posner, "April Woodrow Wilson Tours Calendar"; Posner, "May 2014 Woodrow Wilson Tours Calendar"; Posner, "June 2014 Woodrow Wilson Tours Calendar"; Posner, "July 2014 Woodrow Wilson Tours Calendar"; Posner, "September WW 2014 Calendar"; Kleinfelder, email message to interpretive team, "October Woodrow Wilson Schedule"; Kleinfelder, "November 2014–WWFH Calendar."
131. Kleinfelder, email message to interpretive team, "February WWFH Schedule," January 23, 2015; Kleinfelder, email message to interpretive team, "March Woodrow Wilson Schedule," March 3, 2015; Kleinfelder, email message to interpretive team, "April WWFH Schedule," March 17, 2015; Bacon-Rogers, email message to weekend staff, "Weekend Updates 6/27–6/28," June 25, 2015. The new tour schedule launched April 7, 2015. "New Tour Times," April 2015, Historic Columbia.
132. Bacon-Rogers and Allen, interview by Taylor, Zoom recording, May 11, 2023.
133. Bacon-Rogers and Allen.
134. Historic Columbia, "Hampton-Preston Mansion and Gardens"; Historic Columbia, "1615 Blanding Street"; Andrew, *Wade Hampton*, 3–4, 6–7, 11, 15–17.
135. Bacon-Rogers and Allen, Zoom interview.
136. Bacon-Rogers and Allen.

Chapter 4: Aren't I a Citizen?

1. Deborah G. White, *Ar'n't I a Woman?: Female Slaves in the Plantation South* (New York: Norton, 1985), 5, 11.
2. Welter coined the term "cult of true womanhood," and Kraditor coined "cult of domesticity." Barbara Welter, "The Cult of True Womanhood: 1820-1860," *American Quarterly* 18, no. 2 (July 1, 1966): 151–74; Aileen S. Kraditor, *Up from the Pedestal: Selected Writings in the History of American Feminism* (Chicago: Quadrangle Books, 1968), 8, 10–12; Nancy F. Cott, *The Bonds of Womanhood: "Woman's Sphere" in New England, 1780-1835*, 2nd ed. (Yale University Press, 1997), xii; Suzanne Lebsock, *The Free Women of Petersburg: Status and Culture in a Southern Town, 1784-1860* (New York: Norton, 1984), xv; Joanne V. Hawks and Sheila L. Skemp, eds., *Sex, Race, and the Role of Women in the South: Essays* (Jackson: University Press of Mississippi, 1983), 97, 102.
3. Other classes and races of women left few records, and being a lady carried far less weight in an underprivileged setting. Scott, *Southern Lady*, ix–xii, xv, 4–5, 247, 271–73; Cott, *Bonds of Womanhood*, xi–xii, 2–4, 9–13, 197, 200.
4. Vagnone and Ryan, *Anarchist's Guide to Historic House Museums*, 140.
5. Vagnone and Ryan, 76.
6. Posner, "WW Training Class April 2014"; Posner, "WW Volunteer Training Nov. 2013 Session 4"; Taylor, email message to Bacon-Rogers, "Evaluations," August 29, 2014. This account of the cultural and language sensitivity workshops includes details from a History@Work blog post for the National Council on Public History. Jennifer Whitmer Taylor, "Inclusive Training at Historic Columbia," *National Council on Public History History@Work* (blog), March 6, 2017, http://ncph.org/history-at-work/inclusive-training-at-historic-columbia/.

7. Waites, email message to interpretive team, "Dialoging about Race," November 15, 2013.
8. Cook, email message to Waites, "Follow Up from Training and Next Steps," February 4, 2014; McIntosh, "White Privilege." Also in preparation for the workshop, Cook circulated a link to the second episode of the series *Race: The Power of an Illusion* on the construction of race and the contradictions of American independence and equality in the context of slavery. Episode 2, *Race: The Power of an Illusion*, uploaded by California Newsreel, YouTube, May 28, 2010, https://youtu.be/4UZS8Wb4S5k?si=bjQxzFCIBfXj4v4O; "Ten Things Everyone Should Know about Race," California Newsreel, https://newsreel.org/guides/race/10things.htm (accessed September 4, 2024). A modification of the pamphlet "Cultural Etiquette: A Guide for the Well-Intentioned" by Amoja Three Rivers, the etiquette guide offered thirteen tips. Alison Bailey and Maura Toro-Morn, "Tour Guide Etiquette: A Guide for the Well Intentioned Volunteer," n.d. (quotes); Amoja Three Rivers, "Cultural Etiquette: A Guide for the Well-Intentioned," School of the Americas Watch, http://soaw.org.
9. Posner, email message to Taylor and Quint, "Monday Afternoon Presentation with Portia," [*sic*] April 9, 2014; Quint, email message to Taylor and Posner, "Monday Afternoon Presentation with Portia," April 9, 2014. The exercise in challenging assumptions was from Southern Poverty Law Center, *Writing for Change*, 29–32. Docents circled the "assumptions" in such sentences as "Fashion Tights are available in black, suntan, and flesh color" and "Our founding fathers carved this great state out of the wilderness" and explained their selections.
10. Posner, email message to Taylor and Quint, "Monday Afternoon," April 9, 2014; Quint, email message to Taylor and Posner, "Monday Afternoon," April 9, 2014. At the time Moore was a PhD candidate in library sciences at USC. Today she is assistant professor at the University of Florida in the School of Art + Art History and Museum Studies. Porchia Moore, "Radical Trust," Incluseum (blog), May 7, 2014, https://incluseum.com/2014/05/07/radical-trust/.
11. Posner, email message to Waites, "WW Volunteers," December 19, 2013.
12. Examples of privilege walk activities can be found here: "Privilege Walk Activity," Inclusion and Diversity Education, Lakeland College, n.d., https://www.lakelandcollege.edu, accessed 10/7/2016; "Module 5: Privilege Walk Activity," School of Social Welfare, University of Albany, n.d., http://www.albany.edu, accessed 10/7/2016.
13. Taylor, email message to Kleinfelder, "WWFH Tour," October 21, 2014. The subject of the docent review email has been changed to keep the evaluation process confidential. Jennifer Taylor, email message to Ann Posner, "Docent A," February 26, 2014; Taylor, "Docent A Tour Review," Historic Columbia, February 10, 2014; Posner and Taylor, "Docent P Tour Review," Historic Columbia, February 11, 2014; Cook, "Historic Columbia Foundation WWFH Tour Observation Report," Columbia, SC, March 13, 2014, 2; Wright, "Results of WWFH Volunteer Training," PowerPoint, Historic Columbia, March 10, 2014, Historic Columbia Collection.
14. Taylor, "Woodrow Wilson Family Home Trends," slide 9.
15. Brazier interview; Bacon-Rogers interview; Lee interview; Gunter interview.
16. Morgan, "Historic Columbia Docent Survey"; Westcott interview; Weir, "Historic Columbia Docent Survey"; Docent Doe interview; Scott, "Historic Co-

lumbia Docent Survey"; Storm interview; Stickney interview; Hogan interview; Clark first interview; Clark second interview; Taylor, "Docent I Tour Review."

17. Brazier interview; Bacon-Rogers, "Historic Columbia Docent Survey"; Holmes, "Historic Columbia Docent Survey."
18. Morgan interview. For an introduction to the Mann-Simons site, see "Mann-Simons Site," Historic Columbia, http://www.historiccolumbia.org.
19. Brazier interview; Docent Doe interview; Lee interview; Gunter interview.
20. Hogan interview; Scott, "Historic Columbia Docent Survey"; Weir, "Historic Columbia Docent Survey"; Richardson, "Historic Columbia Docent Survey"; Stickney, "Historic Columbia Docent Survey"; Clark first interview; Westcott interview.
21. Gunter interview; Hogan interview; Storm interview; Clark first interview.
22. Vagnone and Ryan, *Anarchist's Guide to Historic House Museums*, 45, 72; Pustz, *Voices from the Back Stairs*, 34–35, 38–39, 42, 46–47, 50, 57–58, 67, 72, 212n7.
23. Vagnone and Ryan, *Anarchist's Guide to Historic House Museums*, 76, 139–41 (quotes); Pustz, *Voices from the Back Stairs*, 11, 48; Taylor, email message to Waites, "WWFH Follow Up," December 27, 2013; Lee interview; McPherson, *Reconstructing Dixie*, 5, 7.
24. Wamsley, "Staunton's Indomitable Mrs. Herbert McK. Smith."
25. Cynthia Polhill, the coordinator of visitor services and a twelve-year veteran of the WWPLM, conducted my tour. Polhill, guided tour, Woodrow Wilson Birthplace, Staunton, Virginia, June 18, 2015; Polhill, "Behind-the-Scenes Tour"; Pustz, *Voices from the Back Stairs*, 49; Phillips, "Behind-the-Scenes Tour"; Brown, *Woodrow Wilson Presidential Library and Museum*, 5, 7, 23.
26. Polhill, guided tour, Woodrow Wilson Birthplace; Brown, *Woodrow Wilson Presidential Library and Museum*, 11.
27. Brown, *Woodrow Wilson Presidential Library and Museum*, 23 (emphasis added); Scott, "Reimagining Freedom," 74.
28. Eichstedt, "Museums and (In)Justice," 128. This study evaluated 130 plantation museums or related sites.
29. Jennifer Eichstedt, "Museums and (In)Justice," 128, quote 131.
30. Brown, *Woodrow Wilson Presidential Library and Museum*, 7; Berg, *Wilson*, 30.
31. Wilson to Thomas Woodrow, April 27, 1857, Woodrow Wilson Papers, Presidential Papers Microfilm, S. 2 P. 4; Montgomery, *Thomas Woodrow Wilson*, 39.
32. Herzberg, guided tour, Woodrow Wilson Boyhood Home, Augusta, GA, May 28, 2015; Montgomery, *Thomas Woodrow Wilson*, 18, 39, 41, 53–54.
33. Toegel, guided tour, President Woodrow Wilson House, Washington, DC, June 20, 2015.
34. Taylor, "Notes from Meeting with Betty van Iersel," President Woodrow Wilson House, Washington, DC, June 20, 2015.
35. Berg, *Wilson*, 704, 737.
36. EWB to Mrs. H. McK. Smith, 1954, folder 28, 1954, EWBP.
37. President Wilson House, "Tours."
38. Bacon-Rogers interview; Gunter interview; Morgan interview; Brazier interview.
39. Hogan interview; Brazier interview; "Domestic Service," panel, *Woodrow Wilson Family Home*, 2014; Sanborn Map Company, "Image 56 of Sanborn Fire Insurance Map"; Taylor, "WWFH Interpretation Adult Tour Jen's Revision," Historic Columbia, December 10, 2013, 7; Blackwell, "WWFH Interpretation Adult Tour-SAB Edits per 12.11.13 Meeting," Historic Columbia, December 11,

2013, 5; Waites, "WWFH Interpretation Adult Tour Jen's Revision 2 Dec 16 RW Notes," Historic Columbia, December 20, 2013, 4; Taylor, "WWFH Interpretation Adult Tour 01 31 14 Working Draft," Historic Columbia, January 31, 2014, 9; Taylor, "WWFH Interpretation Adult Tour 02 06 14 Working Draft," Historic Columbia, February 6, 2014, 9; Taylor, "WWFH Interpretation Adult Tour Second Training Version," Historic Columbia, April 2014, 9; Waites, Sherrer, and Taylor, "WWFH Adult Tour Summer Revision Marking Changes RW JMS Comments," Historic Columbia, June 3, 2014, 12; Taylor, "Woodrow Wilson Family Home Adult Tour Script," Historic Columbia, June 13, 2014, 12.

40. Storm interview; Clark, Second Interview; Docent Doe interview; Stickney interview.
41. Gunter interview; Holmes, "Historic Columbia Docent Survey."
42. Pustz, *Voices from the Back Stairs*, 60.
43. O. Cox, "'Downton Boom,'" 113, 116.
44. Bacon-Rogers interview.
45. O. Cox, "'Downton Boom,'" 115.
46. Gunter interview.
47. J. Jones, *Labor of Love, Labor of Sorrow*, 56, 58–59; Glymph, *Out of the House of Bondage*, 9–11, 139, 150–51, 168–69, 172–73.
48. Bacon-Rogers interview; Gunter interview; Storm interview.
49. Brazier interview; Gunter interview; Hogan interview.
50. Taylor, "WWFH Interpretation Adult Tour Jen's Dec 30 Revision," Historic Columbia, December 30, 2013, 6; Taylor, "Tour 01 31 14 Working Draft," 10–11; Taylor, "WWFH Interpretation Adult Tour 02 04 14 Working Draft," Historic Columbia, February 4, 2014, 10–11; Waites, Sherrer, and Taylor, "Marking Changes RW JMS," 10; Taylor, "WWFH Script," June 13, 2014, 12.
51. Taylor, "WWFH Script," December 10, 2013, 7; Blackwell, "Tour-SAB Edits," 5; Waites, "Revision 2 Dec 16 RW Notes," 4; Taylor, "Tour Jen's Dec. 30 Revision," 5; Clark second interview; Stickney, "Historic Columbia Docent Survey"; Brazier interview; Morgan interview; Hogan interview; Stickney interview; Jones, *Labor of Love, Labor of Sorrow*, 52, 59, 77–78; "Marriage Divorce Orphans," panel, *Woodrow Wilson Family Home*, 2014.
52. Taylor, "WWFH Script," December 10, 2013, 7; Blackwell, "Tour-SAB Edits," 5; Waites, "Revision 2 Dec 16 RW Notes," 4; "Domestic Service" panel, *Woodrow Wilson Family Home*, 2014.
53. Posner, "Docent D Tour Review"; Posner, "Docent N Tour Review"; Morgan interview; Docent Doe interview; Redfield, "Thoughts on the Scrip[t]."
54. Waites, "WWFH-Tour Review First Floor DC," January 21, 2014, Historic Columbia Collection; Taylor, "WWFH Interpretation Adult Tour 01 10 14 Post Volunteer," Historic Columbia, January 10, 2014, 7.
55. Pustz, *Voices from the Back Stairs*, 47, 63, 64.
56. "Domestic Service" panel; Pustz, *Voices from the Back Stairs*, 52–53; Docent Doe, "Historic Columbia Docent Survey."
57. Bacon-Rogers interview; Docent Doe interview; John Sherrer, "Woodrow Wilson's Perspectives on African Americans," January 8, 2016, Historic Columbia Collection.
58. Pustz, Voices from the Back Stairs, 62–63.
59. Wright, email message to Waites, "Feedback on the WWFH Tour," March 18, 2014; Freed, email message to Sherrer, Taylor, and Blackwell, "Tour Notes,"

January 24, 2014; Waites, email message to interpretive team, "WWFH Action Items," May 21, 2014; Robin Waites, email message to Cook et al., "WWFH Notes from Guides," April 21, 2014; Waites, email message to volunteers, "WWFH June Follow-Up," June 13, 2014; Waites, email message to volunteer docents, "Follow Up from WWFH Feedback Sessions," May 27, 2014; Waites, Sherrer, and Taylor, "Marking Changes RW JMS," 12; Docent Doe interview; Stickney interview; Bacon-Rogers interview; Morgan interview. One volunteer ignored the portrait and gravitated to a formal dress as an example of expensive popular fashion requiring special labor. Redundancy deterred another, since the citizenship video in the next room also highlighted the image. Westcott interview; Clark second interview.

60. Pustz, *Voices from the Back Stairs*, 60–62.
61. Genovese, *Roll, Jordan, Roll*, 413–23, 459–61; Clinton, *Plantation Mistress*, 201, 204, 209, 211–14, 220–22; Jones, "My Mother Was Much of a Woman," 248; Giddings, *When and Where I Enter*, 33–34, 37, 39, 43, 45; White, *Ar'n't I a Woman?*, 5, 9–10, 33–39, 61, 146; Fox-Genovese, *Within the Plantation Household*, 189, 292, 294, 323, 325–26; Jennings, "Us Colored Women," 45–74; Jones, "Race, Sex and Self-Evident Truths," 23–24; King, "Suffer with Them," 148, 158–59.
62. Jones, "My Mother Was Much of a Woman," 248; White, *Ar'n't I a Woman?*, 41–43; Jennings, "Us Colored Women," 56, 63. Glymph was far less forgiving than Fox-Genovese of the plantation mistress's violence. Fox-Genovese, *Within the Plantation Household*, 22–24, 96–97, 139–42, 309, 314–15, 379–80; Glymph, *House of Bondage*, 26, 54, 58–59.
63. Jones, "Race, Sex and Self-Evident Truths," 23. For a discussion of sexual assault at the hands of younger male members of a slave-owning family, see Jennings, "Us Colored Women," 62–63, 66; Fox-Genovese, *Within the Plantation Household*, 295; Davis, *Inhuman Bondage*, 201.
64. Clinton, "Whip in His Hand," 206–11; Clinton, *Tara Revisited*, 36, 128–30; White, *Ar'n't I a Woman?*, 164; Feimster, *Southern Horrors*, 17, 20–22.
65. White, *Ar'n't I a Woman?*, 174–77; Giddings, *When and Where I Enter*, 30–31; Hine, "Rape and the Inner Lives," 912–14, 916. See also Clinton's body of work in the 1990s ("Bloody Terrain," 315–18, 321, 326, 328–32; "Reconstructing Freedwomen," 310–12, 315–19; "With a Whip in His Hand," 206–11); Cardyn, "Sexualized Racism/Gendered Violence," 716–19; McGuire, "Us Had Been Raped," 908–9; Rosen, *Terror in the Heart of Freedom*, 8, 10, 52–53, 62, 67–70, 212–18, 224; Feimster, *Southern Horrors*, 1, 49–51, 81–85, 89–103, 116–18, 203–5.
66. Gilmore, *Gender and Jim Crow*, 68–69, 82–88, 105–13; Feimster, *Southern Horrors*, 130–35; 1898 Wilmington Race Riot Commission, "1898 Wilmington Race Riot—Final Report," North Carolina Department of Cultural Resources, Office of Archives and History, Raleigh, May 31, 2006), 156, http://www.history.ncdcr.gov.
67. The five women who testified were Rebecca Ann Bloom, Harriet Armour, Lucy Tibbs, Lucy Smith, and Frances Thompson. Rosen, *Terror in the Heart of Freedom*, 1, 4–5, 6 (quote), 8–9, 61–62, 69–73, 77–82, 202–20, 224–33, 247–48n19; Bond and O'Donovan, *Remembering the Memphis Massacre*, 1; Rosen, "Words of Resistance," in *Remembering the Memphis Massacre*, 102–4, 107–10, 113.
68. Blank, "Do the Words 'Race Riot'"; Bond and O'Donovan, *Remembering the Memphis Massacre*, 1–3.
69. Jamie Self and Sammy Fretwell, "Essie Mae Washington-Williams, Daughter of Late US Senator, Dies," February 4, 2013, www.thestate.com; The Associated

Press, "National Briefing | South: South Carolina: Biracial Child Added To Thurmond Monument," *New York Times*, June 29, 2004, http://www.nytimes.com/.

70. Pustz, *Voices from the Back Stairs*, 65; Vagnone and Ryan, *Anarchist's Guide to Historic House Museums*, 82 (quotes); Gunter, "Historic Columbia Docent Survey"; Taylor, "General Overview of Reconstruction Lecture and Questions to Consider," November 2013, slide 11; Waites, "Tour Review First Floor."
71. Rosen details South Carolina upstate Klan members rape of Black women in retaliation for Black men exercising their voting rights and hiding in the woods during a wave of terror. Rosen, *Terror in the Heart of Freedom*, 216–17.
72. Vagnone and Ryan note that rape and other "difficult events" like war, slavery, and political unrest affected people who occupied historic house museums in the past, but the stories are often ignored in favor of sharing "the good times of a place." They also write that historic house museums must embrace inclusivity, both in their interpretation and staffing, to reach minority and neighborhood communities. Vagnone and Ryan, *Anarchist's Guide*, 76, 82.

Chapter 5: Interpreting Domestic Terror

1. Christina Marcos, "Pelosi: Trump Is a 'Clear and Present Danger,'" *The Hill*, January 13, 2021, https://thehill.com/.
2. Associated Press, "Transcript of Trump's Speech," https://www.usnews.com.
3. Natasha Bertrand, "Justice Department Warns of National Security Fallout from Capitol Hill Insurrection," *Politico*, January 7, 2021, https://www.politico.com/.
4. Marshall Cohen, "Questions Swirl Around Possible 'Insider' Help for Capitol Attack," CNN, January 13, 2021, https://www.cnn.com/.
5. Jaclyn Diaz, Bill Chappell, and Elena Moore, "Police Confirm Death Of Officer Injured During Attack On Capitol," NPR, January 7, 2021, https://www.npr.org/.
6. Specific attacks include poisoning a water supply with cyanide and bombing infrastructure, a nuclear power plant, and the Hoover Dam. Belew, *Bring the War Home*, 1–10, 15–16, 184, 210, 216, 221, 224, 231–34, 236–37, 239; Pineda, "Turner Diaries," https://www.latimes.com.
7. In 2018 the Southern Poverty Law Center's census identified 1,020 hate groups, the most since the survey began in 1990. In 2019 the Department of Homeland Security added the movement to its priority list of threats to the United States. In 2020 Belew and the Homeland Security threat assessment both agreed that white supremacy was the greatest terrorist threat to the country. Heidi Beirich, GPAHE's founder, political scientist, and an expert in white supremacist movements, agreed that the movement was "more energized and emboldened than it has been in decades." In October more officials, including FBI director Christopher Wray, confirmed their concern over white supremacy's threat and relationship to violence. Brooks, "SPLC Testifies Before Congress"; Beirich, "Testimony of Heidi L. Beirich," 1–2, 22; Mark Hosenball, "Acting U.S. DHS Security Intelligence Chief Says He Agrees with FBI on White Supremacist Threat," *Reuters*, October 2, 2020; Kathleen Belew, "The Plot Against Whitmer Won't Be the Last White Supremacist Threat," *Washington Post*, October 8, 2020; Pineda, "'Turner Diaries' Didn't."
8. Brooks, "SPLC Testifies before Congress"; Belew, *Bring the War Home*, 238.
9. "WWFH Training Session Planning," Historic Columbia, November 13, 2013, Historic Columbia Collection.

10. Clinton, "Bloody Terrain," 314; Zuczek, *State of Rebellion,* 3–6; B. E. Baker, *What Reconstruction Meant,* 6, 11–12, 87, 89, 108–9, 145, 147, 158–60, 162.
11. The official version is a product of cultural leaders, mostly comprising middle-class professionals, who use memory and commemorations, such as anniversaries, monument dedications, landmark designations, reunions, and centennials, to create an idealized reality that can control anxiety over change, promote their goals or reinforce the status quo, eliminate threats to that goal or messaging, and foster citizenship. Vernacular stems from "firsthand experience in small-scale communities" and expresses what "social reality feels like rather that what it should be like." Bodnar, *Remaking America,* 13–16, 19, 246.
12. Author visit to Oakley Park, Edgefield, SC, June 2014; Porter Barron Jr., Oakley Park Museum and Red Shirt Shrinein "Day Trips! 17 Neat Places to Visit That Aren't Very Far from Columbia," *Free Times,* May 7, 2014, http://www.free-times.com; Associated Press, "Nevada Rancher Standoff Turns on a States' Rights Debate," *CBS News,* April 14, 2014, http://www.cbsnews.com.
13. In addition to seditious conspiracy, the fourteen men in the Fort Smith trial stood accused of interstate transport of stolen money and conspiracy to manufacture illegal weapons and murder federal officers. Belew, *Bring the War Home,* 172–73, 237.
14. Blee, *Women of the Klan,* 2; Cox, *Dixie's Daughters,* 1, 3, 5, 26, 29, 65, 95–99, 120, 122–23.
15. Cox, *Dixie's Daughters,* 2, 4; Blight, *Race and Reunion,* 390, 397; B. E. Baker, *What Reconstruction Meant,* 12, 145, 158–60, 162; Gilmore, *Gender and Jim Crow,* xix–xx, 82–90.
16. Belew, *Bring the War Home,* 8, 157–61, 166–70, 173–77, 180–81, 217. Blee argues that Indiana Klanswomen of the 1920s were more than racists and nativists. These white Protestant members believed the Klan would protect women's suffrage and expand women's rights. Blee, *Women of the Klan,* 1–3.
17. Clark first interview.
18. Writers' Program, *South Carolina,* v, 6, 9; Hirsch, *Portrait of America,* 1, 6–7, 9, 48, 51–54, 56, 58, 125; DuBose, interview by Office of Oral History, South Caroliniana Library.
19. Hirsch, *Portrait of America,* 189 (quotes), 191; Duck, *Nation's Region,* 52, 57, 61, 74 (last quote).
20. Writers' Program, *South Carolina,* v, vii, 8–13 (quote from original preface); Hirsch, *Portrait of America,* 123, 125–26, 188–89.
21. Oliphant, *Simms History of South Carolina,* 234–44; Oliphant, Furman, and Oliphant, *History of South Carolina,* 85–90, 299, 305; Writers' Program, *South Carolina,* 38–41.
22. Oliphant, *Simms History of South Carolina,* 245–46; Oliphant, Furman, and Oliphant, *History of South Carolina,* 291–92.
23. Writers' Program, *South Carolina,* 38–41, 254, 399, 426.
24. "Political Terrorism," panel, *Woodrow Wilson Family Home,* 2014.
25. Edgar, *South Carolina,* 398; B. E. Baker, *This Mob Will Surely,* 17–18, 23–24; Zuczek, *State of Rebellion,* 56; Parsons, *Ku-Klux,* 103, 115, 230–31, 233, 236, 288.
26. Oliphant, *Simms History of South Carolina,* 245–46; Oliphant, Furman, and Oliphant, *History of South Carolina,* 291–92.
27. Zuczek, *State of Rebellion,* 88–89; Writers' Program, *South Carolina,* 384.

28. The three representatives were Samuel Nuckles, Junius Mobley, and Simeon Farr. During this time state representative Samuel Nuckles received a threat. The home invasion took place at Silas Hawkins's Yellow House following rumors that armed Black men were there. Parsons, *Ku-Klux*, 235, 244–54, 256, 260; B. E. Baker, *This Mob Will Surely*, 9, 15–16, 18, 20–33, 35–39; Writers' Program, *South Carolina*, 401.
29. Parsons, *Ku-Klux*, 24–25, 163, 236, 264–65, 291–92, 294; Writers' Program, *South Carolina*, 401.
30. Parsons, *Ku-Klux*, 23, 87, 218, 233–35, 237, 239–41, 249, 255–56, 259, 262, 265–66, 269, 276, 278, 280–82, 292, 294. Baker analyzes seven lynchings in the Carolinas from 1871 to 1930 through the peak of the lynching epidemic. B. E. Baker, *This Mob Will Surely*, 1, 4–5, 14, 17.
31. In New Orleans, for example, the local White League defended their armed but short-lived coup d'état (which was memorialized as the Battle of Liberty Place) because the biracial, Republican-controlled police seized a secret arms purchase. The White League also sent messages to white allies who were in biracial coalitions. Emberton, "'Violent Bear It Away,'" 169–70, 172; Prince, "Memory Battles," 190–91.
32. Emberton, "'Violent Bear It Away,'" 173; Prince, "Memory Battles," 190–91.
33. "The Red Shirt Campaign," panel, *Woodrow Wilson Family Home*, 2014.
34. Oliphant, *Simms History of South Carolina*, 248; Oliphant, Furman, and Oliphant, *History of South Carolina*, 294.
35. Writers' Program, *South Carolina*, 160–63; Zuczek, *State of Rebellion*, 163–64, 175–76.
36. Barron, "Day Trips!"
37. "The Red Shirt Campaign" panel; B. E. Baker, *This Mob Will Surely*, 39.
38. Writers' Program, *South Carolina*, 160 (quote), 161–163; Zuczek, *State of Rebellion*, 163–64, 175–76; B. E. Baker, *This Mob Will Surely*, 39.
39. Oliphant, *Simms History of South Carolina*, 249; Oliphant, Furman, and Oliphant, *History of South Carolina*, 294.
40. Oliphant, Furman, and Oliphant, *History of South Carolina*, 297.
41. WPA Writers' Program, *South Carolina*, 161–63.
42. WPA Writers' Program, *South Carolina*, 165–66.
43. WPA Writers' Program, *South Carolina*, 267–69.
44. As Poole describes the scene, a "shadowy figure flung off its chains and cast aside its robe of mourning, revealing a beautiful young woman, white of skin, dressed in gauzy white, and wearing a tiara emblazoned with words South Carolina." He places the battle cry later that evening. Poole, *Never Surrender*, 116-117.
45. Poole, *Never Surrender*, 48, 126–28, 130–32.
46. Tour 9 included two sites: the Hampton family plantation, Millwood, and the governor's last home. The tour also detailed his life, doubts about slavery, and war service, including evacuating Columbia and being falsely accused by Sherman of burning the city. Writers' Program, *South Carolina*, 375–76, 454.
47. Oliphant, *Simms History of South Carolina*, 249; Writers' Program, *South Carolina*, 38–41, 216–17.
48. "Resistance Organizations," panel, *Woodrow Wilson Family Home*, 2014; "The Red Shirt Campaign" panel; B. E. Baker, *This Mob Will Surely*, 39.
49. Oliphant, *Simms History of South Carolina*, 250–251 (quotes); Oliphant, Furman, and Oliphant, *History of South Carolina*, 295.

50. B. E. Baker, *This Mob Will Surely*, 9, 15, 39–40; "Remembering 'Redemption,'" panel, *Woodrow Wilson Family Home*, 2014; Historic Columbia, "Wade Hampton III Monument," HistoricColumbia.org, accessed July 6, 2021, https://www.historiccolumbia.org; B. E. Baker, *What Reconstruction Meant*, 41–43.
51. Westcott interview; Clark second interview; Hogan interview; Stickney interview; Storm interview.
52. Poole, *Never Surrender*, 122–24, 173.
53. Sons of Confederate Veterans Camp 36, "The Red Shirt," Museum and Library of Confederate History.
54. Storm interview; Hogan interview; Morgan interview; Gunter interview.
55. Brazier interview; Bacon-Rogers interview; Gunter interview; Storm, "Historic Columbia Docent Survey"; Belew, *Bring the War Home*, 168.
56. Bacon-Rogers interview; Brazier interview; Posner, email message to Taylor, "Friday," November 14, 2013; Galens, email message to Taylor, "Walt's Tour," June 12, 2014. Walt revealed during training while speaking with evaluators that he was not sure if he wanted to mention his family connections.
57. Lee interview; Bacon-Rogers interview; Morgan interview.
58. Brazier interview; Clark second interview.
59. Brennan Center for Justice, "It's Official"; Grimmer, "No Evidence for Voter Fraud"; Bump, "Despite GOP Rhetoric," https://www.washingtonpost.com.
60. Gunter interview; Storm interview; Morgan interview; Bacon-Rogers interview (quotes); Taylor, "Docent I Tour Review," Historic Columbia, March 17, 2014.
61. Docent Doe interview.
62. Thompson, *Ousting the Carpetbagger*, 59; Bacon-Rogers interview; Sherrer, "Wilson's Perspectives on African Americans," January 8, 2016, Historic Columbia Collection.
63. Sherrer, "Wilson's Perspectives on African Americans."
64. Clark second interview; Docent Doe interview; Bacon-Rogers, "Historic Columbia Docent Survey."
65. Morgan interview; Stickney interview; Bacon-Rogers interview.
66. Conn, *Do Museums Still Need Objects?* 43.
67. Brazier interview.
68. Christopher Blank, "Do the Words 'Race Riot' Belong on A Historic Marker In Memphis?," NPR.org, May 2, 2016, http://www.npr.org/sections/codeswitch/2016/05/02/476450908/in-memphis-a-divide-over-how-to-remember-a-massacre-150-years-later.
69. Bacon-Rogers interview; Hogan interview; Nast, *Union as It Was*; Nast, *One Vote Less*; "Political Terrorism" panel.
70. Lee interview; Hogan interview; Stickney interview; Brazier interview; Clark first interview.
71. Hogan interview; Stickney interview; Clark first interview.
72. Brazier interview; Bacon-Rogers interview.
73. Brazier interview; Gunter interview; Lee interview.
74. Gunter interview; Lee interview.
75. Gunter interview; Storm interview.
76. Vagnone and Ryan, *Anarchist's Guide to Historic House Museums*, 76.
77. Brooks, "SPLC Testifies Before Congress"; Beirich, "Testimony of Heidi L. Beirich," 13–14.

78. Defense Secretary Donald Rumsfeld refused to institute the zero-tolerance policy requested by the Southern Poverty Law Center and forty members of Congress in 2006. The Pentagon denied problems after forty-six active-duty members identified themselves as New Saxons. By 2008 the FBI revealed in a report titled "White Supremacist Recruitment of Military Personnel since 9/11" that there were more than a dozen investigations and crimes involving veterans and active-duty personnel. They discovered two hundred neo-Nazis with military training. Beirich, "Testimony of Heidi L. Beirich," 6–7, 13–14.
79. Beirich, 15, 19.
80. Trump condemned the Proud Boys and other "Western chauvinists" two days later. Hosenball, "Acting U.S. DHS Security"; Belew, *Bring the War Home*, 237; Belew, "Plot Against Whitmer"; Kathleen Belew and Elizabeth Neumann, "Leaving Trump in Office Now Will Just Encourage White Nationalists," *Washington Post*, January 8, 2021, https://www.washingtonpost.com/; Pineda, "'Turner Diaries' Didn't."
81. Brooks, "SPLC Testifies Before Congress"; Beirich, "Testimony of Heidi L. Beirich," 10, 13.
82. Adam Serwer, "The Capitol Rioters Weren't 'Low Class,'" *The Atlantic*, January 12, 2021, https://www.theatlantic.com/; "The End of Reconstruction," panel, *Woodrow Wilson Family Home*, 2014; Oliphant, *Simms History of South Carolina*, 245–46, 249; Oliphant, Furman, and Oliphant, *History of South Carolina*, 291–92, 294; Writers' Program, *South Carolina*, 38–41, 254, 426.
83. Zuczek, *State of Rebellion*, 101–2, 179; Edgar, *South Carolina*, 401–4.
84. "The End of Reconstruction" panel; Oliphant, *Simms History of South Carolina*, 245–46, 249; Oliphant, Furman, and Oliphant, *History of South Carolina*, 291–92, 294; Writers' Program, *South Carolina*, 38–41, 254, 426.
85. As well as a violent white supremist, Tillman was a passionate orator and "crude champion of the farmer," whose populism included the advancement of scientific agriculture and manufacturing schools in the New South. Poole, *Never Surrender*, 157–60, 162–63, 172–73, 175–76; Prince, "Memory Battles," 193–96; Emberton, *Beyond Redemption*, 208; Serwer, "Capitol Rioters." Though Tillman is not featured on the panels, they do include the Hamburg massacre, Martin W. Gary, and the 1895 state constitution. "Red Shirt Campaign" panel; "End of Reconstruction" panel.
86. Most of the Beirich's recommendations spoke to stronger screening measures, data collection, reporting, tracking, enforcement, and study by the military. Beirich, "Testimony of Heidi L. Beirich," 17–18, 20–21.
87. In addition Belew also recommended a swift investigation of infiltration into law enforcement and the military. Belew and Neumann, "Leaving Trump in Office."
88. Sturken, *Tourists of History*, 1–7, 9, 12, 16–17, 25, 31, 94–95, 141.
89. William Luther Pierce, head of the neo-Nazi group the National Alliance, published the book under a pseudonym. Belew, *Bring the War Home*, 35, 56–59, 11, 110–11, 210, 212, 214, 224; Belew and Neumann, "Leaving Trump in Office"; Pineda, "'Turner Diaries' Didn't."
90. Belew and Neumann, "Leaving Trump in Office"; Pineda, "'Turner Diaries' Didn't."
91. Associated Press, "Transcript of Trump's Speech."
92. Associated Press, "Transcript of Trump's Speech."

Chapter 6: Interpreting the Craft

1. Brazier interview.
2. Lowe, "Dwelling in Possibility," 51.
3. Cook, "WWFH Tour Observation Report," 3.
4. Lee interview.
5. Bacon-Rogers interview.
6. Brazier interview; Morgan interview; Docent Doe interview.
7. Clark second interview.
8. Lee interview; Brazier interview; Gunter interview.
9. Grantham, "Southern Historiography," 253–54; O'Brien, "C. Vann Woodward," 591–92; Kirby, *Media-Made Dixie*, 8; Van Tassel, "From Learned Society to Professional Organization," 931, 933, 943, 946, 954; G. E. Hale, *Making Whiteness*, 73; Blight, *Race and Reunion*, 295, 357–59; "New Beginning, 1892–1945," 83–84; Berg, *Wilson*, 93–94; Smith, introduction, 3, 9, 21, 36.
10. Ayers, *What Caused the Civil War?* 148.
11. Smith, introduction, 4–6, 37–38.
12. Grantham, "Southern Historiography," 253; Blight, *Race and Reunion*, 295; Van Tassel, "From Learned Society to Professional Organization," 943, 946; Smith, introduction, 4, 14–18.
13. Ayers, *What Caused the Civil War?* 147; "New Beginning, 1892–1945," 84–85; Behrend, "Facts and Memories," 428–29; Grantham, "Southern Historiography," 254; G. E. Hale, *Making Whiteness*, 75, 80–81; Smith, introduction, 38.
14. B. E. Baker, *What Reconstruction Meant*: 33–36; B. E. Baker, "Whom Is Reconstruction For?," 17–18; Smith, introduction, 7, 9, 16, 20, 25, 38.
15. Macaulay, "South Carolina Reconstruction Historiography," 20–21, 28; Lowery, "Paul Leland Haworth," 211; Smith, introduction, 3, 9, 21, 36; "Politics and the Press," panel, *Woodrow Wilson Family Home*, 2014.
16. Allen used select documents, letters, speeches, and newspaper clippings to write *Governor Chamberlain's Administration in South Carolina*. Macaulay, "South Carolina Reconstruction Historiography," 21–22; Lowery, "Paul Leland Haworth," 211.
17. Dunning directed eight dissertations on Reconstruction in individual states, ten theses on aspects of the Civil War or Reconstruction, several others on other topics in southern history, and numerous dissertations on political theory. Most theses were the first scholarly discussions of their topics, especially on the state level. Ulrich B. Phillips is Dunning's most famous student. John David Smith and J. Vincent Lowery's 2013 chronological anthology on the Dunning School includes a historical reassessment of the founders and eight Columbia doctoral students and their dissertations. Smith, introduction, 1–3, 8–9, 21, 25, 36–37.
18. Macaulay, "South Carolina Reconstruction Historiography," 21, 23; B. E. Baker, *What Reconstruction Meant*, 36–37; Lowery, "Paul Leland Haworth," 211.
19. Haworth took a break from history to farm and write about wilderness adventures. He involved himself in Progressive causes and served in the Indiana state legislature in 1921–22. Afterward he spent the last fifteen years of his life in the Department of History and Political Science at Butler University. Lowery, "Paul Leland Haworth," 203, 211–12, 215–19, 221–23.
20. Ambrosius, "Woodrow Wilson and *The Birth of a Nation*," 690–91; Benbow, "Birth of a Quotation," 525, 526–27.

21. "Woodrow Wilson on Reconstruction," panel, *Woodrow Wilson Family Home,* Columbia, 2014.
22. Wilson's essay was first published in *Atlantic Monthly* in January 1901. Wilson, "Reconstruction of the Southern States," 368, 379, 388–389, 392–394.
23. Fifty years after the Red Shirt movement began, Henry T. Thompson published *Ousting the Carpetbagger from South Carolina,* which heavily drew on Reynolds's and Ambrose Taylor's scholarship but neglected Gary. Three years later Bowers, *Tragic Era,* depicted Gary as "the grimly practical politician quietly superintending the machinery of the movement," while Hampton became the symbol. In 1952 an English professor at Winthrop, Hampton M. Jarrell, revived the Gary debate in *Wade Hampton and the Negro,* which attacked Gary and praised Hampton's moderation. Another extremist view on Gary was Sheppard's *Red Shirts Remembered.* Macaulay, "South Carolina Reconstruction Historiography," 26, 27 (quote), 30–32.
24. The work of Charles and Mary Beard and David Duncan Wallace's three-volume *History of South Carolina* (1934) were also part of the economic turn. Macaulay, "South Carolina Reconstruction Historiography," 28–30; Ayers, *What Caused the Civil War?* 147–48, 157; B. E. Baker, *What Reconstruction Meant,* 110, 117–18, 123–24, 128–32, 145; B. E. Baker, "Whom Is Reconstruction For?," 25–27.
25. Smith, introduction, 3, 9, 31, 35–36, 39; B. E. Baker, *What Reconstruction Meant,* 146–47, 149, 155–57.
26. Smith, introduction, 36; Baker and Frantz, "Against Synthesis," 219–20; Foner, *Reconstruction.*
27. Domby and Lewis, *Freedoms Gained and Lost,* 4–5, 11–12; Pinheiro, "Idealism versus Material," 144–45, 150–53.
28. Ayers also identified ten commonalities of "reconstructions." Ayers, *What Caused the Civil War?* 148, 155–62, 164–65; Doyle, "International History," 181–83; Domby, "Lessons from 'Redemption,'" 233, 236–37, 239–41. Academic Dr. Nicolau Joaquim Moreira, US consul to Brazil Henry Washington Hilliard, and engineer and writer André Rebouças were central to spreading this narrative. Pinto-Handler, "Dream of a Rural Democracy," 212–24; Roberts, *I've Been Here All the While.*
29. Ayers, *What Caused the Civil War?* 147–48, 157; Baker and Frantz, "Against Synthesis," 218–21, 225–30, 232–33, 237–40, 242–44; Domby and Lewis, *Freedoms Gained and Lost,* 3–5; Domby, "Lessons from 'Redemption,'" 3, 5–7.
30. Baker and Frantz, "Against Synthesis," 223–35; Parsons, *Ku-Klux,* 217–18; South Carolina ETV, "40 Acres and a Mule."
31. Baker considers gerrymandering, voting restrictions, the gutting of the Voting Rights Act, corporate personhood, and mass incarceration to be modern issues that threaten the Reconstruction Amendments. B. E. Baker, "Whom Is Reconstruction For?," 17–18, 22, 24.
32. B. E. Baker, *What Reconstruction Meant,* 6, 11–12, 87, 89, 108–9, 145, 147, 158–60, 162.
33. "Remembering 'Redemption'" panel; Anderson and Darby, "Richard T. Greener," 70.
34. Du Bois identified Pike and Reynolds as among those authors who "select and use facts and opinions in order to prove that the South was right in Reconstruction, the North vengeful or deceived and the Negro stupid." Macaulay,

"South Carolina Reconstruction Historiography," 19–26; B. E. Baker, *What Reconstruction Meant*, 36–37, 111, 113–16; Lowery, "Paul Leland Haworth," 211. In 1920 Howard University student Norman P. Andrews criticized J. G. de Roulhac Hamilton's 1914 dissertation *Reconstruction in North Carolina* for overstating Black political rule and Burgess for questioning Republicans' appointing Black officers to positions of power. Woodson, Andrews's mentor, also dismissed the scholarship of Rhodes and the Dunning founders as prejudiced and deficient. Smith, introduction, 16–18, 31–32; Behrend, "Facts and Memories," 428–33, 436, 441–43; Kirby, *Media-Made Dixie*, 5–7, 22.

35. Macaulay, "South Carolina Reconstruction Historiography," 29–30; B. E. Baker, *What Reconstruction Meant*, 122–24; Smith, introduction, 32–35; Baker and Frantz, "Against Synthesis," 219.
36. Ambrosius, "Woodrow Wilson and *The Birth of a Nation*," 691; Wilson, "Reconstruction of the Southern States," 371.
37. Ta-Nehisi Coates, "Hillary Clinton Goes Back to the Dunning School," *The Atlantic*, January 26, 2016; Kevin Drum, "Does Hillary Clinton Know Her Postbellum History?," *Mother Jones*, January 26, 2016; Matthew Yglesias, "Clinton Campaign Clarifies Her Support for Reconstruction," *Vox*, January 26, 2016, http://www.vox.com; Wilson, "Reconstruction of the Southern States," 385, 390; Lee interview.
38. "A Landmark Controversy," panel, *Woodrow Wilson Family Home*, Columbia, 2014; Taylor, "Adult Tour Script," 20–21.
39. Levine, *Highbrow/Lowbrow*, 48; Winter, *Life and Art of Edwin Booth*, 98–99; Wentworth, "First City Hall Opera House," 58; "Edwin Booth," *Daily Register*, November 4, 1875, SCL; "Local Items—Booth as Hamlet," *Daily Register*, January 13, 1876, SCL; "Opera House January 26. Mr. Edwin Booth's Southern Tour," *Daily Register*, January 13, 1876, SCL. This same advertisement ran January 14–16, January 19–22, and January 26, 1876: "Local Items—To See Booth," *Daily Register*, January 21, 1876, SCL; "Local Items—A Card," *Daily Register*, January 23, 1876, SCL; "Local Items—Booth," *Daily Register*, January 24, 1876, SCL; Edwin Booth to William Winter, "Mammoth Cave," March 5, 1876; "Home Gossip," *New York Times*, March 11, 1876; Booth to Winter, "Louisville," March 14, 1876, in Watermeier, *Between Actor and Critic*, 58–59.
40. Cook, "Tour Observation," 3.
41. The transition statement read:

> Woodrow Wilson was certainly a complicated historical figure. The history and memory of Reconstruction proves to be just as complex. Following Reconstruction, citizens who regained power embraced the concept of the Lost Cause. White Americans generally accepted this interpretation in the spirit of national reconciliation but at the expense of racial equality. But it is important to remember the remarkable changes in the South during Reconstruction could be viewed as the first civil rights movement. Wilson's derogatory racial views aligned with the majority of white Americans in the early twentieth century; however, many white and black Americans were working to advance equality. Yet despite his racial biases, which allowed for the segregation of Washington D.C. during his administration, Wilson won a Nobel Prize and eventually endorsed suffrage for women.

Taylor, "Adult Tour Jen's Revision," Historic Columbia, December 10, 2013, 16; Blackwell, "WWFH Interpretation Adult Tour-SAB Edits per 12.11.13 Meeting," Historic Columbia, December 11, 2013, 13; Waites, "WWFH Interpretation Adult Tour Jen's Revision 2 Dec 16 RW Notes," Historic Columbia, December 20, 2013, 13; Taylor, "WWFH Interpretation Adult Tour Jen's Dec 30 Revision," Historic Columbia, December 30, 2013, 12; Taylor, "WWFH Interpretation Adult Tour 01 31 14 Working Draft," Historic Columbia, January 31, 2014, 23; Taylor, "WWFH Interpretation Adult Tour 02 04 14 Working Draft," Historic Columbia, February 4, 2014, 23; "Remembering Woodrow Wilson," panel, *Woodrow Wilson Family Home*, 2014; "Remembering 'Redemption'" panel.

42. Taylor, "Woodrow Wilson Family Home Adult Tour Script," Historic Columbia, June 13, 2014, 28.
43. Lowe, "Dwelling in Possibility," 42–44, 51, 60.
44. Lowe, "Dwelling in Possibility," 44–45, 49–50. Early French and English melodrama was simply musical drama with songs and accompaniment. Levine, *Highbrow/Lowbrow*, 38; Williams, *Playing the Race Card*, 313; Hays and Nikolopoulou, *Melodrama*, quote vii, viii–ix; Meer, *Uncle Tom Mania*, 109–10.
45. Lowe, "Dwelling in Possibility," 47–49; Foner, "Continuing Evolution," 12.
46. Lowe, "Dwelling in Possibility," 51–52.
47. Lowe, "Dwelling in Possibility"; "Visit—Emily Dickinson Museum," Emily Dickinson Museum, https://www.emilydickinsonmuseum.org; *"Emily and Sue,"* Emily Dickinson Museum, https://www.emilydickinsonmuseum.org.
48. Lowe, "Dwelling in Possibility," 45–47, 58.
49. Lowe, "Dwelling in Possibility, 52; Christopher, "House of the Seven Gables," 63.
50. Christopher, "House of the Seven Gables," 63–65, 74.
51. Lowe, "Dwelling in Possibility," 53.
52. Christopher, "House of the Seven Gables," 72, 74.
53. Alexander, *New Jim Crow*; Equal Justice Initiative, "Criminal Justice Reform"; American Civil Liberties Union, "Mass Incarceration"; Álvarez, "Are Today's Voter Suppression Laws"; Katie Nodjimbadem, "The Long, Painful History of Police Brutality in the U.S.," *Smithsonian Magazine*, May 29, 2020, https://www.smithsonianmag.com/; Perry, Steinbaum, and Romer, "Student Loans"; Lawrence Hurley, "Supreme Court Strikes Down College Affirmative Action Programs," NBC News, June 29, 2023, https://www.nbcnews.com/.
54. Only 8 visitors felt bored, and 116 lost track of time. Taylor, "Woodrow Wilson Family Home Trends," slides 6–7. Eight specifically labeled the tour as highly educational, and 7 revealed they learned a great deal. Another visitor remarked that it was an "experience that I will not find in any history books" and, after thanking the site for the Reconstruction education, expressed the desire to buy "a DVD or pamphlet with the info" or an online tour subscription. Of those that described their extensive learning experience, two visitors claimed the information broadened their perspective and knowledge. Sixteen visitors noted the tour and information was interesting. Another dozen remarked on how informative their experience was, with nine specifically calling it "very informative." Wright, "April 2014 Survey," slide 13; Taylor, "May 2014 Survey," slide 12; Taylor, "June 2014 Survey," slide 12; Taylor, "July 2014 Survey," slide 12; Taylor, "August 2014 Survey," slides 11–12; Taylor, "September 2014 Survey," October, 2014 slide 12; Taylor, "October 2014 Survey," slides 12–13; Taylor, "November 2014 Survey," December 2014, slides 12–13; "December 2014 Survey," January 2015, slides 11–13.

55. Lowe, "Dwelling in Possibility," 54–56.
56. Lowe, "Dwelling in Possibility," 46, 57.
57. Harriet Beecher Stowe Center, "Non-traditional Museum."
58. Harriet Beecher Stowe Center, "More Programs."
59. Harriet Beecher Stowe Center, "Board."
60. Bacon-Rogers and Allen, Zoom interview.
61. Dahl et a., "Is Our Fascination," 167; Falk and Gillespie, "Investigating the Role of Emotion," 112–14, 118–19, 122–27.

Chapter 7: (Re)Writing History with Lightning

1. Tom Gerken, "Black Panther Style 'Repatriation Specialist' Required," BBC News, March 1, 2018, https://www.bbc.com/; Mary Carole McCauley, "'Black Panther' Raises Difficult Questions in Museum Community," *Baltimore Sun*, March 2, 2018, https://www.baltimoresun.com/; Cascone, "Museum Heist Scene"; Gaston, "*Black Panther* and the Ethics of Representation"; Feiger, "Colonizers Stole Africa's Art," https://www.vice.com.
2. Conn, *Do Museums Still Need Objects?* 15.
3. As discussed in part I of the book, the interpretive team consisted of executive director Robin Waites and the heads of the programming, education, preservation, and museum wings of Historic Columbia. The organization contracted my labor to write the scripts and conduct the majority of tours in the first year of opening. Robin Waites, email message to Sherrer, Freed, and Taylor, "Room 15 Video," December 7, 2013; Waites, email message to interpretive team, "Birth," January 22, 2014; Sherrer, email message to Taylor, "Birth," January 22, 2014; Waites, email message to Sherrer et al., "Draft Script for Wilson and Reconstruction Video," January 23, 2014; Sherrer, email message to Waites et al., "Draft Script for Wilson and Reconstruction Video," January 22, 2014; Phillips, email message to Waites, "Draft Script for Wilson and Reconstruction Video," January 23, 2014.
4. Ambrosius, "Woodrow Wilson and *The Birth of a Nation*," 711; "A Young Man Finds His Profession," panel, WWPLM, 2015. When I brought up *Birth of a Nation* on an S Street tour, the group discussed how the Ku Klux Klan was romanticized and contemplated whether Wilson enjoyed the film for its spectacle, racist ideology, or both. Toegel, guided tour, June 20, 2015.
5. The discussion about the term *racist* and scene selection occurred over a series of emails and film revisions: Taylor, email message to Sherrer and Waites, "Room 15 Video Voiceover," January 24, 2014; Cook, email message to Waites, "Room 15 Video Voiceover," January 27, 2014; Phillips, "The Legacy of Woodrow Wilson and Reconstruction CP Edits," Historic Columbia, January 23, 2014, 1–3; Taylor, "The Legacy of Woodrow Wilson and Reconstruction Jen's Edits," Historic Columbia, January 27, 2014, 1–3; Cook, "The Legacy of Woodrow Wilson and Reconstruction DAC Edits," Historic Columbia, January 27, 2014, 1–3; Taylor, "The Legacy of Woodrow Wilson and Reconstruction Fielding Edit with Jen's Comments," Historic Columbia, June 12, 2014, 1.
6. "Wade Hampton Day, Boy Scouts—Czarnitzki—Home Movies," video/H264, 1926, Moving Image Research Collections, University of South Carolina, https://digital.tcl.sc.edu/digital/collection/p17173coll6/id/1905/rec/2; B. E. Baker, *What Reconstruction Meant*, 28–29, 54–64, 75–77, 92, 165.

7. In a previous chapter, I discussed that the weekend docents were paid and often came from the University of South Carolina's public history program. Volunteer docents typically worked during the week. Brazier, "Historic Columbia Docent Survey," 2016.
8. Brazier interview; Hogan interview.
9. Grantham, "Southern Historiography," 254; "New Beginning, 1892–1945," 85; G. E. Hale, *Making Whiteness*, 80–81; Cox, *Dreaming of Dixie*, 83, 85, 97; Eileen Jones, "The Cinematic Lost Cause," *Jacobin, Struggle and Progress*, Summer, no. 18 (2015), https://www.jacobinmag.com/, xix.
10. Waites, email message to interpretive team, "WWFH Action Items," May 21, 2014; Waites, email message to volunteers, "WWFH June Follow-Up," June 13, 2014; Waites, email message to interpretive team, "WWFH Videos," July 22, 2014; Freed, email message to Taylor, "2nd Revision," August 7, 2014; Freed, email message to interpretive team, "WW Script First Draft," October 16, 2014; Waites, email message to interpretive team, "WW Script First Draft," October 16, 2014; Waites, email message to interpretive team, "Lee Ann Kornegay Shared a Video with You!," February 5, 2015.
11. Quint, email message to Taylor, "Birth Film 1st Draft Revision," August 1, 2014; Jennifer Taylor, "Jen's First Revision of The Legacy of Wilson and Reconstruction," Historic Columbia, August 1, 2014, 5–6; Taylor and Freed, "Jen's Second Revision of The Legacy of Wilson and Reconstruction-FF Edits," Historic Columbia, August 11, 2014, 6; Blackwell et al., "WilsonReconstruction-2 JMS Edits JTs Edits JQ Edits FF Edits SB Edits," Historic Columbia, October 16, 2014, 4; Freed, Sherrer, and Taylor, "WilsonReconstruction30Oct2014REV," Historic Columbia, November 19, 2014, 4; Sherrer, Taylor, and Waites, "WilsonReconstruction28Nov2014REV," Historic Columbia, November 28, 2014, 6; Taylor, email message to Kornegay, "Lee Ann Kornegay Shared a Video with You!," February 5, 2015; Freed, email message to interpretive team and Kornegay, "HC Wilson Video Input," February 9, 2015; Taylor, email message to Kornegay and interpretive team, "WW Drop Box Link," March 5, 2015; "Remembering 'Redemption'" panel.
12. Taylor, email message to Robin Waites, "WWFH Videos," August 12, 2014; Taylor, "Jen's First Revision of Legacy," 1–3; Taylor and Freed, "Jen's Second Revision FF Edits," 1–3; Taylor et al., "Third Revision of The Legacy of Wilson and Reconstruction Everyone's Comments," Historic Columbia, August 12, 2014, 1–3; Quint, email message to Taylor, "Birth Film 1st Draft Revision," August 1, 2014; Posner, email message to interpretive team, Phillips, and Galens, "WWFH Videos," August 12, 2014; Freed, email message to Taylor, "WWFH Script," November 14, 2014; Galens, email message to interpretive team, "WW Script First Draft," October 14, 2014.
13. Freed, email message to interpretive team and Kornegay, "HC Wilson Video Input," February 9, 2015; Taylor, email message to Kornegay, "Kornegay Shared a Video," February 5, 2015; Richardson interview; Gunter interview; Welch, "Pounding Heart of Woodrow Wilson."
14. The team hoped the audio could be added as a separate exhibit feature on the smart board or as a push-button sound effect on the engraving image of Wilson in the memory room. As of publication there were no plans to include the audio in the current exhibit. Taylor, "Legacy Fielding Edit," 1; Taylor, "Jen's First Revision of Legacy," 1; Taylor and Freed, "Jen's Second Revision FF Edits," 3; Taylor

et al., "Third Revision of Legacy," 2; Celia Galens et al., "WilsonReconstruction-2 JMS Edits JTs Edits JQ Edits CG," Historic Columbia, October 14, 2014, 3; Freed, Sherrer, and Taylor, "WilsonReconstruction30Oct," 1; Galens, email message to interpretive team, "WW Script First Draft," October 14, 2014; Fielding Freed, email message to Robin Waites, "WWFH Script," November 21, 2014; Freed, Sherrer, and Taylor, "WilsonReconstruction30Oct," 1; Sherrer, Taylor, and Waites, "WilsonReconstruction28Nov," 2. Freed sent two emails on the thread on the same day. Fielding Freed, email message to Lee Ann Kornegay and interpretive team, "WW Drop Box Link," March 5, 2015; Kornegay, email message to interpretive team, "Woodrow Wilson Reconstruction Video," March 2, 2015; Taylor, email message to Kornegay and interpretive team, "WW Drop Box Link," March 5, 2015; Robin Waites, email message to Lee Ann Kornegay and interpretive team, "WW Drop Box Link," March 5, 2015; James Quint, email message to Lee Ann Kornegay and interpretive team, "Revised WW," March 9, 2015.

15. Taylor et al., "Third Revision of Legacy," 6.
16. Galens, email message to interpretive team, "WW Script First Draft," October 14, 2014; Galens et al., "WilsonReconstruction-2 JMS JTs JQ CG," 4; Blackwell et al., "WilsonReconstruction-2 JMS JTs JQ CG FF SB," 4.
17. Taylor, email message to Blackwell, "Evaluations," March 26, 2014.
18. There are two emails from Riggins with the same title and date: Riggins, email message to Posner, "Reminder," May 7, 2014; Posner, email message to Taylor, "Reminder," May 8, 2014; Taylor, email message to Posner, "Reminder," May 8, 2014; Waites, email message to interpretive team, "Reminder," May 8, 2014; Freed, email message to Posner and Taylor, "Reminder," May 8, 2014.
19. Riggins, email message to Taylor, "Two Books about Thomas Dixon and Reconstruction in N.C.," June 2, 2014; Riggins, email message to Taylor, "Two Books about Thomas Dixon and Reconstruction in N.C.," June 4, 2014.
20. Ambrosius, "Woodrow Wilson and *The Birth of a Nation*," 702–4; Gilmore, *Gender and Jim Crow*; Benbow, "Birth of a Quotation," 512–13, 529; Cox, *Dreaming of Dixie*, 84–85; Berg, *Wilson*, 348–49. See also the 1915 *New York Globe* review, "Capitalizing Race Hatred"; Staiger, "*Birth of a Nation*," 164–65, 201–2.
21. Galens et al., "WilsonReconstruction-2 JMS JTs JQ CG," 2.
22. Ambrosius, "Woodrow Wilson and *The Birth of a Nation*," 693, 689–90, 710; Berg, *Wilson*, 94; Gilmore, *Gender and Jim Crow*, 67–68; J. H. Moore, "South Carolina Views," 339–40.
23. Dixon delivered the commencement address at Wake Forest and convinced the trustees to give Wilson his first honorary degree, which strengthened Wilson's national profile. Two years before *Birth of a Nation*, Dixon dedicated *The Southerner* to Wilson, for which Wilson thanked him. Ambrosius, "Woodrow Wilson and *The Birth of a Nation*," 693–95, 698–99, 703; Benbow, "Birth of a Quotation,'" 512, 515; Berg, *Wilson*, 349; Wolgemuth, "Woodrow Wilson and Federal Segregation," 158–59; Gilmore, *Gender and Jim Crow*, 66.
24. According to Benbow, MacKaye and *The Rise of the American Film Industry*, released the following year, are generally the sources cited from this point forward. Wilson's quote is frequently and incorrectly attributed to a *New York Evening Post* article of March 4, 1915. Memoirs of movie star Lillian Gish and producer Roy Aitken placed their own spin on the quote, but surprisingly

Dixon's memoir and fictionalized accounts of the Wilson meeting omit it entirely. Benbow, "Birth of a Quotation," 509, 515 (Griffith quote), 517–19, 521–23, 527, 529; Ambrosius, "Woodrow Wilson and *The Birth of a Nation,*" 704; Berg, *Wilson*, 349.

25. The title card reads: "The white men were roused by a mere instinct of self-preservation. . . . until at last there had sprung into existence a great Ku Klux Klan, a veritable empire of the South, to protect the Southern country." "Woodrow Wilson on Reconstruction," panel, *Woodrow Wilson Family Home*, Columbia, 2014; White, "Birth of a Nation," 217; Berg, *Wilson*, 348–50; Ambrosius, "Woodrow Wilson and *The Birth of a Nation,*" 702, 704–5, 710–11; Benbow, "Birth of a Quotation," 512, 514, 520; Taylor, email message to Waites and Freed, "Birth of a Nation," June 10, 2014.
26. Ambrosius, "Woodrow Wilson and *The Birth of a Nation,*" 710–11; Clark, email message to Waites, "Birth of a Nation," June 2, 2014 (quotes); Clark, email message to Taylor, "WWFH 2014 Trends PowerPoint"; Freed, email message to Waites and Taylor, "Birth of a Nation."
27. Mimi White argues that Griffith's use of Wilson quotes was a strategy to grant historical authority to the film's racially biased narratives, such as the rise of the Klan, that risked being construed as invention. White, "Birth of a Nation," 217; Taylor, email message to Clark, "WWFH 2014 Trends PowerPoint," January 28, 2015; Galens et al., "WilsonReconstruction-2 JMS JTs JQ CG," 3; Blackwell et al., "WilsonReconstruction-2 JMS JTs JQ CG FF SB," 3; Taylor, "Jen's First Revision of Legacy," 4–5; Taylor and Freed, "Jen's Second Revision FF Edits," 4–6; Taylor et al., "Third Revision of Legacy," 4; quotes from the following: "Wilson-Reconstruction-2 Jenny's Comment," Historic Columbia, October 8, 2014, 3–4; Freed, Sherrer, and Taylor, "WilsonReconstruction30Oct," 3; Sherrer, Taylor, and Waites, "WilsonReconstruction28Nov," 4;
28. Fielding Freed, email message to Lee Ann Kornegay and interpretive team, "Revised WW," March 9, 2015; Fielding Freed, email message to Lee Ann Kornegay and interpretive team, "Revised WW," March 10, 2015; Kornegay, email message to interpretive team, "Revised WW," March 10, 2015.
29. Taylor, email message to Waites and Freed, "Birth of a Nation," June 10, 2014;
30. Blackwell, email message to interpretive team, "WW Script First Draft," October 16, 2014; Kornegay, email message to Waites, Sherrer, and Freed, "WW Script First Draft"; Storm, interview by Taylor, digital recording, February 4, 2016, DWWHM; Freed, email message to Waites and Taylor, "Birth of a Nation," June 9, 2014; Taylor, email message to Waites and Freed, "Birth of a Nation," June 10, 2014; Galens et al., "WilsonReconstruction-2 JMS JTs JQ CG," 3; Blackwell et al., "WilsonReconstruction-2 JMS JTs JQ CG FF SB," 4.
31. Ambrosius, "Woodrow Wilson and *The Birth of a Nation,*" 704; Berg, *Wilson*, 349; Benbow, "Birth of a Quotation," 514–28.
32. The film is considered the most profitable silent movie ever made as well as the most watched. By 1931 the film grossed eighteen million dollars. Estimates placed global viewership at two hundred million people by 1946. Cox, *Dreaming of Dixie*, 83, 85.
33. I began to analyze *Birth*'s connections to Columbia and South Carolina via my blog, "Reconstructing Reconstruction," https://reconstructingreconstruction

.wordpress.com. Taylor, email message to Waites and Freed, "Birth of a Nation," June 10, 2014; Taylor, "Legacy Fielding Edit," 1.

34. Taylor, "Jen's First Revision of Legacy," 3–4; Taylor and Freed, "Jen's Second Revision FF Edits," 3–4; Taylor et al., "Third Revision of Legacy," 3–4; Blackwell, email message to interpretive team, "WW Script First Draft," October 16, 2014.
35. Taylor et al., "Third Revision of Legacy," 4; Taylor, email message to Kornegay, "Kornegay Shared a Video"; Taylor, email message to Kornegay and interpretive team, "WW Drop Box Link"; "Detail from *Frank Leslie's Illustrated* April 21, 1877," panel, *Woodrow Wilson Family Home,* Columbia, 2014 (a thumbnail of this image can be found at the Library of Congress, http://www.loc.gov); White, "Birth of a Nation," 218.
36. Lipscomb, "D. W. Griffith's 'Historical Facsimile"; Writers' Program, *South Carolina,* 38–41, 254, 426; J. H. Moore, "South Carolina Views," 339, 346; Taylor, email message to Waites and Freed, "Birth of a Nation," June 10, 2014.
37. The exhibit film used less than one minute of footage from *Birth,* which runs three hours and fifteen minutes.
38. Everett, *Returning the Gaze,* 89; Wood, "With the Roar of Thunder," 147.
39. Courtney, *Hollywood Fantasies of Miscengenation,* 69–70; Allen Wallace, "Columbia Unveils Marker Commemorating 1865 Burning of City," ColaDaily.Com, February 17, 2015, http://coladaily.com; Jeff Wilkinson, "Who Was Really Responsible for the Burning of Columbia in 1865?," *The State,* February 7, 2015, http://www.thestate.com/.
40. Zuczek, *State of Rebellion,* 50, 65n15; Edgar, *South Carolina,* 397; "Records of the Field Offices for the State of South Carolina, Bureau of Refugees, Freedmen, and Abandoned Lands, 1865–1872," 3, http://www.archives.gov/research/microfilm/m1910.pdf.
41. Edgar, *South Carolina,* 398, 400–401.
42. Victor B. Howard probably invented the term "military arm of the Democratic Party" to define the Klan in his 1973 article "The Kentucky Press and the Black Suffrage Controversy." Baker and Frantz, "Against Synthesis," 238.
43. Wood, "With the Roar of Thunder," 150; J. H. Moore, "South Carolina Views," 339 (quote), 339–41; Lipscomb, "D. W. Griffith's 'Historical Facsimile,'" 1, 3.
44. Wood, "With the Roar of Thunder," 153, 165–67; Lipscomb, "D. W. Griffith's 'Historical Facsimile,'" 4; J. H. Moore, "South Carolina Views," 337–38 (quotes), 346–47.
45. J. H. Moore, "South Carolina Views," 344–46.
46. Waites, Sherrer, and Taylor, "WWFH Adult Tour Summer Revision Marking Changes RW JMS Comments," 26.
47. Robin Waites, email message to Fielding Freed, John Sherrer, and Jennifer Taylor, "WWFH Script," November 20, 2014; Freed, email message to Waites and Taylor, "Birth of a Nation," June 9, 2014; Freed, email message to Waites, "WWFH Script," November 21, 2014; Jennifer Taylor, email message to Fielding Freed, "Paul Miller Pic," January 28, 2015.
48. DJ Spooky, "Rebirth of a Nation Talk Back," Burn to Shine, Nickelodeon, January 19, 2015; Steedman, *Dust,* 2, 17–18.
49. Andrea Mock, "Nick Theatre Holds Historic Film Screening," WLTX News, January 20, 2015, http://www.wltx.com/; "Burning of Columbia - Events Gallery," 2014, http://burningofcolumbia.com/; "DJ Spooky, Recasting 'Birth of a

Nation,'" NPR, October 17, 2004, http://www.npr.org/; J. H. Moore, "South Carolina Views," 344. Timing prevented the team from asking DJ Spooky to situate his work within a much longer story of Black dissent against *Birth of a Nation.* Waites, email message to Taylor and Freed, "DJ Spooky," January 2, 2015; Freed, email message to Waites, "DJ Spooky," January 7, 2015; Taylor, email message to Freed, "DJ Spooky," January 7, 2015; Waites, email message to Kornegay, "DJS," January 14, 2015; Kornegay, email message to Waites, "DJS," January 14, 2015; Taylor, email message to Waites and Kornegay, "DJS," January 15, 2015.

50. Bacon-Rogers interview; Clark second interview; Lee interview; Morgan interview; Doe interview; Taylor, email message to Kornegay and interpretive team, "WW Drop Box Link"; Waites, email message to Kornegay and interpretive team, "WW Drop Box Link"; Taylor, email message to Kornegay, "Kornegay Shared a Video"; Lee Ann Kornegay, dir., *The Legacy of Woodrow Wilson and Reconstruction,* digital video exhibit, Historic Columbia, 2015.
51. Spooky, "Rebirth Talk Back."
52. Cox, *Dreaming of Dixie,* 83–84; Glick, "Mixed Messages," 174, 180–86; Stewart, *Migrating to the Movies,* 27, 240–44; Ambrosius, "Woodrow Wilson and *The Birth of a Nation,*" 702; Kirby, *Media-Made Dixie,* 3–5, 8.
53. Taylor, "Legacy Fielding Edit," 2; Stewart, *Migrating to the Movies,* 189, 220, 226–27, 230–31, 234–37, 239–44, 277.
54. Taylor, email message to Waites, "WWFH Session 3," December 15, 2013.
55. Stewart, *Migrating to the Movies,* 228–30, 238–41; Gilmore, *Gender and Jim Crow,* 68–80; Benbow, "Birth of a Quotation," 525.
56. Taylor, email message to Sherrer and Waites, "Room 15 Video Voiceover," January 24, 2014; Taylor, "Legacy Jen's Edits," 2; Cook, "Legacy DAC Edits," 2.
57. Taylor, "Legacy Fielding Edit," 2.
58. One team member recommended three *Rebirth* scenes with graphics and music edits that more clearly conveyed DJ Spooky's style and the period of Reconstruction for the revision. But *Legacy* retained the original clip of Union soldiers burning the Cameron home during the Civil War, which at least expressed continuity with the burning of Columbia B-roll from DJ Spooky. Kornegay, email message to Waites, "DJS," January 14, 2015; Waites, email message to Taylor and Freed, "DJ Spooky," January 2, 2015; Waites, email message to Kornegay, "DJS," January 14, 2015; Taylor, email message to Waites and Kornegay, "DJS," January 15, 2015; Waites, email message to Freed, Sherrer, and Taylor, "WWFH Script," November 20, 2014; Jennifer Taylor, email message to Fielding Freed, John Sherrer, and Robin Waites, "WWFH Script," November 20, 2014; Jennifer Taylor, email message to Fielding Freed et al., "WWFH Script Update," November 28, 2014; Taylor, "Jen's First Revision of Legacy," 4; Taylor and Freed, "Jen's Second Revision FF Edits," 5; Taylor et al., "Third Revision of Legacy," 5; Lee Ann Kornegay, email message to interpretive team, "WW Drop Box Link," March 5, 2015. Freed sent two emails on the thread on the same day. Freed, email message to Kornegay and interpretive team, "WW Drop Box Link," March 5, 2015; Waites, email message to Kornegay and interpretive team, "WW Drop Box Link," March 5, 2015; Taylor, email message to Kornegay and interpretive team, "WW Drop Box Link," March 5, 2015; Quint, email message to Kornegay and interpretive team, "Revised WW," March 9, 2015; Freed, email message to Kornegay and Interpretive team, "Revised WW," March 9, 2015; Freed, email

message to interpretive team and Kornegay, "HC Wilson Video Input," February 9, 2015; Taylor, email message to Kornegay, "Kornegay Shared a Video," February 5, 2015; Waites, email message to interpretive team, "Kornegay Shared a Video," February 5, 2015.

59. Freed, email message to Waites, "Final WWFH Video Rollout," March 26, 2015; Freed, email message to Bacon-Rogers and interpretive team, "New and Improved WWFH Video," April 2, 2015; Bacon-Rogers, email message to interpretive team, "New and Improved WWFH Video," April 2, 2015; Taylor, email message to Bacon-Rogers and interpretive team, "New and Improved WWFH Video," April 2, 2015; Kleinfelder, email message to Bacon-Rogers and interpretive team, "New and Improved WWFH Video," April 2, 2015.
60. Blackwell, "Tour-SAB Edits," 13; Waites, "Revision 2 Dec 16 RW Notes," 11/ The previous scripts had these elements as talking points. They became full sentences for this script. Taylor, "Tour Jen's Dec. 30 Revision," 12; Posner, email message to Taylor, "Adult Tour," December 23, 2013.
61. O'Brien, "Woodward and the Burden," 590; "New Beginning, 1892–1945," 84–85; Benbow, "Birth of a Quotation," 524–25.
62. Westcott, "Historic Columbia Docent Survey"; Hogan, "Historic Columbia Docent Survey"; Clark second interview.
63. Welch, "Pounding Heart of Woodrow Wilson."
64. Morgan interview; Clark first interview; Clark second interview; Doe interview; Taylor, "Docent H Tour Review," Historic Columbia, March 12, 2014; Posner, "Docent H Tour Review," Historic Columbia, March 12, 2014; Clements, "Discussion Questions about Woodrow Wilson in Columbia," December 2013, Historic Columbia Collection; Freed, email message to Waites, "WWFH Materials for Ken and Tom," December 4, 2013.
65. B. E. Baker, *What Reconstruction Meant*, 101–2. The quote is a reference to the election of 1876, which ended Reconstruction in South Carolina through white Democratic fraud and violence. See pages 94–102 for Bruce Baker's extensive discussion of how Cotton Ed Smith frequently exploited a white supremacist memory of Reconstruction in 1938. Thomas J. Brown, "Main Points for Training of WWFH Volunteers," November 12, 2013, Historic Columbia Collection; Freed, email message to Waites, "WWFH Materials for Ken and Tom," December 4, 2013.
66. Clark second interview; Westcott interview; Westcott, "Historic Columbia Docent Survey"; Morgan interview; Richardson, "Historic Columbia Docent Survey"; Docent Doe interview; Storm, "Historic Columbia Docent Survey"; Schneider, "Historic Columbia Docent Survey."
67. Clark first interview; Hogan, "Historic Columbia Docent Survey"; Hogan interview; Storm interview; Docent Doe interview; Stickney interview.
68. Storm interview; Clark first interview; Docent Doe interview; Wolgemuth, "Woodrow Wilson and Federal Segregation," 158–59.
69. Docent Doe interview; Wolgemuth, "Woodrow Wilson and Federal Segregation," 163–68, 170; Waites, Sherrer, and Taylor, "Marking Changes RW JMS," 27; Taylor, "WWFH Script," June 13, 2014, 28–29.
70. Lee interview. Vagnone and Ryan argue that "speculative" and "subjective" traits when combined with the professionalized tour make for good museum practice. The blending of the historical record with "presumed life" can create a "relatable

experience." Vagnone and Ryan, *Anarchist's Guide to Historic House Museums*, 34–37, 86, 108.

71. Clark first interview; Clark second interview. For a discussion of southern exceptionalism, see the essays in Griffin and Doyle, *South as an American Problem* (particularly Griffin's "Why Was the South a Problem to America?"); and Lassiter and Crespino, *Myth of Southern Exceptionalism* (particularly the editors' introductory essay).
72. Waites, email message to interpretive team, "Reminder," May 8, 2014; Taylor, email message to Posner, "Reminder," May 8, 2014; Freed, email message to Posner and Taylor, "Reminder," May 8, 2014; Freed, email message to Waites and Taylor, "Birth of a Nation," June 9, 2014; Taylor, email message to Waites and Freed, "Birth of a Nation," June 10, 2014; Morgan interview; Westcott, email message to Taylor, "March Results," April 30, 2015.
73. Randy Barnett, "Expunging Woodrow Wilson from Official Places of Honor," *Washington Post*, June 25, 2015, https://www.washingtonpost.com/; Jennifer Schuessler, "Woodrow Wilson's Legacy Gets Complicated," *New York Times*, November 29, 2015, https://www.nytimes.com/; Andy Newman, "At Princeton, Woodrow Wilson, a Heralded Alum, Is Recast as an Intolerant One," *New York Times*, November 22, 2015, https://www.nytimes.com/; Taylor and Sherrer, "Coming to Terms with Woodrow Wilson's White Supremacy and the Difficulty of Discussing America's Racist Past in Public Spaces."
74. Morgan interview; Docent Doe interview.
75. Storm interview; Gunter interview; Docent Doe interview; Betsy Kleinfelder, email message to Jennifer Taylor et al., "Woodrow Wilson Controversy," December 9, 2015.
76. Stickney interview; Bacon-Rogers, "Historic Columbia Docent Survey"; Bacon-Rogers interview; Hogan interview.
77. Vagnone and Ryan, *Anarchist's Guide to Historic House Museums*, 108, 111, 140.
78. Storm interview; Hogan interview; Stickney interview.
79. The qualitative evidence is lacking in determining whether alteration or reinterpretation with written contextualization makes a difference in the way people think about monuments and memorialization. Most public historians and preservationists prior to Charlottesville in 2017 opposed removal, although "some protesters suggest memorials be placed in less prominent locations or in museums." Labode, "Reconsideration of Memorials and Monuments," *AASLH Blogs* (blog), November 30, 2016, http://blogs.aaslh.org/.
80. Cook, "Tour Observation," 3; Clark, "Historic Columbia Docent Survey"; Taylor, "Docent J Tour Review," Historic Columbia, April 2, 2014.
81. Blackwell, "Tour-SAB Edits," 13–14; Waites, "Revision 2 Dec 16 RW Notes," 11; Taylor, "Tour Jen's Dec. 30 Revision," 12; Taylor, "Tour 01 31 14 Working Draft," 23; Waites, Sherrer, and Taylor, "Marking Changes RW JMS," 27; Taylor, "WWFH Script," June 13, 2014, 28–29.
82. Docent Doe interview; Blackwell, "Tour-SAB Edits," 13–14; Waites, "Revision 2 Dec 16 RW Notes," 11; Taylor, "Tour Jen's Dec. 30 Revision," 12; Taylor, "Tour 01 31 14 Working Draft," 23; Waites, Sherrer, and Taylor, "Marking Changes RW JMS," 27.
83. Bacon-Rogers interview; Lee interview.

84. "State Government," panel, *Woodrow Wilson Family Home,* Columbia, 2014; Historic Columbia, "Hampton-Preston Mansion and Gardens," https://www.historiccolumbia.org; Schaffer, "'Bitter Memory Upon," 203–15.
85. Wilson, "Reconstruction of the Southern States," 369.
86. Hogan interview; Posner, "Docent B Tour Review," Historic Columbia, February 20, 2014; Taylor, "Docent B Tour Review," Historic Columbia, February 20, 2014; Taylor, "Docent I Tour Review," Historic Columbia, March 17, 2014.
87. Kirby, *Media-Made Dixie,* 162.
88. Cox, *Dreaming of Dixie,* 93–96; McPherson, *Reconstructing Dixie,* 44, 46–47.
89. Storm interview.
90. Gunter interview. *Gone with the Wind* is popular in Japan. For example, tourists flock to a rice field in Japan re-creating an iconic image of Rhett Butler and Scarlett O'Hara. genderedjapan, "Takarazuka Revue Does Gone With the Wind," *Gendered Japan,* February 9, 2014, https://genderedjapan.wordpress.com/; "Grown with the Wind: Tourists Wowed by Japanese Rice Art," BBC News, 2015, http://www.bbc.com/.
91. Brazier interview; Rosenberg, "Why We Should Keep Reading 'Gone with the Wind,'" *Washington Post,* July 1, 2015, https://www.washingtonpost.com.
92. Morgan interview.
93. Toegel, guided tour.

Conclusion

1. Simon, *Participatory Museum,* 140–41, 147, 149; Benfield et al., "'Honest Visionary,'" 58–59, 61–62, 70; Taylor, "WWFH Interpretation Adult Tour 02 04 14 Working Draft," Historic Columbia, February 4, 2014, 4; Taylor, "WWFH Interpretation Adult Tour 02 06 14 Working Draft," Historic Columbia, February 6, 2014, 4; Taylor, "WWFH Interpretation Adult Tour Second Training Version," Historic Columbia, April 2014, 4; Waites, Sherrer, and Taylor, "WWFH Adult Tour Summer Revision Marking Changes RW JMS Comments," Historic Columbia, June 3, 2014, 4; Wright, email message to Waites, "Feedback on the WWFH Tour," March 18, 2014. Some guides found that the question worked better for them in the first large exhibit space in the formal parlor. Ann Posner, email message to Taylor, "Revised WWFH Script Summer 2014," May 14, 2014; Brazier interview.
2. Vagnone and Ryan, *Anarchist's Guide to Historic House Museums,* 101; Falk, Identity and the Museum Visitor Experience, 52.
3. Wright, "April 2014 WWFH Visitor Survey Update," PowerPoint, Historic Columbia, May 2014, slide 14.
4. Wright, "Draft: WWFH Visitor Survey," January 14, 2014, Historic Columbia Collection; Taylor, email message to Waites, "Draft of Visitor Survey for WWFH," January 14, 2014; Taylor, email message to Ann Posner, "Visitor Evaluations," March 27, 2014; Weiler and Ham, "Development of a Research Instrument," 188–92; Dahl et al., "Is Our Fascination," 164.
5. Waites, email message to interpretive team, "WWFH Action Items," May 21, 2014; Taylor, "Woodrow Wilson Family Home Trends," slide 11; Taylor, "June 2014 WWFH Visitor Survey Update," PowerPoint, Historic Columbia, July 2014, slide 7; Blackwell, email message to Quint and Taylor, "May Update-WWFH Visitors' Data," June 27, 2014; Waites, email message to volunteers,

"WWFH June Follow-Up," June 13, 2014. In June the education department placed me in charge of processing the evaluations for monthly reports. Taylor, email message to Jowers, "Survey Monkey Intern," July 1, 2014; Taylor, "July 2014 WWFH Visitor Survey Update," PowerPoint, Historic Columbia, August 2014, slide 7; Taylor, "August 2014 WWFH Visitor Survey Update," PowerPoint, Historic Columbia, September 2014, slide 7; Taylor, email message to interpretive team, "August Survey Monkey Results," September 5, 2014; Taylor, email message to James Quint, "October Survey Monkey Results," December 3, 2014; Waites, email message to Taylor, "October WWFH Results," December 9, 2014; Taylor, "November 2014 WWFH Visitor Survey Update," PowerPoint, Historic Columbia, December 2014, slide 7; Jennifer Whitmer Taylor, "December 2014 WWFH Visitor Survey Update," PowerPoint, Historic Columbia, January 2015, slide 7; Taylor, email message to Interpretive Team, "March WWFH Results," April 28, 2015; Stickney, email message to Waites, "WWFH," June 25, 2014; Hogan, interview by Taylor, digital recording, February 16, 2016, DWWHM.

6. The analysis of data is from February through December 2014. In January 2015 Historic Columbia had a year-in-review meeting about the WWFH. The meeting highlighted evaluation data about the exhibit's and tour's strengths and weaknesses, misleading and inaccurate data, visitor statistics by gender, age, and race, and finally the most consistent criticism and lingering questions appearing in the comments section. At that time there had been 2,952 total visitors, 2,549 of them adults. I created the "Trends" presentation using monthly Survey Monkey data. I also ran demographic profiles in Survey Monkey of the data by race and ethnicity, gender, and decade of birth from the 1920s forward. Sixty-six percent of respondents identified as women and 38 percent men, in line with larger museum attendance trends, where six in ten museum visitors are women. Women were thus more likely to complete an evaluation. Baby boomers visited more than other generations. One hundred and thirty-seven visitors born in the 1940s took an evaluation. A close second was 131 visitors born in the 1950s. A distant third was the seventy-eight visitors born in the 1960s. For the purposes of classification, the Greatest Generation includes those born in the 1930s through 1946, when the baby boomers begin. Generation X is considered those born between 1965 and 1984, but those born late to this generation may find themselves among the oldest millennials, which cohort began in 1982 and ended in 2004. Taylor, "WWFH Trends," slide 3, 13–15, 17, 19–20; Taylor, "November 2014 Survey," slide 3; Taylor, "December 2014 Survey," slide 3; Falk, *Identity and the Museum Visitor Experience*, 28; Bump, "Each Generation," https://www.theatlantic.com.
7. No one checked that the overall quality was poor, just as no one reported being disengaged. Two-thirds of respondents were fully engaged throughout the tour, and 32 percent felt engaged at many points. Wright, slides 2–5; Taylor, "WWFH Trends," slides 4–5, 8; Taylor, "July 2014 Survey," slide 3; Taylor, "August 2014 Survey," slide 3; Taylor, "December 2014 Survey," slide 6.
8. Sixteen visitors said that they enjoyed the tour, five of them very much so. Fourteen described the tour or museum as excellent, eleven as great, one as very good, and another as "engaging." Twelve guests thought the tour well done, some extremely well done. Three called the tour a "good presentation." Six visitors described their visit as an "experience," often with positive adjectives such as

"wonderful" and "good." In general five called it wonderful. Similarly others wrote that they "loved" the tour, thought the house was "awesome," and were glad they had taken the tour. Adjectives used to describe the tour ranged from *neat, nice,* and *terrific* to *pretty cool.* Wright, "April 2014 Survey," slide 13; Taylor, "June 2014 Survey," slides 11–12; Taylor, "July 2014 Survey," slide 12; Taylor, "August 2014 Survey," slides 11–12; Taylor, "September 2014 Survey," October 2014, slides 12–13; Taylor, "October 2014 Survey," slides 11–13; Taylor, "November 2014 Survey," December 2014, slides 11–13; Taylor, "December 2014 Survey," slide 13.

9. Four visitors expressed appreciation for "preserving history" and providing "the opportunity to reflect and remember the past." Five visitors remarked on the MoRE's beauty. One visitor called the kitchen frame outlined by the accessibility ramp "brilliant." Annie Wright, "WWFH Visitor Survey Preliminary Findings," PowerPoint, Historic Columbia, March 10, 2014, slide 6, Historic Columbia Collection; Wright, "April 2014 Survey," slide 13; Taylor, "June 2014 Survey," slide 12; Taylor, "August 2014 Survey," slide 12; Taylor, "September 2014 Survey," slides 12–13; Taylor, "November 2014 Survey," slide 13; Taylor, "December 2014 Survey," slides 12–13.
10. Palau-Saumell, Forgas-Coll, and Sánchez-García, "Role of Emotions," 158–59, 168.
11. C. Moore, "Woodrow Wilson Family Home," 190, 192.
12. For example, the Svalbard Museum Study revealed that exhibit displays about which docents told stories fascinated Norwegian teenagers most, especially when content featured large or threatening animals and intense, foreign living conditions. Dahl et al., "Is Our Fascination," 161–67; Palau-Saumell, Forgas-Coll, and Sánchez-García, "Role of Emotions," 157.
13. Of people who responded, 450 said that the docent had their full attention. Less than 8 percent of evaluators preferred self-guided portions of the tour. Taylor, "WWFH Trends," slides 4, 6, 10–11.
14. Nineteen visitors left comments praising docents, with a third of them noting the knowledge of docents. One visitor was "so glad I was able to take this tour with my host," and another one called their guide a "great communicator." Additionally, docents were described as "excellent," "interesting," "absolutely fabulous," "superb," "wonderful," "delightful," "personable," "nice" and "patient." Wright, "April 2014 Survey," slides 13–14; Taylor, "June 2014 Survey," slide 12; Taylor, "July 2014 Survey," slide 12; Taylor, "August 2014 Survey," slide 12; Taylor, "September 2014 Survey," slide 13; Taylor, "October 2014 Survey," slides 12–13; Taylor, "November 2014 Survey," slides 12–13; Taylor, "December 2014 Survey," slide 13.
15. Wright, "April 2014 Survey," slide 14; Taylor, "June 2014 Survey," slide 12; Taylor, "July 2014 Survey," slide 12; Taylor, "August 2014 Survey," slide 12; Taylor, "December 2014 Survey," slide 12.
16. The fifth question on the survey generated 556 responses. Artifacts, panels, and interactives saw significant dips and growth during fluctuations, varying from 5 to 15 percent. Overall the docent received 6 percent of responses, while panels received 23 percent and artifacts 21 percent. Simon, *Participatory Museum,* 37; Taylor, "WWFH Trends," slide 4, 10-11; Taylor, "June 2014 Survey," slide 7; Taylor, "July 2014 Survey," slide 7; Taylor, "August 2014 Survey," slide 7; Taylor, email message to interpretive team, "August Survey Monkey Results,"

September 5, 2014; Taylor, "November 2014 Survey," slide 7; Taylor, "December 2014 Survey," slide.

17. Six visitors positively mentioned the material culture, appreciating that "the home was not over crowded" with random artifacts and finding it "refreshing to be on a tour that focused more on substance of information than related artifacts." Fourteen visitors wanted more objects in the traditional HHM staged style or furnished for the Wilsons rather than a "modern" museum presentation that left the rooms spartan and heavy on text panels. Taylor, "WWFH Trends," slide 22; Wright, "April 2014 Survey," slide 12; Jennifer Whitmer Taylor, "May 2014 WWFH Visitor Survey Update," PowerPoint, Historic Columbia, June 2014, slides 11–12; Taylor, "June 2014 Survey," slides 11–12; Taylor, "July 2014 Survey," slides 11–12; Taylor, "August 2014 Survey," slides 11–12; Taylor, "October 2014 Survey," slides 7, 11–12; Taylor, "November 2014 Survey," slide 11; Taylor, "December 2014 Survey," slides 11–12; Wright, "WWFH Visitor Survey Preliminary Findings," slide 6; Robin Waites, email message to Cook et al., "WWFH Notes from Guides," April 21, 2014.
18. Bacon-Rogers interview; Docent Doe interview; Clark first interview.
19. Taylor, "May 2014 Survey," slide 11; Taylor, "June 2014 Survey," slide 11; Taylor, "November 2014 Survey," slide 11; Weiler and Ham, "Development of a Research Instrument," 204.
20. Historic Columbia modified the survey so visitors could make multiple selections for the most interesting types of information. The organization wanted to see what other information visitors valued beyond what was provided by the docent. Initially visitors chose only one option on the mobile device. Visitors completing paper copies sometimes took the initiative to mark more than one option. After the update the two weakest categories started registering with visitors at 10 percent. This was a 2 percent increase for interactives and a 6 percent surge for questions. Taylor, "WWFH Trends," slides 4, 10–11; Taylor, "July 2014 Survey," slide 7; Taylor, "August 2014 Survey," slide 7; Taylor, email message to interpretive team, "August Survey Monkey Results," September 5, 2014; Taylor, "September 2014 Survey," slide 7; Taylor, "October 2014 Survey," slide 7; Taylor, "November 2014 Survey," slide 7; Taylor, "December 2014 Survey," slide 7.
21. Visitors mentioned interactives in general, one welcoming them as "ingenious and informative" tools that needed ample time for exploration. Two visitors praised the concept of the museum and how the combination of components worked together. Others listed specific interactives. The favorite part of one visitor's "breathtaking" experience was dressing up as the president using reproduction clothing located in a trunk in Tommy's bedroom. Several docents commented on the map's popularity, with Bacon-Rogers calling it "one of the coolest things" Historic Columbia had ever done. Seven docents revealed that visitors rarely interacted with the family tree or only "fiddled" with it before losing interest. One lone visitor commented on evaluations that the exhibit was too digitized. Wright, "WWFH Visitor Survey Preliminary Findings," slides 4, 6; Taylor, "May 2014 Survey," slides 11–12.
22. One study dealt with active recruitment as part of research on how long participants spent with an interactive math exhibit. The results suggested that when visitors are cued to an interactive and observed, they spend 10 to 100 percent more time than visitors who are not cued. In another study of 128 families using

a laser light show activity in a Design Zone exhibition at the Oregon Museum of Science and Industry, those that were actively recruited spent on average over four minutes longer at the interactive and created six more laser patterns than visitors passively recruited through signage. Pattison and Shagott, "Participant Reactivity in Museum Research," 216–18, 222–24, 226; Yalowitz and Bronnenkant, "Timing and Tracking," 58; Taylor, "June 2014 Survey," slide 11; Morgan interview; Gunter interview; Bacon-Rogers interview; Clark second interview; Westcott interview; Lee interview; Storm interview.

23. Simon, *Participatory Museum*, iii–iv, 18, 26–28.
24. For example, some visitors associated Jim Crow with the period immediately after the Civil War. They learned that Black people were temporarily allowed to vote and that Reconstruction's failure allowed Jim Crow to be codified with the new state constitutions in the mid-1890s. Storm interview; Hogan interview; Clark second interview; Gunter, "Historic Columbia Docent Survey"; Bacon-Rogers interview; Docent Doe interview; Morgan interview.
25. Stickney, email message to Waites, "WWFH," June 25, 2014; Hogan interview; Richardson, "Historic Columbia Docent Survey"; Menne, "Historic Columbia Docent Survey," 2016; Gunter interview; Stickney interview; Morgan interview.
26. Falk, *Identity and the Museum Visitor Experience*, 27; Dahl et al., "Is Our Fascination," 163, 175–76.
27. Clark first interview; Lee interview; Bacon-Rogers, "Historic Columbia Docent Survey."
28. Lee interview; Gunter, "Historic Columbia Docent Survey"; Gunter interview; Storm interview.
29. Wright, "WWFH Visitor Survey Preliminary Findings," slide 6; Taylor, "May 2014 Survey," slide 12; Taylor, "July 2014 Survey," slide 12; Taylor, "September 2014 Survey," slide 12.
30. Morgan, email message to Taylor, "WWFH," May 4, 2015; Storm interview.
31. Lee interview; Storm interview.
32. Safranek, "Historic House Museum Review," 122–23.
33. C. Moore, "Woodrow Wilson Family Home," 191.
34. Simon, *Participatory Museum*, iv; Luke, "Museum," 24.
35. Fifteen percent of evaluations were left blank in the section asking racial and ethnic identity, making it the least answered question. Although the MoRE was visited primarily by white patrons, people of color had positive responses to the site, and in some cases their evaluation selections were higher than average. For example, 3 percent more Black respondents than average gained a new appreciation for people unlike themselves. All four Native American and twelve Hispanic/Latino visitors found the tour excellent. The latter were also all fully engaged and believed the site handled sensitive issues extremely well. All Native American visitors and all seven Asian/Pacific Islanders responded that they received new information that they found interesting. Taylor, "WWFH Trends," slides 3, 6–7, 16–20; Taylor, "August 2014 Survey," slide 4.
36. Taylor, "May 2014 Survey," slide 12; Taylor, "July 2014 Survey," slide 12; Taylor, "August 2014 Survey," slide 12; Taylor, "September 2014 Survey," slide 13; Taylor, "October 2014 Survey," slide 12; Taylor, "November 2014 Survey," slide 12; Taylor, "December 2014 Survey," slide 12.
37. Both Doe and Stickney used the language *open* rather than *open-minded*.

38. The exhibit films received eight comments by evaluators. Wright, "WWFH Visitor Survey Preliminary Findings," slide 6; Taylor, "May 2014 Survey," slides 11–12; Taylor, "July 2014 Survey," slide 12; Taylor, "August 2014 Survey," slide 12; Taylor, "October 2014 Survey," slides 7, 12; Taylor, "December 2014 Survey," slide 12.
39. C. Moore, "Woodrow Wilson Family Home," 192.
40. Moore, 190; Safranek, "Historic House Museum Review," 122.
41. C. Moore, "Woodrow Wilson Family Home," 192.
42. Safranek, "Historic House Museum Review," 120, 123; C. Moore, "Woodrow Wilson Family Home," 192.
43. The board named Waites executive director in 2004. She brought eight years of museum experience, two with the organization and six at the South Carolina State Museum. As of early 2024, Historic Columbia employed twenty-one full-time and twenty part-time staff. Waites, "Robin Waites Announces Retirement"; Nicholson, "Historic Columbia's Robin Waites to Retire after 20 Years of 'Reconstructing History,'" https://www.postandcourier.com.
44. West, *Domesticating History*, xi–xii, 1–2, 37, 43–45, 102, 159–60.
45. C. Moore, "Woodrow Wilson Family Home," 189; Taylor and Miller, "Postscript to 'Reconstructing Memory,'" http://journalofthecivilwarera.org.
46. Downs and Masur, "Perfect Spot."
47. West, Domesticating History, 162.
48. Pharaon et al., "Safe Containers for Dangerous Memories," 61–62, 68–71.
49. Downs and Masur, "Perfect Spot."
50. C. Moore, "Woodrow Wilson Family Home," 189, 193.
51. Gordon-Reed, "What If Reconstruction Hadn't Failed?," https://www.theatlantic.comThe seminal work detailing the Hemings family relationship with Thomas Jefferson, including the offspring he produced with Sally, is Gordon-Reed, *Hemingses of Monticello*. See also Thomas Jefferson Foundation, "Plantation and Slavery," https://www.monticello.org; Thomas Jefferson Foundation, "Landscape of Slavery: Mulberry Row," Monticellohttps://www.monticello.org.
52. C. Moore, "Woodrow Wilson Family Home," 191–92.
53. Graham, *Framing the South*, 191–92.
54. Carpio, "'I Like the Way You Die, Boy,'" 1; Gates, "'Unfathomable Place,'" 51–53.
55. Barnes and Buckley, "Nate Parker's Heralded Film," https://www.nytimes.com; Alexander, "Epic Fail," https://www.thenation.com.
56. Newkirk, "Faux-Enlightened," http://www.theatlantic.com; Scott, "Review: Matthew McConaughey," http://www.nytimes.com; Schuessler, "Confederate Dissident," http://www.nytimes.com; Taylor and Miller, "Reconstructing Memory," 58.
57. Wilson, "Reconstruction of the Southern States," 369.
58. B. E. Baker, *What Reconstruction Meant*, 10, 136–38; B. E. Baker, "Whom Is Reconstruction For?," 26; Binette, "Pulitzer Prize Winner," http://www.sc.edu; Duncan, "Celebrating the 70th Anniversary," http://auntiebellum.org.
59. Bacon-Rogers and Allen, Zoom interview.
60. Taylor, "June 2014 Survey," slide 11; Taylor, "July 2014 Survey," slide 11; Taylor, "November 2014 Survey," slide 11; Clark second interview; Lee interview.
61. Wright, email message to Waites, "Visitor Feedback," March 10, 2014; Wright, "April 2014 Survey," slide 12; Taylor, "July 2014 Survey," slide 11; Taylor, "December

2014 Survey," slides 6, 11; Jowers, email message to Taylor and Quint, "Mailed in WW Survey," June 30, 2014; Jowers, email message to Blackwell, "Tour Comment," April 25, 2014; "The Building Is Nice," Woodrow Wilson Family Home Visitor Survey, June 2014, Historic Columbia Collection; Bacon-Rogers and Allen, Zoom interview; State of California, "Governor Newsom Statement on Constitutional Amendment to Repeal Prop. 8," California Governor, February 15, 2023, https://www.gov.ca.gov/2023/02/14/governor-newsom-statement-on-constitutional-amendment-to-repeal-prop-8/.

62. For example, the Pauli Murray Project Working Zone Venn diagram visually expresses intersectional overlap. Pharaon et al., "Safe Containers for Dangerous Memories," 62–64, 66–69.
63. Taylor, email message to Booraem, "Letter for AASLH Grant," February 26, 2015; Taylor, "July 2014 Survey," slide 11.
64. Bacon-Rogers and Allen, Zoom interview; Historic Columbia, "Modjeska Monteith Simkins House." For a discussion of the long civil rights movement, see Hall, "Long Civil Rights Movement," 1233–63, https://doi.org/10.2307/3660172.
65. Safranek, "Historic House Museum Review," 120, 123; C. Moore, "Woodrow Wilson Family Home," 192.
66. Thirteen visitors left comments about the home's importance. Related comments included that the home avoided being a presidential shrine while "tackling a difficult subject in the south." Having taken the tour at Staunton, a visitor exclaimed, "You stand up well against Wilson birthplace considering your size in comparison." The tour inspired another to visit Wilson HHMs "to see the whole picture." Wright, "April 2014 Survey," slide 14; Taylor, "May 2014 Survey," slide 12; Taylor, "June 2014 Survey," slide 12; Taylor, "August 2014 Survey," slide 12; Taylor, "September 2014 Survey," slide 12; Taylor, "October 2014 Survey," slides 12–13; Taylor, "November 2014 Survey," slide 12; Taylor, "December 2014 Survey," slide 12.
67. Taylor, "March Results," April 30, 2015; Taylor, "WWFH Trends," slides 21–22; Taylor, "May 2014 Survey," slide 12; Taylor, "June 2014 Survey," slide 11; Taylor, "July 2014 Survey," slide 11; Taylor, "August 2014 Survey," slide 11; Taylor, "September 2014 Survey," October 2014, slide 12; Taylor, "October 2014 Survey," slide 11; Taylor, "November 2014 Survey," December 2014, slide 11.
68. Bacon-Rogers and Allen, Zoom interview.
69. Four docents expressed concerns about backlash in their oral histories. Bacon-Rogers, "Historic Columbia Docent Survey"; Brazier interview; Hogan interview; Docent Doe, "Historic Columbia Docent Survey"; "WWFH Training Session Planning," Historic Columbia, November 13, 2013, Historic Columbia Collection; Taylor and Miller, "Reconstructing Memory," 39, 57. "Heritage, Not Hate" is a white supremacist slogan from the 1990s representing support for Confederate iconography and flags. P. Charles Lunsford, a Sons of Confederate Veterans member with links to more radical heritage groups with white supremacist ties, coined the phrase. Beirich, "Struggle for the Sons of Confederate Veterans," 286.
70. In September 2007 the preservation firm conducting the study of the home, which included structural, archeological, and paint analysis, told the press that the home had "so much to tell about Columbia and South Carolina during Reconstruction"; however, Historic Columbia's executive director, Robin Waites, said the organization would approach the WWFH "as the preservation of an

historic Columbia home and landscape and as a look at Wilson as the president of the United States." Wilkinson, "Building Our City." Other sources made no mention of Reconstruction. Knauss, "Funds Sought"; "The State Briefly," *Columbia (SC) State;* Smith, "$1.5 Million Needed"; Smith, "Saving a Part of History"; "Welcome, Tourists," *Columbia (SC) State;* Chourey, "Haley Vetoes Money"; Cope, "State Boasts $87," 3.

71. Menne, "Historic Columbia Docent Survey"; Bacon-Rogers, "Historic Columbia Docent Survey"; Lee interview; Clark first interview; Clark second interview; Schneider, "Historic Columbia Docent Survey"; Stickney interview; Gunter, "Historic Columbia Docent Survey." Other docents experienced mild microaggressions, such as a visitor's calling the Civil War the "War of Northern Aggression" throughout the tour. The tour never caused any backlash in person for three docents. Hogan interview; Brazier interview; Docent Doe interview; Holmes, "Historic Columbia Docent Survey."
72. Clark first interview; Clark second interview; Schneider, "Historic Columbia Docent Survey"; Stickney interview; Gunter interview; Bacon-Rogers interview; Docent Doe interview.
73. Nearly 84 percent of 628 respondents thought sensitive or controversial issues were treated extremely well. Taylor, "WWFH Trends," slides 4, 9; Taylor, "August 2014 Survey," slide 5; Taylor, "September 2014 Survey," slide 5; Taylor, "October 2014 Survey," slide 13.
74. Wright, email message to Waites, "Visitor Feedback," March 10, 2014; Wright, "April 2014 Survey," slide 12; Taylor, "July 2014 Survey," slide 11; Taylor, "December 2014 Survey," slides 6, 11; Jowers, email message to Taylor and Quint, "Mailed in WW Survey," June 30, 2014; Jowers, email message to Blackwell, "Tour Comment," April 25, 2014; "The Building Is Nice"; Ham, "Monday Letters: Visit to Wilson House Disappointing," *Columbia (SC) State,* September 15, 2014, http://www.thestate.com.
75. The interpretive team discussed details of the encounter via email immediately following Morgan's tour. Morgan interview; Freed, email message to interpretive team, "Follow Up Call from Jean Morgan," January 26, 2015.
76. Bacon-Rogers and Allen, Zoom interview; Benson, "Getting New Name."
77. Only 36 percent of 1980s millennials found the guide most interesting. Over a third of late millennials and the oldest zoomers preferred the self-guided portions. Just over 35 percent of 1990s millennials were fully engaged, and 16 percent were more likely to believe no sensitive issues were raised. Twenty percent of millennials found the interactives most interesting, 12 percent higher than the average. They also liked the question prompts more than most visitors. Most astonishing, nearly two-thirds gained a new appreciation for people different from themselves, an impressive 38 percent above average. Taylor, "WWFH Trends," slides 19–20.
78. Wilson, "Reconstruction of the Southern States," 388; C. Moore, "Woodrow Wilson Family Home," 139.

Bibliography

Primary Sources

Docent Oral Histories and Surveys

Bacon-Rogers, Heather. "Historic Columbia Docent Survey for Jen Taylor's Dissertation," 2016.

Bacon-Rogers, Heather. Interview by Jennifer Whitmer Taylor. Digital recording, March 4, 2016. Docents of the Woodrow Wilson Home Museum Oral History Collection. South Caroliniana Library, University of South Carolina, Columbia.

Brazier, Halie. "Historic Columbia Docent Survey for Jen Taylor's Dissertation," 2016.

Brazier, Halie. Interview by Jennifer Whitmer Taylor. Digital recording, January 27, 2016. Docents of the Woodrow Wilson Home Museum Oral History Collection. South Caroliniana Library, University of South Carolina, Columbia.

Clark, John. First Interview by Jennifer Whitmer Taylor. Digital recording, January 27, 2016. Docents of the Woodrow Wilson Home Museum Oral History Collection. South Caroliniana Library, University of South Carolina, Columbia.

Clark, John. "Historic Columbia Docent Survey for Jen Taylor's Dissertation," 2016.

Clark, John. Second Interview by Jennifer Whitmer Taylor. Digital recording, February 11, 2016. Docents of the Woodrow Wilson Home Museum Oral History Collection. South Caroliniana Library, University of South Carolina, Columbia.

Docent Doe. Interview by Jennifer Whitmer Taylor. Digital recording, February 17, 2016. Docents of the Woodrow Wilson Home Museum Oral History Collection. South Caroliniana Library, University of South Carolina, Columbia.

Gunter, Jennifer. "Historic Columbia Docent Survey for Jen Taylor's Dissertation," 2016.

Gunter, Jennifer. Interview by Jennifer Whitmer Taylor. Digital recording, March 27, 2016. Docents of the Woodrow Wilson Home Museum Oral History Collection. South Caroliniana Library, University of South Carolina, Columbia.

Hogan, Kathy. "Historic Columbia Docent Survey for Jen Taylor's Dissertation," 2016.

Hogan, Kathy. Interview by Jennifer Whitmer Taylor. Digital recording, February 16, 2016. Docents of the Woodrow Wilson Home Museum Oral History Collection. South Caroliniana Library, University of South Carolina, Columbia.

Holmes, Erin. "Historic Columbia Docent Survey for Jen Taylor's Dissertation," 2016.

Lee, Casey. Interview by Jennifer Whitmer Taylor. Digital recording, March 27, 2016. Docents of the Woodrow Wilson Home Museum Oral History Collection. South Caroliniana Library, University of South Carolina, Columbia.

Menne, Katie. "Historic Columbia Docent Survey for Jen Taylor's Dissertation," 2016.

Morgan, Jean. "Historic Columbia Docent Survey for Jen Taylor's Dissertation," 2016.

Morgan, Jean. Interview by Jennifer Whitmer Taylor. Digital recording, January 25, 2016. Docents of the Woodrow Wilson Home Museum Oral History Collection. South Caroliniana Library, University of South Carolina, Columbia.

Richardson, Margie. "Historic Columbia Docent Survey for Jen Taylor's Dissertation," 2016.

Schneider, Maria. "Historic Columbia Docent Survey for Jen Taylor's Dissertation," 2016.

Scott, Bernadette. "Historic Columbia Docent Survey for Jen Taylor's Dissertation," 2016.

Stickney, Pris. "Historic Columbia Docent Survey for Jen Taylor's Dissertation," 2016.

Stickney, Pris. Interview by Jennifer Whitmer Taylor. Digital recording, January 28, 2016. Docents of the Woodrow Wilson Home Museum Oral History Collection. South Caroliniana Library, University of South Carolina, Columbia.

Storm, Cyndy. "Historic Columbia Docent Survey for Jen Taylor's Dissertation," 2016.

Storm, Cyndy. Interview by Jennifer Whitmer Taylor. Digital recording, February 4, 2016. Docents of the Woodrow Wilson Home Museum Oral History Collection. South Caroliniana Library, University of South Carolina, Columbia.

Weir, Anne. "Historic Columbia Docent Survey for Jen Taylor's Dissertation," 2016.

Westcott, Holly. "Historic Columbia Docent Survey for Jen Taylor's Dissertation," 2016.

Westcott, Holly. Interview by Jennifer Whitmer Taylor. Digital recording, February 26, 2016. Docents of the Woodrow Wilson Home Museum Oral History Collection. South Caroliniana Library, University of South Carolina, Columbia.

Woodrow Wilson Family Home Scripts (Authored by Jennifer Taylor)

"WWFH Interpretation Adult Tour Jen's Revision." Historic Columbia, December 10, 2013.

"WWFH Interpretation Adult Tour Jen's Dec 30 Revision." Historic Columbia, December 30, 2013.

"Woodrow Wilson Family Home Adult Tour Script." Historic Columbia, January 2, 2014.

"WWFH Interpretation Adult Tour 01 10 14 Post Volunteer." Historic Columbia, January 10, 2014.

"WWFH Interpretation Adult Tour 01 31 14 Working Draft." Historic Columbia, January 31, 2014.

"WWFH Interpretation Adult Tour 02 04 14 Working Draft." Historic Columbia, February 4, 2014.

"Woodrow Wilson Family Home Adult Tour Script." Historic Columbia, February 6, 2014.

"WWFH Interpretation Adult Tour Second Training Version." Historic Columbia, April 2014.

"Woodrow Wilson Family Home Adult Tour Script." Historic Columbia, June 13, 2014.

Docent Tour Evaluations

Freed, Fielding. "Docent P Tour Review." April 18, 2014. Historic Columbia.

Posner, Ann. "Docent B Tour Review." February 20, 2014. Historic Columbia.

Posner, Ann. "Docent D Tour Review." February 24, 2014. Historic Columbia.

Posner, Ann. "Docent F Tour Review." March 4, 2014. Historic Columbia.

Posner, Ann. "Docent G Tour Review." March 6, 2014. Historic Columbia.

Posner, Ann. "Docent H Tour Review." March 12, 2014. Historic Columbia.

Posner, Ann. "Docent N Tour Review." October 30, 2014. Historic Columbia.

Posner, Ann. "Docent O Tour Review." n.d. Historic Columbia.

Posner, Ann, and Jennifer Taylor. "Docent P Tour Review." February 11, 2014. Historic Columbia.

Quint, James. "Docent C Tour Review." February 20, 2014. Historic Columbia

Sherrer, John. "Docent P Tour Review." June 4, 2014. Historic Columbia.

Taylor, Jennifer. "Docent A Tour Review." February 10, 2014. Historic Columbia.

Taylor, Jennifer. "Docent B Tour Review." February 20, 2014. Historic Columbia.

Taylor, Jennifer. "Docent E Tour Review." February 28, 2014. Historic Columbia.

Taylor, Jennifer. "Docent G Tour Review." March 20, 2014. Historic Columbia.

Taylor, Jennifer. "Docent H Tour Review." March 12, 2014. Historic Columbia.

Taylor, Jennifer. "Docent I Tour Review." March 17, 2014. Historic Columbia.

Taylor, Jennifer. "Docent J Tour Review." April 2, 2014. Historic Columbia.

Taylor, Jennifer. "Docent K Tour Review." October 30, 2014. Historic Columbia.

Taylor, Jennifer. "Docent L Tour Review." June 6, 2014. Historic Columbia.

Taylor, Jennifer. "Docent M Tour Review." August 21, 2014. Historic Columbia.

Taylor, Jennifer. "Docent P Tour Review." March 26, 2014. Historic Columbia.

Taylor, Jennifer. "Docent P Tour Review." June 4, 2014. Historic Columbia.

Taylor, Jennifer. "Docent Q Tour Review." October 1, 2014. Historic Columbia.

Taylor, Jennifer. "Docent R Tour Review." July 24, 2014. Historic Columbia.

Taylor, Jennifer. "Docent S Informal Tour Review." June 18, 2014. Historic Columbia.

Taylor, Jennifer. "Docent S Tour Review." July 18, 2014. Historic Columbia.

Manuscript Collections

Dreher, Jennie Clarkson. Papers. South Caroliniana Library, University of South Carolina, Columbia.

DuBose, Louise Jones. Interview by Office of Oral History, South Caroliniana Library. Audio recording, September 21, 1981. South Caroliniana Library, University of South Carolina, Columbia.

Smith, Emily P. Papers. The Woodrow Wilson Presidential Library, Staunton, Virginia.

Wilson, Edith Bolling. Papers. The Woodrow Wilson Presidential Library, Staunton, Virginia.

Woodrow Wilson Boyhood Home Records. South Caroliniana Library, University of South Carolina, Columbia.

Woodrow Wilson Family Home Files. Historic Columbia, Columbia, South Carolina. Includes all visitor evaluation data from Survey Monkey, email correspondence, and internal documents, except scripts and docent tour evaluations, created during my time as Woodrow Wilson Family Home tour facilitator.

Woodrow Wilson Memorial MS. South Caroliniana Library, University of South Carolina, Columbia.

Films, Media, and Images

The Birth of a Nation. Directed by D.W. Griffith. 1915. MPEG video, 180 min. https://archive.org.
The Birth of a Nation. Directed by Nate Parker. 2016. 20th Century Fox, 2017. DVD, 120 min.
The Butler. Directed by Lee Daniels. 2013. Anchor Bay Entertainment, 2014. DVD, 132 min.
Django Unchained. Directed by Quentin Tarantino. 2012. Weinstein Company, 2013. DVD, 165 min.
Forrest Gump. Directed by Robert Zemeckis. 1994. Paramount, 2001. DVD, 142 min.
Free State of Jones. Directed by Gary Ross. 2016. Universal Studios, 2016. DVD, 142 min.
Gone with the Wind. Directed by Victor Fleming. 1939. Warner Home Video, 2010. DVD, 233 min.
Harris & Ewing, photographer. Edith Bolling Galt Wilson, full-length portrait, standing, facing front, hands behind waist. ca. 1913. Photograph. https://www.loc.gov
Kornegay, Lee Ann. *The Legacy of Woodrow Wilson and Reconstruction*. Digital video exhibit. Historic Columbia, 2015. https://www.youtube.com.
Kornegay, Lee Ann. *13th, 14th & 15th Amendments*. Digital video exhibit. Historic Columbia, 2015. https://www.youtube.com.
Nast, Thomas. *"One Vote Less"—Richmond Whig*, 1872. Art and Picture Collection, New York Public Library. http://digitalcollections.nypl.org.
Nast, Thomas. *The Union as It Was—The Lost Cause, Worse Than Slavery*. Cartoon, 1874. *Harper's Weekly*, October 24, 1874, 848. Library of Congress, Prints and Photographs Online Catalog. http://www.loc.gov.
Ogden, Harry, Artist. South Carolina—The November election—The dead-lock in the state legislature at Columbia / from sketches by Harry Ogden. South Carolina Columbia, 1876. Photograph. https://www.loc.gov.
Rebirth of a Nation. Directed by DJ Spooky. 2004. Starz Productions, 2007. DVD, 140 min.
Twelve Years a Slave. Directed by Steve McQueen. 2013. 20th Century Fox Home Entertainment, 2014. DVD, 134 min.
"Wade Hampton Day, Boy Scouts—Czarnitzki—Home Movies." Directed by William Esper Czarnitzki. December 14, 1926. Video/H264, 15 min. https://digital.tcl.sc.edu.
Wilson Family. Photograph. 1892. Woodrow Wilson Presidential Library, Staunton, Virginia. https://presidentwilson.org.
Within Our Gates. Directed by Oscar Micheaux. 1919. MPEG video, 79 min. https://archive.org.

Newspapers and Magazines

Aljazeera America
AP News
The Atlantic

Baltimore Sun
BBC News
CBS News
Columbia (SC) Star
CNN
Charlotte Observer
Columbia (SC) Daily Register
Columbia (SC) Free Times
Daily Camera (Boulder, CO)
The Hill
Jacobin
Los Angeles Times
Mother Jones
The Nation
National Public Radio
NBC News
New York Times
PBS NewsHour
Politico
Charleston (SC) Post and Courier
Reuters
SC Patch (Irmo-Seven Oaks)
Smithsonian Magazine
The State (Columbia, SC)
USA Today College
US News & World Report
Vice
Washington Post

Museum Websites and Tours

Egner, Kate. "Ann Pamela Cunningham." The Digital Encyclopedia of George Washington. Accessed March 10, 2017. http://www.mountvernon.org/digital-encyclopedia/article/ann-pamela-cunningham/.

Emily Dickinson Museum. "Emily and Sue." Accessed July 11, 2023. https://www.emilydickinsonmuseum.org.

Emily Dickinson Museum. "Visit—Emily Dickinson Museum." Accessed July 11, 2023. https://www.emilydickinsonmuseum.org.

Equal Justice Initiative. "Criminal Justice Reform." Accessed July 21, 2023. https://eji.org.

Explore Mitchelville. "About Us," June 16, 2021. https://exploremitchelville.org.

Explore Mitchelville. Accessed June 16, 2021. https://exploremitchelville.org.

Explore Mitchelville. "https://exploremitchelville.org/timeline/mitchelville-today/." Accessed November 8, 2023.

Harriet Beecher Stowe Center. "A Non-traditional Museum." Accessed July 3, 2023. https://www.harrietbeecherstowecenter.org.

Harriet Beecher Stowe Center. "Board." Accessed July 3, 2023. https://www.harrietbeecherstowecenter.org.

Harriet Beecher Stowe Center. "More Programs." Accessed July 3, 2023. https://www.harrietbeecherstowecenter.org.
Healy, John McD. "November 2022 Year End Update." NC History Center on the Civil War, Emancipation and Reconstruction, November 25, 2022. https://nccivilwarcenter.org.
Herzberg, Stephanie. Guided Tour. Woodrow Wilson Boyhood Home. Augusta, Georgia, May 28, 2015.
Historic Columbia. "Wade Hampton III Monument." Accessed July 6, 2021. https://www.historiccolumbia.org.
Historic Columbia. "Modjeska Monteith Simkins House." Accessed July 20, 2023. https://www.historiccolumbia.org.
Historic Columbia. "Hampton-Preston Mansion and Gardens." Accessed August 3, 2021. https://www.historiccolumbia.org.
Historic Columbia. "1615 Blanding Street." Accessed June 8, 2023. https://www.historiccolumbia.org.
Historic Columbia. "Hampton-Preston Turns 200." Accessed February 4, 2023. https://www.historiccolumbia.org.
Historic Columbia. "House Tours." Accessed February 4, 2023. https://www.historiccolumbia.org.
National Constitution Center. "Civil War and Reconstruction: The Battle for Freedom and Equality." Constitution Center. Accessed December 23, 2023. https://constitutioncenter.org.
National Park Service. "Discover the Reconstruction Era National Historic Network." Reconstruction Era. Accessed December 23, 2023. https://www.nps.gov.
National Park Service. "Washington's Headquarters." Valley Forge National Historical Park. Accessed November 18, 2021. https://www.nps.gov.
National Trust for Historic Preservation. "The President Woodrow Wilson House," August 2, 2021. https://savingplaces.org.
NC Civil War Center. "Groundbreaking Ceremony Speeches." Accessed December 23, 2023. https://nccivilwarcenter.org.
NC History Center on the Civil War, Emancipation and Reconstruction. "Community Foundation Announces $500,000 Grant Investment," March 14, 2014. https://nccivilwarcenter.org.
New York State Parks, Recreation and Historic Preservation. "Washington's Headquarters State Historic Site." Accessed November 18, 2021. https://parks.ny.gov.
Pennsylvania Conservation Heritage Project. "Anna Morris Holstein." Accessed November 18, 2021. https://paconservationheritage.org.
Phillips, Andrew. "Behind-the-Scenes Tour of the Woodrow Wilson Presidential Library and Museum." Guided tour. Staunton, Virginia, June 18, 2015.
Polhill, Cynthia. "Behind-the-Scenes Tour of the Woodrow Wilson Presidential Library and Museum." Guided tour. Staunton, Virginia, June 18, 2015.
Polhill, Cynthia. Guided tour. Woodrow Wilson Presidential Library and Museum Manse. Staunton, Virginia, June 18, 2015.
President Woodrow Wilson House. "About Us." President Wilson House. Accessed November 22, 2021. https://www.woodrowwilsonhouse.org.
President Woodrow Wilson House. "Tours." President Wilson House. Accessed June 23, 2023. https://woodrowwilsonhouse.org.
Sons of Confederate Veterans Camp 36. "The Red Shirt." Museum and Library of Confederate History, n.d. Accessed February 2, 2024. http://www.confederatemuseum.org.

South Carolina Department of Archives and History. "South Carolina's Reconstruction: A Digital Exhibit." June 16, 2021. https://scdah.sc.gov.

South Carolina Department of Archives and History. "Constitutional Convention, Article 10, S 131081," 1868.

South Carolina ETV. "40 Acres and a Mule." Reconstruction 360. Accessed January 31, 2022. https://reconstruction360.org.

South Carolina ETV. "A Seat at the Table." Reconstruction 360. Accessed January 31, 2022. https://reconstruction360.org.

South Carolina State Museum. "Fourth Floor Galleries." Accessed December 29, 2023. https://scmuseum.org.

South Carolina State Museum. "South Carolina and Reconstruction: A Virtual 360 Exhibit." South Carolina State Museum. Accessed January 3, 2024. https://www.scmuseum.org.

Toegel, Alex. Guided tour. President Woodrow Wilson House. Washington, DC, June 20, 2015.

Whitney Plantation. "Tours of Whitney Plantation Museum." Accessed July 26, 2022. https://www.whitneyplantation.org.

Woodrow Wilson: His Life and Times. Exhibit. The Woodrow Wilson Presidential Library and Museum, Staunton, Virginia, June 2015.

Woodrow Wilson Family Home. Exhibit. Historic Columbia, Columbia, SC. June 2015.

Other

Álvarez, Brenda. "Are Today's Voter Suppression Laws the New Jim Crow?" National Education Association, January 16, 2022. https://www.nea.org.

Baker, Ray Stannard. *Youth 1856–1890.* Vol. 1 of *Woodrow Wilson: Life and Letters.* Garden City, NY: Doubleday, Page, 1927.

Beirich, Heidi. "Testimony of Heidi L. Beirich, Ph.D. Co-Founder Global Project Against Hate and Extremism, 'Alarming Incidents of White Supremacy in the Military—How to Stop It?,'" February 11, 2020. https://www.congress.gov.

Brennan Center for Justice. "It's Official: The Election Was Secure." Brennan Center, December 11, 2020. https://www.brennancenter.org.

Brooks, Lecia. "SPLC Testifies before Congress on Alarming Incidents of White Supremacy in the Military." Testimony before the Subcommittee on Military Personnel. Southern Poverty Law Center, February 11, 2020. https://www.splcenter.org.

Cascone, Sarah. "The Museum Heist Scene in 'Black Panther' Adds Fuel to the Debate about African Art Restitution." *Artnet,* March 5, 2018. https://news.artnet.com.

Courson, Sen. John E., Sen. Darrell Jackson Sr., and Sen. Greg Hembree. "Senate Education Oversight Subcommittee Summary Report on the SC Confederate Relic Room and Military Museum." Senate of South Carolina, March 2016. https://www.scstatehouse.gov/CommitteeInfo/SenateEducationCommittee/.

Grimmer, Justin. "No Evidence for Voter Fraud: A Guide to Statistical Claims About the 2020 Election." Text. Hoover Institution, February 3, 2021. https://www.hoover.org.

Oliphant, Mary C. Simms. *The Simms History of South Carolina.* Columbia: State Company, 1932.

Oliphant, Mary C. Simms, Mary C. Simms Oliphant Furman, and W. Gilmore Simms Oliphant. *The History of South Carolina.* Columbia: Laidlaw Brothers, 1970.

Perry, Andrew M., Marshall Steinbaum, and Carl Romer. "Student Loans, the Racial Wealth Divide, and Why We Need Full Student Debt Cancellation." Brookings, June 23, 2021. https://www.brookings.edu.

Sanborn Map Company. "Image 56 of Sanborn Fire Insurance Map from Columbia, Richland County, South Carolina." Image. Library of Congress, 1919. https://www.loc.gov.

Spearman, Molly M. "South Carolina Social Studies College-and Career-Ready Standards." Columbia: South Carolina Department of Education, 2019. https://ed.sc.gov.

State of California. "Governor Newsom Statement on Constitutional Amendment to Repeal Prop. 8." California Governor, February 15, 2023. https://www.gov.ca.gov/2023/02/14/governor-newsom-statement-on-constitutional-amendment-to-repeal-prop-8/.

Taylor, Jennifer. "Woodrow Wilson Family Home Trends." PowerPoint. Historic Columbia, January 12, 2015.

Waites, Robin. "Robin Waites Announces Retirement from Historic Columbia in June 2024." Historic Columbia, October 19, 2023. https://www.historiccolumbia.org.

Watermeier, Daniel J., ed. *Between Actor and Critic: Selected Letters of Edwin Booth and William Winter.* Princeton, NJ: Princeton University Press, 1971.

Wearn & Hix. *Woodrow Wilson, Head-and-Shoulders Portrait, Facing Right.* Still image, 1873. https://www.loc.gov.

Wilson, Woodrow. Presidential Papers Microfilm. Washington: Library of Congress, 1969. Thomas Cooper Library Microforms, University of South Carolina, Columbia.

Wilson, Woodrow. "The Reconstruction of the Southern States." In *The Public Papers of Woodrow Wilson. Authorized Edition,* edited by Ray Stannard Baker and William Edward Dodd, 2:368–95. College and State: Educational, Literary and Political Papers (1875–1913). New York: Kraus Reprint, 1970.

Writers' Program of the Work Projects Administration in the State of South Carolina. *South Carolina: The WPA Guide to the Palmetto State.* Edited by Walter B. Edgar. Columbia: University of South Carolina Press, 1988.

Zais, Mick. "South Carolina Social Studies Academic Standards." Columbia: South Carolina Department of Educations, 2011. https://artsandsciences.sc.edu.

Secondary Sources

Alexander, Michelle. The New Jim Crow: Mass Incarceration in the Age of Colorblindness. New York: New Press, 2012.

Ambar, Saladin. "Woodrow Wilson: Life Before the Presidency." Miller Center, October 4, 2016. https://millercenter.org.

Ambrosius, Lloyd E. "Woodrow Wilson and *The Birth of a Nation:* American Democracy and International Relations." *Diplomacy and Statecraft* 18, no. 4 (December 2007): 689–718.

American Association for State and Local History. "Woodrow Wilson Family Home: A Museum of Reconstruction in Columbia and Richland County." Accessed December 23, 2023. https://aaslh.org.

American Civil Liberties Union. "Mass Incarceration." Accessed July 21, 2023. https://www.aclu.org.

American Legion Auxiliary. "History." American Legion Auxiliary. Accessed January 7, 2024. https://www.legion-aux.org.
Anderson, Christian K., and Jason C. Darby. "Richard T. Greener at the Reconstruction-Era University." In *Invisible No More: The African American Experience at the University of South Carolina*, edited by Robert Greene II and Tyler D. Parry, 51–72. Columbia: University of South Carolina Press, 2021.
Andrew, Rod, Jr. *Wade Hampton: Confederate Warrior to Southern Redeemer*. Civil War America. Chapel Hill: University of North Carolina Press, 2008.
Ayers, Edward L. *What Caused the Civil War? Reflections on the South and Southern History*. New York: Norton, 2005.
Baker, Bruce E. *This Mob Will Surely Take My Life: Lynchings in the Carolinas, 1871–1947*. London: Continuum, 2008.
Baker, Bruce E. *What Reconstruction Meant: Historical Memory in the American South*. Charlottesville: University of Virginia Press, 2007.
Baker, Bruce E. "Whom Is Reconstruction For?" In Domby and Lewis, *Freedoms Gained and Lost*, 17-38.
Baker, Bruce E., and Elaine S. Frantz. "Against Synthesis: Diverse Approaches to the History of Reconstruction." In *Reinterpreting Southern Histories: Essays in Historiography*, edited by Craig Thompson Friend and Lorri Glover, 218–44. Baton Rouge: Louisiana State University Press, 2020.
Behrend, Justin. "Facts and Memories: John R. Lynch and the Revising of Reconstruction History in the Era of Jim Crow." *Journal of African American History* 97, no. 4 (2012): 427–48.
Beirich, Heidi. "The Struggle for the Sons of Confederate Veterans: A Return to White Supremacy in the Early Twenty-First Century?" In *Neo-Confederacy: A Critical Introduction*, edited by Euan Hague, Edward H. Sebesta, and Heidi Beirich, 280–308. Austin: University of Texas Press, 2008.
Belew, Kathleen. *Bring the War Home: The White Power Movement and Paramilitary America*. Cambridge, MA: Harvard University Press, 2018.
Benbow, Mark E. "Birth of a Quotation: Woodrow Wilson and 'Like Writing History with Lightning.'" *Journal of the Gilded Age and Progressive Era* 9, no. 4 (October 2010): 509–33.
Benfield, Jacob A., Robert D. Jakubowski, William J. Szlemko, Ross J. Loomis, Juti Winchester, and Robert Pickering. "An 'Honest Visionary' and 'Dishonest Scallywag': Blending Fact, Opinion, and Interest into a Front-End Evaluation." *Visitor Studies* 11, no. 1 (March 2008): 55–72.
Bennett, Tony. *The Birth of the Museum: History, Theory, Politics*. New York: Routledge, 1995.
Berg, Andrew Scott. *Wilson*. New York: Putnam, 2013.
Berry, Daina Ramey, and Kali Nicole Gross. *A Black Women's History of the United States*. Boston, MA: Beacon Press, 2020.
Bertellini, Giorgio. *The Divo and the Duce: Promoting Film Stardom and Political Leadership in 1920s America*. Oakland: University of California Press, 2019.
Blank, Christopher. "Do the Words 'Race Riot' Belong on a Historic Marker in Memphis?" NPR.org, May 2, 2016. http://www.npr.org.
Blee, Kathleen M. *Women of the Klan: Racism and Gender in the 1920s*. Berkeley: University of California Press, 1991.
Bleick, Charles. "A Volunteer in Art Education: The Art Museum Docent." *Art Education* 33, no. 1 (January 1980): 19–20.

Blight, David W. *Race and Reunion: The Civil War in American Memory*. Cambridge, MA: Belknap Press of Harvard University Press, 2001.

Bodnar, John E. *Remaking America: Public Memory, Commemoration, and Patriotism in the Twentieth Century*. Princeton, NJ: Princeton University Press, 1994.

Bond, Beverly Greene, and Susan Eva O'Donovan. *Remembering the Memphis Massacre: An American Story*. Athens: University of Georgia Press, 2020.

Brown, Katherine L. *The Woodrow Wilson Presidential Library and Museum Staunton, Virginia*. Staunton, VA: Woodrow Wilson Presidential Library Foundation, 2009.

Brundage, W. Fitzhugh. *The Southern Past: A Clash of Race and Memory*. Cambridge, MA: Belknap Press of Harvard University Press, 2005.

Brundage, W. Fitzhugh. "Introduction." In *Remembering Reconstruction: Struggles Over the Meaning of America's Most Turbulent Era*, edited by Carole Emberton and Bruce E. Baker, 1–14. Baton Rouge: Louisiana State University Press, 2017.

Burns, Andrea. *From Storefront to Monument: Tracing the Public History of the Black Museum Movement*. Amherst: University of Massachusetts Press, 2013.

Cardyn, Lisa. "Sexualized Racism/Gendered Violence: Outraging the Body Politic in the Reconstruction South." *Michigan Law Review* 100, no. 4 (February 1, 2002): 675–867.

Carpio, Glenda R. "'I Like the Way You Die, Boy': Fantasy's Role in *Django Unchained*." *Transition* 112, no. 1 (2013): iv–12.

Chen, Chia-Li, and Chen-Gia Tsai. "The Influence of Background Music on the Visitor Museum Experience: A Case Study of the Laiho Memorial Museum, Taiwan." *Visitor Studies* 18, no. 2 (July 2015): 183–95.

Christopher, Tami. "The House of the Seven Gables: A House Museum's Adaptation to Changing Societal Expectations since 1910." In *Defining Memory: Local Museums and the Construction of History in America's Changing Communities*, edited by Amy K. Levin, 63–76. Lanham, MD: AltaMira, 2007.

Clements, Kendrick A. *The Presidency of Woodrow Wilson*. American Presidency Series. Lawrence, Kan: University Press of Kansas, 1992.

Clements, Kendrick A. *Woodrow Wilson, World Statesman*. Twayne's Twentieth-Century American Biography Series 7. Boston: Twayne, 1987.

Clinton, Catherine. "Bloody Terrain: Freedwomen, Sexuality, and Violence during Reconstruction." *The Georgia Historical Quarterly* 76, no. 2 (Summer 1992): 313–32.

Clinton, Catherine. *The Plantation Mistress: Woman's World in the Old South*. New York: Pantheon Books, 1982.

Clinton, Catherine. *Tara Revisited: Women, War & the Plantation Legend*. 1st ed. New York: Abbeville Press, 1995.

Clinton, Catherine. "With a Whip in His Hand." In *History and Memory in African American Culture*, edited by Geneviève Fabre and Robert G. O'Meally. New York: Oxford University Press, 1994.

Coleman, Christy S. "African American Museums in the Twenty-First Century." In Genoways, *Museum Philosophy*, 151–60.

Coleman, Laurence Vail. *Historic House Museums: With a Directory*. Detroit, MI: Gale Research Company, 1973.

Commander, Michelle D. "Plantation Counternarratives: Disrupting Master Accounts in Contemporary Cultural Production." *Journal of American Culture* 41, no. 1 (2018): 28–44.

Conn, Steven. *Do Museums Still Need Objects?* Philadelphia: University of Pennsylvania Press, 2010.

Cooper, John Milton. *Breaking the Heart of the World: Woodrow Wilson and the Fight for the League of Nations.* Cambridge and New York: Cambridge University Press, 2001.

Corley, Florence Fleming. *Confederate City: Augusta, Georgia, 1860–1865.* Columbia: University of South Carolina Press, 1960.

Courtney, Susan. *Hollywood Fantasies of Miscegenation: Spectacular Narratives of Gender and Race, 1903–1967.* Princeton, NJ: Princeton University Press, 2005.

Cox, Karen L. *Dixie's Daughters: The United Daughters of the Confederacy and the Preservation of Confederate Culture.* New Perspectives on the History of the South. Gainesville: University Press of Florida, 2003.

Cox, Karen L. *Dreaming of Dixie: How the South Was Created in American Popular Culture.* Chapel Hill: University of North Carolina Press, 2011.

Cox, Karen L. *No Common Ground: Confederate Monuments and the Ongoing Fight for Racial Justice.* Chapel Hill: University of North Carolina Press, 2021.

Cox, Oliver. "The 'Downton Boom': Country Houses, Popular Culture, and Curatorial Culture." *Public Historian* 37, no. 2 (May 2015): 112–19.

Coxall, Helen. "Open Minds: Inclusive Practice." In Genoways, *Museum Philosophy,* 139–49.

Crane, Susan A. "Memory, Distortion, and History in the Museum." *History and Theory* 36, no. 4 (December 1997): 44–63.

Dagbovie, Pero Gaglo. "Reflections on Black Public History: Past, Present, Future." In *Radical Roots: Public History and a Tradition of Social Justice Activism,* edited by Denise D. Meringolo, 523–540. Amherst: Amherst College Press, 2021.

Dahl, Tove I., Pia Silvana Entner, Ann-Mari Horn Johansen, and Joar Vittersø. "Is Our Fascination with Museum Displays More about What We Think or How We Feel?" *Visitor Studies* 16, no. 2 (July 2013): 160–80.

Davidson, Lee, and Pamela Sibley. "Audiences at the 'New' Museum: Visitor Commitment, Diversity and Leisure at the Museum of New Zealand Te Papa Tongarewa." *Visitor Studies* 14, no. 2 (July 2011): 176–94.

Davis, David Brion. *Inhuman Bondage: The Rise and Fall of Slavery in the New World.* New York: Oxford University Press, 2008.

Dawson, Emily, and Eric Jensen. "Towards a Contextual Turn in Visitor Studies: Evaluating Visitor Segmentation and Identity-Related Motivations." *Visitor Studies* 14, no. 2 (July 2011): 127–40.

Department of History. "Public History." University of South Carolina. Accessed January 8, 2024. https://sc.edu.

Domby, Adam H. "Lessons from 'Redemption:' Memories of Reconstruction Violence in Colonial Policy." In *Freedoms Gained and Lost: Reconstruction and Its Meanings 150 Years Later,* edited by Adam H. Domby and Simon Lewis, 232–48. Reconstructing America. New York: Fordham University Press, 2022.

Domby, Adam H., and Simon Lewis, eds. *Freedoms Gained and Lost: Reconstruction and Its Meanings 150 Years Later.* Reconstructing America. New York: Fordham University Press, 2022.

D'Oney, J. Daniel. "Louisiana's Old State Capitol Museum: Castle on the Mississippi." In *Defining Memory: Local Museums and the Construction of History in America's Changing Communities,* edited by Amy K. Levin, 77–91. Lanham, MD: AltaMira, 2007.

Downs, Gregory P., and Kate Masur. "The Era of Reconstruction, 1861–1900: A National Historic Landmarks Theme Study." National Historic Landmarks Program, National Park Service, US Department of the Interior, 2017. http://www.npshistory.com.

Doyle, Don. "Toward an International History of Reconstruction." In *Freedoms Gained and Lost: Reconstruction and Its Meanings 150 Years Later*, edited by Adam H. Domby and Simon Lewis, 181–211. Reconstructing America. New York: Fordham University Press, 2022.

Du Bois, W. E. B. *Black Reconstruction in America; An Essay toward a History of the Part Which Black Folk Played in the Attempt to Reconstruct Democracy in America, 1860–1880*. New York: Atheneum, 1969.

Duck, Leigh Anne. *The Nation's Region: Southern Modernism, Segregation, and U.S. Nationalism*. Athens: University of Georgia Press, 2009.

Edgar, Walter B. *South Carolina: A History*. Columbia: University of South Carolina Press, 1998.

Eichstedt, Jennifer. "Museums and (In)Justice." In Genoways, *Museum Philosophy*, 127–37.

1898 Wilmington Race Riot Commission. "1898 Wilmington Race Riot—Final Report." Raleigh: North Carolina Department of Cultural Resources, Office of Archives and History, May 31, 2006. http://www.history.ncdcr.gov.

Emberton, Carole. *Beyond Redemption: Race, Violence, and the American South after the Civil War*. Chicago: University of Chicago Press, 2013.

Emberton, Carole. "'The Violent Bear It Away:' White Responses to Black Political Mobilization during Reconstruction." In *Remembering the Memphis Massacre: An American Story*, edited by Beverly Greene Bond and Susan Eva O'Donovan, 166–77. Athens: University of Georgia Press, 2020.

Emberton, Carole, and Bruce E. Baker, eds. *Remembering Reconstruction: Struggles over the Meaning of America's Most Turbulent Era*. Baton Rouge: Louisiana State University Press, 2017.

Everett, Anna. *Returning the Gaze: A Genealogy of Black Film Criticism, 1909–1949*. Durham, NC: Duke University Press, 2001.

Falk, John H. *Identity and the Museum Visitor Experience*. Walnut Creek, CA: Left Coast, 2009.

Falk, John H., and Katie L. Gillespie. "Investigating the Role of Emotion in Science Center Visitor Learning." *Visitor Studies* 12, no. 2 (September 2009): 112–32.

Farmer, James Oscar. "Playing Rebels: Reenactment as Nostalgia and Defense of the Confederacy in the Battle of Aiken." *Southern Cultures* 11, no. 1 (February 2005): 46–73. doi:10.1353/scu.2005.0003.

Feimster, Crystal Nicole. *Southern Horrors: Women and the Politics of Rape and Lynching*. Cambridge, Mass: Harvard University Press, 2009.

Foner, Eric. "The Continuing Evolution of Reconstruction History." *OAH Magazine of History* 4, no. 1 (Winter 1989): 11–13.

Foner, Eric. *Reconstruction: America's Unfinished Revolution, 1863–1877*. New York: Harper & Row, 1988.

Forrest, Regan. "Museum Atmospherics: The Role of the Exhibition Environment in the Visitor Experience." *Visitor Studies* 16, no. 2 (July 2013): 201–16.

Fox-Genovese, Elizabeth. *Within the Plantation Household: Black and White Women of the Old South*. 7th ed. The University of North Carolina Press, 1988.

Gaston, Hannah. "*Black Panther* and the Ethics of Representation in Museums." *Institute of Museum Ethics* (blog), April 1, 2019. http://www.museumethics.org.

Gates, Henry Louis, Jr. "'An Unfathomable Place': A Conversation with Quentin Tarantino about *Django Unchained* (2012)." *Transition* 112, no. 1 (2013): 47–66.

Genovese, Eugene D. *Roll, Jordan, Roll: The World the Slaves Made*. New York: Vintage Books, 1976.

Genoways, Hugh H., ed. *Museum Philosophy for the Twenty-First Century*. Lantham, MD: AltaMira, 2006.

Giddings, Paula J. *When and Where I Enter: The Impact of Black Women On Race and Sex in America*. New York: W. Morrow, 1984.

Gilmore, Glenda Elizabeth. *Gender and Jim Crow: Women and the Politics of White Supremacy in North Carolina, 1896–1920*. Chapel Hill: University of North Carolina Press, 1996.

Glick, Josh. "Mixed Messages: D. W. Griffith and the Black Press, 1916–1931." *Film History* 23, no. 2 (2011): 174–95.

Glymph, Thavolia. *Out of the House of Bondage: The Transformation of the Plantation Household*. Cambridge: Cambridge University Press, 2008.

Golanska, Dorota. "Against the 'Moonlight and Magnolia' Myth of the American South. A New Materialist Approach to the Dissonant Heritage of Slavery in the US: The Case of Whitney Plantation in Wallace, LA." *Muzeológia a Kultúrne Dedičstvo* 8 (January 2020): 137–60.

Gordon-Reed, Annette. *The Hemingses of Monticello: An American Family*. New York: Norton, 2008.

Graham, Allison. *Framing the South: Hollywood, Television, and Race during the Civil Rights Struggle*. Baltimore: Johns Hopkins University Press, 2003.

Grantham, Dewey W. "Southern Historiography and a History of the South." *American Quarterly* 5, no. 3 (1953): 252–68.

Griffin, Larry J., and Don Harrison Doyle, eds. *The South as an American Problem*. Athens: University of Georgia Press, 1995.

Hale, Grace Elizabeth. *Making Whiteness: The Culture of Segregation in the South, 1890–1940*. New York: Vintage Books, 1999.

Hale, William Bayard. *Woodrow Wilson: The Story of His Life*. Garden City, NY: Doubleday, Page, 1912.

Halifax, Shawn. "McLeod Planation Historic Site: Sowing Truth and Change." *Public Historian* 40, no. 3 (August 2018): 252–77.

Hall, Jacquelyn Dowd. *Sisters and Rebels: A Struggle for the Soul of America*. Illustrated ed. New York: Norton, 2019.

Harnay, Melaine. "Slavery and Plantation Tourism in Louisiana: Deconstructing the Romanticized Narrative of the Plantation Tours." *Mondes du tourisme*, no. 21 (June 2022) : 1-18. https://journals.openedition.org.

Hays, Michael, and Anastasia Nikolopoulou, eds. *Melodrama: The Cultural Emergence of a Genre*. New York: St. Martin's, 1996.

Hayward, Jeff, and Christine Larouche. "The Emergence of the Field of African American Museums." *Public Historian* 40, no. 3 (August 2018): 163–72.

Hein, Hilde. "Assuming Responsibility: Lessons from Aesthetics." In Genoways, *Museum Philosophy*, 1–9.

Hine, Darlene Clark. "Rape and the Inner Lives of Black Women in the Middle West." *Signs* 14, no. 4 (July 1, 1989): 912–20.

Hirsch, Jerrold. *Portrait of America: A Cultural History of the Federal Writers' Project.* Chapel Hill: University of North Carolina Press, 2003.

Holt, Thomas. *Black over White: Negro State Legislators in South Carolina during Reconstruction.* Urbana: University of Illinois Press, 1979.

Jennings, Thelma. "'Us Colored Women Had to Go Though A Plenty': Sexual Exploitation of African-American Slave Women." *Journal of Women's History* 1, no. 3 (1990): 45–74.

Jensen, Eric, Emily Dawson, and John H. Falk. "Dialogue and Synthesis: Developing Consensus in Visitor Research Methodology." *Visitor Studies* 14, no. 2 (July 2011): 158–61.

Johnson, Anna, Nancy Cutler, Melissa Bingmann, Tim Grove, and Kimberly Huber. *The Museum Educator's Manual: Educators Share Successful Techniques.* American Association for State and Local History Book Series. Lanham, MD: AltaMira, 2009.

Jones, Jacqueline. *Labor of Love, Labor of Sorrow: Black Women, Work, and the Family from Slavery to the Present.* New York: Basic Books, 1985.

Jones, Jacqueline. "'My Mother Was Much of a Woman': Black Women, Work, and the Family under Slavery." *Feminist Studies* 8, no. 2 (July 1, 1982): 235–69.

Jones, Jacqueline. "'Race, Sex and Self-Evident Truths: The Status of Slave Women during the Era of the American Revolution.'" In *Half Sisters of History: Southern Women and the American Past,* edited by Catherine Clinton. Durham, NC: Duke University Press, 1994.

Jones, Lois Swan. "Volunteer-Guides and Classroom Teachers in School-Visitation Programs in European and North American Art Museums." *Studies in Art Education* 18, no. 3 (January 1977): 31–41.

King, Jean A. "Taking What Action for Change? Dare Evaluation Build a New Social Order?" *Visitor Studies* 19, no. 1 (January 2016): 3–11.

King, Wilma. "'Suffer with Them Till Death': Slave Women and Their Children in Nineteenth-Century America." In *More Than Chattel: Black Women and Slavery in the Americas,* edited by David Barry Gaspar and Darlene Clark Hine. Bloomington: Indiana University Press, 1996.

Kirby, Jack Temple. *Media-Made Dixie: The South in the American Imagination.* Athens: University of Georgia Press, 1986.

Knock, Thomas J. *To End All Wars: Woodrow Wilson and the Quest for a New World Order.* Princeton, N.J.: Princeton University Press, 1995.

Labode, Modupe. "Reconsideration of Memorials and Monuments." *AASLH Blogs* (blog), November 30, 2016. http://blogs.aaslh.org/reconsideration-of-memorials-and-monuments/.

Lassiter, Matthew D., and Joseph Crespino, eds. *The Myth of Southern Exceptionalism.* New York: Oxford University Press, 2010.

Lears, T. J. Jackson. *Rebirth of a Nation: The Making of Modern America, 1877–1920.* New York: HarperCollins, 2009.

Lemann, Nicholas. *Redemption: The Last Battle of the Civil War.* New York: Farrar, Straus and Giroux, 2007.

Levine, Lawrence W. *Highbrow/Lowbrow: The Emergence of Cultural Hierarchy in America.* 1986. Cambridge, MA: Harvard University Press, 1988.

Lewis, George. "The Curation of American Patriotism: The American Legion and The Story of Our American People." *History and Memory: Studies in Representation of the Past* 35, no. 2 (September 22, 2023): 79–110.

Link, Arthur S. *Wilson: The Road to the White House*. Vol. 1. V vols. Princeton, N.J.: Princeton University Press, 1947.

Link, Arthur S. *Wilson: The New Freedom*. Vol. II. V vols. Princeton, NJ: Princeton University Press, 1956.

Link, Arthur S. *Wilson: The Struggle for Neutrality, 1914-1915*. Vol. III. V vols. Princeton, NJ: Princeton University Press, 1960.

Link, Arthur S. *Wilson: Confusions and Crises, 1915-1916*. Vol. IV. V vols. Princeton, NJ: Princeton University Press, 1964.

Link, Arthur S. *Wilson: Campaigns for Progressivism and Peace, 1916-1917*. Vol. V. V vols. Princeton, NJ: Princeton University Press, 1965.

Link, Arthur S. *Wilson the Diplomatist: A Look at His Major Foreign Policies*. Chicago: Quadrangle Books, 1963.

Link, Arthur S. *Woodrow Wilson: Revolution, War, and Peace*. Arlington Heights, IL: AHM Pub. Corp, 1979.

Lipscomb, Terry. "D. W. Griffith's 'Historical Facsimile': How the South Carolina State House Became a Movie Set." *Caroliniana Columns*, Spring 2002, 1, 3–4.

Lopez, Lisa Junkin. "Open House: Reimagining the Historic House Museum." *Public Historian* 37, no. 2 (May 2015): 10–13.

Lowe, Hilary Iris. "Dwelling in Possibility: Revisiting Narrative in the Historic House Museum." *Public Historian* 37, no. 2 (May 2015): 42–60.

Lowery, J. Vincent. "Paul Leland Haworth: The 'Black Republican' in the Old Chief's Court." In *The Dunning School: Historians, Race, and the Meaning of Reconstruction*, edited by John David Smith and J. Vincent Lowery, 203–28. University Press of Kentucky, 2013.

Luke, Timothy W. "The Museum: Where Civilizations Clash or Clash Civilizes?" In Genoways, *Museum Philosophy*, 19–25.

Macaulay, Neill W., Jr. "South Carolina Reconstruction Historiography." *South Carolina Historical Magazine* 65, no. 1 (January 1964): 20–32.

Manela, Erez. *The Wilsonian Moment: Self-Determination and the International Origins of Anticolonial Nationalism*. New York: Oxford University Press, 2007.

McGuire, Danielle L. "'It Was like All of Us Had Been Raped': Sexual Violence, Community Mobilization, and the African American Freedom Struggle." *Journal of American History* 91, no. 3 (December 1, 2004): 906–31.

McIntosh, Peggy. "White Privilege: Unpacking the Invisible Knapsack." In *White Privilege: Essential Readings on the Other Side of Racism*, edited by Paula S. Rothenberg and Soniya Munshi, 97–101. New York: Worth, 2016.

McPherson, Tara. *Reconstructing Dixie: Race, Gender, and Nostalgia in the Imagined South*. Durham, NC: Duke University Press, 2003.

Meer, Sarah. *Uncle Tom Mania: Slavery, Minstrelsy, and Transatlantic Culture in the 1850s*. Athens: University of Georgia Press, 2005.

Montgomery, Erick. *Thomas Woodrow Wilson: Family Ties and Southern Perspectives*. Augusta, GA: Historic Augusta, 2006.

Moore, Cecelia. "Woodrow Wilson Family Home: A Museum of Reconstruction in Columbia and Richland County." *Journal of American History* 102, no. 1 (June 2015): 188–93.

Moore, John Hammond. "South Carolina Views *The Birth of a Nation*." In *Perspectives in South Carolina History: The First 300 Years*, edited by Ernest M. Lander and Robert K. Ackerman, 337–47. Columbia: University of South Carolina Press, 1973.

O'Brien, Michael. "C. Vann Woodward and the Burden of Southern Liberalism." *American Historical Review* 78, no. 3 (1973): 589–604.

Olsen, Cindy. "Are Guided Tours at Historic Houses Dead?" American Association for State and Local History blog, December 19, 2014. http://blogs.aaslh.org.

Palau-Saumell, Ramon, Santiago Forgas-Coll, and Javier Sánchez-García. "The Role of Emotions in a Model of Behavioral Intentions of Visitors to the Gaudí Historic House Museums in Barcelona, Spain." *Visitor Studies* 19, no. 2 (July 2016): 156–77.

Parsons, Elaine Frantz. *Ku-Klux: The Birth of the Klan during Reconstruction*. Chapel Hill: University of North Carolina Press, 2016.

Pattison, Scott A., and Lynn D. Dierking. "Staff-Mediated Learning in Museums: A Social Interaction Perspective." *Visitor Studies* 16, no. 2 (July 2013): 117–43.

Pattison, Scott A., and Todd Shagott. "Participant Reactivity in Museum Research: The Effect of Cueing Visitors at an Interactive Exhibit." *Visitor Studies* 18, no. 2 (July 2015): 214–32.

Pharaon, Sarah, Sally Roesch Wagner, Barbara Lau, and María José Bolaña Caballero. "Safe Containers for Dangerous Memories." *Public Historian* 37, no. 2 (May 2015): 61–72.

Pinheiro, Jr., Holly A. "Idealism versus Material Realities: Economic Woes for Northern African American Soldiers and Their Families." In *Freedoms Gained and Lost: Reconstruction and Its Meanings 150 Years Later*, edited by Adam H. Domby and Simon Lewis, 143–58. Reconstructing America. New York: Fordham University Press, 2022.

Pinto-Handler, Sergio. "The Dream of a Rural Democracy: US Reconstruction and Abolitionist Propaganda in Rio de Janeiro, 1880-1890." In *Freedoms Gained and Lost: Reconstruction and Its Meanings 150 Years Later*, edited by Adam H. Domby and Simon Lewis, 212–31. Reconstructing America. New York: Fordham University Press, 2022.

Poole, W. Scott. *Never Surrender: Confederate Memory and Conservatism in the South Carolina Upcountry*. Athens: University of Georgia Press, 2004.

Prince, K. Stephen. "Memory Battles: History, Memory and the Meanings of Reconstruction." In *Remembering the Memphis Massacre: An American Story*, edited by Beverly Greene Bond and Susan Eva O'Donovan, 190–203. Athens: University of Georgia Press, 2020.

Pustz, Jennifer. *Voices from the Back Stairs: Interpreting Servants' Lives at Historic House Museums*. DeKalb: Northern Illinois University Press, 2010.

Pyatt, Robert E., Tracie Rosser, and Kelly Powell. "Undergraduates as Science Museum Docents: Training Students to Be the Teachers Using Peer Led Team Learning." *American Biology Teacher* 71, no. 1 (January 2009): 16–19.

Rhea, Gordon C. *Stephen A. Swails: Black Freedom Fighter in the Civil War and Reconstruction*. Southern Biography Series. Baton Rouge: Louisiana State University Press, 2021.

Ritchie, Donald A. *Doing Oral History: A Practical Guide*. 3rd ed. Oxford: Oxford University Press, 2014.

Roberts, Alaina E. *I've Been Here All the While: Black Freedom on Native Land*. Philadelphia: University of Pennsylvania Press, 2021.

Rose, Julia. "Collective Memories and the Changing Representations of American Slavery." *Journal of Museum Education* 29, no. 2/3 (2004): 26–31.

Rose, Willie Lee. *Rehearsal for Reconstruction: The Port Royal Experiment*. New York: Vintage Books, 1964.
Rosen, Hannah. *Terror in the Heart of Freedom: Citizenship, Sexual Violence, and the Meaning of Race in the Postemancipation South*. Gender and American Culture. Chapel Hill: University of North Carolina Press, 2009.
Rosen, Hannah. "Words of Resistance: African American Women's Testimony about Sexual Violence during the Memphis Massacre." In *Remembering the Memphis Massacre: An American Story*, edited by Beverly Greene Bond and Susan Eva O'Donovan, 102–19. Athens: University of Georgia Press, 2020.
Ruffins, Fath Davis. "Building Homes for Black History: Museum Founders, Founding Directors, and Pioneers, 1915–95." *Public Historian* 40, no. 3 (August 2018): 13–43.
Rutherford, Janice Williams, and Steven E. Shay. "Peopling the Age of Elegance: Reinterpreting Spokane's Campbell House—A Collaboration." *Public Historian* 26, no. 3 (August 2004): 27–48.
Safranek, Lauren. "Historic House Museum Review: Woodrow Wilson Family Home." *Public Historian* 37, no. 2 (May 2015): 120–23.
Schaffer, Samuel L. "'A Bitter Memory Upon Which Terms of Peace Would Rest:' Woodrow Wilson, the Reconstruction of the South, and the Reconstruction of Europe." In *Remembering Reconstruction: Struggles Over the Meaning of America's Most Turbulent Era*, edited by Carole Emberton and Bruce E. Baker, 203–22. Baton Rouge: Louisiana State University Press, 2017.
Scott, Anne Firor. *Natural Allies: Women's Associations in American History*. University of Illinois Press, 1992.
Scott, Jennifer. "Reimagining Freedom in the Twenty-First Century at a Post-emancipation Site." *Public Historian* 37, no. 2 (May 2015): 73–88.
Serrell, Beverly. *Exhibit Labels: An Interpretive Approach*. Lanham, MD: AltaMira, 1996.
Shopes, Linda. "Legal and Ethical Issues in Oral History." In *History of Oral History: Foundations and Methodology*, edited by Thomas L. Charlton, Lois E. Myers, and Rebecca Sharpless, 125–59. Lanham, MD: AltaMira Press, 2007.
Simkins, Francis Butler, and Robert H. Woody. *South Carolina during Reconstruction*. Gloucester, MA: Smith, 1966.
Simon, Nina. *The Participatory Museum*. Santa Cruz, CA: Museum 2.0, 2010.
Smith, John David. Introduction to *The Dunning School: Historians, Race, and the Meaning of Reconstruction*, edited by John David Smith and J. Vincent Lowery. Lexington: University Press of Kentucky, 2013: 1-48.
Staiger, Janet. "The Birth of a Nation: Reconsider Its Reception." In *The Birth of a Nation: D.W. Griffith, Director*, edited by Robert Lang, 195–213. Rutgers Films in Print, v. 21. New Brunswick, NJ: Rutgers University Press, 1994.
Steedman, Carolyn Kay. *Dust: The Archive and Cultural History*. New Brunswick, NJ: Rutgers University Press, 2002.
Stewart, Jacqueline Najuma. *Migrating to the Movies: Cinema and Black Urban Modernity*. Berkeley: University of California Press, 2005.
Sturken, Marita. *Tourists of History: Memory, Kitsch, and Consumerism from Oklahoma City to Ground Zero*. Durham, NC: Duke University Press, 2007.
Stylianou-Lambert, Theopisti. "Re-conceptualizing Museum Audiences: Power, Activity, Responsibility." *Visitor Studies* 13, no. 2 (July 2010): 130–44.

Tamura, Eileen H. "Ethnic Museums in Hawai'i: Exhibits, Interpreters, and Reenactments." *Journal of American Ethnic History* 28, no. 3 (April 2009): 66–73.

Taylor, Jennifer Whitmer. "Inclusive Training at Historic Columbia." *National Council on Public History History@Work* (blog), March 6, 2017. http://ncph.org/history-at-work/inclusive-training-at-historic-columbia/.

Taylor, Jennifer Whitmer, and Page Putnam Miller. "Reconstructing Memory: The Attempt to Designate Beaufort, South Carolina, the National Park Service's First Reconstruction Unit." *Journal of the Civil War Era* 7, no. 1 (March 2017): 39–66.

Taylor, Jennifer Whitmer, and Page Putnam Miller. "Postscript to 'Reconstructing Memory.'" *Muster from the Journal of the Civil War Era* (blog), March 7, 2017. http://journalofthecivilwarera.org/2017/03/postscript-reconstructing-memory/.

Thompson, Henry Tazewell. *Ousting the Carpetbagger from South Carolina*. Columbia: Bryan, 1926.

Throntveit, Trygve. "The Fable of the Fourteen Points: Woodrow Wilson and National Self-Determination." *Diplomatic History* 35, no. 3 (2011): 445–81.

Tyson, Amy M. *The Wages of History: Emotional Labor on Public History's Front Lines*. Amherst: University of Massachusetts Press, 2013.

Upton, Dell. *What Can and Can't Be Said: Race, Uplift, and Monument Building in the Contemporary South*. New Haven, CT: Yale University Press, 2015.

Urofsky, Melvin I. "A New Beginning, 1892–1945." *Virginia Magazine of History and Biography* 114, no. 1 (2006): 80–113.

Vagnone, Franklin D., and Deborah E. Ryan. *Anarchist's Guide to Historic House Museums*. Walnut Creek, CA: Routledge, 2015.

Van Tassel, David D. "From Learned Society to Professional Organization: The American Historical Association, 1884–1900." *American Historical Review* 89, no. 4 (1984): 929–56.

Vaughan, Charles. "Official Social Studies Curriculum Standards: An Analysis of Southern Political, Cultural, and Historical Contexts." *Theses and Dissertations*, January 1, 2012. https://scholarcommons.sc.edu/etd/878.

Vivian, Daniel J. *A New Plantation World: Sporting Estates in the South Carolina Lowcountry, 1900–1940*. New York: Cambridge University Press, 2018.

Weiler, Betty, and Sam H. Ham. "Development of a Research Instrument for Evaluating the Visitor Outcomes of Face-to-Face Interpretation." *Visitor Studies* 13, no. 2 (July 2010): 187–205.

Wentworth, Brenda Kathryn. "The First City Hall Opera House in Columbia, South Carolina, 1875–1899." MA Thesis, University of South Carolina, 1978.

West, Patricia. *Domesticating History: The Political Origins of America's House Museums*. Washington, DC: Smithsonian Institution Press, 1999.

White, Deborah G. *Ar'n't I a Woman? Female Slaves in the Plantation South*. New York: Norton, 1999.

White, Mimi. "The Birth of a Nation: History as Pretext." In *The Birth of a Nation: D.W. Griffith, Director*, edited by Robert Lang, 214–24. Rutgers Films in Print, v. 21. New Brunswick, NJ: Rutgers University Press, 1994.

Williams, Heather Andrea. *Self-Taught: African American Education in Slavery and Freedom*. Chapel Hill: University of North Carolina Press, 2007.

Williams, Linda. *Playing the Race Card: Melodramas of Black and White from Uncle Tom to O.J. Simpson*. Princeton, NJ: Princeton University Press, 2001.

Wilson, Mabel O. *Negro Building: Black Americans in the World of Fairs and Museums*. Oakland: University of California Press, 2012.

Wilson, Woodrow. "The Reconstruction of the Southern States." In *The Public Papers of Woodrow Wilson. Authorized Edition*, edited by Ray Stannard Baker and William Edward Dodd, 2:368–95. College and State: Educational, Literary and Political Papers (1875-1913). New York: Kraus Reprint Co., 1970.

Wilson, Woodrow. "Robert E. Lee: An Interpretation." In *The Public Papers of Woodrow Wilson. Authorized Edition*, edited by Ray Stannard Baker and William Edward Dodd, Vol. 2. College and State: Educational, Literary and Political Papers (1875-1913). New York: Kraus Reprint Co., 1970.

Wilson, Woodrow. "The Young People and the Church, An Address Delivered before the Pennsylvania State Sabbath School Association, at Pittsburgh, October 23, 1904." In *The Public Papers of Woodrow Wilson. Authorized Edition*, edited by Ray Stannard Baker and William Edward Dodd, 1:474–86. College and State: Educational, Literary and Political Papers (1875-1913). New York: Kraus Reprint Co., 1970.

Winter, William. *Life and Art of Edwin Booth*. New York: Macmillan, 1893.

Wolgemuth, Kathleen L. "Woodrow Wilson and Federal Segregation." *Journal of Negro History* 44, no. 2 (April 1959): 158–73.

Wood, Amy Louise. "With the Roar of Thunder: *The Birth of a Nation*." In *Lynching and Spectacle: Witnessing Racial Violence in America, 1890-1940*, 148–76. Chapel Hill: University of North Carolina Press, 2009.

The Woodrow Wilson Museum. Digital video. The Woodrow Wilson Presidential Library and Museum. (Staunton, Virginia, n.d.). Accessed June 22, 2015.

Woodward, C. Vann. *Origins of the New South, 1877-1913*. Revised. Louisiana State University Press, 1972.

Yalowitz, Steven S., and Kerry Bronnenkant. "Timing and Tracking: Unlocking Visitor Behavior." *Visitor Studies* 12, no. 1 (March 2009): 47–64.

Yuhl, Stephanie E. *A Golden Haze of Memory: The Making of Historic Charleston*. Chapel Hill: University of North Carolina Press, 2005.

Zuczek, Richard. *State of Rebellion: Reconstruction in South Carolina*. Columbia, SC: University of South Carolina Press, 2009.

Index